Snow-capped peaks, turquoise-green rivers and an Adriatic coastline inspired by Venice. Throughout Slovenia, a culinary and cultural sophistication hides behind a rural, rustic charm.

(left) Piran (p122)
(below) Vršič Pass (p92), Julian Alps

Friendly Faces

The people are the 'X' factor in any visit to a foreign land, and rest assured you'll find plenty of friendly people here. Wherever you go, you'll get an enthusiastic, helpful, welcoming response, often in English. Numbering only around two million people, Slovenes punch well above their weight class in international sport, science, academics and even philosophy. In the days of old Yugoslavia, Slovenia was regarded as the most open of the country's republics, and it's not any different today. Slovenes are proud of their country and happy to show it off.

Fresh-Air Pursuits

Slovenia is an outdoor destination. Of course, there are great museums and historic churches here too, but the locals seem to favour active holidays, and you'll be invited – even expected – to join in. The most popular pursuits remain mountain walks and hikes, though increasingly Slovenes are discovering cycling (especially in the capital, Ljubljana). Fast rivers like the Soča cry out to be rafted and there are ample chances to try out more esoteric activities like horse riding, ballooning, caving and diving. If all this sounds a bit much, you can always decamp to the coast and sunbathe by the Adriatic.

❭ Slovenia

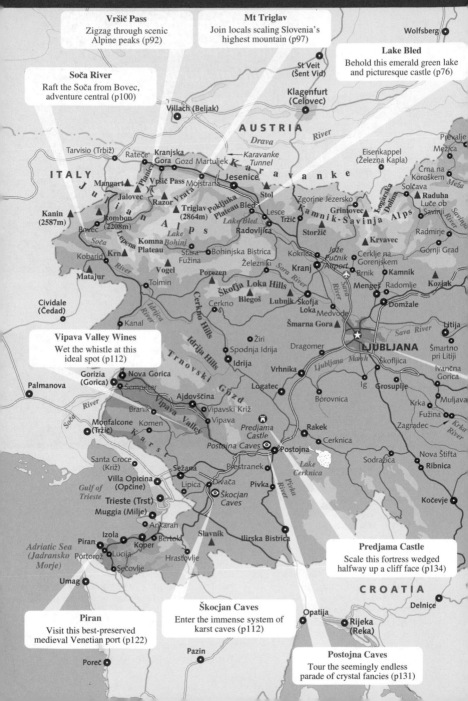

Vršič Pass
Zigzag through scenic Alpine peaks (p92)

Mt Triglav
Join locals scaling Slovenia's highest mountain (p97)

Wolfsberg

Lake Bled
Behold this emerald green lake and picturesque castle (p76)

Soča River
Raft the Soča from Bovec, adventure central (p100)

St Veit (Šent Vid)

Klagenfurt (Celovec)

Villach (Beljak)

AUSTRIA

Drava   *River*

Prevalje

Mežica

Soča River Mangart

Tarvisio (Trbiž) Rateče Kranjska Gora Gozd Martuljek

Karavanke Tunnel

Eisenkappel (Železna Kapla)

Črna na Koroškem Meža

ITALY

Mangart Planica Vršič Pass Mojstrana

Jesenice

Stol

Zgornje Jezersko

Solčava Raduha

Luče ob Savinji

Jalovec

Razor Vrata Triglav (2864m) Pokljuka Plateau Bled

Lesce

Tržič

Grintovec Kamnik-Savinja Alps

Radmirje

Gornji Grad

Kanin (2587m) Kombon (2208m) Bovec

Lake Bohinj Stara Fužina Bohinjska Bistrica Železniki

Radovljica Storžič Krvavec Kozjak

Kamnik-Savinja Alps

Kobarid Krn Komna Plateau

Soča

Lepena

River

Matajur

Vogel

Tolmin

Porezen

Škofja Loka Hills

Cerkno

Blegoš

Kokrica

Jože Pučnik Airport Brnik Menges Radomlje

Cerklje na Gorenjskem Kamnik

Domžale

Litija

Cividale (Čedad)

Kanal

Cerkno

Škofja Loka Medvode

Lubnik

Šmarna Gora

Sava River

Šmartno pri Litiji

Vipava Valley Wines
Wet the whistle at this ideal spot (p112)

Žiri Spodnja Idrija Dragomer

Idrija

Vrhnika

Ljubljana Marsh

LJUBLJANA

Škofljica

Ivančna Gorica

Grosuplje

Gorizia (Gorica) Nova Gorica Šempeter

Logatec

Ig

Krka Muljava

Palmanova

Ajdovščina Vipavski Križ

Borovnica

Fužina

Zagradec

Krka River

Branik Komen Vipava

Predjama Castle

Rakek

Cerknica

Nova Štifta

Monfalcone (Tržič)

Postojna Caves Postojna

Sodražica

Ribnica

Santa Croce (Križ)

Sežana Prestranek

Lake Cerknica

Villa Opicina (Opčine) Lipica

Divača Pivka

Pivka River

Kočevje

Gulf of Trieste

Trieste (Trst) Muggia (Milje)

Škocjan Caves

Ankaran

Izola Bertoki

Slavnik

Ilirska Bistrica

Piran Koper

Predjama Castle
Scale this fortress wedged halfway up a cliff face (p134)

Adriatic Sea (Jadransko Morje)

Portorož Lucija

Hrastovlje

Sečovlje

CROATIA

Umag

Delnice

Piran
Visit this best-preserved medieval Venetian port (p122)

Škocjan Caves
Enter the immense system of karst caves (p112)

Opatija Rijeka (Reka)

Poreč Pazin

Postojna Caves
Tour the seemingly endless parade of crystal fancies (p131)

Ptuj
Enjoy a maze of red roofs and medieval streets (p172)

Ljubljana
Indulge in the perfect balance of size and quality of life (p34)

ELEVATION

1500m
1000m
500m
100m
0

0   20 km
0   10 miles

HUNGARY

CROATIA

★ ZAGREB

12
TOP
EXPERIENCES

Ljubljana

1 Slovenia's capital city (p34) strikes that perfect yet elusive balance between size and quality of life. It's big enough to be interesting, yet small enough to walk – or better yet, bike – across at a leisurely pace. The term 'jewel box' gets tossed around all too frequently to describe attractive smaller cities, but in Ljubljana's case the words are apt. What better way to describe architect Jože Plečnik's wondrously decorative pillars, obelisks and orbs that seem to top every bridge, fountain and lamp post?
Triple Bridge (p37), Ljubljana

Climbing Mt Triglav

2 Nothing quite says 'I'm a Slovene' like climbing to the top of the country's tallest mountain. Indeed, for Slovenes, it's practically stamped in their passports once they've made the trek. The good news for the rest of us is that Mt Triglav (p94) is a challenging but accessible peak that just about anyone in decent shape can summit with an experienced guide. There are several popular approaches, each with its own attractions and degrees of difficulty. Whichever path you choose, the reward is the same: sheer exhilaration. Triglav National Park (p94)

3

4

Piran

3 Venice in Slovenia? Of course! That busy merchant empire left its mark up and down the Adriatic coast, and Slovenia was lucky to end up with the best-preserved medieval Venetian port outside Venice, well, possibly anywhere. It's true that Piran (p122) attracts tourist numbers on a near-Venetian scale, but the beautiful setting means it's never less than a constant delight. Eat fresh seafood on the harbour, then get lost wandering the narrow streets and end up for drinks and people-watching in a glorious central square.

River Adventures

4 Rarely does a river beckon to be rafted as convincingly as Slovenia's Soča (p100). Maybe it's that piercing sky-blue-bordering-on-green – or is it turquoise? – colour of the water, or the river's refreshing froth and foam as it tumbles down the mountains. Even if you're not the rafting type, you'll soon find yourself strapping on a wetsuit for that exhilarating ride of the summer. Several outfitters in Bovec and Kobarid specialise in guided rafting trips. For the more intrepid there's always canyoning. For gentler floats, try the Krka River (p144).
Kayakers, Soča River

Lake Bled

5 Bled (p76), Slovenia's biggest tourist draw, looks like it came off the drawing board of a gifted architect or interior designer. Start with a crystal-clear blue lake, add a tiny island over here, top it with an impossibly cute church, and then put a dramatic, cliffside castle over there. Now add some Alpine peaks to the backdrop. Voila! It really is that lovely, but Bled is more than just good looks. There's a raucous adventure scene too, with diving, cycling and rafting, among other active pursuits. There are excellent hotels and restaurants here as well.

Postojna Cave System

6 The caves at Postojna (p131) are Slovenia's biggest subterranean attraction. The entrance might look like nothing, but when you get whisked 4km underground on a train and only then start exploring, you begin to get a sense of the scale. The caverns are a seemingly endless parade of crystal fancies – from frilly chandeliers and dripping spaghetti formations, to paper-thin sheets and stupendous stalagmites, all patiently laid down over the centuries by the simple drip of mineral-rich water. A theatrical experience in silent stone.

Crossing the Vršič Pass

7 Making your way – whether by car or (yikes) bike – across this mind-bogglingly scenic Alpine pass (p92), as it zigzags through peaks and promontories, it's hard not to think of those poor Russian POWs who built the road during WWI. They're given their due, and the passage is now called the Ruska cesta (Russian Road), but talk about hard work. This summer-only roadway links Kranjska Gora with Bovec, 50km to the southwest, and includes a number of photo-op rest stops and several mountain huts along the way.

Škocjan Caves

8 Where Postojna is baroque, the caves at Škocjan (p112) are positively Gothic. It's all about melo-drama here – think Jules Verne, Tolkien and Wagner all wrapped into one. Forget crawling in tiny underground spaces: the Murmuring Cave has walls reaching a hundred metres high, while the Cerkevnik Bridge crosses a gloomy chasm with a 45m plunge to where the Reka River still carves its way through the rock. The remains of pre-historic humans have been found here – what must they have made of this place?

Traditional Spas

9 A 'spa' in Central Europe can often mean a fusty 19th-century royal relic with lots of great architecture but not much in the way of fun or modern treatments. Slovenia's natural and thermal spas have the architecture, but more importantly they offer a wealth of high-quality wellness and beauty treat-ments including massage, mud baths, saunas, warm seawater baths and more. Most of the spas are situated in the eastern half of the coun-try and usually feature great food and accommodation as well. Spa architecture, Rogaška Slatina (p169)

8

9

Predjama Castle

10 Two things Slovenia seems to specialise in: castles and caves. The country is dotted with both, but a castle in a cave? That's something special. Few fortresses have a setting as grand as this, wedged halfway up a cliff face at the foot of a valley (p134). The location has a story behind it that's equally dramatic: Slovenia's 'Robin Hood', Erazem Lueger, apparently taunted besieging troops here by hurling fresh cherries at them that he collected via a secret passage. He came to a swift and rather embarrassing end.

Vipava Valley Wines

11 Slovenes like to enjoy the good things in life, and their country is blessed with the means to produce some of the best. The Karst region's Vipava Valley (p112) particularly stands out. It enjoys a warm Mediterranean climate freshened by cold winter winds, making it the ideal destination for those wanting to treat their palates. Wineries with some of the best merlots in the world? Check. The best air-dried *pršut* ham? Yep. Have some with the local fruits and olives and you've got a Slovenian picnic to remember.

Vineyards, Štanjel (p112)

10

JOHN WOOLDWORTH / GETTY IMAGES ©

Ptuj

12 To English speakers' ears the name might sound like a cartoon character spitting, but Ptuj (p172) is far more than a cheap one-liner. Instead, it's one of Slovenia's richest historical towns. Everyone since the Romans has left their mark, and the centre is still a maze of red roofs and medieval streets, dotted with churches, towers and museums, as well as street cafes where you can enjoy the passing views. If you're there in February, look for the riotous street theatre of the Kurentovanje festivities (p175). Ptuj is also within easy reach of some of the country's best wine regions.
City Tower (p173)

need to know

Currency
» Euro (€)

Language
» Slovene
(slovenščina)

When to Go

Warm to hot summers, mild winters
Warm to hot summers, cold winters
Mild summers, cold winters
Cold climate

Kranjska Gora
GO Dec–Mar

Bovec
GO May–Jul

Maribor
GO Apr–Jun

Ljubljana
GO Sep–Oct

Piran
GO Jun–Aug

High Season
(Jun–Aug)
» Mostly sunny skies with occasional rain.

» Crowds in Ljubljana and the coast; advance booking essential.

» Museums and other attractions open for business.

» Best time for hikes.

Shoulder
(Apr & May, Sep & Oct)
» Sunny, dry September is a great time for climbing Mt Triglav.

» Lower tariffs are in effect at many hotels.

» Rafting is great by late May; swimming is over by October.

Low Season
(Nov–Mar)
» Ski season runs from mid-December to March or even April.

» Christmas through New Year can be crowded.

» Attractions in smaller towns may close or have limited hours.

Your Daily Budget

Budget less than
€40
» Hostel dorm bed or low-cost guesthouse: €15

» Street food and self-catering: €10

» Train/bus tickets: €10

» Museum/attraction entry: €5

Midrange around
€80
» Room in a midrange hotel or pension: €30

» Lunch and dinner in good restaurants: €30

» Train/bus tickets: €10

» Museum/attraction entry: €10

Top End more than
€100
» Room in the best place in town: €50

» Lunch and dinner in good restaurants: €30

» Train/bus/taxi: €20

» Museum/attraction entry: €10

Money
» ATMs widely available. Credit and debit cards accepted in most hotels and restaurants.

Visas
» Generally not required for stays of up to 90 days. Some nationalities will need an EU Schengen visa.

Mobile Phones
» Local SIM cards can be used in European, Australian and some American phones. Other phones must be set to roaming.

Transport
» Mostly trains for long-distance travel; buses within regions.

Websites
» **Slovenian Tourist Board** (www.slovenia .info) Info on every conceivable sight and activity.

» **Slovenia Times** (www.sloveniatimes .com) Website of the independent magazine.

» **E-uprava** (http://e-uprava.gov .si/e-uprava/en/ portal.euprava) Official government portal has just about everything you could want to know about the country.

» **Lonely Planet** (www .lonelyplanet.com) Ask questions or dispense advice via the Thorn Tree forum.

Exchange Rates
Prices are quoted in euros (€) unless otherwise stated. €1 = 100 cents.

Australia	A$1	€0.78
Canada	C$1	€0.78
Japan	¥100	€0.97
New Zealand	NZ$1	€0.62
UK	UK£1	€1.23
USA	US$1	€0.77

For current exchange rates see www.xe.com.

Important Numbers
All landline phone numbers have an area code followed by a seven-digit number. Mobile phone numbers start with a three-digit prefix, which is followed by six digits.

Ambulance (Reševalci)	☎112
Fire brigade (Gasilci)	☎112
First aid (Prva Pomoč)	☎112
Police (Policija)	☎113 (emergencies)
Road emergency or towing (AMZS)	☎1987

Arriving in Slovenia
» **Ljubljana, Jože Pučnik Airport**
City Bus – €4.10; 45 minutes to the centre
Shuttle Van – €9; 30 minutes to the centre
Taxi – about €40; 30 minutes to the centre

» **Overland Travel**
Ljubljana's **bus** (p65) and **train** (p65) stations are the main points of entry for overland travel from the rest of Europe.

Booking Rooms Well in Advance
While Slovenia has lots of different accommodation options, it's always a good idea to book as far in advance as possible. Lodging in Ljubljana can be very tight. In spring and autumn, rooms book up during the week, as this is the prime season for business travel. In summer, weekdays are generally OK, but weekends can get crowded. This is doubly true during festivals. We've listed major events in our Month by Month chapter (p18), so that you can time your arrival to coincide with (or to avoid) major events.

Outside the capital, the lodging situation eases somewhat, though each region has its peak travel season. Naturally, mountain areas near ski resorts become crowded during the ski season, particularly over weekends. The week between Christmas and New Year, and in mid-February, when schoolkids have a weeklong ski holiday, are especially crowded. Similarly, summer resorts are crowded most weekends in July and August.

if you like...

Dramatic Scenery

For such a small country, Slovenia packs an amazing amount of diversity and stunning natural beauty. Snow-capped Alps; long, green valleys; and lakes and rivers so blue they almost hurt your eyes.

Vršič Pass This curving WWI-era highway crosses the Alps at an elevation of 1611m as it runs from near Kranjska Gora to Bovec (p92)

Velika Planina High-altitude Alpine pastureland that offers some of the best mountain photo ops we've seen (p72)

Soča River Valley It's not just the river's hair-raising setting of narrow gorges and steep verdant valleys that makes it so unforgettable, it's also the electrified aquamarine colour of the water (p100)

Lake Bohinj Bled's lesser-known sister lake is no wallflower; it's an emerald-green mountain paradise with a quieter, more rustic feel and a glimpse of Mt Triglav (p85)

Logarska Dolina The 'pearl of the Alpine region' offers caves, springs, rock towers and waterfalls – as well as rare fauna like mountain eagles (p191)

Historical Locations

From Roman times through to the rough and tumble Middle Ages, the Napoleonic Wars, WWI, WWII and the Communist era, there's been something afoot on Slovenian territory.

Predjama Castle Could easily be called 'pre-drama' for its dramatic perch tucked high inside a cliffside cage (p134)

Ptuj One of the oldest towns in Slovenia, this former metropolis from the Middle Ages boasts a symphony of red-tiled roofs (p172)

Škofja Loka The 'Bishop's Meadow' is a perfectly preserved medieval town with an intact square and a spooky hilltop castle (p68)

Kropa This one-horse, former iron-working town is a perfectly preserved living museum of the country's once-mighty industrial tradition (p77)

Piran It's hard to imagine a more romantic spot anywhere than this little Venetian port jutting out into the Adriatic (p122)

Ljubljana Castle For history, look no further than the capital's hilltop fortress that's been around since at least the 12th century and probably much earlier (p37)

Walks & Hikes

Slovenia is crossed by thousands of kilometres of hiking trails, many passing through points of considerable natural beauty or paired to teach the lessons of the country's moving history.

Climbing Mt Triglav The ultimate Slovenian hike involves a trek to the top of Mt 'Three Heads'; at 2864m it's a point of considerable national pride, especially for those who've reach the top (p97)

Trail of Remembrance This trail snakes 34km around the capital along the boundary where German barbed wire once enclosed the city during WWII (p51)

Walk of Peace This pretty 5km-long trail starting from Kobarid is an open-air museum of the atrocities committed during WWI (p103)

Jeruzalem-Ljutomer wine road Walk or cycle this lovely trail that begins at Ormož and continues for 18km north to Ljutomer, passing many wine cellars and restaurants en route (p178)

Lake Bled If you're looking for something easy and relaxing, this two-hour circuit around lovely Lake Bled is just the ticket (p76)

» Velika Planina (p72)

Food & Wine

Slovenia is in the midst of a slow-food, organic-food, local-food revolution that prizes original recipes and fresh, quality ingredients. The country's excellent wine is sorely underrated.

Gostilna na Gradu Ljubljana's castle-top restaurant – local food only – is a great reason to make that long slog to the top (p55)

Izola The port of Piran likes to think it has the country's best seafood, but for our money the freshest fish is a few kilometres east in Izola (p120)

Teran Wine This ruby-red, peppery wine with high acidity is made from Slovenian Refošk grapes and pairs beautifully with *pršut* and black olives

Groats If Slovenian cooking has a signature side, it would have to be these stick-to-your-ribs barley or buckwheat groats

Prekmurska gibanica Slovenia's tongue-twister dessert is a rich concoction of pastry filled with poppy seeds, walnuts, apples, raisins and cheese and topped with cream

Outdoor Activities

Slovenia is an active holiday destination. And while hiking and biking are still the most popular ways to play, there are lots of chances to swim, boat, raft or jump out of a plane.

Rafting the Soča The signature Slovenian outdoor adventure involves a breath-taking float down one of Europe's fastest and most beautiful rivers (p100)

Adrenaline A growing number of operators, particularly at Bovec, Bled and Bohinj – offer the chance to try ballooning, canyoning and paragliding, among other instant rushes

Caving Slovenia has dozens of caves; the one at Škocjan has walls that run 100m high. Postojna Cave is pretty amazing as well. (p112) (p131)

Skiing The Julian Alps offers myriad chances to hit the slopes. Kranjska Gora is the centre of the country's ski universe, but is just one of several popular resorts. (p91)

Mt Triglav Slovenia's only national park covers a huge swath of Slovenian turf in the northwest; it's a world of rivers, streams, waterfalls and hiking trails (p94)

Unique Sleeps

Why stay in a hotel when a bunk in a former prison beckons or a shepherd offers his lean-to with a view of the starry night sky free of charge?

Glamping 'Glam camping' (or 'glamping') is all the rage at Lake Bled. Forget bedrolls and rent an ecofriendly, all-natural, A-frame hut with a hot tub. (p82)

Celica Hostel In Ljubljana, this stylishly revamped former prison has 20 'cells' interior-designed by different artists (p52)

MCC Hostel, Celje Another creative take on the hostel model is situated in a converted brew house, with each room decorated by local artists (p189)

Kaki Plac Escape the package-tour feel of popular Portorož by sleeping in a tent under an Istrian shepherd's lean-to (p129)

Farmstays One of the best ways to experience rural life is to stay with a family on a working farm

month by month

February

A normally cold and snowy month keeps things busy on the ski slopes near Kranjska Gora. Watch for crowds around mid-month, when schoolkids have their annual winter break.

⭐ Kurentovanje

Ptuj's 'rite of spring' (p175) is celebrated for 10 days before Shrove Tuesday (February or early March) and is the most popular Mardi Gras celebration in Slovenia.

March

Still plenty of good skiing in the higher elevations; elsewhere the country is relatively quiet.

☆ Men's Slalom & Giant Slalom Vitranc Cup Competition

The number one downhill ski event of the year for men takes place at Kranjska Gora (www.pokal-vitranc .com) in mid-March.

April

Flowers bloom and trees blossom in lower elevations. Depending on the winter, there's skiing at higher elevations. The Vršič Pass opens to cars by mid-month.

👁 Spring Flower Show & Gardening Fair

Slovenia's largest flower and gardening show takes place at an arboretum in Volčji Potok (www.arbore tum-vp.si), near Kamnik, in mid-April.

May

Hit the Alpine valleys for a burst of mountain wildflowers. Expect sunshine and warm daytime temps. It's too cold yet to swim in the Adriatic, but days are ideal for a portside promenade.

⭐ Druga Godba

Held in mid-May, this is a festival of alter-native and world music (p51) in the Križanke in Ljubljana.

June

June can be gloriously sunny or depressingly rainy. It's the best time for white-water rafting: rivers swell after the spring thaw and it's warm enough to make the idea palatable.

☆ International Rowing Regatta

One of the country's most exciting (and fastest) sport-ing events (p81) is held over three days in mid-June on Lake Bled.

⭐ Idrija Lace-Making Festival

This red-letter annual event (p109) held in late June ends with a contest of up to 100 competitors.

⭐ Lent Festival

A two-week extrava ganza (p179) of folklore in Maribor's Old Town.

July

Mostly warm and sunny, this is the biggest month for festivals. Trekkers, watch out for freak storms in higher elevations.

Primorska Summer Festival

Concerts, theatre and dance events held in various venues in Ankaran, Izola, Koper, Piran and Portorož over four weeks from late July to early August. (www.portoroz.si)

Rock Otočec

Slovenia's biggest open-air rock concert (www.rock-otocec.com) is held over three days in late June or early July near the Krka River, not far from Novo Mesto.

Ljubljana Festival

The nation's premier festival of classical entertainment (music, theatre and dance) held from early July to mid-August (p52).

August

The traditional summer holiday month for Europeans finds resorts like Piran and Portorož filled to brimming. Campgrounds are packed, and the waters of lakes Bohinj and Bled warm up enough to swim.

Trnfest

Probably the most popular annual festival in the capital, this month-long party (p52) at the KUD France Prešeren cultural centre showcases music, dance and theatre from around the world.

Radovljica Festival of Classical Music

One of the most important festivals of ancient classical music in Europe is staged over 10 days from early to late August (www.festival-radovljica.si).

September

The first autumn chill comes to the mountains. Swimming winds down on the Adriatic coast and resorts like Bled and Bohinj hold their last big shindigs of the season. Mushroom-hunting shifts into high gear.

Cows' Ball

Zany weekend of folk dance, music, eating and drinking in Bohinj to mark the return of the cows from their high pastures to the valleys in mid-September (p87).

Dormouse Night, Cerknica

A celebration and feast during the very short dormouse-hunting season of late September in the forests around Snežnik Castle.

Slovenian Film Festival

A pivotal event in the Slovenian cinema world, this three-day festival in Portorož in late September or early October sees screenings and awards. (www.fsf.si)

October

Coastal areas quieten down for the year and the action shifts to big cities like Ljubljana, where the cultural season of classical concerts, ballet and theatre is in full swing.

City of Women

Ljubljana's two-week international festival focusing on contemporary arts and culture created by women (p52).

Ljubljana Marathon

First run in 1996, this marathon (p52) draws an increasingly international field.

November

The solemn holiday of All Souls' Day (1 November) sets the tone for the rest of this mostly dark, chilly month. On this day, Slovenes bring candles to cemeteries to remember departed loved ones.

St Martin's Day

Nationwide celebration to mark the day (11 November) when *mošt* (must; fermenting grape juice) officially becomes new wine.

December

Christmas (25 December) is the high point of this dark and cold month. Ski season gets underway in the mountains.

Christmas Concerts

Held throughout Slovenia, but the most famous are in Postojna Cave (p131), where you can also attend the Live Christmas Crib, a re-enactment of the Nativity. Held early to mid-December.

itineraries

Whether you've got six days or 60, these itineraries provide the starting point for the trip of a lifetime. Want more inspiration? Head online to lonelyplanet .com/thorntree to chat with other travellers.

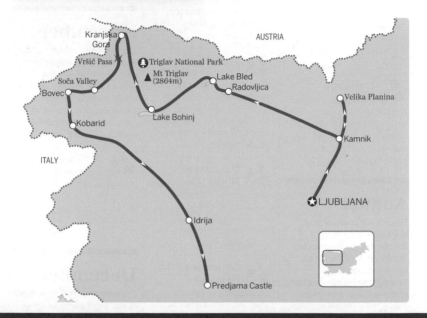

One Week
Mountain Majesty

Slovenia has mountains in spades. From Ljubljana to Predjama Castle, this itinerary is perfect for active travellers looking to make the most of their time.

Begin in **Ljubljana**, where you can buy any hiking gear you might need and bookstores stock excellent regional maps. From **Ljubljana**, make your way to **Kamnik** and the picturesque, high-altitude pastureland of **Velika Planina**. Then head back toward Kranj and continue north to impossibly cute **Radovljica**. Overnight here or a few kilometres north at **Lake Bled**.

Use Bled or nearby **Lake Bohinj** for forays into **Triglav National Park**. Both are popular approaches for scaling **Mt Triglav**. Proceed northward to the ski centre **Kranjska Gora** and the heart-stopping **Vršič Pass**. (Note the pass is closed in winter.) The road down deposits you in Primorska's **Soča Valley**. Following the Soča River will bring you to the activities centre of **Bovec** and the WWI battlegrounds around **Kobarid**. From here, head down through Tolmin to **Idrija**. Keep going south and you'll reach stunning **Predjama Castle**.

10 to 14 Days
Essential Slovenia

Travellers wanting to experience the highlights of the country's alpine, karst and coastal regions should begin in the country's capital, **Ljubljana**. Allow at least two nights to take in the sights, restaurants and beautiful riverside setting. Drive, train or take the bus north to Lake Bled. If you've got time, stop at one or both of the historic towns of **Škofja Loka** or **Radovljica** on your way.

Lake Bled merits at least a night's stay to allow time to walk around the lake and take a *pletna* (gondola) to Bled Island. Plan for a longer sojourn if you intend to try an adventure outing, like rafting or canyoning.

Lovely **Lake Bohinj**, 26km southwest of Lake Bled and accessible by bus, makes for a more rustic, less touristy base and has the added advantage of direct views to Mt Triglav. Both Bled and Bohinj are good starting points for further exploration of **Triglav National Park**.

Make your way northward to **Kranjska Gora**, the country's skiing capital and another good base for walking and hiking. It's also the northern terminus of the spectacularly beautiful **Vršič Pass**, a high-altitude roadway that can be traversed by car, bus or bike during summer, but is closed to vehicles from November to April.

The Vršič Pass twists and turns for some 50km down to the country's white-water rafting capital of **Bovec**. Overnight here or in nearby **Kobarid**, a pretty town with a Mediterranean feel, amazing WWI history and some of the country's best restaurants.

Continue southward through **Nova Gorica** to the **Vipava Valley**, the centre of the Karst region that stretches southeast to the Croatian border. Little towns here, like **Štanjel** to the west, are rich in olives, ruby-red Teran wine, *pršut* (dry-cured ham) and red-tiled roofs.

Further south, following the main Hwy E70 to the coast near Divača, is the awe-inspiring **Škocjan Caves**, part of an immense system of limestone caves in this region.

From here, it's just a skip to the coastal resorts of **Portorož** and **Piran**. If you're looking for romance, choose Piran; if it's sun and fun, Portorož is the centre of the action.

The return journey to Ljubljana passes through **Postojna**, another amazing cave.

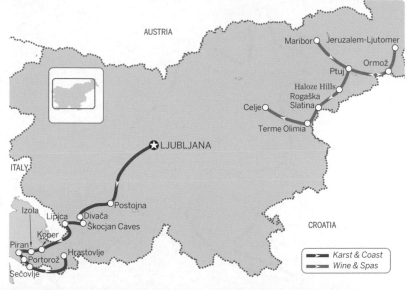

AUSTRIA

Maribor   Jeruzalem-Ljutomer

Ormož

Ptuj

Haloze Hills

Rogaška
Slatina

Celje

Terme Olimia

⭐ LJUBLJANA

ITALY

Postojna

Izola

Lipica   Divača

Škocjan Caves

Koper

Piran

Portorož   Hrastovlje

Sečovlje

CROATIA

—► *Karst & Coast*
—► *Wine & Spas*

One Week
Wine & Spas

> Eastern Slovenia is known for both wines and spas. This tour includes the best of each.

Start in **Maribor**, the region's biggest city and cultural hub. Make your way south to the former Roman stronghold and thoroughly charming town of **Ptuj**.

Head east to **Ormož**, for the start of the important **Jeruzalem-Ljutomer** wine district, home to the country's best whites. Walk or hike the wine trail here.

Return to Ptuj and head southwest into another important wine region, the **Haloze Hills**, celebrated for its pinot blanc, sauvignon and riesling. There's a wonderful footpath here, too: the Haloze Highlands Trail.

Head southwest from the Haloze Hills to find atmospheric **Rogaška Slatina**, Slovenia's oldest and largest spa. It's a veritable 'cure factory' with a dozen hotels, treatments and therapies.

To the south stretches another well-known wine region: the Bizeljsko-Sremič area. This region is noted for its medium-dry whites and reds and for *repnice*, which are caves for storing wine. Not surprisingly, you'll find another inviting spa nearby, the **Terme Olimia**. Return to Maribor via **Celje**.

Two Days to One Week
Karst & Coast

> Combining the best of two worlds – the fun-filled coast and the evocative, sun-baked Karst – this itinerary is designed to be driven, but most major points can be reached by train or bus.

From **Ljubljana** follow the A1 motorway to **Postojna**, then continue to **Divača** and the awesome **Škocjan Caves**. If you have your own wheels, take some R&R at the bucolic oasis of **Lipica**.

Return to Divača and head southwest to **Koper**, an affordable coastal place to stay, then follow the coast to **Izola**, **Piran**, and **Portorož**, with all types of accommodation for different budgets.

To the south along the coast is **Sečovlje** and its famous salt pans, a relaxing antidote to brash Portorož.

A spur road just before the Croatian border crosses the Drnica River and links up with Route 11, which takes you back to Ljubljana. At the Rižana exit, take a detour south for the Karst village of **Hrastovlje** and its wonderful church.

Outdoor Slovenia

The Best...

Hiking
Julian Alps, Triglav National Park, Kamnik-Savinja Alps, Pohorje Massif

Skiing
Maribor Pohorje, Kranjska Gora, Vogel, Kanin

Cycling
Lake Bohinj, Krka Valley

Rafting
Soča Valley, Krka River, Kolpa River

Caving
Škocjan, Postojna

Summer Activities
Hiking walking, cycling and swimming.

Spring Activities
White-water rafting and birdwatching.

Autumn Activities
Early autumn is a good time to climb Mt Triglav.

Winter Activities
Skiing: the season runs from mid-December to early April.

Slovenes are naturally outdoorsy and the country is blessed with a magnificent natural environment of mountains, lakes and rivers that lend a breathtaking backdrop to any activity. The most popular pursuits include walking and hiking, cycling and skiing, though the range of possible activities encompasses white-water rafting, boating, horse riding, caving and fishing, among others.

The **Slovenian Tourist Board** (www.slovenia.info) publishes comprehensive brochures and maps on all of these activities as well as the country's top spas and heath resorts.

Hiking & Walking

Hiking is a national pastime. The country has an excellent system of well-marked trails that run to a total length of nearly 10,000km. Most trails are marked by a red circle with a white centre, with periodic updater signs along the way indicating distances and walking times. In addition, most regional tourist offices and bookshops stock a comprehensive selection of hiking maps.

The most popular areas for hikes include the Julian Alps and the Kamnik-Savinja Alps in Gorenjska as well as the Pohorje Massif in Štajerska & Koroška, but there are wonderful trails in all of the country's regions. Some of the best of these are linked with less obviously salubrious activities like wine drinking.

Many trails can also be cycled, with the notable exception being the trails in the

Triglav National Park. Maps usually indicate which trails are suitable for cycling with a bicycle sign.

Great Slovenian Hikes

» The **Slovenian Mountain Trail** runs for 500km from Maribor to Ankaran on the coast via the Pohorje Massif, the Kamnik-Savinja Alps, the Julian Alps and the Cerkno and Idrija hills. It was opened back in 1953 and was the first such national trail in Europe.

» The 470km-long **Sub-Alpine Trail** covers Slovenia's hill country – from Cerkno and Idrija to Posavje via Notranjska – and is for less-ambitious, but equally keen, walkers and hikers.

» A great 'wine trail' is the **Jeruzalem-Ljutomer wine road** in Štajerska & Koroška, which begins at Ormož and continues for 18km north to Ljutomer, via the hilltop village of Jeruzalem. There are many wine cellars along the way, and this road can also be biked.

» The **Haloze Highlands Trail** is a lovely wine-oriented footpath that takes in the gentle landscape of the Haloze Hills wine region. It is accessible from near Štatenberg.

Major European Trails

» The 350km **E6 European Hiking Trail** runs from the Baltic to the Adriatic Seas and enters Slovenia at Radlje ob Dravi in Koroška. It continues on to a point south of Snežnik in Notranjska.

» The 600km **E7 European Hiking Trail** connects the Atlantic with the Black Sea. It crosses into Slovenia at Robič in Primorska and runs along the Soča Valley. From here, it continues through the southern part of the country eastward to Bistrica ob Sotli in Štajerska before exiting into Croatia.

» Slovenia has joined Austria, Germany, Liechtenstein, Switzerland, Italy, France and Monaco to develop the **Via Alpina** (www.via-alpina.com), a system of five long trails that follow the entire arc of the Alps from Trieste to Monaco. Two of the trails pass through northern Slovenia: the 14-stage Red Trail (220km) and the 10-stage Purple Trail (120km).

Skiing

Skiing rivals hiking as the most popular recreational pursuit in Slovenia. On the basis of written references that go back to the 17th century, many believe that skiing was actually invented here, on the slopes of the Bloke Plateau in Notranjska. Today an estimated 300,000 people – some 15% of the population – ski regularly. Just about everyone takes to the slopes or trails in season, and you can too on the more than two dozen ski grounds and resorts of varying sizes listed in the Slovenian Tourist Board's useful *Ski Centers of Slovenia.*

Most of Slovenia's ski areas are small and relatively unchallenging compared to the Alpine resorts of France, Switzerland and Italy, but they do have the attraction of lower prices and easy access. The latest weather and snow reports are available from the **Snow Telephone** (Snežni Telefon; ☎031 182 500, 041 182 500; www.snezni-telefon.si).

Gorenjska

» **Kranjska Gora** (810m to 1291m), has 20km of pistes, but the skiing here is fairly straightforward and suited mostly to beginners and intermediates. Nevertheless, for foreign visitors, it is probably Slovenia's best-known and most popular ski resort, being easily accessible from Austria and Italy.

» **Vogel** (570m to 1800m), above shimmering Lake Bohinj, offers dazzling views of Mt Triglav and reliable snow cover.

» **Krvavec** (1450m to 1971m), in the hills northeast of Kranj, is one of the best-equipped ski areas in the country, with 20km of pistes and

» (above) Mountain biking, Triglav National Park (p94)
» (left) Hiking, Mt Triglav (p97)

BEDDING DOWN ON HIGH

» A bivouac is the most basic hut in the mountains of Slovenia, provides shelter only.

» A refuge has refreshments, and sometimes accommodation, but usually no running water.

» A *koča* (hut) or *dom* (house) can be a simple cottage or a fairly grand establishment.

» A bed for the night runs from €18 to €27 in a Category I hut, the most remote hut, depending on the number of beds in the room, and from €12 to €20 in a Category II, defined as being within an hour's walk of motor transport.

» There are some 60 mountain huts (41 of them Category I) in the Julian Alps, most of them open at least between June and September; some huts at lower altitudes are open all year.

» Huts are never more than five hours' walk apart. You'll never be turned away if the weather looks bad, but some huts on Triglav can be unbearably crowded at weekends – especially in August and September.

40km of trails. In addition, you'll find a number of ski (alpine and telemark) and snowboard schools, equipment rental, a ski shop and some good restaurants and bars. However, as it's only an hour's drive from Ljubljana, it's best avoided at the weekends.

Primorska

» For spectacular scenery, you can't beat Slovenia's highest ski resort, **Kanin** (1600m to 2300m), which perches above Bovec and can have snow until May. You'll get stunning views north to Mt Triglav and the Julian Alps, and from the top station you can even glimpse the Adriatic Sea.

Štajerska & Koroška

» The biggest downhill skiing area is **Maribor Pohorje** (325m to 1347m) in the hills south of Maribor, with 40km of linked pistes and 36km of cross-country trails suitable for skiers of all levels. It offers a ski and snowboard school, equipment rental and floodlit night skiing, as well as being a good starting point for ski touring through the forested hills of the Pohorje.

Cycling & Mountain Biking

Cycling is a popular pastime in Slovenia and the country is an excellent cycling destination. Ljubljana is a bike-friendly big city, with marked cycling paths, an active bike-riding population, and several rental outfits, including an innovative rent-as-you-go cycling scheme, called Bicike(lj) (p66).

The Slovenian Tourist Board publishes a brochure called *Cycling in Slovenia*, with information for on- and off-road biking. On its website, the tourist board identifies 14 areas that it considers to be true 'cycling destinations', based on the existence of marked bike trails, good signage, and rental and repair shops.

Mountain bikers will want to focus on Gorenjska and Primorska, particularly around Bovec, Lake Bohinj and Kranjska Gora, the latter of which also offers free-riding possibilities, where cyclists are whisked up the hill on a ski lift and then hurtle downward at breakneck speed. Around Lake Bohinj, look for the book *Bohinj by Mountain Bike*, available at the tourist information centre, which marks out 15 routes, from family friendly to downright crazy. Another popular adrenaline destination is the Upper Savinja Valley in Štajerska.

Slower, more scenic rides can be found around Lake Bled, and in the Krka Valley in Dolenjska, which has become something of a cycling centre.

Other Popular Pursuits

Birdwatching

Slovenia has some of the best birdwatching in Central Europe. Some 376 species have been sighted here, 219 of which are breeders and 11 of which are under threat.

The Ljubljana Marsh (Ljubljansko Barje), south of Ljubljana, Lake Cerknica in Notranjska, and the Sečovlje salt pans in Primorska are especially good for sighting waterbirds and waders, as is the Drava River and its reservoirs in northeast Slovenia.

An especially wonderful (though messy) sight is the arrival of the white storks in Prekmurje in March/April. Other important habitats are the Julian and Savinja Alps, the Karst area and the Krakovski Forest north of Kostanjevica na Krki in Dolenjska.

For more information, contact the Ljubljana-based **Bird Watching & Study Association of Slovenia** (Društvo za Opazovanje in Proučevanje Ptic Slovenije; www.ptice.si), a member of Bird Life International.

Caving

It is hardly surprising that the country that gave the world the word 'karst' is riddled with caves – around 7500 have been recorded and described. For information on club contacts and expeditions, contact the **Speleological Association of Slovenia** (Jamarska Zveza Slovenije; 01-429 34 44; www.jamarska-zveza.si; Lepi pot 6) in Ljubljana.

There are about 20 'show caves' open to visitors, but the top two are Škocjan and Postojna in Primorska and Notranjska.

The main potholing regions in Slovenia are the Notranjska karst, centred around Postojna, and the Julian Alps of Gorenjska and Primorska.

Diving

You can dive in all Slovenian rivers, lakes and of course the sea, with the exceptions of the fish hatchery in Lake Bohinj and the shipping lanes and harbour areas.

The sport is popular in Lake Bled, in the Kolpa River in Bela Krajina, and at Ankaran, Portorož and Piran on the coast, where you can take lessons. For more information, contact the **Slovenian Diving Federation** (Slovenska Potapljaška Zveza; 01-433 93 08; www.spz.si; 25 Celovška cesta) in Ljubljana.

Cave diving is a popular sport in Slovenia but is permitted only under the supervision of a professional guide. Cave diving has been done at Postojna, Škocjan and in the tunnel at Wild Lake (Divje Jezero) near Idrija.

Fishing

Slovenia's mountain streams are teeming with brown and rainbow trout and grayling, and its lakes and more-sluggish rivers are home to pike, perch, carp, chub and other fish. The best rivers for angling are the Soča, the Krka, the Kolpa, the Sava Bohinjka near Bohinj, and the Unica in Notranjska.

Fishing is not cheap in Slovenia – a permit at the more popular rivers will cost

SLOVENIA'S LONE NATIONAL PARK

Slovenia has a few regional parks and a few dozen small 'landscape' parks, but **Triglav National Park** (Triglavski Narodni Park; TNP), in the far northwestern corner, is the country's only true national park. Covering about 84,000 hectares (4% of the country's total land area), it's one of the European continent's largest protected natural landscapes.

The park's main attraction is **Mt Triglav**, which at 2864m is both the country's tallest mountain and the highest peak in the Julian Alps range. In addition to this and several other peaks that top 2500m, the park boasts scenic waterfalls, gorges, ravines, rivers, streams and the source lands of two major river systems: the Sava and Soča.

The national park straddles two Slovenian regions: Gorenjska in the east and Primorska in the south and west. The border between the two regions lies just to the west of the Vršič Pass.

The main Triglav National Park Information Centre (p92) is located in the village of Trenta, about 24km south of Kranjska Gora along the Vršič Pass highway. In addition to providing general information on the park, there's a small museum, a gift shop and a small restaurant.

Recommended hiking and trekking maps include the PZS 1:50,000-scale *Triglavski Narodni Park* (*Triglav National Park*; €8.50) and Freytag & Berndt's 1:50, 000 *Julische Alpen* (*Julian Alps*) for €9.

'TAKING THE CURE' SLOVENIAN STYLE

Taking the waters is one of the most enjoyable ways to relax in Slovenia, especially after a day on the slopes or mountain trails.

Slovenia has a score of thermal spa resorts – two on the coast at Portorož and Strunjan and the rest in the eastern half of the country in Štajerska, Dolenjska and Prekmurje. They are excellent places not only for 'taking the cure' but also for relaxing and meeting people. Many resorts use the Italian *terme* for 'spa' instead of the Slovene words *toplice* (thermal spring) or *zdravilišč p*.

Only two – Dolenjske Toplice in Dolenjska and Rogaška Slatina in Štajerska – are really spa towns as such, with that distinctive 19th-century feel about them. Others, like Terme Ptuj in Štajerska, are loud, brash places dedicated to all the hedonistic pursuits you care to imagine, complete with swimming pools, waterslides, tennis courts, saunas, massage services and wellness centres.

from €50 to €100 a day. Catch-and-release permits are cheaper. You can usually buy short-term fishing permits at local tourist information offices.

For information on licences and seasons, contact the **Slovenian Fishing Institute** (Zavod za Ribištvo Slovenije; ☑01-244 34 00; www .zzrs.si; Župančičeva ulica 9) in Ljubljana.

Horse Riding

Slovenia is a nation of horse riders. The world's most famous horse – the Lipizzaner of the Spanish Riding School in Vienna – was first bred at Lipica in Primorska.

Among the best places for serious riders to improve their skills are the Lipica Stud Farm in Primorska and the Novo Mesto Sport Equestrian Centre in Dolenjska.

For a simple day out on the horses, the Mrcina Ranč in Studor near Lake Bohinj in Gorenjska, offers a range of guided tours on horseback, many of which are suitable for children.

Mountaineering & Rock Climbing

The principal rock- and ice-climbing areas in Slovenia include Mt Triglav's magnificent north face – where routes range from the classic 'Slovene Route' (Slovenski Pot; Grade II/III; 750m) to the modern 'Sphinx Face' (Obraz Sfinge; Grade IX+/X-; 140m), with a crux 6m roof – as well as the impressive northern buttresses of Prisank overlooking the Vršič Pass.

The best mountaineering guidebook readily available is *Mountaineering in Slovenia* (Sidarta) by the late Tine Mihelič, which describes some 85 tours in the Julian

Alps as well as the Kamnik-Savinja Alps and the Karavanke.

Športno plezanje (sport climbing) is very popular here too. The revised *Slovenija Športnoplezalni Vodnik* (*Sport Climbing Guide to Slovenia*; Sidarta) by climber Janez Skok et al covers 85 crags, with good topos and descriptions in English, German and Italian as well as Slovene.

Paragliding, Ballooning & Flying

Paragliding has taken off in Slovenia, especially in Gorenjska around Lake Bohinj and at Bovec, where you can take a tandem flight from the upper cable-car station on Kanin peak and descend 2000m into the Bovec Valley.

The tourist information centre in Ljubljana (p64) organises hot-air balloon flights.

Every self-respecting town in Slovenia seems to have an airstrip or aerodrome, complete with an *aeroklub* whose enthusiastic members will take you 'flight-seeing'. The Ljubljana-based **Aeronautical Association of Slovenia** (Letalska Zveza Slovenije; ☑01-422 33 33; www.lzs-zveza.si; Tržaška cesta 2) has a list.

Rafting, Kayaking, Canoeing & Canyoning

River sports are hugely popular and practised anywhere there's running water in Slovenia.

The centre for rafting and canoeing is the Soča River at Bovec in Primorska. The Soča is famed as one of the best white-water rafting and kayaking rivers in Europe, and it is one of only half a dozen rivers in the European Alps whose upper waters are still unspoiled.

Other rafting centres include the Krka River, the Kolpa in Bela Krajina, the Sava River at Bohinj in Gorenjska, the Savinja River at Logarska Dolina in Štajerska, and the Drava River near Dravograd in Koroška.

Canyoning, a relatively new sport that has grown by leaps and bounds in recent years, will have you descending through gorges, jumping over and sliding down waterfalls, swimming in rock pools and abseiling. It's been described as being in one huge, natural water park. Operators at Lake Bled can set you up for the day.

For something a little less adrenaline filled, you can rent rowboats and paddle boats on lakes all around the country. The best backdrops are at Lake Bohinj and Lake Bled in Gorenjska.

regions at a glance

Ljubljana

Museums ✓✓✓
Entertainment ✓✓✓
Food ✓✓

Museums

Ljubljana is home to Slovenia's most important museums of art, history and natural science, among others. Admirers of architect and designer extraordinaire Jože Plečnik can tour the house he lived and worked in for almost 40 years.

Entertainment

Ljubljana has a thriving cultural scene, with something for everyone. From autumn through spring, the calendar is filled with classical music, drama and opera. In summer, nearly every weekend brings a festival or event, including the city's two-month Ljubljana Festival.

Food

We can't say for sure if Ljubljana has the country's best restaurants, but certainly the capital offers the most variety. Naturally you'll find excellent Slovenian restaurants, but also very good Balkan, Italian and Turkish cooking, and much more.

p34

Gorenjska

Views ✓✓✓
Hiking ✓✓
Activities ✓✓

Scenic Views

The Vršič Pass, lakes Bled and Bohinj, Mt Triglav: if you're seeking awe-inspiring natural beauty and mountain vistas, you've come to the right place. Views range from dramatic to sublime.

Hiking & Walking

The area around Kranjska Gora is filled with great day hikes or longer treks. The mother of all Slovenian hikes is an ascent of Mt Triglav.

Adrenalin Sports

The rivers and gorges of Triglav National Park supply thrills for fast-paced water sports like rafting and canyoning. In winter, Lake Bohinj has paragliding, while Kranjska Gora is a centre for downhill skiing and ski jumping.

p67

Primorska & Notranjska

Activities ✓✓✓
Caves ✓✓✓
Coastal Fun ✓✓

Outdoor Activities

The Soča Valley is one of Slovenia's best outdoor playgrounds. The stunning Soča River is made for rafting, kayaking and canyoning, the trails for trekking and biking, or opt to paraglide above it all.

Caves

Primorska's Karst region and Notranjska hide many of their most spectacular landscapes underground. The epic Postojna and Škocjan caves reveal the surprising Slovenia hidden below the surface.

Coastal Fun

Explore the fantastic architecture and wonderful seafood of one of the Adriatic's true jewels, the medieval Venetian port of Piran. Koper, another historic town, is a stone's throw away.

p98

Dolenjska & Bela Krajina

History ✓✓✓
Wine ✓✓
Activities ✓✓

Štajerska & Koroška

Activities ✓✓
History ✓✓
Spas ✓✓

Prekmurje

Food ✓✓
Spas ✓✓✓
Churches ✓✓

Historic Sights

Discover the history of WWII at a restored Partisan camp hidden in the Kočevski Rog landscape. Bogenšperk and Kostanjevica castles offer more grand military and cultural history.

Wine

Bela Krajina is justly celebrated for its wines. The Metlika wine region produces ruby reds and sweet whites, which can be sampled in the many vineyards and farmhouses.

Outdoor Activities

The Krka and Kolpa river valleys wend their way through this region, and are particularly good for rafting, with plenty of hiking and cycling opportunities beyond their banks. Everywhere there are beautiful walks.

p138

Outdoor Activities

Hike or mountainbike through the green valleys of Logarska Dolina or the Maribor Pohorje highlands, where, if you wait until winter, you can explore the same slopes on skis.

Historic Towns

Štajerska and Koroška have a host of fascinating historic towns, from gorgeous medieval Ptuj to Celje, with its grand castle and old centre rich in museums. Don't overlook Maribor's charming historic areas.

Spas

At Rogaška Slatina you'll find an entire town dedicated to the fine art of taking to Slovenia's mineral-rich spring waters for pleasure and health, and a goodly amount of beauty pampering.

p164

Food

Prekmurje's cuisine has a strong Hungarian influence, so help yourself to a plate of paprika-rich *golaž* (goulash). For dessert try *prekmurska gibanica*, a pastry with walnuts, fruit, cheese and cream.

Spas

Slovenia's eastern regions are fine places to take the waters. The two biggest spa centres are Moravske Toplice and Radenci, home to the country's most famous mineral water.

Church Architecture

There are several gems tucked into Prekmurje, foremost the Church of St Martin in Martjanci, with its 14th-century frescoes. Nearby Ižakovci has one of the last floating mills in the country.

p196

> Every listing is recommended by our authors, and their
favourite places are listed first

> Look out for these icons:

 Our author's top
recommendation

 A green or
sustainable option

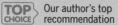 No payment
required

See the Index for a full list of destinations covered in this book.

On the Road

Ljubljana

☑01 / POP 272,554 / ELEV 295M

Best Places to Eat

» Gostilna na Gradu (p55)
» Ribca (p55)
» Špajza (p55)
» Julija (p55)
» Falafel (p57)

Best Places to Stay

» Antiq Palace Hotel & Spa (p52)
» Cubo (p52)
» Celica Hostel (p52)
» H2O (p53)
» Allegro Hotel (p53)

Why Go?

Slovenia's capital and largest city also happens to be one of Europe's greenest and most liveable capitals. Car traffic is restricted in the centre, leaving the leafy banks of the emerald-green Ljubljanica River, which flows through the city's heart, free for pedestrians and cyclists. In summer, cafes set up terrace seating along the river, lending the feel of a perpetual street party. Slovenia's master of early-modern, minimalist design, Jože Plečnik, graced Ljubljana with beautiful alabaster bridges and baubles, pylons and pyramids that are both elegant and playful. Attractive cities are often described as 'jewel boxes', but here the name really fits. The city's 64,000 students support an active clubbing and cultural scene, and the museums, hotels and restaurants are among the best in the country.

When to Go
Ljubljana

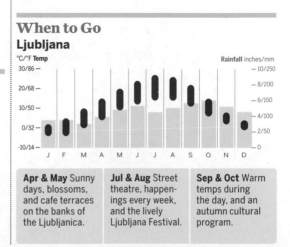

Apr & May Sunny days, blossoms, and cafe terraces on the banks of the Ljubljanica.

Jul & Aug Street theatre, happenings every week, and the lively Ljubljana Festival.

Sep & Oct Warm temps during the day, and an autumn cultural program.

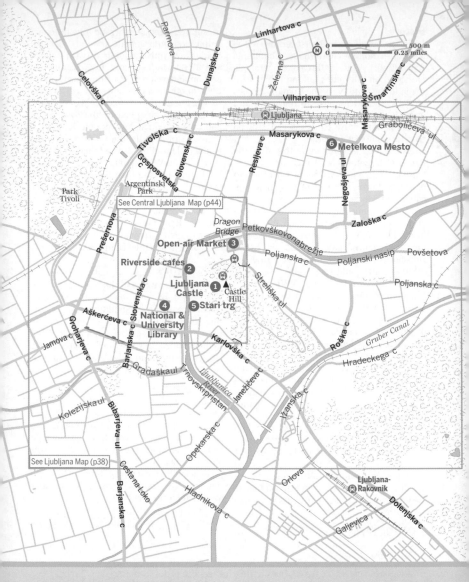

Ljubljana Highlights

1 Enjoy a ride on the funicular to **Ljubljana Castle** (p37) for an overview of the city's past and present

2 Spend an evening at an outside table at **Maček** (p59) or any other riverside cafe

3 Indulge in fresh fruits, vegetables and some delicious fish at the Ljubljana **open-air market** (p42)

4 Consider the genius of Slovenian architect and designer Jože Plečnik at the **National & University Library** (p43)

5 Stroll through lovely **Stari trg** (p41) and marvel that this pretty place is actually the capital of a European country

6 Crawl through the waterfront pubs of the Old Town and end up at an alternative club in **Metelkova Mesto** (p61)

History

Ljubljana began life in the 1st century AD as a smallish Roman city of 5000 inhabitants called Emona. The city thrived as a strategic crossroad on the routes linking Upper Pannonia in the south with the Roman colonies at Noricum and Aquileia to the north and west. Remnants of the old Roman walls, dwellings and early churches can still be seen throughout Ljubljana.

Emona was sacked and destroyed by the Huns, Ostrogoths and Langobards (Lombards) from the mid-5th century; by the end of the next century tribes of early Slavs began to settle here.

First mentioned in writing as 'Laibach' in 1144, Ljubljana changed hands frequently in the Middle Ages. The last and most momentous change came in 1335, when the Habsburgs became the town's new rulers, a position they would retain almost without interruption until the end of WWI in 1918.

The town and its hilltop castle were able to repel the Turks in the late 15th century, but a devastating earthquake in 1511 reduced much of medieval Ljubljana to a pile of rubble. This led to a period of frantic construction in the 17th and 18th centuries that provided the city with many of its pale-coloured baroque churches and mansions – and the nickname 'Bela (White) Ljubljana'.

When Napoléon established his Illyrian Provinces in 1809 in a bid to cut Habsburg Austria's access to the Adriatic, he made Ljubljana the capital (though Austrian rule was restored just four years later). In 1821 Ljubljana walked onto the world stage when the four members of the Holy Alliance (Austria, Prussia, Russia and Naples) met at the Congress of Laibach to discuss measures to suppress the democratic revolutionary and national movements in Italy.

Railways linked Ljubljana with Vienna and Trieste in 1849 and 1857, stimulating economic development of the town. But in 1895 another, more powerful earthquake struck, forcing the city to rebuild once again. To Ljubljana's great benefit, the Secessionist and art-nouveau styles were all the rage in Central Europe at the time, and many of the wonderful buildings erected then still stand.

During WWII Ljubljana was occupied by the Italians and then the Germans, who encircled the city with a barbed-wire fence creating, in effect, an urban concentration camp. Ljubljana became the capital of the Socialist Republic of Slovenia within Yugoslavia in 1945 and remained the capital after Slovenia's independence in 1991.

⊙ Sights

The easiest way to see Ljubljana is on foot. The oldest part of town, with the most important historical buildings and sights (including Ljubljana Castle) lies on the right (east) bank of the Ljubljanica River. Center, which has the lion's share of the city's museums and galleries, is on the left (west) side of the river.

CASTLE HILL

Begin an exploration of the city by making the trek up to **Castle Hill** (Grajska Planota) to poke around grand Ljubljana Castle. The castle area offers a couple of worthwhile exhibitions, and the castle watchtower affords amazing views over the city. The prospect of lunch at one of the city's best restaurants, Gostilna na Gradu (p55), provides an added inducement.

LJUBLJANA IN...

One Day

Take the funicular up to **Ljubljana Castle** to get an idea of the lay of the land. Come down and explore the **Central Market**. After a seafood lunch at **Ribca**, explore the **Old Town** then cross the Ljubljanica River via St James Bridge and walk north along Vegova ulica to **Kongresni trg** and **Prešernov trg**. Plan your evening over a fortifying libation at one of the many cafes along the Ljubljanica: low key at **Jazz Club Gajo**, chichi at **Top: Eat & Party**, trashy at **Ultra** or alternative at **Metelkova Mesto**.

Two Days

On your second day check out some of the city's excellent **museums** and **galleries,** and then stroll or cycle on a **Ljubljana Bike** through **Park Tivoli**, stopping for an oh-so-local horse burger at **Hot Horse** along the way. In the evening take in a performance at the **Križanke** or **Cankarjev Dom** and then visit one of the **clubs** you missed last night.

FREE **Ljubljana Castle** CASTLE

(Ljubljanski Grad; Map p44; ☑306 42 93; www
.ljubljanskigrad.si; Grajska Planota 1; adult/child incl
funicular and castle attractions €8/5, castle attractions only €6/3; with guided tour €10/8; ☺9am-
11pm May-Sep, 10am-9pm Oct-Apr) There's been
a human settlement here since at least Celtic
times, but the oldest structures these days
date from around the 16th century, and
were built following an earthquake in 1511.
It's free to ramble around the castle grounds,
but you'll have to pay to enter the Watchtower, the Chapel of St George and to see the
worthwhile exhibition on Slovenian history.

There are several ways to access the
castle, with the easiest (and for kids, the
most fun) being a 70m-long funicular that
leaves from Old Town not far from the market on Vodnikov trg. There's also an hourly
tourist train that departs from south of the
Ljubljana Tourist Information Centre. If
you'd like to get some exercise, you can hike
the hill in about 20 minutes. There are three
main walking routes: Študentovska ulica,
which runs south from Ciril Metodov trg;
steep Reber ulica from Stari trg; and Ulica
na Grad from Gornji trg.

There are several admission options
available; some include the price of the
funicular ride, while others include a castle
tour. Consult the castle website for details.
The **Ljubljana Castle Information Centre**
(☑306 42 93; www.ljubljanskigrad.si; Grajska Planota 1; ☺9am-9pm Apr-Sep, 9am-6pm Oct-Mar) can
advise on tours and events that might be on
during your visit.

Watchtower

(Razgledni Stolp; Map p44; ☑306 42 93; www
.ljubljanskigrad.si; included in general castle admission; ☺9am-9pm May-Sep, 10am-6pm Oct-Apr)
The 19th-century watchtower is located on
the southwestern side of the castle courtyard. The climb to the top, via a double
wrought-iron staircase (95 steps from the
museum level) and a walk along the ramparts, is worth the effort for the views down
into the Old Town and across the river to
Center.

Virtual Museum

(Virtualni Muzej; Map p44; ☑306 42 93; www
.ljubljanskigrad.si; included in general castle admission; ☺9am-9pm May-Sep, 10am-6pm Oct-Apr)
Situated in the watchtower, this is a short
video tour of Ljubljana and its history in several languages.

Slovenian History Exhibition

(Map p44; ☑306 42 93; www.ljubljanskigrad.si;
included in general castle admission; ☺9am-9pm
May-Sep, 10am-6pm Oct-Apr) Interesting and
well-presented interactive exhibition on
Slovenian history through the ages, running
from the very earliest Roman times, through
the Middle Ages, the 19th century, WWI and
WWII, and ending with socialist Yugoslavia
and independence.

Chapel of St George

(Kapela Sv Jurija; Map p44; ☑306 42 93; www
.ljubljanskigrad.si; included in general castle admission) This chapel, situated below the watchtower down a small flight of stairs, is one of
the oldest surviving remnants of the castle,
dating from 1489. It is covered in frescoes and
the coats of arms of the Dukes of Carniola.

PREŠERNOV TRG

This central and very beautiful **square** (Map
p44) forms the link between Center and
the Old Town. Taking pride of place is the
Prešeren monument (1905) designed by
Maks Fabiani and Ivan Zajc, and erected in
honour of Slovenia's greatest poet, France
Prešeren (1800–49). On the plinth are motifs from his poems. Just south of the monument is the **Triple Bridge** (Tromostovje),
called the Špital (Hospital) Bridge when it
was built as a single span in 1842, which
leads to the Old Town. The prolific architect
Jože Plečnik added the two sides in 1931.

To the east of the monument at No 5 is
the Italianate Central Pharmacy (Centralna
Lekarna), an erstwhile cafe frequented by
intellectuals in the 19th century. To the
north, on the corner of Trubarjeva cesta
and Miklošičeva cesta, is the delightful Secessionist **Palača Urbanc** (Urbanc Palace)
building from 1903. Diagonally across the
square at No 1 is another Secessionist gem:
the **Hauptman House**. Two doors down
Wolfova ulica at No 4 you'll see a terracotta
figure peeking out from a window. It's Julija Primič looking at the monument to her
lifelong admirer France Prešeren.

**Franciscan Church of the
Annunciation** CHURCH

(Frančiškanska Cerkev Marijinega Oznanjanja; Map
p44; ☑242 93 00; Prešernov trg 4; ☺10am-6pm)
The 17th-century salmon-pink Franciscan
Church of the Annunciation stands on the
northern side of the square. The interior has
six side altars and an enormous choir stall.
The main altar was designed by the Italian
sculptor Francesco Robba (1698–1757). To the

Ljubljana

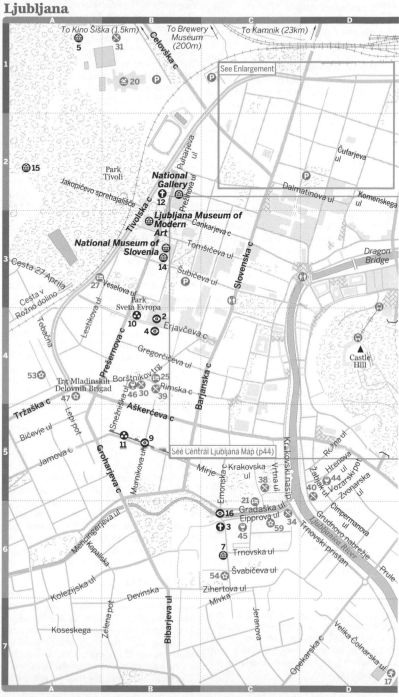

To Kino Šiška (1.5km)
To Brewery Museum (200m)
To Kamnik (23km)

5
31
20
P

See Enlargement

Čufarjeva ul

Park Tivoli

Jakopičevo sprehajališče

National Gallery 12

Puharjeva ul

Prešernova ul

P

Dalmatinova ul

Komenskega ul

Ljubljana Museum of Modern Art

Cankarjeva c

National Museum of Slovenia 14

Cesta 27 Aprila

Tomšičeva ul

Subičeva ul

Slovenska c

Dragon Bridge

Cesta v Rožno dolino

27 Veselova ul

Park Sveta Evropa

10 2 4

Erjavčeva c

P

Trobačna

Lestnikova ul

Gregorčičeva ul

Barjanska c

Castle Hill

53

Trg Mladinskih Delovnih Brigad

Prešernova c

Borštnikov trg 25

46 30

Rimska c

39

47

Tržaška c

Lepi pot

Snežniška ul

Aškerčeva c

Bičevje ul

Jamova c

Groharjeva c

Murnikova ul

11 9

See Central Ljubljana Map (p44)

Mirje

Krakovska ul

Emonska c

38

Vrtna ul

Krakovski nasip

Zabiac c

44

Hrenova ul

Zvonarska ul

Vozarski pot

40

Cimpermanova

Grudnovo nabrežje

21 Gradaška ul

16

3

Eipprova ul

45

59

34

Ljubljanica River

Trnovski pristan

Prule

Menicngerjeva ul

Kopališka

7 Trnovska ul

54

Švabičeva ul

Koležijska ul

Devinska

Bibarjeva ul

Zihertova ul

Mivka

Jeranova

Koseskega

Zelena pot

Opekarska c

Velika Čolnarska ul

17

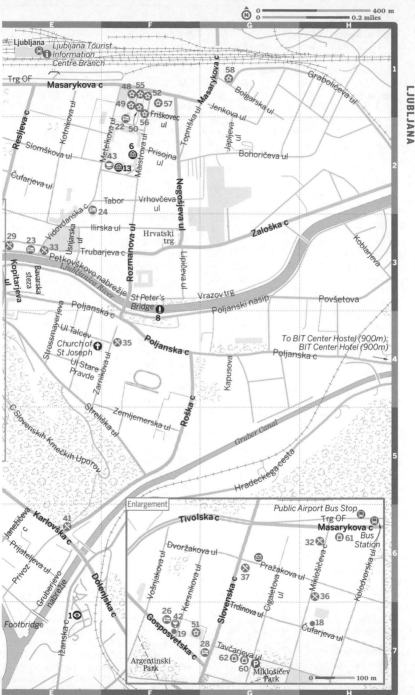

0 400 m
0 0.2 miles

Ljubljana
Ljubljana Tourist
Information
Centre Branch

Trg OF
Masarykova c

58
Bolgarska ul
Graboličeva ul

48 55
49 52 57
Friškovec ul
22 50 56
Jenkova ul
Bohoričeva ul

6
43
13

Tabor
24
Vrhovčeva ul

Ilirska ul
Hrvatski trg

29
23
33

Topniška ul
Masarykova c
Negošjeva ul
Zaloška c
Koblarjeva

Kotnikova ul
Metelkova ul
Mainstrova ul
Prisojna ul
Rozmanova ul

Resljeva c
Slomškova ul
Čufarjeva ul
Vidovdanska c
Usnjarska ul
Trubarjeva c
Petkovškovo nabrežje
Ljubljanica River

Kopitarjeva ul
Bavarska steza

St Peter's
Bridge
8
Vrazov trg
Poljanski nasip
Povšetova

Poljanska c
Ul Talcev
Church of
St Joseph
35

Strossmayerjeva
Zarnikova ul
Ul Stare Pravde
Streliška ul
Zemljemerska ul
Roška c
Kapusova
Poljanska c

To BIT Center Hostel (900m);
BIT Center Hotel (900m)
Poljanska c

C Slovenskih Kmečkih Uporov
Gruber Canal
Hradeckega cesta

Karlovška c
41
Janežičeva c
Prijateljeva ul
Privoz
Gruberjevo nabrežje
Dolenjska c

Footbridge
Ižanska c
1

Enlargement

Tivolska c

Public Airport Bus Stop
Trg OF
Masarykova c
Bus Station
61
32

Dvoržakova ul

Vošnjakova ul
Kersnikova ul
Slovenska c
Cigaletova ul
Miklošičeva ul
Kolodvorska ul

Pražakova ul
37
36

26 42
51
19
Trdinova ul
18
Čufarjeva ul

Gosposvetska c
28
Tavčarjeva ul
62 60
Miklošičev Park

Argentinski Park

0 100 m

Ljubljana

left of the main altar is a glass-fronted coffin with the spooky remains of St Deodatus.

Miklošičeva Cesta   STREET
This 650m-long thoroughfare links Prešernov trg with Trg OF and the train and bus stations; the southern end boasts a splendid array of fine Secessionist buildings. The cream-coloured former **People's Loan Bank** (1908) at No 4 is topped with blue tiles and the figures of two women holding symbols of industry (a beehive) and wealth (a purse). The one-time **Cooperative Bank** (Map p44) at No 8 was designed

by Ivan Vurnik, and the red, yellow and blue geometric patterns were painted by his wife Helena in 1922. Just opposite is the **Grand Hotel Union** (Map p44), the grande dame of Ljubljana hotels built in 1905. About 150m to the north is **Miklošičev Park,** laid out by Fabiani in 1902. Many of the buildings facing it are art-nouveau masterpieces.

OLD TOWN

Ljubljana's Old Town (Staro Mesto) occupies a narrow swath of land along the right (eastern) bank of the Ljubljanica River. This is the city's oldest and most important historical quarter. It's comprised of three contiguous town squares that include Mestni trg (Town Square), Stari trg (Old Square) and Gornji trg (Upper Square) as you move south and east. A large portion of the buildings here are baroque, although some houses along Stari trg and Gornji trg have retained their medieval layout.

MESTNI TRG

The first of the Old Town's three 'squares' (the next two are more like narrow cobbled streets), Mestni trg is dominated by the town hall. In front of the town hall stands the 1751 **Robba Fountain** (Map p44); the three titans with their gushing urns represent the three rivers of Carniola – the Sava, Krka and Ljubljanica – but are modern copies. The originals, worn down by time and eaten away by urban pollution, are now housed in the National Gallery (p48).

Town Hall   TOWN HALL
(Mestna Hiša; Map p44; ☏306 30 00; Mestni trg; ☺7.30am-4pm Mon-Fri) The seat of the city government and sometimes referred to as the Magistrat or Rotovž, the town hall was erected in the late 15th century and rebuilt in 1718. The Gothic courtyard inside, arcaded on three levels, is where theatrical performances once took place and contains some lovely graffiti.

If you look above the south portal leading to a second courtyard you'll see a relief map of Ljubljana as it appeared in the second half of the 17th century.

STARI TRG

The 'Old Square' is the true heart of the Old Town. It is lined with 19th-century wooden shopfronts, quiet courtyards and cobblestone passageways. From behind the medieval houses on the eastern side, paths once led to Castle Hill, which was a source of water. The buildings fronting the river had

large passageways built to allow drainage in case of flooding.

Where No 2 is today, a prison called **Tranča** (Map p44) stood until the 18th century, and those condemned to death were executed at a spot nearby. The great polymath Janez Vajkard Valvasor was born at No 4, now called the **Valvasor House** (Map p44), in 1641.

A small street to the north called Pod Trančo ('Below Tranča') leads to **Cobbler Bridge** (Čevljarski Most). During the Middle Ages this was a place of trade, and a tolled gateway led to the town. Craftsmen worked and lived on bridges (in this case 16 shoemakers) to catch the traffic and avoid paying town taxes – a medieval version of duty-free.

Between Stari trg Nos 11 and 15 – the house that should bear the number 13 – there's a lovely rococo building called **Schweiger House** (Map p44) with a large Atlas supporting the upper balcony. The figure has his finger raised to his lips as if asking passers-by to be quiet (the owner's name means 'Silent One' in German). In this part of the world, bordellos were traditionally located at house No 13 of a street, and he probably got quite a few unsolicited calls.

GORNJI TRG

'Upper Square' is the southeastern extension of Stari trg. The five **medieval houses** (Map p44) at Nos 7 to 15 have narrow side passages

LJUBLJANA'S DRAGONS

Ljubljana's town hall is topped with a golden dragon, a symbol of Ljubljana, but not an ancient one as many people assume. Just before the turn of the 20th century a wily mayor named Ivan Hribar apparently persuaded the authorities in Vienna that Ljubljana needed a new crossing over the Ljubljanica, and he submitted plans for a 'Jubilee Bridge' to mark 50 years of the reign of Franz Joseph. The result was the much-loved **Dragon Bridge** (Zmajski Most) that stands north of Mestni trg, just beyond Vodnikov trg. City folk, both male and female, joke that the winged bronze dragons supposedly wag their tails whenever a virgin crosses the bridge, which is usually followed up with a smile and observation that they've never seen it happen.

JOŽE PLEČNIK, ARCHITECT EXTRAORDINAIRE

Few architects anywhere in the world have had as great an impact on the city of their birth as Jože Plečnik. His work is eclectic, inspired, unique – and found everywhere in the capital.

Born in Ljubljana in 1872, Plečnik was educated at the College of Arts in Graz and studied under the architect Otto Wagner in Vienna. From 1911 he spent a decade in Prague teaching and later helping to renovate Prague Castle.

Plečnik's work in his hometown began in 1921. Almost single-handedly, he transformed the city, adding elements of classical Greek and Roman architecture with Byzantine, Islamic, ancient Egyptian and folkloric motifs to its baroque and Secessionist faces. The list of his creations and renovations is endless – from the National & University Library and the colonnaded Central Market (p42) to the magnificent cemetery at Žale (p50).

Plečnik was also a city planner and designer. Not only did he redesign the banks of the Ljubljanica River (including Triple Bridge and the monumental lock downstream, entire streets (Zoisova ulica) and Park Tivoli, but he also set his sights elsewhere: on monumental stairways (Kranj), public buildings (Kamnik), chapels (Kamnik) and outdoor shrines (Bled). An intensely religious man, Plečnik designed many furnishings and liturgical objects – chalices, candlesticks, lanterns – for churches throughout the land (eg Škofja Loka's Parish Church of St James p69). One of Plečnik's designs that was never realised was an extravagant parliament, complete with an enormous cone-shaped structure, to be built on Castle Hill after WWII.

Plečnik's eclecticism and individuality alienated him from the mainstream of modern architecture during his lifetime, and he was relatively unknown (much less appreciated) outside Eastern and Central Europe when he died in 1957. Today he is hailed as a prophet of post-modernism.

(some with doors) where rubbish was once deposited so that it could be washed down into the river. An important building on this elongated square is the **Church of St Florian** (Cerkev Sv Florijana). It was built in 1672 and dedicated to the patron saint of fires after a serious blaze destroyed much of the Old Town. Plečnik renovated it in 1934.

The footpath **Ulica na Grad**, leading up from the church, is an easy way to reach the castle.

FREE **Botanical Garden**　　PUBLIC GARDEN
(Botanični Vrt; Map p38; ☑ 427 12 80; www.botanicni-vrt.si; Ižanska cesta 15; ☉ 7am-8pm Jul & Aug, 7am-7pm Apr-Jun, Sep & Oct, 7am-5pm Nov-Mar) About 800m southeast of the Old Town along Karlovška cesta and over the Ljubljanica River, this 2.5-hectare botanical garden was founded in 1810 as a sanctuary of native flora. It contains 4500 species of plants and trees, about a third of which are indigenous.

Gruber Palace　　PALACE
(Gruberjeva Palača; Map p44; Zvezdarska ulica 1) Across Karlovška cesta is Gruber Palace. Gabriel Gruber, the Jesuit who built the

Gruber Canal (Gruberjev Prekop) that regulates the Ljubljanica, lived here until 1784. The palace is in Zopf style, a transitional art style between late baroque and neoclassicism, and now contains the **national archives** (Arhiv Republike Slovenije; ☑ 241 42 00; www.arhiv.gov.si; Gruber Palace, Zvezdarska ulica 1; ☉ 8am-?pm Mon-Fri)

Church of St James　　CHURCH
(Cerkev Sv Jakoba; Map p44; ☑ 252 17 27; Gornji trg 18; ☉ 7am-8pm) The Church of St James was built in 1615. Inside the church, far more interesting than Robba's main altar (1732) is the one in the church's Chapel of St Francis Xavier to the left, with statues of a 'White Queen' and a 'Black King'.

CENTRAL MARKET AREA

The Central Market area extends northeast of the Triple Bridge along the eastern edge of the Ljubljanica River, following Adamič-Lundrovo nabrežje. There are not many traditional sights here, but it's a great place to stroll and naturally pay a visit to the covered market, fish market and enormous open-air market on Vodnikov trg (p54).

Cathedral of St Nicholas CHURCH
(Stolna Cerkev Sv Nikolaja; Map p44; ☑234 26 90; http://lj-stolnica.rkc.si; Dolničarjeva ulica 1; ⊗10am-noon & 3-6pm) A church has stood here since the 13th century, but the existing twin-towered building dates from the start of the 18th century. Inside it's a vision of pink marble, white stucco and gilt and contains a panoply of baroque frescoes. Have a look at the magnificent carved choir stalls, the organ and the angels on the main altar.

Two stunning bronze doors were added in 1996 to commemorate the late Pope John Paul II's visit – the (main) west door facing the Bishop's Palace symbolises 1250 years of Christianity in Slovenia; the six bishops on the south door fronting Ciril Metodov trg depict the history of the Ljubljana diocese.

CENTER
This large district on the left bank of the Ljubljanica is the nerve centre of modern Ljubljana. It is filled with shops, commercial offices, government departments and embassies. The region is divided into several distinct neighbourhoods centred on town squares.

NOVI TRG
'New Square', south of Cobbler Bridge, was a walled settlement of fisherfolk outside the town administration in the Middle Ages, but it became more aristocratic from the 16th century. It suffered extensive damage in the 1895 earthquake, but medieval remnants include the very narrow street to the north called **Židovska ulica** and its offshoot Židovska steza (Jewish Lane), once the site of a synagogue and the centre of Jewish life here in the Middle Ages. **Breg**, the city's port when the Ljubljanica River was still navigable this far inland, runs south from the square and is now almost entirely pedestrianised.

TOP CHOICE **National & University Library** HISTORIC BUILDING
(Map p44; ☑200 11 09; Turjaška ulica 1; ⊗9am-6pm Mon-Fri, 9am-2pm Sat) This library is Plečnik's masterpiece, completed in 1941. To appreciate this great man's philosophy, enter through the main door (note the horse-head doorknobs) on Turjaška ulica – you'll find yourself in near darkness, entombed in black marble. As you ascend the steps, you'll emerge into a colonnade suffused with light – the light of knowledge, according to the architect's plans.

The **Main Reading Room** (Velika Čitalnica), now open to nonstudents only by group tour in summer, has huge glass walls and some stunning lamps, also designed by Plečnik.

Slovenian Academy of Arts & Sciences HISTORIC BUILDING
(Slovenska Akademija Znanosti in Umetnosti; Map p44; Novi trg 3) At Novi trg's western end is the Slovenian Academy of Arts and Sciences, housed in a 16th-century building that was the seat of the provincial diet (parliament) under the Habsburgs.

KONGRESSNI TRG
This lovely square, with leafy **Zvevda Park** (Star Park) at its centre, was named in honour of the Congress of the Holy Alliance, convened by Austria, Prussia, Russia and Naples in 1821 and hosted by Ljubljana. Today the square is a popular venue for open-air concerts. It also contains several important buildings. To the south at No 12 is the central building of Ljubljana University, erected as a ducal palace in 1902.

Ursuline Church of the Holy Trinity CHURCH
(Uršulinska Cerkev Sv Trojice; Map p44; ☑252 48 64; Slovenska cesta 21; ⊗6-7.30am, 9-11am & 4-7pm) This church, which faces the square from across Slovenska cesta and dates from 1726, is the most beautiful baroque building in the city. It contains a multicoloured altar by Robba made of African marble.

The small gilded statue on top of a column nearby is a copy (the original is in the National Museum) of the Roman-era **Citizen of Emona** (Map p44), dating from the 4th century and unearthed not far from here in 1836.

Philharmonic Hall HISTORIC BUILDING
(Filharmonija; Map p44; ☑241 08 00; www.filharmonija.si; Kongresni trg 10) Situated in the square's southeast corner, this building is home to the Slovenian Philharmonic Orchestra, which was founded in 1701 and is one of the oldest in the world. Haydn, Beethoven and Brahms were honorary members, and Gustav Mahler was resident conductor for a season (1881–82).

Slovenian School Museum MUSEUM
(Slovenski Šolski Muzej; Map p44; ☑251 30 24; www.ssolski-muzej.si; Plečnikov trg 1; adult/child €2/1; ⊗9am-1pm Mon-Fri) This rather esoteric museum explores how Slovene kids learned the three Rs in the 19th century.

Central Ljubljana

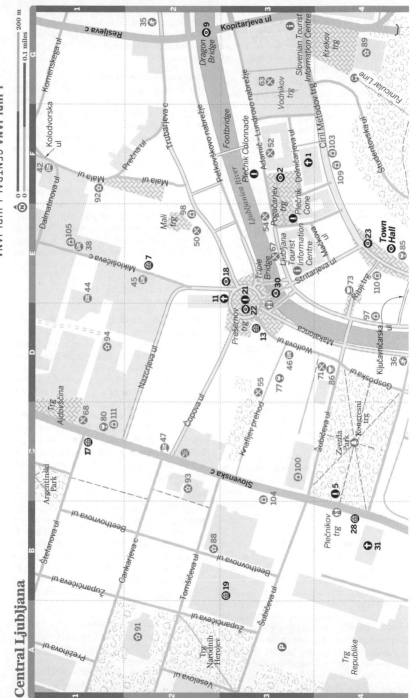

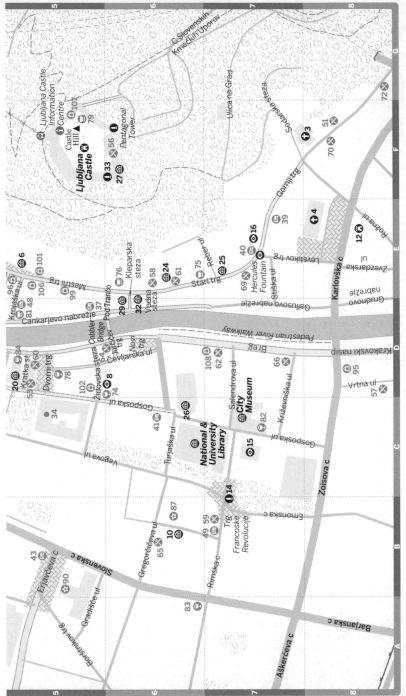

C. Slovenskih
Kmečkih Uporov

Ljubljana Castle
Information
Centre 107
79

Castle
Hill ▲

Ljubljana
Castle 33
56
27
Pentagonal
Tower

Ulica na Grad

Sodarska steza

3
51
70
72

Gornji trg

4
39

16
40
12

6
101
Mestni trg
76
Kleparska
steza
58 24
61 75
Stari trg 25
Reber ul
Levstikov trg
Hercules
Fountain
Šiška ul
69
Karlovška c
Zvezdarska
ul
Rožna ul
96
Krojaška ul
106
99
81 48
Cankarjevo nabrežje
37
Pod Trančo
29
32
Vodna
steza
Gallusovo nabrežje
Grudnovo
nabrežje

Pedestrian River Walkway
Krakovski nasip

84
60
Kratka st
Dvorni trg
53
20
102
Židovska steza
64
Cobbler
Bridge
Jurčičev
trg
Novi
trg
Čevljarska ul
8
74
78
Gosposka ul
Vegova ul
34
41
26
108
62
66
Breg
Salendrova ul
City
Museum
82
Križevniška ul
95
57
Vrtna ul

National &
University
Library
Turjaška ul
15
Gosposka ul
Zoisova c

14
Trg
Francoske
Revolucije
87
59
49
65
10
Rimska c
Emonska c

43
Enjavčeva c
90
Gradišče ul
Gregorčičeva ul
83
Slovenska c
Barjanska c
Aškerčeva c
Borštnikov trg

Central Ljubljana

Top Sights

Sights

Activities, Courses & Tours

Sleeping

Eating

TRG FRANCOSKE REVOLUCIJE

'French Revolution Sq' was for centuries the headquarters of the Teutonic Knights of the Cross (Križniki). They built a commandery here in the early 13th century, which was transformed into the **Križanke** (Map p44; ☎241 60 00; Trg Francoske Revolucije 1-2) monastery complex in the early 18th century. Today it serves as the headquarters of the Ljubljana Festival (p52), with an open-air theatre seating 1400 people, and hosts concerts at other times of the year. The **Ilirija Column** in the centre of the square recalls Napoléon's Illyrian Provinces (1809–13), when Slovene was taught in schools for the first time.

City Museum — MUSEUM

(Mestni Muzej; Map p44; ☎241 25 00; www.mestnimuzej.si; Gosposka ulica 15; adult/child €4/2.50; ⏰10am-6pm Tue & Wed, Fri-Sun, 10am-9pm Thu) The excellent city museum focuses on Ljubljana's history, culture and politics via imaginative multimedia and interactive displays. The reconstructed Roman street that linked the eastern gates of Emona to the Ljubljanica, and the collection of well-preserved classical finds in the basement are worth a visit in themselves.

The permanent 'Faces of Ljubljana' exhibit of celebrated and lesser-known *žabarji* ('froggers', as natives of the capital are known) is memorable. The museum hosts some very good special exhibitions too.

53 Delikatesa Ljubljanski Dvor D5
54 Fish Market..E3
55 Gostilna As.. D3
56 Gostilna na Gradu....................................F6
57 Harambaša... D8
58 Julija..E6
59 Le Petit Restaurant............................. B7
60 Ljubljanski Dvor.................................... D5
61 Lunch Café Marley & Me E6
62 Namasté.. D7
63 Open-Air Market G3
64 Paninoteka... D6
65 Pizzeria Foculus B6
66 Pri Vitezu... D7
67 Ribca...E3
68 Šestica...C1
69 Slaščičarna Pri Vodnjaku......................E7
70 Špajza..F8
71 Sushimama... D4
72 Taverna Tatjana G8

⊕ Drinking
73 Abecedarium Cafe.................................E4
74 BiKoFe... D6
75 Café Antico..E6
76 Čajna Hiša...E6
77 Cutty Sark Pub..................................... D3
78 Dvorni Bar.. D5
79 Grajska Kavarna.....................................F5
80 Juice Box..C1
   Le Petit Café...................................(see 59)
81 Maček D5
   Nebotičnik..................................... (see 17)
82 Pod Skalco.. C7
83 Pr' Semaforju A6
84 Solist.. D5

85 Vinoteka Movia.....................................E4
86 Zvezda..D4

⊕ Entertainment
   As Lounge...(see 55)
87 Glej Theatre..B6
88 Jazz Club Gajo B2
   Križanke..(see 15)
89 Ljubljana Puppet Theatre......................G4
90 National Drama Theatre........................B5
91 Opera & Ballet Ljubljana A2
   Philharmonic Hall ....(see 20)
92 Roxly Cafe Bar F1
93 Top: Eat & Party C2
94 Ultra..D1

⊕ Shopping
95 Annapurna...D8
96 Antika Ferjan..E5
97 Antiques & Flea Market D4
98 Carniola Antiqua....................................E2
   Galerija Fortuna.............................(see 25)
99 Galerija Idrijske Čipke...........................E5
100 Geonavtik...C3
101 Honey House...E5
   Katarina Silk..................................(see 16)
102 Knjigarna Behemot D5
103 Kraševka...F4
104 Mladinska Knjiga C3
105 Peko E1
106 Piranske Soline E5
107 Rustika..F5
108 Skrina..D7
109 Trgovina Ika..F4
110 Trubarjev Antikvariat.............................E4
111 Vino Boutique C1

TRG REPUBLIKE

'Republic Sq' is Center's main plaza. Unfortunately, it is basically a car park dominated by a pair of glowering, grey tower blocks – TR3, housing offices and embassies, and the headquarters of Nova Ljubljanska Banka – and a couple of garish revolutionary monuments.

FREE **Parliament Building**   HISTORIC BUILDING
(Map p44; ☑to arrange a tour 478 97 88; www.dz-rs
.si; Šubičeva ulica 4; ⊙tours by prior arrangement)
The renovated parliament building, built between 1954 and 1959 at the northeast corner of the square, is no beauty-pageant winner on the outside but the mammoth portal festooned with bronze sculptures is noteworthy. If you can time it right, it's

worth booking a guided tour to see the inside, especially the period-piece mural by Slavko Pengov.

Cankarjev Dom   CULTURAL CENTRE
(Map p38; ☑241 71 00; www.cd-cc.si; Prešernova cesta 10) The city's premier cultural and conference centre squats behind the TR3 building to the southwest.

Ferant Garden   HISTORIC REMNANTS
(Map p38; ☑241 25 06; Erjavčeva cesta 18; ⊙by appointment Apr-Oct) Behind Cankarjev Dom is this garden, with the remains of an early Christian church porch and baptistery with mosaics from the 4th century visible from the locked gate. To visit you must first contact the City Museum. Opposite and

LJUBLJANA'S OTHER MUSEUMS

Ljubljana contains many more interesting museums, some of them a bit further out from the centre.

Brewery Museum (Pivovarski Muzej; ☑to arrange group tours 471 73 40; www.pivo-union .si; Union Brewery, Pivovarniška ulica 2; admission free; ⊗8am-1pm every 1st Tue of month; ☐1, 3 or 5 to Tivoli) This museum at the Union Brewery offers various displays of brewing, a film, a tour of the brewery and a tasting. Note the limited opening hours.

Museum of Architecture & Design (Muzej za arhitekturo in oblikovanje; www.mao.si; Fužine Castle, Pot na Fužine 2; adult/child €3/1.50; ⊗9am-3pm Mon-Fri, 10am-6pm Sat, 10am-3pm Sun; ☐20 or 22 to Fužine) Much emphasis on Plečnik, focusing on his work at home and abroad, and some stunning unrealised projects. Hosts temporary exhibitions and also has strong permanent collections on architecture and photography.

Railway Museum (Železniški Muzej; www.slo-zeleznice.si; Parmova ulica 35; adult/senior, student & child €3.50/2.50; ⊗10am-6pm Tue-Sun; ☐14 Parmova) A boiler room full of locomotives (one going back to 1861), carriages, uniforms and signalling equipment, located north of Center.

to the west of the Cankarjev Dom are the remains of a **Roman wall** (Map p38) dating from 14–15 AD.

MUSEUM AREA

Four of Ljubljana's most important museums are located in this area, which is only a short distance to the northwest of Trg Republike.

National Museum of Slovenia MUSEUM
(Narodni Muzej Slovenije; Map p38; ☑241 44 00; www.nms.si; Prešernova cesta 20; adult/child €3/2.50, free 1st Sun of month; ⊗10am-6pm Fri-Wed, 10am-8pm Thu) Highlights include a highly embossed *Vače situla*, a Celtic pail from the late 6th century BC unearthed in a town east of Ljubljana, and a Stone Age bone flute discovered near Cerkno in western Slovenia in 1995. There are also examples of Roman glass and jewellery found in 6th-century Slavic graves, along with many other historical finds.

Check out the ceiling fresco in the foyer, which features an allegorical Carniola surrounded by important Slovenes from the past and the statues of the Muses and Fates relaxing on the stairway banisters.

Slovenian Museum of Natural History MUSEUM
(Prirodoslovni Muzej Slovenije; Map p38; ☑241 09 40; www2.pms-lj.si; Prešernova cesta 20; adult/student €3/2.50, incl National Museum €5/4; ⊗10am-6pm Fri-Wed, 10am-8pm Thu) Housed in the same impressive building as the National Museum, the Natural History Museum contains the usual reassembled mammoth and whale skeletons, stuffed birds, reptiles and mammals. However, the mineral collections amassed by the philanthropic Baron Žiga Zois in the early 19th century and the display on Slovenia's unique salamander *Proteus anguinus* (p132) are worth a visit.

National Gallery MUSEUM
(Map p38; ☑241 54 18; www.ng-slo.si; Prešernova cesta 24; adult/child €7/5, free 1st Sun of month; ⊗10am-6pm Tue-Sun) Slovenia's foremost assembly of fine art is housed over two floors in an old building dating to 1896 and an impressive modern wing.

Ljubljana Museum of Modern Art MUSEUM
(Map p38; ☑241 68 00; www.mg-lj.si; Tomšičeva ulica 14; adult/student €5/2.50; ⊗10am-6pm Tue-Sun) This museum houses the very best in Slovenian modern art. Keep an eye out for works by painters Tone Kralj (*Peasant Wedding*), the expressionist France Mihelič (*The Quintet*) and the surrealist Štefan Planinc (*Primeval World* series) as well as sculptors such as Jakob Savinšek (*Protest*).

The museum also owns works by the influential 1980s and '90s multimedia group Neue Slowenische Kunst (NSK; *Suitcase for Spiritual Use: Baptism under Triglav*) and the artists' cooperative Irwin (*Kapital*).

Nebotičnik HISTORIC BUILDING
(Skyscraper; Map p44; www.neboticnik.si; Štefanova ulica 1; ⊗9am-2am Sun-Wed, 9am-3am Thu-Sat) Along busy Slovenska cesta is the impressive art-deco Nebotičnik, designed by Vladimir

Šubič (1933). At nine storeys, this was Ljubljana's tallest building for decades after it was built. After languishing for years, it has now been renovated and houses a popular rooftop restaurant and cafe (p59), with amazing views on all sides.

Serbian Orthodox Church CHURCH
(Srbska Pravoslavna Cerkev; Map p38; www.spco-lj .si; Prešernova cesta; ☺9am-noon & 2-6pm Tue-Sun) The interior of the Serbian Orthodox Church, built in 1936 and dedicated to Sts Cyril and Methodius, is covered from floor to ceiling with colourful modern frescoes. There is a richly carved iconostasis separating the nave from the sanctuary.

PARK TIVOLI
This enormous, 510-hectare park is Ljubljana's leafy playground and the perfect spot for a walk or bike ride. The park was laid out in 1813. One of the highlights is the **Jakopičevo sprehajališče**, the monumental 'Jakopič Promenade', designed by Plečnik in the 1920s and '30s.

International Centre of
Graphic Arts MUSEUM
(Mednarodni Grafični Likovni Center; Map p38; www .mglc-lj.si; Pod Turnom 3; adult/senior & student €3.40/1.70, at biennial €6/3; ☺11am-6pm Tue-Sun) This museum and gallery dedicated to the graphic arts regularly hosts rotating exhibitions and is home to the International Biennial of Graphic Arts every odd-numbered year. The centre is located in the 17th-century **Tivoli Mansion** (Grad Tivoli) and has a delightful terrace cafe (open from 10am to 5pm) with views over the park.

Museum of Contemporary
History of Slovenia MUSEUM
(Muzej Novejše Zgodovine Slovenije; Map p38; www .muzej-nz.si; Celovška cesta 23; adult/student €3.50/2.50; ☺10am-6pm Tue-Sat) This museum, housed in the 18th-century Cekin Mansion (Grad Cekinov), traces the history of Slovenia in the 20th century through multimedia and artefacts. Note the contrast between the sober earnestness of the communist-era rooms and the exuberant, logo-mad commercialism of the industrial exhibits. The sections focusing on Ljubljana under occupation during WWII are very effective.

Ljubljana Zoo ZOO
(Živalski Vrt Ljubljana; www.zoo-ljubljana.si; Večna pot 70; adult/child €7/5; ☺9am-7pm May-Aug, 9am-6pm Apr & Sep, 9am-5pm Mar & Oct, 9am-4pm Nov-Feb) The 20-hectare zoo, on the southern slope of **Rožnik Hill** (394m), contains some 500 animals representing almost 120 species and is an upbeat and well-landscaped menagerie. There's a petting zoo and lots of other activities for children; consult the website for feeding schedules.

KRAKOVO & TRNOVO
These two attractive districts south of Center are Ljubljana's oldest suburbs, and they have a number of interesting buildings and historic sites. The neighbourhood around Krakovska ulica, with all its two-storey cottages, was once called the Montmartre of Ljubljana because of all the artists living there.

The **Roman wall** (Map p38) running along Mirje from Barjanska cesta dates from about AD 15; the archway topped with a **pyramid** is a Plečnik addition. Spanning the picturesque canal called Gradaščica to the south is little **Trnovo Bridge** (Map p38), designed in 1932 by Plečnik, who added five of his trademark pyramids.

Plečnik Collection MUSEUM
(Map p38; ☎280 16 00; www.aml.si; Karunova ulica 4-6; adult/child €4/2; ☺10am-6pm Tue-Thu, 9am-3pm Sat, by appointment Mon & Fri) This house is where Jože Plečnik lived and worked for almost 40 years. There's an excellent introduction by guided tour to this almost ascetically religious man's life, inspiration and work.

Church of St John the Baptist CHURCH
(Cerkev Sv Janeza Krstnika; Map p38; Kolezijska ulica 1; ☺8am-6pm) This is the church where the poet Prešeren met the love of his life, Julija Primic, and Plečnik worshipped.

SLOVENIAN HERITAGE

If you are searching for your Slovenian roots, check first with the *mestna občina* (municipal government office) or *občina* (county office); they usually have birth and death certificates going back a century. Vital records beyond the 100-year limit are kept at the Archives of the Republic of Slovenia (p42). Ethnic Slovenes living abroad might be interested in contacting the **Slovenian Emigrants Centre** (Slovenska Izseljenska Matica; ☎241 02 80; www.zdruzenje -sim.si; 2nd fl, Cankarjeva cesta 1; ☺by appointment).

A GALLERY OF GALLERIES

Ljubljana is awash with galleries, both public and commercial. The following are among the best:

» **City Gallery** (Mestna Galerija; Map p44; ☑241 17 70; www.mestna-galerija.si; Mestni trg 5; admission free; ☉11am-7pm Tue-Sat, 11am-3pm Sun) Rotating displays of modern and contemporary painting, sculpture, graphic art and photography.

» **DESSA Architectural Gallery** (Map p44; ☑251 40 74; www.dessa.si; Židovska steza 4; admission free; ☉10am-3pm Mon-Fri) Small gallery spotlighting contemporary Slovenian and international architecture and architects.

» **Equrna Gallery** (Galerija Equrna; Map p44; ☑252 71 23; www.equrna.si; Gregorčičeva ulica 3; admission free; ☉10am-7pm Mon-Fri, 10am-1pm Sat) Among the most innovative modern galleries in town.

» **Škuc Gallery** (Galerija Škuc; Map p44; ☑421 31 40; www.skuc.si; Stari trg 21; admission free; ☉noon-8pm Tue-Sun) Cutting-edge with a studenty vibe in the heart of the Old Town.

TABOR

North of Castle Hill across the Ljubljanica River, this neighbourhood is leafy, residential and home to the pulsating Metelkova district of alternative culture. The region is also morphing into an important cultural centre, built around a couple of key museums.

Slovenian Ethnographic Museum MUSEUM
(Slovenski Etnografski Muzej; Map p38; ☑300 87 45; www.etno-muzej.si; Metelkova ulica 2; adult/student & senior €4.50/2.50, last Sun of month admission free; ☉10am-6pm Tue-Sun) Housed in the 1886 Belgian Barracks on the southern edge of Metelkova, the museum has a permanent collection on the 3rd floor. There's traditional Slovenian trades and handicrafts – everything from beekeeping and blacksmithing to glass-painting and pottery making – and some excellent exhibits directed at children. There's also a good cafe here.

**National Museum of
Slovenia Collection** MUSEUM
(Zbirka Narodnega Muzeja Slovenije; Map p38; ☑230 70 30; www.nms.si; Maistrova ulica 1; adult/student & senior/family €3/2.50/6, 1st Sun of month admission free; ☉10am-6pm Tue-Sun) The modern building across the courtyard to the northeast of the Slovenian Ethnographic Museum contains a bizarre assortment of mostly applied art and objets d'art (furniture, religious items, paintings etc) that are tenuously linked through themes. Surely this is a home away from home for these goodies until the main museum site is sorted.

ŽALE

Žale Cemetery CEMETERY
(Pokopališče Žale; ☑420 17 00; www.zale.si; Med Hmeljniki 2; ☉6am-8pm Apr-Sep, 7am-6pm Oct-Mar; ☐2, 7 or 22 to Žale) This suburb about 2km northeast of Tabor is Ljubljana's answer to Père Lachaise or Highgate, but is best known for the ornamental gates and chapels and colonnades known as 'Plečnik Žale', which were designed by the architectural master in 1940. The Plečnik buildings are used for pre-burial ceremonies.

🏃 Activities

Adventure Sports

Agencies like **Label** (Map p44; ☑051-200 743; www.label.si; Hribarjevo nabrežje 13) and Trek Trek (p65) can organise a wide range of outdoor activities around Ljubljana and the rest of Slovenia between May and October, including trekking, mountaineering, rock climbing, ski touring, cross-country skiing, mountain biking, rafting, kayaking, canyoning, caving and paragliding.

Ballooning

The Ljubljana TIC organises **hot-air balloon rides** (☑306 12 15; www.visitljubljana.si; adult/child €80/40; ☉6am & 8pm Apr-Aug, 8am & 5pm Sep-Mar) year-round lasting three to four hours (with one to 1½ hours actually in the air) departing from the Slovenian Tourist Information Centre (p240).

Boating & Rafting

Ljubljana Rowing Club BOATING
(Veslaški Klub Ljubljana; Map p38; ☑283 87 12; www.vesl-klub-ljubljanica.si; Velika Čolnarska ulica 20;

per hr from €4; ⊘11am-10pm mid-May–Sep) This club in Trnovo has dinghies and larger rowing boats for hire on the Ljubljanica River.

Skok Sport TRAVEL AGENCY
(☑512 44 02; www.skok-sport.si; Marinovševa cesta 8; ⊘8am-1pm, 3pm-8pm May-Oct) In Šentvid, 8km northwest of Center, this place organises rafting trips on the nearby Sava, from Medvode to Brod (1½ hours) for around €25 and from Boka to Trnovo (two hours) for around €45. It can also arrange kayak and canoe excursions on the Ljubljanica and runs a kayaking school. Take bus 8 to Brod.

Swimming & Sauna

Atlantis SWIMMING
(☑585 21 00; www.atlantis-vodnomesto.si; BTC City, Šmartinska cesta 152; day pass adult/child Mon-Fri €14.60/12.30, Sat & Sun €16.70/14.50; ⊘9am-9pm Mon-Thu, 9am-10pm Fri-Sun) The largest and fanciest of Ljubljana's water parks, with separate theme areas: Adventure World, with a half-dozen pools and water slides; Thermal Temple, with indoor and outdoor thermal pools; and Land of Saunas, with a dozen different types of saunas. Get there by bus 27, stop BTC Emporium.

Tivoli Recreation Centre SWIMMING
(Map p38; ☑431 51 55; Celovška cesta 25) In Park Tivoli, this centre has an indoor swimming pool (open mid-September to June), a fitness centre, clay tennis courts and a roller-skating rink, which becomes an ice rink in winter. It also has a popular sauna.

Walking & Hiking
Popular with walkers and joggers, the marked **Trail of Remembrance** (Pot Spominov) runs for 34km around Ljubljana where German barbed wire once completely enclosed the city during WWII. The easiest places to reach the trail are from the AMZS headquarters (Slovenian Automobile Association; take bus 6, 8 or 11 to the AMZS stop), or from Trg Komandanta Staneta just northwest of the central office of the public transport authority LPP (take bus 1 to the Remiza stop). You can also join it from the northwestern side of Žale Cemetery (take bus 19 to the Nove Žale stop), or south of Trnovo (take bus 9 to the Veliki Štradon stop).

An easy and very popular hiking destination from Ljubljana is **Šmarna Gora**, a 669m-high hill above the Sava River, 12km northwest of Ljubljana. Take bus 25 from Slovenska cesta or Gosposvetska cesta to the Medno stop, or bus 8 to Brod and begin walking. Another way to go is via the Smlednik bus from the main station and then follow the marked path from the 12th-century Smlednik Castle.

⚓ Courses

Centre for Slovene as a Second/Foreign Language LANGUAGE COURSE
(Center za Slovenščino kot Drugi/Tuji Jezik; Map p44; ☑241 86 47; www.centerslo.net; Kongresni trg 12) The Centre for Slovene as a Second/Foreign Language offers a full palette of Slovene language courses suited to short-term visitors, students or serious linguistic study. The centre offers a free 90-minute survival course in Slovene every Wednesday from 5pm to 6.30pm at the Slovenian Tourist Information Centre (p64).

☞ Tours

The Ljubljana Tourist Information Centre (p64) organises a number of guided tours of the city and even has a **digital tour guide** (€10) taking in 17 sights and lasting about two hours.

A glass-enclosed vessel offers guided one-hour English-language **boat tours** (adult/child €10/5; ⊘sailings 10am, 11am & 1pm, hourly 5-8pm) on the Ljubljanica River, departing from near the little Ribji trg Pier along Cankarjevo nabrežje.

Segway Tours Ljubljana (☑041 683 184; www.segway-slovenia.com), run by Bled-based 3glav Adventures (p80), will have you seeing the capital at a different level altogether – from a two-wheeled, self-balancing electric-powered conveyance. Two–hour tours (€65) of up to eight people depart at 10am and 2pm daily; see the website for exact departure points.

🎭 Festivals & Events

Ljubljana is at its most vibrant in July and August during the so-called **Summer in the Old Town** season, when there are four or five free cultural events a week in the city's historic squares, courtyards and bridges.

Druga Godba WORLD MUSIC
(http://festival.drugagodba.si; ⊘May-Jun) This festival of alternative and world music takes place in the Križanke from late May to early June.

Ljubljanska Vinska Pot
WINE TASTING

(Ljubljana Wine Route; www.ljubljanskavinskapot
.si; ☉Jun) Held on a Saturday in June, this
event brings wine makers from around the
country to central Ljubljana, where visitors
spend the day wandering around sampling
the offerings.

Ana Desetnica International
Street Theatre Festival
THEATRE

(www.anadesetnica.org; ☉Jun-Jul) Organised by
the Ana Monro Theatre in late June/early
July, this festival is not to be missed.

Ljubljana Festival
MUSIC & THEATRE

(www.ljubljanafestival.si; ☉Jul-Aug) The number-
one event on Ljubljana's social calendar is
the Ljubljana Festival, a celebration from
early July to late August of music, opera,
theatre and dance held at venues throughout the city, but principally in the open-air
theatre at the Križanke.

Trnfest
ALTERNATIVE

(www.kud.si; ☉Jul-Aug) An international festival of alternative arts and culture – and
many Ljubljančans' favourite annual event –
takes place at the KUD France Prešeren (p60)
in Trnovo and at other venues from late July
to late August.

City of Women
PERFORMANCE ART

(www.cityofwomen.org; ☉Oct) Held in the
first half of October in venues throughout
Ljubljana, it showcases all forms of artistic
expression by women.

International Ljubljana Marathon
MARATHON

(www.ljubljanskimaraton.si; ☉Oct) Takes off on
the last Saturday in October.

🛏 Sleeping

Accommodation prices in Ljubljana are the
highest in the country, so expect to shell
out a bit more here than elsewhere. For
tighter budgets there is a growing number
of higher-quality modern hostels, some
with private singles and doubles. For longer stays of more than a couple of nights,
there's the option of renting out a private
apartment. The TIC website maintains a
comprehensive list of hotels and sleeping
options, including private rooms (single/
double from €30/50). Unfortunately, only a
few of these are in the centre; most require a
bus trip north to Bežigrad or beyond.

Antiq Palace Hotel & Spa
BOUTIQUE HOTEL €€€

(Map p44; ☎051-364 124; www.antiqpalace.com;
Gosposka ulica 10 & Vegova ulica 5a; s/d €180/210;

❄@🌐) Easily the city's most luxurious
sleeping option, the Antiq Palace occupies a
16th-century town house about a block from
the river. Accommodation is in 13 individually designed suites, each with several rooms
and some stretching to 250 sq metres in size.
The list of amenities is a mile long. Perfect
for upscale honeymooners and businessmen
on expenses.

Cubo
BOUTIQUE HOTEL €€€

(Map p44; ☎425 60 00; www.hotelcubo.com;
Slovenska cesta 15; s/d €120/140; ❄🌐) This
sleek boutique hotel in the centre of town
boasts high-end, minimalist design that
could have stepped out of the pages of
Wallpaper magazine. The owners have
placed great emphasis on using the best
construction materials and high-quality
bedding to ensure a good night's sleep. The
in-house restaurant is very good.

🔝Celica Hostel
HOSTEL €€
TOP CHOICE

(Map p38; ☎230 97 00; www.hostelcelica.com; Metelkova ulica 8; dm €19-25, s/d/tr cell €53/60/70;
🅿@🌐) This stylishly revamped former
prison (1882) in Metelkova has 20 'cells', designed by different artists and architects and
complete with original bars. There are nine
rooms and apartments with three to seven
beds and a packed, popular 12-bed dorm.
The ground floor is home to a cafe and
restaurant (set lunch €5 to €7, open from
7.30am to midnight) and the hostel boasts
its own gallery where everyone can show
their work.

Slamič B&B
PENSION €€

(Map p38; ☎433 82 33; www.slamic.si; Kersnikova
ulica 1; s €65-75, d €95-100, ste from €135;
🅿❄@🌐) It's slightly away from the
action but Slamič, a B&B above a famous
cafe and teahouse, offers 11 bright rooms
with antique(ish) furnishings and parquet
floors. Choice rooms include the ones looking on to a back garden and the one just off
an enormous terrace used by the cafe.

Penzion Pod Lipo
PENSION €€

(Map p38; ☎031-809 893; www.penzion-podlipo.
com; Borštnikov trg 3; d/tr/q/ste €65/75/100/125;
@) Sitting atop one of Ljubljana's oldest
gostilna (inn-like restaurant), with a
400-year-old linden tree, this 10-room inn
offers plain rooms but excellent value in a
part of the city that is filling up with bars and
restaurants. We love the communal kitchen,
the original hardwood floors and the east-

facing terrace with deckchairs that catch the morning sun.

Antiq Hotel
BOUTIQUE HOTEL €€€

(Map p44; ☑421 35 60; www.antiqhotel.si; Gornji trg 3; s €75-120, d €85-150; ❄@☎) This attractive boutique hotel has been cobbled together from several town houses in the Old Town. There are 16 spacious rooms and a multitiered back garden. The decor is kitsch with a smirk and there are fabulous touches everywhere. Among our favourite rooms are enormous No 8, with views of the Hercules Fountain, and No 13, with glimpses of Ljubljana Castle.

Allegro Hotel
BOUTIQUE HOTEL €€€

(Map p44; ☑059-119 620; www.allegrohotel.si; Gornji trg 6; s €95-115, d €130-150, tr €185; P❄@☎) Another historic boutique hotel in Old Town, the 17-room Allegro is a symphony of designer chic with rooms that give on to Gornji trg and a charming back courtyard. Room No 3 has a balcony and No 12 at the top sleeps four. The front lounge – a parlour, really – is on two levels and we love the original wood staircase.

Ljubljana Resort
CAMPGROUND €

(☑568 39 13; www.ljubljanaresort.si; Dunajska cesta 270; adult €8-17, child €6-13; P❄@☀) It's got a grandiose name, but wait till you see the facilities at this attractive 6-hectare camping ground-cum-resort 4km north of the centre. Along with a 62-room hotel (singles/doubles €67/104) and five stationary mobile homes (€84 to €108), there's the Laguna water park next door, which is free for guests. Take bus 6, 8 or 11 to the Ježica stop.

Zeppelin Hostel
HOSTEL €

(Map p38; ☑059-191 427; www.zeppelinhostel.com; 2nd fl, Slovenska cesta 47; dm €18-24, d €49-60; @☎) Located in the historic Evropa building on the corner of Gosposvetska cesta, this hostel offers clean and bright dorm rooms (four to eight beds) and doubles and is run by a young team of international travellers who keep their guests informed on parties and happenings around town.

Pri Mraku
HOTEL €€€

(Map p44; ☑421 96 00; www.daj-dam.si; Rimska cesta 4; s €70-86, d €105-120; P❄@☎) Although it calls itself a *gostilna*, 'At Twilight' is really just a smallish hotel with 36 rooms in an old building with no lift and a garden. Rooms on the 1st and 4th floors have aircon. Almost opposite the Križanke on Trg

---

RENTING A PLACE OF YOUR OWN

If you plan on staying for an extended period (longer than three nights), renting an apartment can be cheaper and more comfortable than a hotel. While you sacrifice a 24-hour reception desk and someone to cook your breakfast, you gain a bit more privacy, a washing machine and a fully-equipped kitchen. **Apartments In Ljubljana** (Map p38; ☑051-666 400; www.apartmentsinljubljana.com; Gradaska 8a; per night €70-145) offers several apartments, ranging from a studio to a 150-sq-metre, three-bedroom affair, about a 10-minute walk south of the centre. The apartments have been fully renovated and furnished in tastefully modern, minimalist style. Rates vary depending on the size of the apartment and the time of year.

Francoske Revolucije, it's ideally located for culture vultures.

Maček Rooms
PRIVATE ROOMS €€

(Map p44; ☑425 37 91; www.sobe-macek.si; Krojaška ulica 5; s/d/apt €61/96/126; ❄@) In a building that once took the overflow from the Alibi Hostel just downriver, these four gorgeous rooms and one apartment (all but one of which overlook the river) are owned by the city's most popular riverfront cafebar and are among the most sought-after in town (so book well in advance).

H2O
HOSTEL €

(Map p38; ☑041-662 266; www.h2ohostel.com; Petkovškovo nabrežje 47; dm €17-22, d €36-52, q €68-88; @☎) One of our favourite hostels in Ljubljana, this six-room place wraps around a tiny courtyard bordering the Ljubljanica River and one room has views of the castle. Private doubles are available and guests have access to a common kitchen.

Hotel Park
HOTEL €€

(Map p38; ☑300 25 00; www.hotelpark.si; Tabor 9; s €55-90, d €70-130; P❄@☎) A recladding outside and a facelift within have turned this 243-room tower-block hotel into a good-value midrange choice in central Ljubljana. The 200 pleasant, well-renovated 'standard' and 'comfort' (air-conditioned) rooms are bright and unpretentiously well equipped. Cheaper 'hostel' rooms are available on the 7th and

12th floors; some have shared facilities and others en suite shower (dorm €20 to €23).

City Hotel Ljubljana
HOTEL €€€

(Map p44; ☑239 00 00; www.cityhotel.si; Dalmatinova ulica 15; s €65-85, d €96-128; ᴘ✳@☎) An attractive high-rise hotel offering clean, basic rooms and a central location. Rooms vary from 'basic' to 'superior', with the primary difference being the more-expensive rooms are larger and have air-conditioning. Some 'superior' rooms have parquet flooring and hypoallergenic bed linens.

Hotel Slon Best Western Premier
HOTEL €€€

(Map p44; ☑470 11 31; www.hotelslon.com; Slovenska cesta 34; s €90-115, d €130-150; ᴘ✳@☎) The 168-room 'Hotel Elephant' is a smart business-class hotel, with tastefully decorated, well-appointed rooms, a fitness centre and a very good restaurant. There are several categories of rooms, some with a Jacuzzi in the bathroom.

Grand Hotel Union Executive
HOTEL €€€

(Map p44; ☑308 12 70; www.gh-union.si; Miklošičeva cesta 1; s €99-194, d €109-224, ste €150-455; ᴘ✳@☎⛱) The 187-room Grand Hotel Union Executive, the art-nouveau southern wing of a two-part hostelry, was built in 1905 and remains one of the most desirable addresses in town. It has glorious public areas and guests can use the indoor pool and fitness centre of the adjacent 133-room **Grand Hotel Union Business** (Map p44; ☑308 12 70; www.gh-union.si; Miklošičeva cesta 3; s €85-178, d €99-208, ste €150-372; ᴘ✳@⛱), the Grand Hotel Union's renovated modern wing.

Vila Veselova
PENSION €€

(Map p38; ☑059-926 721; www.v-v.si; Veselova ulica 14; dm/d/q €21/68/100; ᴘ✳@) This attractive yellow villa, with its own garden and 42 beds in the centre of the museum district, offers mostly hostel accommodation in five colourful rooms with four to eight beds. A double and two apartments with attached facilities and access to a kitchen make it an attractive midrange option, however. Some rooms face Park Tivoli across busy Tivolska cesta.

Hotel Emonec
HOTEL €€

(Map p44; ☑200 15 20; www.hotel-emonec.com; Wolfova ulica 12; d €69-77, s/tr/q €64/96/111; ᴘ@) The decor is simple and functionally modern at this 41-room hotel. Everything is spotless and you can't beat the central location. Internet connection in the rooms is via LAN/Ethernet cable.

BIT Center Hotel
HOTEL €€

(☑548 00 55; www.bit-center.net; Litijska cesta 57; s/d €35/55; ᴘ@☎) The BIT Center offers one of the best-value deals in Ljubljana although, at 3km east of the centre (bus 5, 9 or 13 to Emona stop), it's a bit far from the action. The hotel was completely renovated in 2012, with clean, light, modern decor. Guests receive a 50% discount at the sports centre next door.

Bit Center Hostel
HOSTEL €

(☑548 00 55; www.bit-center.net; Litijska cesta 57; dm €16; ᴘ@☎) Occupying the same building as the Bit Center Hotel, this 35-bed hostel is clean and well run, with dorm accommodation offered in six rooms.

Alibi Hostel
HOSTEL €

(Map p44; ☑251 12 44; www.alibi.si; Cankarjevo nabrežje 27; dm €15-18, d €40-50; ✳@) This very well-situated 106-bed hostel on the Ljubljanica has brightly painted, airy dorms with four to eight wooden bunks and a dozen doubles. There's a private suite at the top for six people.

Alibi M14 Hostel
HOSTEL €

(Map p44; ☑232 27 70; www.alibi.si; 3rd fl, Miklošičeva cesta 14; dm €15-18, d €40-50; ✳@) In the heart of Center is this pint-sized property, which has six rooms, including a 10-bed dormitory, just south of Miklošičev Park.

🍴 Eating

Ljubljana has Slovenia's best selection of restaurants. In addition to excellent Slovenian cooking, you'll find several good restaurants featuring Balkan cuisine (mostly grilled meats and the like) from former Yugoslav compatriots Serbia, Croatia and Bosnia. Although prices tend to be higher in Ljubljana than elsewhere, it is still possible to eat well at moderate cost; even the more-expensive restaurants usually offer an excellent-value three-course *dnevno kosilo* (set lunch) for as little as €8.

Self-caterers and those on a tight budget will want to head directly to Ljubljana's vast **open-air market** (Map p44; Vodnikov trg; ☺6am-6pm Mon-Fri, 6am-4pm Sat summer, 6am-4pm Mon-Sat winter) just across the Triple Bridge to the southeast of Prešernov trg. Here you'll find stalls selling everything from wild mushrooms and forest berries to honey and homemade cheeses. The **covered market** (Map p44; Pogačarjev trg 1; ☺7am-2pm Mon-Wed & Sat, 7am-4pm Thu & Fri) nearby also

LJUBLJANA FOR CHILDREN

The Ljubljana Tourist Information Centre website (www.visitljubljana.si) is a good source of quick info for events suitable for children that might be taking place during your visit.

Park Tivoli, with a couple of children's playgrounds, swimming pools (p51) and a zoo (p49), is an excellent place to take children, as are the two water parks, **Laguna** (☑568 39 13; www.laguna.si; Dunajska cesta 270; adult/child from €16/7.50; ☉9am-8pm May-Oct) and Atlantis (p51).

In the warmer months the **Mini Summer for Children International Festival** (☑434 36 20; www.mini-teater.si; Grajska planota 1; ☉11am & 6.30pm Sun late Jun–Aug) stages puppet shows from around the world for kids at Ljubljana Castle. At other times of the year, check out the program at the Ljubljana Puppet Theatre (p60).

A super place for kids is the **House of Experiments** (Hiša Eksperimentov; Map p44; ☑300 68 88; www.h-e.si; Trubarjeva cesta 39; admission €5; ☉11am-7pm Sat & Sun), a hands-on science centre with almost four dozen inventive and challenging exhibits that successfully mix learning with humour. There's a science adventure show at 5pm.

sells meats and cheeses, and there's a **fish market** (Map p44; Adamič-Lundrovo nabrežje 1; ☉7am-4pm Mon-Fri, 7am-2pm Sat) too. You'll also find open-air fish stands selling plates of fried calamari for as low as €6. Another budget option is *burek*, pastry stuffed with cheese, meat or even apple. Reputedly the best places in town are **Olimpije** (Map p38; Pražakova ulica 2; burek €2; ☉24hr), southwest of the train and bus stations, and **Nobel Burek** (Map p38; ☑232 33 92; Miklošičeva cesta 30; burek €2, pizza slices €1.40; ☉24hr).

Gostilna na Gradu
TOP CHOICE — SLOVENIAN €

(Map p44; ☑031-523 760; www.nagradu.si; Grajska planota 1; mains €8-14; ☉10am-midnight Mon-Sat, noon-6pm Sun) Be sure to plan a meal at this marvellous traditional Slovenian restaurant during your visit to the castle. The chefs pride themselves on using only Slovenian-sourced breads, cheeses and meats, and age-old recipes to prepare a meal to remember. The castle setting is ideal. Book at table in advance to avoid disappointment.

Julija
MEDITERRANEAN €€

(Map p44; ☑425 64 63; http://julijarestaurant.com; Stari trg 9; mains €10.90-18.90; ☉noon-10pm) This is arguably the best of a trio of restaurants standing side by side on touristy Stari trg. We love the three-course set lunches served on the sidewalk terrace for €9. The cuisine here revolves around risottos and pastas, though the chicken breast special served in a spicy peanut sauce was one of the best meals on our trip.

Ribca
SEAFOOD €

(Map p44; ☑425 15 44; www.ribca.si; Adamič-Lundrovo nabrežje 1; dishes €5-8; ☉8am-4pm Mon-Fri, to 2pm Sat) One of the culinary joys of a visit to Ljubljana is the chance to sample inexpensive and well-prepared fish dishes. This basement seafood bar below the Plečnik Colonnade in Pogačarjev trg is one of the best for tasty fried squid, sardines and herrings. The setting is informal, though the cuisine is top-notch. Set lunch on weekdays is €7.50.

Pri Škofu
SLOVENIAN €€

(Map p38; ☑426 45 08; Rečna ulica 8; mains €8-22; ☉7am-11pm; ☏) This wonderful little place in tranquil Krakovo south of the centre serves some of the best-prepared local dishes and salads in Ljubljana, with an ever-changing menu. Weekday set lunches are good value at €8.

Špajza
SLOVENIAN €€

(Map p44; ☑425 30 94; www.spajza-restaurant.si; Gornji trg 28; mains €15-25; ☉noon-11pm) This popular Old Town restaurant is the perfect spot for a splurge or romantic meal for two. The interior is decorated with rough-hewn tables and chairs, wooden floors, frescoed ceilings and nostalgic bits and pieces. The terrace in summer is a delight. The cooking is traditional Slovenian, with an emphasis on less-common mains like rabbit and veal.

Trta
ITALIAN €

(Map p38; ☑426 50 66; www.trta.si; Grudnovo nabrežje 21; pizza €8-10; ☉11am-10pm Mon-Fri, noon-10.30pm Sat; ☏) This award-winning pizzeria, with large pies cooked in a wood-fired oven, is slightly south of the centre, across the river opposite Trnovo.

Le Petit Restaurant
FRENCH €€

(Map p44; ☑️426 14 88; Trg Francoske Revolucije 4; mains €12-20; ⏱️7.30am-1am; 🔊) Opposite the Križanke, what has always been a popular French-style cafe on French Revolution Sq has now opened a wonderful restaurant on the 1st floor with a provincial decor and menu. The pleasant, boho cafe still offers great coffee and a wide range of breakfast goodies (€2.20 to €6.50) and lunches (sandwiches €2.90 to €4.50).

Harambaša
BALKAN €

(Map p44; ☑️041-843 106; www.harambasa.si; Vrtna ulica 8; dishes €5-7; ⏱️10am-10pm Mon-Fri, noon-10pm Sat, noon-6pm Sun) At this small place in Krakovo you'll find authentic Bosnian – Sarajevan to be precise – dishes like *čevapčiči* (spicy meatballs of beef or pork) and *pljeskavica* (spicy meat patties) served at low tables in a charming cottage with a fireplace.

Sushimama
JAPANESE €€

(Map p44; ☑️040-702 070; www.sushimama.si; Wolfova ulica 12; mains €15-25; ⏱️11am-11pm Mon-Sat; 🔊) Ljubljana's first and still arguably the best Japanese restaurant has simple, restful decor and the full range of Japanese dishes – from miso soups to rice and noodle dishes – but with fish this fresh it would be a shame not to indulge in the mixed sushi or sashimi.

Kavalino
ITALIAN €€

(Map p38; ☑️232 09 90; http://kaval-group.si; Trubarjeva cesta 52; mains €10-15; ⏱️8am-10pm Mon-Thu, to 11pm Fri & Sat) Our favourite Italian (they say Tuscan) place at the moment, Kavalino serves pizza like everybody does but it excels with its pasta, especially its four types of ravioli. Excellent seating in the courtyard and upstairs gallery.

Gostilna Rimska XXI
SLOVENIAN €€

(Map p38; ☑️256 56 54; Rimska cesta 21; mains €8-20; ⏱️11am-11pm Mon-Fri, noon-5pm Sat) This popular inn specialises in traditional Slovenian cooking, using locally sourced ingredients and lots of homemade extras, including its own very good home-brewed beer. There's no English menu, so ask the server what looks good in the kitchen. The steak served with mashed potatoes comes highly recommended.

Namasté
INDIAN €€

(Map p44; ☑️425 01 59; www.restavracija-namaste.si; Breg 8; mains €8-18; ⏱️11am-midnight Mon-Sat, to 10pm Sun; 🔊) Should you fancy a bit of Indian, head for this place on the left bank of the Ljubljanica. You won't get high-street-quality curry but the thalis and tandoori dishes are very good. The choice of vegetarian dishes is better than average and set lunch is €6.50 to €8.50. Eat along the river in nice weather.

Yildiz Han
TURKISH €

(Map p38; ☑️426 57 17; http://yildiz-han.com; Karlovška cesta 19; mains €8.50-15; ⏱️11am-midnight Mon-Sat) If Turkish is your thing, head for authentic (trust us) 'Star House', which features belly dancing on Friday night. There's a small terrace for outside dining on warm evenings. The restaurant is a little hard to find, tucked away in a small house below the road.

Lunch Café Marley & Me
INTERNATIONAL €€

(Map p44; ☑️040-564 188; www.lunchcafe.si; Stari trg 9; mains from €7-20; ⏱️11am-11pm; 🔊) The name couldn't be more misleading. It's more than a lunch cafe... and the 'Marley' bit? We just don't get it. Still, it's a very popular spot for lunch or dinner with salads, pastas and a variety of meats and seafood. There's sidewalk dining in nice weather.

Taverna Tatjana
SEAFOOD €€

(Map p44; ☑️421 00 87; Gornji trg 38; mains €8.50-25; ⏱️5pm-midnight Mon-Sat) A wooden-beamed cottage pub with a nautical theme (think nets and seascapes), this is actually a rather exclusive fish restaurant with a lovely (and protected) back courtyard for the warmer months.

Ljubljanski Dvor
ITALIAN €

(Map p44; ☑️251 65 55; Dvorni trg 1; pizza €7-10; ⏱️10am-midnight Mon-Sat, noon-10pm Sun) The competition for best pizza in Ljubljana is a heated one, and this place, with a huge terrace overlooking the Ljubljanica, can certainly make a claim. There are some 100 different pizzas on the menu, though the popularity of the restaurant often means that service suffers. There's takeaway pizza at nearby **Delikatesa Ljubljanski Dvor** (Map p44; ☑️426 93 27; Kongresni trg 11; pizza slices €1.70-3; ⏱️10am-midnight Mon-Sat).

Pizzeria Foculus
ITALIAN €

(Map p44; ☑️421 92 95; www.picerija.net/foculus.htm; Gregorčičeva ulica 3; pizza €6-8.50; ⏱️11am-midnight) This popular pizzeria, with a wood-fired pizza oven, boasts comfy outdoor seating and a vaulted indoor ceiling painted with spring and autumn leaves for when the weather turns nasty.

Falafel
MIDDLE EASTERN €

(Map p38; ✍041-640 166; Trubarjeva cesta 40; sandwiches €4-6; ⏰11am-midnight Mon-Fri, noon-midnight Sat, 1-10pm Sun) Authentic Middle Eastern food, like falafel and hummus, served up to go, or eat in at a few tables and chairs scattered about. Perfect choice for a quick meal on the run or the late-night munchies.

Šestica
SLOVENIAN €€

(Sixth; Map p44; ✍242 08 55; www.sestica.si; Slovenska cesta 40; mains €13-19; ⏰10am-11pm Mon-Fri, noon-11pm Sat, noon-5pm Sun) Šestica has been around since 1776 and serves up plates of *goveji golaž s pečeno polento* (beef goulash with baked polenta) and *svinjska pečenka* (roast pork) to devoted patrons. The back courtyard is pleasant in summer, and the staff try hard to please. It holds a weekly Slovenian Night (€37, from 8pm to 11pm Friday) with folk music.

Mencigar Nobile
SLOVENIAN €€

(Map p38; ✍051-482 808; www.prekmurska-gostil na.si; Zarnikova ulica 3; mains €9.50-23; ⏰10am-5pm Mon-Wed, 10am-10pm Thu & Fri) A rare breed indeed, this is a regional Slovenian restaurant serving dishes from Prekmurje, Slovenia's flat-as a-pancake province in the far north-east. By all means try the *orehoje palačinke* (walnut pancakes) but start off with Hungarian-inspired savouries such as *bograč* (beef goulash), the Gypsy-style cutlet (*kotlet po ciganjsko*) or anything with *kaša* (groats).

Gostilna Čad
BALKAN €€

(Pod Rožnikom; ✍251 34 46; www.gostilna-cad .si; Cesta na Rožnik 18; mains €5-17; ⏰10am-11pm Mon-Fri, 11am-11pm Sat & Sun) This place under Rožnik Hill, just downwind from the zoo in Park Tivoli and known locally as Čad, serves southern Slav-style grills, like *pljeskavica* (spicy meat patties) with *ajvar* (roasted red peppers, tomatoes and eggplant cooked into a purée) and starters such as *prebranac* (onions and beans cooked in an earthenware pot).

Sofra
BALKAN €€

(✍565 68 00; Dunajska cesta 145; mains €8-15; ⏰11am-11pm Mon-Fri, noon-11pm Sat) Often touted as the most authentic Bosnian restaurant in town, with a good selection of grilled meats. There's often live music from September to June, when your fellow diners are likely to provide as much entertainment as those performing. Service can be on the slow side.

Manna
SLOVENIAN €€€

(Map p38; ✍051-315 220; www.kulinarika-manna. si; Eipprova ulica 1a; mains €14-35; ⏰7am-midnight Mon-Wed, 7am-1am Thu-Sat, 8am-4pm Sun) Festooned across the front of this canal-side restaurant in Trnovo is the slogan '*Manna – Bžanske Jedi na Zemlji*' (Manna – Heavenly Food on Earth). A Chaîne des Rôtisseurs establishment, it has very stylish decor, there's a wonderful covered inner courtyard for dining almost al fresco and the setting is pretty nice.

Gostilna As
INTERNATIONAL €€€

(Map p44; ✍425 88 22; www.gostilnaas.si; Čopova ulica 5a; mains €16.70-32; ⏰noon-midnight) The Ace Inn, in the passage linking Wolfova ulica and Slovenska cesta, is the place for a special occasion, with an embarrassment of caviar and truffles, a good wine list, and a few classic Slovenian dishes to balance the menu. The As Lounge in the cellar and garden is much more informal, with cheaper sandwiches and salads.

Pri Vitezu
SLOVENIAN €€

(Map p44; ✍426 60 58; www.privitezu.si; Breg 18-20; mains €17-25; ⏰noon-11pm Mon-Sat) Located directly on the left bank of the Ljubljanica, 'At the Knight' is the place for a special meal (Mediterranean-style grills and Adriatic fish dishes), whether in the brasserie, the salon or the very cosy Knight's Room.

JB Restavracija
INTERNATIONAL €€€

(Map p38; ✍433 13 58; www.jb-slo.com; Miklošičeva cesta 17; mains €20-30; ⏰11am-11pm Mon-Fri, 6-11pm Sat) Old-world charm, a hybrid international menu, a top-notch wine list and very stylish decor have made this restaurant one of the most popular in town for a fancy meal.

Castello
ITALIAN €

(Map p44; ✍051-383 902; Gornji trg 33; dishes €5-9; ⏰noon-midnight Mon-Sat) Very good pizza and pasta in a lovely setting in a quiet part of town, along the outer section of Gornji trg.

Thai Inn Pub
ASIAN €

(Map p38; ✍421 03 77; http://thaipub.si; Rimska cesta 17; mains €6-8; ⏰11am-10pm Mon-Fri, noon-10pm Sat; ☞) This Thai and Asian restaurant is popular with students, who come for the well-above-average food as well as the general party atmosphere. There's a lovely garden beside a park, which makes for a perfect lunchtime setting.

Ajdovo Zrno
VEGETARIAN €

(Map p44; ☑040-832 446; www.ajdovo-zrno.si; Trubarjeva cesta 7; soups & sandwiches €2-4, set lunch €6; ☺10am-7pm Mon-Fri; ☑) 'Buckwheat Grain' serves soups, sandwiches, fried vegetables and lots of different salads. And it has terrific, freshly squeezed juices, including the unusual rose-petal juice with lemon. Enter from Mali trg.

Paninoteka
SANDWICHES €

(Map p44; ☑040-349 329; Jurčičev trg 3; soups & toasted sandwiches €4-7; ☺8am-11pm Mon-Thu, 8am-midnight Fri, 9am-midnight Sat, 9am-10pm Sun; ☎) Healthy sandwich creations and salads on a lovely little square by the river.

Hot Horse
BURGERS €

(Map p38; ☑521 14 27; www.hot-horse.si; Park Tivoli, Celovška cesta 25; snacks & burgers €3-6; ☺9am-6pm Tue-Sun, 10am-6pm Mon) This little place in the city's biggest park supplies Ljubljančani (local people) with their favourite treat: horse burgers (€4). It's just down the hill from the Museum of Contemporary History.

Slaščičarna Pri Vodnjaku
ICE CREAM €

(Map p44; ☑425 07 12; Stari trg 30; ☺8am-midnight) This popular ice-cream parlour offers almost three dozen different flavours as well as coffee, hot chocolate, tea and fresh juices.

🍷 Drinking

Ljubljana offers a dizzying array of drinking options, whether your tipple is beer, wine and spirits or tea and coffee. In summer the banks of the Ljubljanica River are transformed into essentially one long terrace and serve as the perfect spot on which to perch yourself, drink and people-watch. In practice there's often little distinction between 'pubs and bars' and 'cafes and teahouses'. Most cafes also serve beer and wine, and many pubs and bars start the day out as cafes before morphing into nightspots after sundown.

Pubs & Bars

TOP CHOICE ⟩ Žmavc
BAR

(Map p38; ☑251 03 24; Rimska cesta 21; ☺7.30am-1am Mon-Fri, from 10am Sat, from 6pm Sun; ☎) A super-popular student hang-out west of Slovenska cesta, with manga comic-strip scenes and figures running halfway up the walls. There's a great garden terrace for summer evening drinking, but try to ar-

rive early to snag a table. Also excellent for morning coffee.

BiKoFe
BAR

(Map p44; ☑425 93 93; Židovska steza 2; ☺7am-1am Mon-Fri, 10am-1am Sat & Sun; ☎) A favourite with the hipster crowd, this cupboard of a bar has mosaic tables, studenty art on the walls, soul and jazz on the stereo, and a giant water pipe on the menu for that long, lingering smoke outside. The shady outdoor patio is a great place to enjoy a recent purchase from the Behemot (p62) bookshop across the street.

Vinoteka Movia
WINE BAR

(Map p44; ☑452 54 48; www.movia.si; Mestni trg 2; ☺noon-11pm Mon-Sat) If you're more interested in the grape than the grain, hop over to this excellent wine bar where, with due ceremony and ritual, you can taste your way through some award-winning Slovenian wines. It does retail as well.

Dvorni Bar
WINE BAR

(Map p44; ☑251 12 57; www.dvornibar.net; Dvorni trg 2; ☺8am-1am Mon-Sat, 9am-midnight Sun; ☎) This wine bar is an excellent place to taste Slovenian vintages; it stocks more than 100 varieties and has wine tastings every month (usually the second Wednesday).

Šank Pub
PUB

(Map p38; Eipprova ulica 19; ☺7am-1am; ☎) Down in studenty Trnovo, this raggedy little place with brick ceiling and wooden floor is a relaxed option. The Šank is one of a number of inviting bars and cafes along this stretch of Eipprova ulica.

Pr' Semaforju
BAR

(Map p44; Slovenska cesta 5; ☺7am-midnight Mon-Fri; ☎) Student hang-out par excellence, 'At the Traffic Light' (the name is translated into a dozen languages outside) is a slightly grotty cafe-bar that rocks over two floors later in the evening.

Cutty Sark Pub
PUB

(Map p44; ☑051-286 609; www.cuttysarkpub.si; Knafljev prehod 1; ☺9am-1am Mon-Sat, noon-1am Sun; ☎) A pleasant and well-stocked pub with colourful windows in the courtyard behind Wolfova ulica 6, the Cutty Sark is a congenial place for a *pivo* (beer) or glass of *vino* (wine). Happy hour is from 5pm to 7pm.

Solist
BAR

(Map p44; ☑040-206 400; Kongresni trg 10; ☺8.30am-1am; ☎) Nowhere near as pretentious as it sounds, this stylish bar attached to the rear of the Filharmonija, and facing the Ljubljanica, plays only classical music. Makes for a nice change.

Pod Skalco
BAR

(Under the Rock; Map p44; ☑426 58 20; www.pod skalco.si; Gosposka ulica 19; ☺6.30am-3am Mon-Thu, 5pm-3am Fri-Sun) The only thing this dive due south of the City Museum has going for it is that it keeps late hours when you need them most. Enjoy.

Cafes & Teahouses

TOP CHOICE Nebotičnik
CAFE

(Map p44; ☑040-601 787; www.neboticnik.si; 12th fl, Štefanova ulica 1; ☺9am-1am Sun-Wed, 9am-3am Thu-Sat; ☎) After a decade-long hibernation, this elegant cafe with its breathtaking terrace atop Ljubljana's famed art-deco Skyscraper (1933) has reopened, and the 360-degree views are spectacular.

Le Petit Café
CAFE

(Map p44; ☑251 25 75; www.lepetit.si; Trg Francoske Revolucije 4; ☺7.30am-1am; ☎) Just opposite the Križanke, this pleasant, boho place offers great coffee and a wide range of breakfast goodies, lunches and light meals, plus a good restaurant on the 1st floor.

Čajna Hiša
TEAHOUSE

(Map p44; ☑421 24 40; Stari trg 3; ☺9am-10.30pm Mon-Fri, 9am-3pm & 6-10pm Sat; ☎) This elegant and centrally located teahouse takes its teas very seriously. It also serves light meals and there's a tea shop next door.

Maček
CAFE

(Map p44; ☑425 37 91; http://sobe-macek.si; Krojaška ulica 5; ☺9am-12.30am Mon-Sat, to 11pm Sun; ☎) The place to be seen on a sunny summer afternoon, the 'Cat' is one of a number of spots on the right bank of the Ljubljanica to relax over a coffee or alcoholic beverage. Starts to really hop after sundown, when it morphs pretty seamlessly into a cocktail bar.

Kavarna SEM
CAFE

(Map p38; ☑041-729 619; www.etno-muzej.si; Metelkova ulica 2; ☺7am-1am Sun-Wed, 7am-2am Thu-Sat; ☎) This wonderful cafe in the Slovenian Ethnographic Museum is all glass and modern art with views of the attached pottery workshop and live ethno music on Tuesday and Friday.

Café Antico
CAFE

(Map p44; Stari trg 17; ☺9am-midnight Mon-Thu, 9am-1am Fri, 10am-10pm Sat, 11am-10pm Sun; ☎)

With frescoed walls, painted ceiling and retro-style furniture, this pretty place is perfect for a quiet tête-à-tête over a cup of coffee or glass of wine. Also does small food items, like soups and stews.

Open Cafe
GAY & LESBIAN

(Map p38; ☑041-391 371; www.open.si; Hrenova ulica 19; ☺4pm-midnight; ☎) This very stylish gay-owned and run cafe south of the Old Town has become the meeting point for Ljubljana's burgeoning queer culture. In June 2009 it was attacked by fascist homophobics who attempted to torch the place, and some patrons fought back.

Zvezda
CAFE

(Map p44; ☑421 90 90; Kongresni trg 4 & Wolfova ulica 14; ☺7am-11pm Mon-Sat, 10am-8pm Sun; ☎) The 'Star' has all the usual varieties of coffee and tea but is celebrated for its shop-made cakes, especially *skutina pečena* (€3), an eggy cheesecake.

KavaČaj
CAFE

(Map p38; ☑433 82 33; Kersnikova ulica 1; ☺7.30am-10pm Mon-Thu, 7.30am-9pm Fri, 9am-2pm Sat; ☎) This gem of a place, though a bit off the beaten track, serves excellent tea and coffee, and sells the stuff (and accoutrements) as well. There's a smokers' area upstairs on the terrace.

Grajska Kavarna
CAFE

(Map p44; ☑439 41 40; www.ljubljanskigrad.si; Ljubljana Castle, Grajska planota 1; ☺9am-midnight May-Sep, 9am-11pm Oct-Apr) This welcoming cafe at Ljubljana Castle offers a respite on a hot day and a great place to kick back with a coffee, beer or light meal after a long slog up the hill.

Abecedarium Cafe
CAFE

(Map p44; ☑426 95 14; Ribji trg 2; ☺8am-11pm; ☎) Ensconced in the oldest house (1528) in Ljubljana and one-time residence of the writer Primož Trubar (who wrote *Abecedarium*) this place – as much a restaurant as a cafe these days – oozes atmosphere.

Juice Box
JUICE BAR

(Map p44; ☑051-614 545; www.juicebox.si; Slovenska cesta 38; juices & smoothies €3.60-5; ☺7am-8pm Mon-Fri, 8am-3pm Sat; ☎) Of the crop of juice bars that have sprouted up in Ljubljana, this is the most central and the best, with some excellent fruit and vegetable combinations.

☆ Entertainment

Ljubljana in Your Pocket (www.inyourpocket.com), which comes out every two months, is a good English-language source for what's on in the capital. Buy tickets for shows and events at the venue box office, online through **Eventim** (☏430 24 05; www.eventim.si), or at Ljubljana Tourist Information Centre (p64). Expect to pay around €10 to €20 for tickets to live acts, and less for club entry and DJ nights.

Theatre

Ljubljana has half a dozen theatres so there should be something on stage for everyone. Slovenian theatre is usually quite visual with a lot of mixed media, so you don't always have to speak the lingo to enjoy the production. In addition to concerts and other musical events, Cankarjev Dom regularly stages theatrical productions.

National Drama Theatre   THEATRE
(Narodno Gledališče Drama; Map p44; ☏252 14 62, box office 252 15 11; www.drama.si; Erjavčeva cesta 1; ⊙box office 2-5pm & 6-8pm Mon-Fri, 6pm-showtime Sat) Built as a German-language theatre in 1911, this wonderful art-nouveau building is home to the national theatre company. Performances are in Slovene.

KUD France Prešeren   THEATRE
(Map p38; ☏283 22 88; www.kud-fp.si; Karunova ulica 14; ⊙10am-10pm Mon-Sat, 1-10pm Sun) This 'noninstitutional culture and arts society' in Trnovo stages concerts as well as performances, literary events, exhibitions, workshops etc on most nights.

Glej Theatre   THEATRE
(Gledališče Glej; Map p44; ☏251 66 79, 421 92 40; www.glej.si; Gregorčičeva ulica 3; performances €10-15) Glej (Look) has been Ljubljana's foremost experimental theatre since the 1970s, working with companies that include Betontanc (dance) and Grejpfrut (drama). It stages about five productions – theatre, mime, puppetry, multimedia – a year.

Ljubljana Puppet Theatre   THEATRE
(Lutkovno Gledališče Ljubljana; Map p44; ☏box office 300 09 82; www.lgl.si; Krekov trg 2; ⊙box office 4-6pm Mon-Fri, 10am-noon Sat & 1hr before performance) The Ljubljana Puppet Theatre stages its own shows throughout the year and hosts Lutke, the International Puppet Festival (Mednarodni Lutkovni Festival), every other (even-numbered) year in September.

Live Music
JAZZ & ROCK

Gala Hala   INDIE & ROCK
(Map p38; ☏431 70 63; www.galahala.com; Metelkova Mesto, Masarykova cesta 24) Metelkova's biggest and best venue to catch live alternative, indie and rock music several nights a week. There's an open-air performance space from May to September.

Kino Šiška   INDIE & ROCK
(☏box office 030-310 110; www.kinosiska.si; Trg Prekomorskih brigad 3; ⊙5-8pm Mon-Fri, 10am-1pm Sat) This renovated old movie theatre has been reopened as an urban cultural centre, hosting mainly indie, rock and alternative bands from around Slovenia and the rest of Europe.

Jazz Club Gajo   JAZZ
(Map p44; ☏425 32 06; www.jazzclubgajo.com; Beethovnova ulica 8; ⊙7pm-2am Mon-Sat) Now in its 18th year, Gajo is the city's premier venue for live jazz and attracts both local and international talent. Jam sessions are at 8.30pm Monday.

Sax Pub   ROCK
(Map p38; ☏283 90 09; Eipprova ulica 7; ⊙noon-1am Mon, 10am-1am Tue-Sat, 4-10pm Sun) Two decades in Trnovo and decorated with colourful murals and graffiti inside and out, the tiny Sax has live jazz at 9pm or 9.30pm on Thursday from late August to December and February to June. Canned stuff rules at other times.

Roxly Cafe Bar   BLUES & ROCK
(Map p44; ☏430 10 21; www.roxly.si; Mala ulica 5; ⊙8am-2am Mon-Wed, 8am-3am Thu & Fri, 10am-3am Sat) This cafe, bar and restaurant north of the Ljubljanica features occasional live music (mostly blues and rock) from 10pm.

Orto Bar   ROCK
(Map p38; ☏232 16 74; www.orto-bar.com; Grabolličeva ulica 1; ⊙9pm-4am Tue & Wed, to 5am Thu-Sat) A popular bar-club for late-night drinking and dancing with occasional live music, Orto is just five minutes' walk from Metelkova. Note the program takes a two-month hiatus in summer during July and August.

OPERA & CLASSICAL

Cankarjev Dom   CLASSICAL, OPERA, DANCE
(Map p38; ☏241 71 00, box office 241 72 99; www.cd-cc.si; Prešernova cesta 10; ⊙box office 1am-1pm & 3-8pm Mon-Fri, 11am-1pm Sat, 1hr before

SOMETHING COMPLETELY DIFFERENT: METELKOVO MESTO

For a scruffy antidote to trendy clubs, try **Metelkova Mesto** (Metelkova Town; Map p38; www.metelkova.org; Masarykova cesta 24), an ex-army garrison taken over by squatters in the 1990s and converted into a free-living commune – a miniature version of Copenhagen's Christiania. In this two-courtyard block, a dozen idiosyncratic venues hide behind brightly tagged doorways, coming to life generally after midnight daily in summer and on Friday and Saturday the rest of the year. While it's certainly not for the genteel and the quality of the acts and performances varies with the night, there's usually a little of something for everyone on hand.

Entering the main 'city gate' from Masarykova cesta, the building to the right houses **Gala Hala**, with live bands and club nights, and **Klub Channel Zero** (www .ch0.org), with punk and hardcore. Above it on the 1st floor is **Galerija Mizzart** (www .mizzart.net) with a great exhibition space (the name is no comment on the quality of the creations – promise!). Easy to miss in the first building to the left is the **Kulturni Center Q** (Q Cultural Centre) including Tiffany (p62) for gay men and Klub Monokel (p62) for lesbians. Due south is the ever-popular **Jalla Jalla Club**, a congenial pub with concerts. Beyond the first courtyard to the southwest, **Klub Gromka** (www.klubgromka .org) has folk concerts, theatre and lectures. Next door is **Menza pri Koritu** (☑434 03 45; www.menzaprikoritu.org), under the creepy ET-like figures, with performance and concerts. If you're staying at the Hostel Celica (p52), all of the action is just around the corner.

performance) Ljubljana's premier cultural and conference centre has two large auditoriums (the Gallus Hall is said to have perfect accoustics) and a dozen smaller performance spaces offering a remarkable smorgasbord of performance arts.

Opera & Ballet Ljubljana OPERA & DANCE
(Map p44; ☑box office 241 59 59; www.opera.si; Župančičeva ulica 1; ☺box office 10am-5pm Mon-Fri, 1hr before performance) Home to the Slovenian National Opera and Ballet companies, this historic neo-Renaissance theatre was fully renovated in 2011 and restored to its former lustre.

Philharmonic Hall CLASSICAL
(Slovenska Filharmonija; Map p44; ☑241 08 00; www.filharmonija.si; Kongresni trg 10; ☺7am-10pm) Home to the Slovenian Philharmonic Orchestra, this smaller but more atmospheric venue also stages concerts and hosts performances of the Slovenian Chamber Choir (Slovenski Komorni Zbor), which was founded in 1991.

Križanke CLASSICAL, DANCE, THEATRE
(Map p44; ☑241 60 00, box office 241 60 26; www .ljubljanafestival.si; Trg Francoske Revolucije 1-2; ☺box office 10am-8pm Mon-Fri, 10am-1pm Sat Apr-Sep) The open-air theatre at this sprawling 18th-century monastery hosts the events of the Ljubljana Summer Festival. The smaller

Knights' Hall (Viteška Dvorana) is the venue for chamber concerts.

Nightclubs

Cirkus CLUB
(Kinoklub Vič; Map p38; ☑051-631 631; www.cirkus klub.si; Trg Mladinskih Delovnih Brigad 7; admission €5; ☺8pm-5am Tue-Sat) This popular dance club, with DJs at the weekends, occupies the former Kinoklub Vič.

Klub K4 CLUB
(Map p38; ☑040-212 292; www.klubk4.org; Kersnikova ulica 4; ☺10pm-2am Tue, 11pm-4am Wed & Thu, 11pm-6am Fri & Sat, 10pm-4am Sun) This evergreen venue in the basement of the Student Organisation of Ljubljana University (ŠOU) headquarters features rave-electronic music Friday and Saturday, with other styles of music on weeknights, and a popular gay and lesbian night on Sunday.

KMŠ CLUB
(Map p38; ☑425 74 80; www.klubkms.si; Tržaška ulica 2; ☺8am-10pm Mon-Fri, 9pm-5am Sat) Located in the deep recesses of a former tobacco factory complex, the Maribor Student Club stays comatose till Saturday when it turns into a raucous place with music and dancers all over the shop.

Top: Eat & Party
CLUB

(Map p44; ☑040-667 722; www.klubtop.si; Tomšičeva ulica 2; ☺11pm-5am) This retro restaurant and cocktail bar, on the 6th floor of the Nama department store with fabulous views, becomes a popular dance venue nightly and attracts a very chichi crowd. Take the glass-bubble lift from along Slovenska cesta or the lift in the passageway linking Cankarjeva ulica and Tomšičeva ulica.

Ultra
CLUB

(Map p44; www.ultra-club.si; Nazorjeva ulica 6; ☺10pm-6am Wed-Sat) Ultra is a popular dance venue with four different theme nights and a switched-on raucous crowd.

As Lounge
CLUB

(Map p44; ☑425 88 22; www.gostilnaas.si; Čopova ulica 5a; ☺11pm-3am Wed-Sat; 🛜) DJs transform this candlelit basement bar into a pumping, crowd-pulling nightclub four nights a week. The way the name sounds in Slovene might have you thinking you're going to get lucky, but it just means 'ace'. Enter from Knafljev prehod.

Gay & Lesbian Venues

Ljubljana may not be the most gay-friendly city in Central Europe, but there are a few decent options. For general information and advice, call Klub Roza, which is made up of the gay and lesbian branches of Škuc (Študentski Kulturni Center or Student Cultural Centre), or the **Škuc Information Centre** (☑251 65 40; www.skuc.org; Stari trg 21; ☺noon-8pm). Open Cafe (p59) is a gay-friendly watering hole, located south of the Old Town.

Klub Roza
GAY & LESBIAN

(Klub K4; Map p38; ☑438 02 61; www.klubk4.org; Kersnikova ulica 4; ☺10pm-6am Sun Sep-Jun) A popular spot for gays and lesbians alike is this Sunday (and occasionally Saturday) night disco at Klub K4. The music takes no risks, but the crowd is lively. See the website for dates and details.

Tiffany
GAY & LESBIAN

(Map p38; www.kulturnicenterq.org/tiffany/klub/; Metelkovo Mesto, Masarykova cesta 24; ☺varies) On-again, off-again club for gay men located in the Metelkova Mesto complex.

Klub Monokel
GAY & LESBIAN

(Map p38; www.klubmonokel.com; Metelkovo Mesto, Masarykova cesta 24; ☺varies) Club for lesbians situated in the Metelkova Mesto complex.

🛍 Shopping

Ljubljana has plenty on offer in the way of folk art, antiques, music, wine, food and, increasingly, fashion. If you want everything under one roof, head for **BTC City** (☑585 22 22; www.btc-city.com; Šmartinska cesta 152; ☺9am-8pm Mon-Sat) or **City Park** (☑587 30 50; www.citypark.si; Šmartinska cesta 152g; ☺9am-9pm Mon-Sat, 9am-3pm Sun), sprawling malls side by side with hundreds of shops in Moste, northeast of Center. They can be reached on bus 2, 7 and 27.

Art & Antiques

Carniola Antiqua
ART & ANTIQUES

(Map p44; ☑231 63 97; Trubarjeva cesta 9; ☺4-7pm Mon, 10am-1pm & 4-7pm Tue-Fri, 10am-1pm Sat) Newly expanded, with a large selection of items from the 1950s and '60s, this is among the best and most helpful antique galleries in town.

Antika Ferjan
ART & ANTIQUES

(Map p44; ☑426 18 15; 1st fl, Mestni trg 21; ☺9am-7pm Mon-Fri, 10am-2pm Sat) Ferjan is a large shop with Slovenian and other European art and antique glass, furniture and clocks.

Trubarjev Antikvariat
ART & ANTIQUES

(Map p44; ☑244 26 83; www.mladinska.com; Mestni trg 25; ☺8.30am-1.30pm & 3.30-7.30pm Mon-Fri, 8.30am-1.30pm Sat) Come here for antiquarian and secondhand books. There's a good selection of antique maps upstairs.

Galerija Fortuna
ART & ANTIQUES

(Map p44; ☑425 01 87; Gornji trg 1; ☺10am-1pm & 4-8pm Mon-Fri, 10am-1pm Sat) Packed into this shop in the Old Town are some really beautiful antiques, especially glassware from the 1920s and other art-nouveau treasures.

Antiques & Flea Market
ART & ANTIQUES

(Cankarjevo nabrežje; Map p44; ☺8am-2pm Sun) Worth checking out is the weekly antiques and flea market held year-round on the embankment between Triple and Cobbler Bridges.

Bookshops

🄳 Knjigarna Behemot
BOOKS

(Map p44; ☑251 13 92; www.behemot.si; Židovska steza 3; ☺10am-8pm Mon-Fri, 10am-3pm Sat) Ljubljana's pint-sized English bookshop is packed with high-quality reading. It's especially strong on current events, nonfiction and the translated works of Slovenia's own philosopher-king Slavoj Žižek. A must-visit for bibliophiles.

Mladinska Knjiga BOOKS
(Map p44; ☑241 46 84; www.mladinska.com; 1st fl, Slovenska cesta 29; ☺9am-7.30pm Mon-Fri, 9am-2pm Sat) 'MK' is the city's biggest and best-stocked bookshop, with lots of guidebooks, maps, pictorials, fiction, and newspapers and periodicals in English. There's a **branch** (Map p38; ☑234 27 80; Miklošičeva cesta 40; ☺8.30am-7pm Mon-Fri, 9am-noon Sat) on Miklošičeva cesta.

Geonavtik BOOKS
(Map p44; ☑252 70 27; www.geonavtik.com; Kongresni trg 1; ☺8.30am-8.30pm Mon-Fri, 8.30am-4pm Sat) Superb shop with travel and nautical guides, maps, books about Slovenia in English and a popular cafe-bar.

Clothing & Accessories
Almira Sadar FASHION
(Map p38; ☑430 13 29; www.almirasadar.com; Tavčarjeva ulica 6; ☺10am-7pm Mon-Fri, 10am-2pm Sat) On offer here are uniquely patterned women's foundation pieces and accessories in natural materials from one of Slovenia's leading designers.

Torbice Marjeta Grošelj ACCESSORIES
(Marjeta Grošelj Bags; Map p38; ☑231 89 84; Tavčarjeva ulica 4; ☺8.30am-12.30pm & 3.30-7pm Mon-Fri, 8.30am-noon Sat) Sells upscale handbags by designer Marjeta Grošelj in top-quality leather.

Peko ACCESSORIES
(Map p44; ☑059-089 068; www.peko.si; Miklošičeva cesta 14; ☺9am-8pm Mon-Sat) Once the provenance of good solid socialist shoes manufactured in the good solid socialist town of Tržič, northwest of Ljubljana, Peko has gone all trendy and its shoes vie in quality only with its new line of handbags.

Katarina Silk ACCESSORIES
(Map p44; ☑425 00 10; www.katarina-silk.si; Gornji trg 5; ☺10am-7pm Mon-Fri, 10am-2pm Sat May-Sep, noon-7pm Mon-Fri, 10am-2pm Sat Oct-Apr) Silk scarves so fine they'll pass through a ring, and unique costume jewellery.

Folk Art & Gifts
Trgovina Ika FOLK ART, GIFTS
(Map p44; ☑232 17 43; www.trgovina-ika.si; Ciril-Metodov trg 13; ☺10am-7.30pm Mon-Fri, 9am-6pm Sat, 10am-2pm Sun) This cute shop opposite the cathedral and market sells handmade items that put a modern spin on traditional forms and motifs. More than 100 designers have clothing, jewellery, porcelain etc on sale here.

Skrina FOLK ART
(Map p44; ☑425 51 61; www.skrina.si; Breg 8; ☺9am-7pm Mon-Fri, 9am-1pm Sat) This is a good shop for distinctly Slovenian (and affordable) folk craft, like Prekmurje black pottery, Idrija lace, beehive panels with folk motifs, decorated heart-shaped honey cakes, painted Easter eggs, Rogaška glassware, colourful bridal chests and stepped stools.

Piranske Soline GIFTS
(Piran Salt Pans; Map p44; ☑425 01 90; www.soline.si; Mestni trg 19; ☺9am-8pm Mon-Fri, 10am-3pm Sat & Sun) This place in the Old Town sells bath sea salts and other products from Sečovlje.

Rustika FOLK ART
(Map p44; ☑031 383 247; Ljubljanski grad; ☺10am-7pm) This attractive gallery and shop, with wooden floors and a really 'rustic' feel, is conveniently located in Ljubljana Castle and is good for folk art.

Galerija Idrijske Čipke GIFTS
(Idrija Lace Gallery; Map p44; ☑425 00 51; www.idrija-lace.com; Mestni trg 17; ☺10am-1pm & 3-7pm Mon-Fri, 10am-2pm Sat) If Idrija in Primorska is not on your itinerary but you hanker for some of the fine lace for which that town is renowned, visit this shop. It has the stuff in spades.

Food & Wine
Kraševka FOOD, WINE
(Map p44; ☑232 14 45; www.krasevka.si; Ciril Metodov trg 10; ☺9am-7pm Mon-Fri, 8am-2pm Sat) This fantastic delicatessen with stuff from farms (mostly) in the Karst stocks *pršut* (dry-cured ham) in all its variations and cheeses, as well as wines and spirits, oils and vinegars, and honeys and marmalades.

Honey House FOOD
(Map p44; Mestni trg 7; ☺9am-7pm) Slovenia is one of the largest producers of honey and honey-related products in Europe and this place stocks enough varieties of the sweet sticky stuff to satisfy any taste. Mead, propolis and royal jelly available too.

Wine Cellars of Slovenia WINE
(Vinske Kleti Slovenije; ☑431 50 15; Jurček Pavilion, Dunajska cesta 18; ☺10am-7pm Mon-Fri, 9am-1pm Sat, restaurant 10am-11pm Mon-Sat) If you're serious about wine, this enormous wine cellar and restaurant north of Center is for you. It has a selection of more than 800 wines, most of which are Slovenian.

Vino Boutique
WINE

(Map p44; ☑425 26 80; Slovenska cesta 38; ☺10am-7pm Mon-Fri, 10am-1pm Sat) This small wine boutique is located in a narrow central passageway, and the owners are well informed and helpful.

Sporting Goods

Annapurna
OUTDOOR EQUIPMENT

(Map p44; ☑031 740 838; www.annapurna.si; Krakovski nasip 4; ☺9am-7pm Mon-Fri, 9am-1pm Sat) If you've forgotten your sleeping bag, ski poles, hiking boots, climbing gear or rucksack, this shop in Krakovo can supply you with all of it – and more.

Lovec
OUTDOOR EQUIPMENT

(☑585 17 99; www.koptex.com; BTC City - Hall A, Šmartinska cesta 152; ☺9am-8pm Mon-Sat) For those into ridin', fishin' and shootin', Hunter has all the kit and equipment you'll need.

❶ Information

Discount Cards

The **Urbana-Ljubljana Tourist Card** (www .visitljubljana.si/en/ljubljana-and-more/ ljubljana-tourist-card), available from the tourist office for 24/48/72 hours (€23/30/35), offers free admission to most museums and galleries, walking and boat tours, and unlimited travel on city buses.

Internet Access

Many cafes and restaurants offer free wi-fi for customers. Most hostels, and some hotels, maintain a public computer for guests to surf the internet. The Slovenian Tourist Information Centre has computers on-hand to check email (€1 per 30 minutes).

Cyber Cafe Xplorer (☑430 19 91; Petkovškovo nabrežje 23; per 30min/hr €2.50/4; ☺10am-10pm Mon-Fri, 2-10pm Sat & Sun; ☞) Ljubljana's best internet cafe; also has wi-fi and offers discount international calling.

Internet Resources

In addition to the websites of the Slovenian Tourist Information Centre (www.slovenia.info) and Ljubljana Tourist Information Centre (www.vis itljubljana.si), the following sites might be useful:

City of Ljubljana (www.ljubljana.si) Comprehensive information portal on every aspect of life and tourism direct from city hall.

In Your Pocket (www.inyourpocket.com) Insider info on the capital updated regularly.

Left Luggage

Left Luggage in Bus Station (Trg OF 4; per day €2; ☺5.30am-10.30pm Sun-Fri, 5am-10pm Sat) Window No 3.

Left Luggage in Train Station (Trg OF 6; per day €2-3; ☺24hr) Coin lockers on platform 1.

Medical Services

University Medical Centre Ljubljana (Univerzitetni Klinični Center Ljubljana; ☑522 50 50, emergencies 522 84 08; www4.kclj.si; Zaloška cesta 2; ☺24hr) University medical clinic with 24-hour accident and emergency service.

Health Centre Ljubljana (Zdravstveni Dom Ljubljana; ☑472 37 00; www.zd-lj.si; Metelkova ulica 9; ☺7.30am-7pm) For non-emergencies.

Barsos-MC (☑242 07 00; www.barsos.net; Gregorčičeva ulica 11; ☺8am-3pm Mon, Wed & Fri, 8am-2pm Tue & Thu) Private clinic, with prices starting at around €40 per consultation.

Central Pharmacy (Centralna Lekarna; ☑230 61 00; Prešernov trg 5; ☺8am-7.30pm Mon-Fri, 8am-3pm Sat)

Money

There are ATMs at every turn, including a row of them outside the main Ljubljana Tourist Information Centre office. At the train station you'll find a **bureau de change** (☺7am-8pm) changing cash for no commission but not travellers cheques.

Abanka (☑300 15 00; www.abanka.si; Slovenska cesta 50; ☺9am-1pm & 3-5pm Mon-Fri)

Nova Ljubljanska Banka (☑476 39 00; www .nlb.si; Trg Republike 2; ☺8am-6pm Mon-Fri)

Post

Main Post Office (Slovenska cesta 32; ☺8am-7pm Mon-Fri, to 1pm Sat) Holds poste restante for 30 days and changes money.

Post Office Branch (Pražakova ulica 3; ☺8am-7pm Mon-Fri, to noon Sat) Just southwest of the bus and train stations.

Tourist Information

Ljubljana Tourist Information Centre (TIC; ☑306 12 15; www.visitljubljana.si; Adamič-Lundrovo nabrežje 2; ☺8am-9pm Jun-Sep, 8am-7pm Oct-May) Knowledgeable and enthusiastic staff dispense information, maps and useful literature and help with accommodation. Maintains an excellent website. Has a helpful **branch** (☑433 94 75; www.visitljubljana.si; Trg OF 6; ☺8am-10pm Jun-Sep, 10am-7pm Mon-Fri, 8am-3pm Sat Oct-May) at the train station.

Slovenian Tourist Information Centre (STIC; ☑306 45 76; www.slovenia.info; Krekov trg 10; ☺8am-9pm Jun-Sep, 8am-7pm Oct-May) Good source of information for the rest of Slovenia, with internet and bicycle rental also available.

Travel Agencies

STA Ljubljana (☑041 612 711, 439 16 90; www .sta-lj.com; 1st fl, Trg Ajdovščina 1; ☺10am-5pm

Mon-Fri) Discount air fares for students. Its cafe has internet access.

Trek Trek (📞425 13 92; www.trektrek.si; Bičevje ulica 5; ⊙10am-5pm Mon-Fri) Specialising in adventure travel in Slovenia, with an emphasis on trekking and cycling holidays.

ℹ Getting There & Away

Air

There are no regularly scheduled passenger flights within Slovenia. For flights to and from Ljubljana from abroad, see p241.

Bus

Buses to destinations within Slovenia and abroad leave from the **bus station** (Avtobusna Postaja Ljubljana; 📞234 46 00; www .ap-ljubljana.si; Trg Osvobodilne Fronte 4; ⊙5.30am-10.30pm Sun-Fri, 5am-10pm Sat) just next to train station. Next to the ticket windows are multilingual information phones and a touchscreen computer. There's another touch-screen computer outside too.

You do not usually have to buy your ticket in advance; just pay as you board the bus. But for long-distance trips on Friday, just before the school break and public holidays, you are running the risk of not getting a seat – book one the day before and reserve a seat (€1.20/3.70 domestic/international).

You can reach almost anywhere in the country by bus – as close as Kamnik (€3.30, 50 minutes, 25km, every half-hour) or as far away as Murska Sobota (€18, 4¼ hours, 199km, one or two a day).

Car & Motorcycle

Most of the big international car-hire firms have offices in Ljubljana. You can rent locally on the spot or often snag a better deal renting in advance over the company website.

Avis (📞430 80 10; www.avis.si; Čufarjeva ulica 2; ⊙8am-7pm Mon-Fri, 6am-1pm Sat, 8am-noon Sun)

Budget (📞421 73 40; www.budget.si; Grand Hotel Union Business, Miklošičeva cesta 3; ⊙8am-4pm Mon-Fri, 9am-noon Sat & Sun)

Atet Rent a Car (📞513 70 17; www.atet.si; Devova ulica 6a; ⊙8am-6pm Mon-Fri, 8am-1pm Sat & Sun)

Train

Domestic and international trains arrive at and depart from central Ljubljana's **train station** (Železniška Postaja; 📞291 33 32; www.slo -zeleznice.si; Trg Osvobodilne Fronte 6; ⊙6am-10pm) where you'll find a separate Info Center next to the Ljubljana Tourist Information Centre branch. Buy domestic tickets from windows No 1 to 8 and international ones from either window No 9 or the Info Center. See p66 for a sample of trains from Ljubljana.

Note that there's a surcharge of €1.55 on domestic InterCity (IC) and EuroCity (EC) train tickets.

ℹ Getting Around

To/From the Airport

The cheapest way to Ljubljana's Jože Pučnik Airport is by **public bus** (€4.10, 45 minutes, 27km) from stop No 28 at the bus station. These run at 5.20am and hourly from 6.10am to 8.10pm Monday to Friday; at the weekend there's a bus at 6.10am and then one every two hours from 9.10am to 7.10pm. Buy tickets from the driver.

A **private airport van** (📞051 321 414; www .airport-shuttle.si) also links Trg OF, near the bus station, with the airport (€9) up to 11 times daily between 5.20am and 10.30pm, and is a 30-minute trip. It goes from the airport to Ljubljana 10 times a day between 5.45am and 11pm.

A taxi from the airport to Ljubljana will cost from €40 to €45.

Bicycle

Ljubljana is a pleasure for cyclists, and there are bike lanes and special traffic lights everywhere.

BUSES FROM LJUBLJANA

DESTINATION	PRICE (ONE WAY)	DURATION	DISTANCE	FREQUENCY
Bled	€6.50	1½hr	57km	hourly
Bohinj	€9	2hr	91km	hourly
Koper	€12	2½hr	122km	5 daily with more in summer
Maribor	€14	3hr	141km	2-4 daily
Novo Mesto	€8	1hr	72km	up to 7 daily
Piran	€14	3hr	140km	up to 7 daily
Postojna	€7	1hr	53km	up to 24 daily

TRAINS FROM LJUBLJANA

DESTINATION	PRICE (ONE WAY, 2ND CLASS)	DURATION	DISTANCE	FREQUENCY
Bled	€6.22	55min	51km	up to 21 daily
Koper	€9	2½hr	153km	up to 4 daily with more in summer
Maribor	€15	1¾hr	156km	up to 25 daily
Murska Sobota	€14	3¼hr	216km	up to 5 daily
Novo Mesto	€6	1½hr	75km	up to 14 daily

Ljubljana Bike (⌕306 45 76; www.visitljubljana.si; Krekov trg 10; per 2hr/day €2/8; ☻8am-7pm or 9pm Apr-Oct) rents two-wheelers in two-hour or full-day increments from April through October from the Slovenian Tourist Information Centre (p64).

For short rides, you can hire bikes as needed from **Bicike(lj)** (www.bicikelj.si; subscription weekly/yearly €1/€3 plus hourly rate; ☻24hr) bike stands located around the city. To rent a bike requires pre-registration and subscription over the company website plus a valid credit or debit card. After registration simply submit your card or an Urbana card plus a PIN. The first hour of the rental is free, the second hour costs €1, the third hour €2, and each additional hour €4. Bikes must be returned within 24 hours.

Car & Motorcycle

The centre is walkable and many streets are off limits to motor vehicle traffic, so you're best advised to stow your car on arrival and walk or take public transport as needed to get around. Parking in Ljubljana is tight, especially on workdays. Most parking in the centre is metered parking (per hour €0.80 to €1, from 8am to 6pm Monday to Friday, and 8am to 1pm Saturday). There are enclosed car parks throughout the city, and their locations are indicated on most maps. Parking rates normally start at €1 to €2 per hour; expect to pay a day rate of around €30.

Public Transport

Ljubljana's city buses operate every five to 15 minutes from 5am (6am on Sunday) to around 10.30pm, though some routes start as early as 3.30am and run until midnight or later. A flat fare of €1.20 (good for 90 minutes of unlimited travel, including transfers) is paid with a stored-value magnetic **Urbana** (⌕430 51 74; www.jh-lj.si/urbana) card, which can be purchased at newsstands, tourist offices and the **LPP Information Centre** (⌕430 51 75; www.jhl.si; Slovenska cesta 56; ☻7am-7pm Mon-Fri) for €2; credit can then be added from €1 to €50. The central area is perfectly walkable, though, so buses are really only necessary to reach destinations well outside of the centre.

Taxi

Metered taxis can be hailed on the street or hired from ranks near the train station, at the Ljubljana TIC on Stritarjeva ulica, in front of the Grand Hotel Union, or on Mestni trg. Flagfall is €0.83 to €1.50 and the per-kilometre charge ranges from €1 to €1.50, depending on the company and whether you call ahead (cheaper) or hail a taxi on the street.

Laguna Taxi (⌕511 23 14; www.taxi-laguna .com; Celovška cesta 228) Reliable radio taxi with English-speaking operators.

Gorenjska

Best Places to Eat

» Gostilna Mihovc (p89)
» Zeleni Rob (p72)
» Gostilna Rupa (p89)
» Gostilna Lectar (p75)
» Gostilna Pr' Kovač (p77)

Best Places to Stay

» Penzion Gasperin (p87)
» Camping Bled (p82)
» Gostilna Lectar (p74)
» Eko Camp (p92)
» Traveller's Haven (p82)

Why Go?

Mountains and lakes are the big draws in Gorenjska, and if you're into adventure sports, this is the province to head for. The Triglav National Park, with hiking and biking trails galore as well as Slovenia's share of the Julian Alps, is the epicentre for all things outdoors. A mountain trek is an excellent way to meet other Slovenes in a relaxed environment, so take advantage of this opportunity if you get the chance. The beautiful Alpine lakes at Bled and Bohinj offer boating and swimming amid shimmering mountain backdrops. But Gorenjska is not just about nature pursuits; it also contains some of the country's most attractive and important historical towns. Škofja Loka and Radovljica – to name just a couple – are treasure troves of Gothic, Renaissance and baroque architecture.

When to Go
Bled

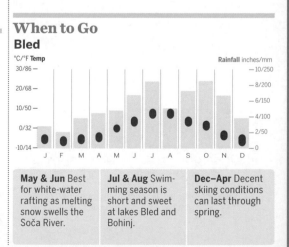

May & Jun Best for white-water rafting as melting snow swells the Soča River.

Jul & Aug Swimming season is short and sweet at lakes Bled and Bohinj.

Dec–Apr Decent skiing conditions can last through spring.

Škofja Loka

📞 04 / POP 11,970 / ELEV 354M

Škofja Loka (Bishop's Meadow), just 26km from Ljubljana, is among the most beautiful and oldest settlements in Slovenia. Its evocative Old Town has been protected as a historical monument since 1987. It can be explored as a day trip from the capital or as an overnight stay (though book accommodation in advance since there's just a handful of lodging options). When the castle and other old buildings are illuminated on weekend nights, Škofja Loka takes on the appearance of a fairy tale. It's also an excellent springboard for walking in the Škofja Loka Hills to the west.

◉ Sights

Loka Castle & Museum   MUSEUM
(Loški Grad & Muzej; www.loski-muzej.si; Grajska pot 13; adult/child €5/3; ⊙10am-6pm Tue-Sun)

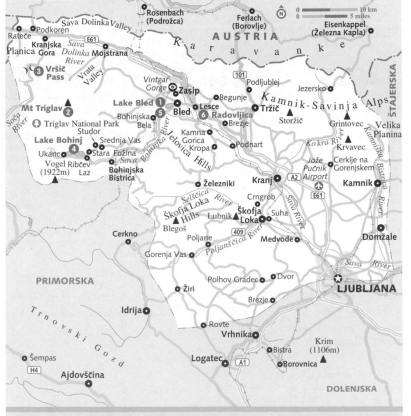

Gorenjska Highlights

1 Hire a *pletna* (gondola) and sail the crystal-clear waters of **Lake Bled** (p76)

2 Climb to the top of **Mt Triglav** (p97), Slovenia's tallest peak, and proclaim yourself Slovene

3 Drive or bike over the hair-raising (and spine-tingling) **Vršič Pass** (p92) in the Julian Alps

4 Commune with nature *au naturel* at the naturist beach on the northern shore of **Lake Bohinj** (p85)

5 Spend an unforgettable day **canyoning**, **rafting** or **ballooning** starting from **Lake Bled** (p76)

6 Treat yourself to a meal to remember at one of **Radovljica's** excellent restaurants (p75)

The town's premier sight is this commanding castle, dating from the 13th century and extensively renovated after an earthquake in 1511, that overlooks the town from a grassy hill west of Mestni trg. The castle houses the **Loka Museum**, which boasts one of the best ethnographic collections in Slovenia spread out over two dozen galleries on two floors.

Highlights of the museum include several ornate guild chests, reflecting the fact that the area around Škofja Loka was famous for smiths and lace-makers. In the garden, you'll find a typical peasant house from nearby Pušta dating from the 16th century. Don't miss the four spectacular golden altars in the castle **chapel**. They were taken from a church destroyed during WWII in Dražgoše, northwest of Škofja Loka. Two paths lead up to the castle; the most convenient starts just opposite Kavarna Homan (p72).

Mestni Trg   TOWN SQUARE

The group of colourful 16th-century **burghers' houses** on this square have earned the town the nickname 'Painted Loka'. Almost every one is of historical and architectural importance, but arguably the most impressive is **Homan House** (Homanova Hiša; Mestni trg 2), dating from 1511 with graffiti and bits of frescoes of St Christopher and of a soldier.

Another building to look out for is the former **Town Hall** (Stari Rotovž; Mestni trg 35), remarkable for its stunning three-storey Gothic courtyard and the 17th-century frescoes on its facade. Further south, 17th-century **Martin House** (Martinova Hiša; Mestni trg 26) leans on part of the old town wall. It has a wooden 1st floor, a late-Gothic portal and a vaulted entrance hall. The **plague pillar**, in the centre of Mestni trg, was erected in 1751.

Parish Church of St James   CHURCH

(Župnijska Cerkev Sv Jakoba; http://zupnije.rkc .si; Cankarjev trg; ☉7am-6pm) The town's most important church dates back to the 13th century, with key features like the **nave**, **presbytery** with star vaulting (1524), and the tall **bell tower** (1532) added over the next three centuries. The dozen or so distinctive ceiling lamps and the **baptismal font** were designed by Jože Plečnik.

Inside the church, look up to the vaulted ceiling to see bosses with portraits of the Freising bishops (the town's founders), saints, workers with shears, and a blacksmith; the

two crescent moons in the presbytery are reminders of the Turkish presence. Outside the church, on the south side, is the church's **rectory**, part of a fortified aristocratic manor house built in the late 16th century.

Spodnji Trg   PUBLIC SQUARE

The main square to the east of Mestni trg was where the poorer folk lived in the Middle Ages; today it is a busy thoroughfare with admittedly not much to see. The 16th-century **Granary** (kašča; Spodnji trg 1) at the northern end is where the town's grain stores, collected as taxes, were once kept.

Over two floors in the granary you'll find **France Mihelič Gallery** (Galerija Franceta Miheliča; ☏517 04 00; www.loski-muzej.si; Spodnji trg 1; adult/child €2/1.50; ☉by appointment), which displays the works of the eponymous artist born in nearby Virmaše in 1907.

Capuchin Monastery   MONASTERY

(Kapucinski Samostan; ☏512 09 70; Kapucinski trg 2; ☉by appointment) The 18th-century Capuchin monastery, west of the bus station, has a priceless **library** of medieval manuscripts, as well as the *Škofja Loka Passion*, a processional with dramatic elements, from around 1720.

Capuchin (or Stone)
Bridge   HISTORIC ARCHITECTURE

(Kapucinski Most) The stone Capuchin Bridge leading from the Capuchin monastery originally dated from the 14th century and is an excellent vantage point for the Old Town and castle as well as the river, with its deep gorge, dams, abandoned mills and 18th-century barracks.

Church of the Annunciation   CHURCH

(Cerkev Marijinega Oznanenja; Crngrob; ☉by appointment) This small church in the village of Crngrob, 4km north of Škofja Loka, has one of the most treasured frescoes in Slovenia. Called 'Holy Sunday' *(Sveta Nedelja)* and produced in 1460, it explains in pictures what good Christians do on Sunday (pray, go to Mass, help the sick) and what they don't do (gamble, drink or fight).

🏃 Activities

The **Škofja Loka Hills** to the west, a region of steep slopes, deep valleys and ravines, is an excellent area for walks or hikes, and there are several huts with accommodation in the area. Before you set out, buy a copy of the 1:50,000 hiking map *Škofjeloško in Cerkljansko Hribovje (Škofja Loka and*

GORENJSKA ŠKOFJA LOKA

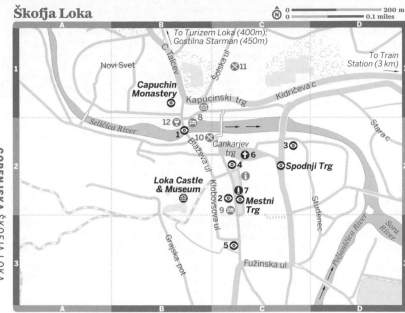

Škofja Loka

◎ Top Sights

◎ Sights

🛏 Sleeping

⊗ Eating

⊙ Drinking

Cerkno Hills; €9) and ask the TIC for the pamphlet *Škofja Loka Walk around the Town and Surroundings,* which will direct you to Crngrob on foot.

One of the easiest trips in the brochure is to **Lubnik**, a 1025m peak northwest of the Old Town, which can be reached on foot in two hours via Vincarje or the castle ruins near Gabrovo. Start the walk from Klobovsova ulica in Mestni trg. A mountain hut near the summit, Category II **Dom na Lubniku**

(☎031 727 046, 512 05 01; info@pd-skofjaloka.com; Lubnik; ⊙daily Mar-Dec, Sat & Sun Jan & Feb), has seven triple rooms.

A hike to 1562m **Blegoš**, further west, would be much more demanding, but it takes only about three hours from Hotavlje, a village about 2km from Gorenja Vas and accessible by bus from Škofja Loka. There is a mountain hut in the area: Category II **Koča na Blegošu** (☎051 614 587, 512 06 67; info@pd-skofjaloka.com; Blegoš; ⊙daily late Apr–late Oct, Sat & Sun late Oct–late Apr), at 1391m, with 61 beds.

The **Stari Vrh ski centre** (☑518 81 36, 041 650 849; www.starivrh.si; Stari Vrh; day pass adult/child/student €26/15/21), 12km west of Škofja Loka, is situated at altitudes of 580m to 1216m and covers 12km of ski slopes and trails. There are five T-bar tows and a chairlift.

✯✯ Festivals & Events

Škofja Loka Passion Play RELIGIOUS FESTIVAL
(http://pasijon.skofjaloka.si; ☻late Mar–Apr) The staging of the Škofja Loka Passion Play throughout the Old Town in the three weeks before Easter (late March/April) involves as many as 800 actors and 80 horses, and is Škofja Loka's biggest annual event.

Venerina Pot MEDIEVAL FESTIVAL
(Path of Venus; http://venera.skofjaloka.si; ☻late Jun) A medieval-inspired festival held on the last weekend in June.

Pod Homanovo Lipo MUSIC
(☻Jul-Aug) This music festival takes place under the big linden tree in front of Homan House on Mestni trg on certain nights in July and August.

🛏 Sleeping

Hotel Garni Paleta HOTEL €€
(☑512 64 00; www.hotel-skofjaloka.si; Kapucinski trg 17; s/d €41/62; P❄�) This colourful and upbeat place next door to an art-supplies shop (thus the name) just over Capuchin Bridge has six plain but clean rooms, all with exceptional bathrooms. Room 1, 3, 5 and 6 have views of the river and the castle, but the upper-floor rooms (just under the roof) can get very hot in summer. Book in advance, particularly in summer.

Kavarna Vahtnca PENSION €
(☑512 14 79; www.vahtnca.si; Mestni trg 31; s/d €30/48; P�)) This attractive, modern cafe in the heart of Škofja Loka's Old Town has two upscale rooms upstairs that will put you in the centre of the action.

Turizem Loka PENSION €€
(☑515 09 86; www.loka.si; Stara Loka 8a, Stara Loka; s/d €40/60; P@�)) Though this comfortable, remodelled farmhouse pension styles itself as a farmstay option, it's actually in the middle of the village of Stara Loka. It offers spotless rooms, a small wellness centre, and

a quieter environment than Škofja Loka, plus it's just a few minutes' walk to Gostilna Starman. On the downside, it's a 20-minute walk from the centre of Škofja Loka.

Camp Smlednik CAMPGROUND €
(☑01-362 70 02; www.dm-campsmlednik.si; Dragočajna 14a, Drago čajna; per adult €7-8, child €3.50-4, 2-/3-/4-person bungalows €40/50/60; ☻May–mid-Oct; P☁) This 4-hectare campground for 400 guests in Drago čajna, 11km to the east, is the closest one to Škofja Loka. It is situated on the left bank of the Sava River and beside Lake Zbilje. There is also a beach with separate facilities set aside for naturists.

🍴 Eating

TOP CHOICE **Gostilna Starman** SLOVENIAN €
(Stara Loka 22, Stara Loka; mains €7-12; ☻9am-11pm Mon, Tue, Thu-Sat, 9am-6pm Sun) This popular *gostilna* (inn-like restaurant) about 3km out of the centre (a 15- to 20-minute walk) in the charming village of Stara Loka. It serves authentic traditional Slovenian cooking in an informal tavern setting. There's a small terrace for dining outside in hot weather.

Kašča SLOVENIAN €€
(☑512 43 00; www.kasca-plevna.com; Spodnji trg 1; mains €8-15; ☻noon-midnight; �)) This attractive (and huge) pub and wine bar in the cellar of the town's 16th-century granary is Škofja Loka's most upscale dining option, and the perfect venue for a big meal out. The menu is heavy on traditional Slovenian food but there's also an appealing range of pizzas on the menu. There's a small terrace outside.

Jesharna ITALIAN €
(☑512 25 61; Blaževa ulica 10; pizza & pasta €6-9; ☻9am-11pm Mon-Fri, 10am-11pm Sat, 11.30am-10pm Sun; 🐾) This friendly, upbeat pizzeria and spaghetti house serves the town's best pizza, good salads and pasta dishes that are so big they could easily be shared. Book in advance for one of the few riverside tables. It's a little tricky to find, but more or less directly across the river from the post office.

Market FOOD MARKET €
(Šolska ulica; ☻7am-1pm Thu & Sat) The food market is northeast of the Nama department store.

KAMNIK & VELIKA PLANINA

The town of Kamnik and the nearby Alpine pastureland of Velika Planina are less travelled by visitors but worth a detour if you've got an extra day.

Start your exploration in Kamnik, with its attractive medieval core. From near central Glavni trg, climb to the **Little Castle** (Mali Grad), which dates to the 11th century, for a look at the adjoining **Romanesque Chapel** (adult/child €5/3; ⊙9am-7pm mid-Jun–mid-Sep), with its 15th-century frescoes and Gothic stone reliefs. Other important sights include the **Church of St James** (Cerkev Sv Jakoba; Frančiškanski trg; admission free; ⊙8am-6pm) and its tent-like **Chapel of the Holy Sepulchre** (Kapela Božjega Groba; Frančiškanski trg; admission free; ⊙8am-6pm), designed by Jože Plečnik in 1952, just off the main altar.

Leave at least half a day for Velika Planina, situated about 11km northeast of Kamnik. The journey to the top unfolds in two stages: first a dramatic **cable-car ride** (žičnica; ☎01-839 71 77; www.velikaplanina.si; adult/child return €16/14, cable car only €11/10, chairlift only €5/4.50; ⊙hourly 8am-6pm Mon-Thu, 8am-8pm Fri-Sun mid-Jun–mid-Sep, shorter hrs rest of year) and then a 15-minute chairlift. Once on top, there's not much to do except walk the pristine fields and admire a herding and dairy economy little changed for hundreds of years. The pastures are scattered with around 50 traditional shepherds' huts that are unique to Velika Planina. Regrettably, all but one of these, the tiny two-room **Preskar's Hut** (Preskarjeva Bajta; www.velikaplanina.si; Velika Planina; admission €2.50; ⊙10am-5pm Sat & Sun late Jun–early Sep) that's now a small museum, are replicas. The originals, dating from the early 20th century, were burned to the ground by Germans in WWII.

While at the top, have a meal at **Zeleni Rob** (www.velikaplanina.si; Velika Planina; mains €6-8; ⊙8am-8pm Jun-Sep, 8am-8pm Fri-Sun Oct-May), a small restaurant situated a short walk from the first (lower) stop on the chairlift. It's rumoured to have Slovenia's best *štruklji* (sweet dumplings stuffed with curd cheese) – something we can personally attest to.

Transport from Kamnik to the cable-car station is limited to a few buses daily (inquire at the Kamnik TIC) or arrange transport through your hotel.

Back in Kamnik, there are two acceptable choices for lodging, depending on your budget: the **Hotel Malograjski Dvor** (☎01-830 31 00; www.hotelkamnik.si; Maistrova ulica 13; s/d €68/92; P@🖘), a family-run, three-star hotel with 21 stylishly appointed rooms, and **Hostel Pod Skalo** (☎01-839 12 33; www.hi-kamnik.com; Maistrova ulica 32; s/d/tr from €30.50/45/67.50; P@🖘) with around a dozen doubles and triples, all with en suite baths, and a lively pub next door. If you have your own wheels, head out of town a couple of kilometres to **Gostilna Repnik** (☎01-839 12 93; www.gostilna-repnik.si; Vrhpolje 186; mains €10-15; ⊙10am-10pm Tue-Fri, noon-10pm Sat, noon-3pm Sun; P🖘) for gourmet-quality Slovenian cooking, based on locally sourced ingredients and traditional recipes.

Kamnik's helpful **Tourist Information Centre** (TIC; ☎01-831 82 50; www.kamnik-tourism.si; Glavni trg 2; city tours adult/child €5/3; ⊙9am-8pm Jul & Aug, 10am-6pm Mon-Sat, 10am-2pm Sun Jun & Sep, 8am-4pm Mon-Fri, 8am-noon Sat Oct-May; 🖘) has a wealth of brochures and free internet access, and can assist in working out transport details to Velika Planina.

Buses from Ljubljana (€3, 50 minutes, 25km) run almost every 20 minutes on weekdays, half-hourly on Saturday and hourly on Sunday. Kamnik is on a direct rail line to/from Ljubljana (€2.50, 45 minutes, 23km, up to 15 a day).

🍷 Drinking

Kavarna Vahtnca　　　　CAFE
(www.vahtnca.si; Mestni trg 31; ⊙11am-midnight Mon-Fri, 8am-11pm Sat & Sun; 🖘) With a tiered back terrace peeking up at the castle, and tables on the main square, this attractive modern cafe in the heart of the Old Town should be your first port of call. The cafe rents rooms on the upper floor.

Kavarna Homan　　　　CAFE
(Mestni trg 2; ⊙8am-11pm Mon-Thu, 8am-midnight Fri & Sat, 8am-10pm Sun) This ground-floor cafe in historical Homan House is always busy, especially in the warm weather when tables are set out on Mestni trg under the giant linden tree.

Bar pri Ziherlu　　　　BAR
(Kapucinski trg 22; ⊙6.30am-midnight Mon-Fri; 9am-midnight Sat & Sun; 🖘) This little bar-

cafe just beside the Capuchin Bridge serves decent espresso by day and is practically the only venue in town for more intoxicating stuff later on. The pretty back terrace, with a view over the river, makes for a picturesque repose on a hot summer day.

❶ Information

Most practical facilities for visitors are located a short walk from the bus station on Kapucinski trg. These include branches of **Gorenjska Banka** (Kapucinski trg 7), diagonally opposite the bus station, **SKB Banka** (Kapucinski trg 4), and the **post office** (Kapucinski trg 14). The **Tourist Information Centre** (TIC; ☑512 02 68; www .skofjaloka.info; Mestni trg 7; ⊙8.30am-7pm Mon-Fri, 8.30am-2pm Sat & Sun mid-Jun–mid-Sep, 8.30am-7pm Mon-Fri, 8.30am-12.30pm & 5-7pm Sat & Sun mid-Sep–mid-Jun) is located in the centre of the Old Town. It's a good source of general information and has books and maps on the area.

❶ Getting There & Away

BUS Škofja Loka is well served by regional buses. Count on at least hourly buses weekdays between 4.35am and 9.10pm to Ljubljana (€3.10, 40 minutes, 25km). There are far fewer departures at the weekend.

TRAIN Škofja Loka can be reached by up to 15 trains a day from Ljubljana (€1.60, 25 minutes, 20km) via Medvode. Almost 20 services go to Jesenice (€3.60 to €5.20, 50 minutes, 44km) via Radovljica and Lesce-Bled. Up to eight of these cross the border for Villach, 87km to the north in Austria.

Radovljica

☑04 / POP 18.164 / ELEV 491M

The town of Radovljica is filled with charming, historic buildings and blessed with stunning views of the Alps, including Mt Triglav. It was settled by the early Slavs, and by the 14th century had grown into an important market town centred on a large rectangular square, today's Linhartov trg, and fortified with high stone walls. Amazingly, much of the original architecture is still standing and looks remarkably unchanged from those early days. Radovljica has just a couple of places to stay, so it's advisable to book accommodation in advance or turn to the tourist information centre to snag a private room. It's an easy day trip from Bled, just 7km away.

◉ Sights

Radovljica's tiny but colourful **main square** (Linhartov trg) is the town's leading attraction. The square is lined with houses from the 16th century. Look especially for **Thurn Manor** (Linhartov trg 1); **Koman House** (Komanova Hiša; Linhartov trg 23), identified by a baroque painting of St Florian on its facade; **Mali House** (Malijeva Hiša; Linhartov trg 24) and **Vidič House** (Vidičeva Hiša; Linhartov trg 3).

Beekeeping Museum   MUSEUM
(Čebelarski Muzej; www.muzeji-radovljica.si; Linhartov trg 1; adult/child €3/2; ⊙10am-6pm Tue-Sun May-Oct, 8am-3pm Tue, Thu & Fri, 10am-noon & 3-5pm Wed, Sat & Sun Mar, Apr, Nov & Dec, 8am-3pm Tue-Fri Jan & Feb) More interesting than it sounds, this museum takes a closer look at beekeeping in Slovenia. The museum's collection of illustrated beehive panels from the 18th and 19th centuries, a folk art unique to Slovenia, is the largest in the country. Ask to see the short, instructive video in English.

Bees are still kept in Slovenia for their honey and wax but much more lucrative are such by-products as pollen, propolis and royal jelly, used as elixirs and in homeopathic medicine. Propolis is a brownish, waxy substance collected from certain trees by bees and used to cement or caulk their hives. Royal jelly, so beloved by the European aristocracy of the 1920s and 1930s and by the Chinese today, is the substance fed to the queen bee by the workers.

Šivec House   MUSEUM
(Šivčeva Hiša; Linhartov trg 22; adult/child €2/1.50; ⊙10am-1pm & 5-8pm Tue-Sun Jul & Aug, 10am-1pm & 4-7pm Tue-Sun May, Jun, Sep & Oct, 10am-noon & 4-6pm Tue-Sun Nov-Apr) This small museum, in perhaps the most important house on the square, displays a wood-panelled, late-Gothic drawing room with a beamed ceiling. There is also a chimney-less 'black kitchen' and an interesting collection of children's book illustrations by celebrated Slovenian artists.

Gingerbread Museum   MUSEUM
(Lectarski Museum; Linhartov trg 2; admission €1; ⊙noon-10pm Wed-Mon) Opposite Šivec House, in the cellar of the Gostilna Lectar (p75), is a small Gingerbread Museum that exhibits and demonstrates in living colour the particularly Slovenian art of *lectarstvo*, the making and shaping of honey dough into hearts, figures and so on.

Radovljica

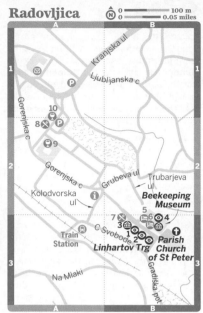

Parish Church of St Peter   CHURCH

(Župnijska Cerkev Sv Petra; Linhartov trg; ⊙7am-8pm) At the end of Linhartov trg is the Gothic Parish Church of St Peter, a hall church modelled after the one in Kranj. The three portals are flamboyant Gothic, and the sculptures inside were done by Angelo Pozzo in 1713. The building with the arcaded courtyard south of the church is the **rectory** *(župnišče)*, where exhibitions are sometimes held.

✸ Festivals & Events

Festival Radovljica   CLASSICAL MUSIC

(www.festival-radovljica.si; ⊙Aug) The biggest event of the year is the two-week Festival Radovljica, one of the most important festivals of ancient classical music in Europe.

🛏 Sleeping

TOP CHOICE Gostilna Lectar   PENSION €€

(☑537 48 00; www.lectar.com; Linhartov trg 2; s/d €50/80; ✳🛜) The nicest place in town, this delightful B&B in the heart of the Old Town has nine individually decorated rooms done up in folk motif – painted headboards and rooms signs (each is named differently) made of *lect* (gingerbread) – that could have ended up kitsch but instead feel like those in a village farmhouse from the 19th century.

Vidic House   HOSTEL €

(Vidičevi Hiši; ☑031 810 767; www.vidichouse.com; Linhartov trg 3; per person €17-22; 🛜) This 400-year-old historic town house on the main square offers accommodation in three large, airy apartments, with postcard views over Linhartov trg. Two of the apartments can be rented as private doubles or singles. Skip the €4 breakfast and have a coffee in one of the cafes instead.

Sport Penzion Manca   PENSION €€

(☑531 40 51; www.manca-sp.si; Gradnikova cesta 2; s €45-60, d €68-76, tr €88-96; 🅿@🛜🏊) This excellent-value pension about 2.5km north of Linhartov trg has 17 spic-and-span modern rooms and all sorts of sports facilities – from swimming pool and sauna to bicycles. Some rooms have views of the Karavanke range, others of Mt Triglav itself.

Camping Šobec   CAMPGROUND €

(☑535 37 00; www.sobec.si; Šobčeva cesta 25; camping per adult €10.60-13.30, child €8-9.90, bungalows for 2 €75-120, for 3-6 €94-150; ⊙late Apr–Sep; 🅿) The largest (15 hectares with

500 sites) and arguably the best-equipped campground in Slovenia is in Lesce, about 2.5km northwest of Radovljica. Situated on a small lake near a bend of the Sava Dolinka River, the campground can accommodate up to 1500 people in tents and bungalows.

✖ Eating

TOP CHOICE **Gostilna Lectar** SLOVENIAN €€
(☎537 48 00; www.lectar.com; Linhartov trg 2; mains €9-15; ⊘noon-11pm; 🛜) This inviting guesthouse on the main square may just be the best restaurant in Gorenjska. Everything from relatively common dishes like veal goulash to harder-to-find items like beef tongue and kohlrabi are given a gourmet touch. Book ahead on weekends or to snag a table on the back terrace with stunning mountain views.

Grajska Gostilnica SLOVENIAN €€
(☎531 44 45; www.grajska-gostilnica.si; Kranjska cesta 2; mains €9-15; ⊘11am-11pm) This traditional wine cellar and small terrace may lack the picturesque setting of the town's other good restaurants, but it's no slouch when it comes to cooking. The menu is filled with grilled meats and seafood, pasta and pizza.

The grilled calamari stuffed with prosciutto and mozzarella was one our best meals in Slovenia.

Gostilna Augustin SLOVENIAN €€
(☎531 41 63; Linhartov trg 15; mains €10-17; ⊘10am-10pm) This delightful restaurant is one of the most welcoming in Gorenjska. It serves excellent Slovenian dishes to order and bans pizzas altogether. Don't miss the cellar dining room, which was once part of a prison (and may have seen an execution or two), and the wonderful back terrace with stunning views of Mt Triglav.

🍷 Drinking

Caffeteria CAFE
(Kranjska cesta 4; coffee €1-1.20; ⊘7am-10pm; 🛜) This modern, centrally located cafe serves excellent coffees and small bites like toasts. It has a convenient terrace and free, reliable wi-fi. What else could you ask for?

Vidic House CAFE
(Vidičevi Hiši; www.vidichouse.com; Linhartov trg 3; coffee €1; ⊘9am-9pm; 🛜) The nicest and most charming of several cafes located along historic Linhartov trg. Specialises in coffee, cakes and ice cream. The interior is jammed

GORENJSKA RADOVLJICA

THE BOARDS & THE BEES

Radovljica is known throughout Slovenia as a centre for beekeeping, an integral part of Slovenian agriculture since the 16th century. Slovenians were at the forefront in developing early ways to improve beekeeping techniques, including the invention of what became known as the *kranjič* hive, with removable boxes that resembled a chest of drawers. This created multiple hives and solved an early problem of damaging an entire hive when the honeycomb was removed. It also led to the development of one of Slovenia's most important forms of folk art.

The *kranjič* hives are constructed with front boards above the entrance, and enterprising beekeepers soon began the practice of painting and decorating these panels with religious and other motifs. Radovljica's Beekeeping Museum (p73) has an extensive collection on hand, and some of the artwork is nothing short of phenomenal.

The first panels, dating back to the mid-18th century, were painted in a 'folk baroque' style and the subjects were taken from the Old and New Testaments (Adam and Eve, the Virgin Mary, and especially patient Job, the patron of beekeepers), and history (the Turkish invasions, Napoléon, and the Counter-Reformation, with Martin Luther being driven to hell by a devil).

The most interesting panels show the foibles, rivalries and humour of the human condition. A devil may be sharpening a gossip's tongue on a grindstone or two women fighting over a man's trousers (ie his hand in marriage). A very common illustration shows the devil exchanging old wives for nubile young women – to the delight of the husbands.

The painting of beehive panels in Slovenia enjoyed its golden age between about 1820 and 1880; after that the art form went into decline. The introduction of a new and much larger hive by Anton Žnidaršič at the end of the 19th century obviated the need for small illustrations, and the art degenerated into kitsch.

with found items; our favourite is a retro turntable from the 1960s.

Grajski Pub PUB
(Kranjska cesta 2; ⏱noon-2am; 🛜) The pub adjacent to the Grajska Gostilnica is the only place outside the Beekeeping Museum where you're likely to find a buzz in Radovljica. The terrace stays busy into the wee hours, and some nights bring live music and DJs.

❶ Information

The **Tourist Information Centre Radovljica** (TIC; 📞531 51 12; www.radolca.si; Linhartov trg 9; ⏱9am-7pm May-Sep, 9am-4pm Mon-Fri, 9am-1pm Sat Oct-Apr; 🛜) is centrally located, helps book rooms and has a computer on hand for a few minutes of gratis surfing. The office also sells local souvenirs, including jars of the best honey you're likely to ever taste. Most other conveniences for tourists are centrally located, including branches of **Gorenjska Banka** (Gorenjska cesta 16) and **SKB Banka** (Gorenjska cesta 10), and the **post office** (Kranjska cesta 1).

❶ Getting There & Away

BUS Buses depart for Bled (€1.80, 15 minutes, 7km) almost every 30 minutes from just before 5.30am to 10.40pm, and for Ljubljana (€6, 70 minutes, 50km) between 5.14am and 9.14pm. There are also buses to Kranjska Gora (€5.50, 50 minutes, 41km, up to eight a day) and Kropa (€2.10, 20 minutes, 13km, seven to 12 a day). The bus station is 400m northwest of Linhartov trg on Kranjska cesta.

TRAIN Radovljica is on a main rail line linking Ljubljana (€4, one hour, 48km) with Jesenice (€1.75, 20 minutes, 16km) via Škofja Loka, Kranj and Lesce-Bled. Around eight trains a day pass through the town in each direction. The train station is 100m below the Old Town on Cesta Svobode. International trains use the nearby station at Lesce-Bled.

Bled

📞04 / POP 10,900 / ELEV 501M

With its emerald-green lake, picture-postcard church on an islet, a medieval castle clinging to a rocky cliff and some of the highest peaks of the Julian Alps and the Karavanke as backdrops, Bled is Slovenia's most popular resort, drawing everyone from honeymooners lured by the over-the-top romantic setting to backpackers, who come for the hiking, biking, boating and canyoning possibilities. Not surprisingly, Bled can be overpriced and swarming with tourists in mid-summer. But as is the case with many popular destinations around the world, people come in droves – and will continue to do so – because the place is special.

History
Bled was the site of a Hallstatt settlement in the early Iron Age, but as it was far from the main trade routes the Romans gave it short shrift. From the 7th century the early Slavs came in waves, establishing themselves at Pristava below the castle, on the tiny island and at a dozen other sites around the lake.

Around the turn of the first millennium, the German Emperor Henry II presented Bled Castle and its lands to the Bishops of Brixen in South Tyrol, who retained secular control of the area until the early 19th century when the Habsburgs took it over.

Bled's beauty and its warm waters were well known to medieval pilgrims who came to pray at the island church; the place made it into print in 1689 when Janez Vajkard Valvasor described the lake's thermal springs in *The Glory of the Duchy of Carniola*. But Bled's wealth was not fully appreciated at that time, and in the late 18th century the keeper of the castle seriously considered draining Lake Bled and using the clay to make bricks.

Fortunately, along came a Swiss doctor named Arnold Rikli, who saw the lake's full potential. In 1855 he opened baths where the casino now stands, taking advantage of the springs, the clean air and the mountain light. With the opening of the railway from Ljubljana to Tarvisio (Trbiž) in 1870, more and more guests came to Bled and the resort was a favourite of wealthy Europeans from the turn of the 20th century right up to WWII. In fact, under the Kingdom of Serbs, Croats and Slovenes, Bled was the summer residence of the Yugoslav royal family.

◉ Sights

Lake Bled LAKE
(Blejsko jezero) Bled's greatest attraction is its crystal-clear blue-green lake, measuring just 2km by 1.4km. The lake is lovely to behold from almost any vantage point, and makes a beautiful backdrop for the 6km walk along the shore. Mild thermal springs warm the water to a swimmable 26°C from June through August. You can rent boats, go diving or simply snap countless photos.

THE FORMER FORGING VILLAGE OF KROPA

In the early years of the Industrial Revolution, the towns and villages around Radovljica grew wealthy through forging and metal working. While much of that activity was stilled decades ago, the custom still lives on in the pretty hillside village of Kropa, 13km southeast Radovljica and an easy 20-minute bus ride away.

Kropa has been a 'workhorse' for centuries, mining iron ore and hammering out the nails and decorative wrought iron that can still be seen in many parts of Slovenia. Today, the village has turned its attention to screws – the German-owned Novi Plamen factory is based here – but artisans continue their work, clanging away in the workshop on the village's single street, unsurprisingly called 'Kropa'. The work of their forebears is evident in weather vanes, shutters and ornamental street lamps shaped like birds and dragons.

Kropa's charm lies in the town's remote feel and the lovely, centuries-old former workers' housing that lines a fast-flowing mountain stream, the Kroparica, that runs right through the centre of town.

The main sight is the **Blacksmith Museum** (Kovaški Muzej; www.muzeji-radovljica .si; Kropa 10; adult/child €3/2; ☺10am-6pm Tue-Sun May-Oct, reduced hrs & days rest of year), which traces the history of iron mining and forging in Kropa and nearby Kamna Gorica from the 14th to the early 20th centuries. Nail and spike manufacturing was the town's main industry for most of that period; from giant ones that held the pylons below Venice together to little studs for snow boots, Kropa produced more than 100 varieties in huge quantities. The museum also has working models of forges, a couple of rooms showing how workers and their families lived in very cramped quarters (up to 45 people in one house) and a special exhibit devoted to the work of Jože Bertoncelj (1901–76), who turned out exquisite wrought-iron gratings, candlesticks, chandeliers and even masks. The museum shows two films, one on nail production and one on local customs.

Just across the street from the museum, be sure to pop in at the **UKO Kropa forgers' workshop** (www.uko.si; Kropa 7a; ☺7am-6pm Mon-Fri, 9am-noon Sat Jul & Aug, 7am-3pm Mon-Fri, 9am-noon Sat Sep-Jun), which sells all manner of articles made of wrought iron – from lamps and doorknobs to garden gates – including some very trendy-looking brushed metal trays and vases.

Kropa is not exactly awash with dining and lodging options, though don't miss a chance to try the traditional Slovenian cooking at **Gostilna Pr' Kovač** (At the Smith's; ☎04-533 63 20; Kropa 30; mains €7.50-12; ☺10am-11pm Tue-Sun). On our visit, the veal stew flavored with a hint of coriander and served with a side of buckwheat groats laced with pork crackling was a meal to remember. Sit outside in hot weather or dine in an evocative period setting inside the 400-year-old house. The gostilna has one room to let upstairs (per person 30€), but you'll have to book well in advance.

Most days are fairly quiet in Kropa, though **Smith's Day** (Kovaški Dan; www.uko.si; ☺2 Jul), brings a bit more excitement in the form of sporting and cultural events.

If you don't have your own car, the best way to get here is by bus from Radovljica. Seven to 12 buses a day run between the towns (€2.20, 20 minutes, 13km). Buses stop in front of the **Mercator** (Kropa 3a; ☺8am-6pm Mon-Fri, 7am-1pm Sat) supermarket at the bottom of the village.

Bled Castle   CASTLE, MUSEUM
(Blejski Grad; www.blejski-grad.si; Grajska cesta 25; adult/child €8/3.50; ☺8am-8pm Apr-Oct, 8am-6pm Nov-Mar) Perched atop a steep cliff more than 100m above the lake, Bled Castle is how most people imagine a medieval fortress to be, with towers, ramparts, moats and a terrace offering magnificent views. The castle houses a museum collection that traces the lake's history from earliest times to the de-

velopment of Bled as a resort in the 19th century.

The castle, built on two levels, dates back to the early 11th century, although most of what stands here now is from the 16th century. For 800 years, it was the seat of the Bishops of Brixen. Among the museum holdings, there's a large collection of armour and weapons (swords, halberds and firearms from the 16th to 18th centuries), jewellery found at the

GORENJSKA BLED

Bled

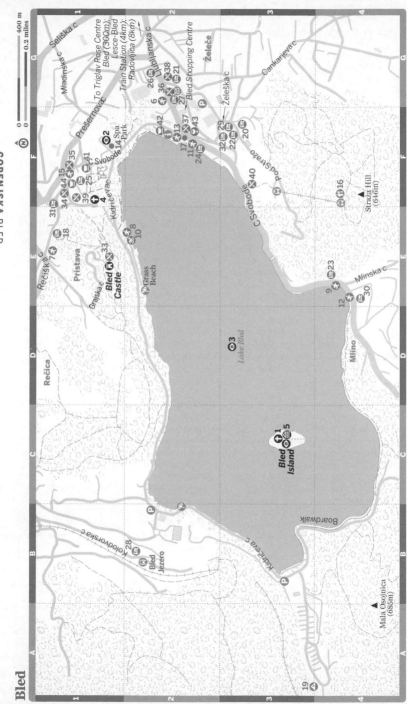

0   400 m
0   0.2 miles

Mladinska c
Seliška c
To Triglav Rose Centre
Bled (300m);
Lesce-Bled
Train Station (4km);
Radovljica (8km)
Prešernova c
Spa
14 Park
C Svobode
Ljubljanska c
Bled Shopping Centre
Želeče
Cankarjeva c
26
36
38
6
27
21
42
13
37
17 11
24
43
32 29
22
20
Želeška c
Pod Stražo
40
C Svobode
16
Straža Hill
(646m)
Rečiška c
7
18
31
34 44 15
39 25 41
4
35
Pristava
33
Bled
Castle
Grajska c
Kidričeva c
8
10
Grass
Beach
3
Lake Bled
23
9
Minska c
12
30
Mlino
1
5
Bled
Island
Boardwalk
Kidričeva c
Rečica
Kolodvorska c
28
Bled
Jezero
Mala Osojnica
(685m)
19

Bled

early Slav burial pits at Pristava, and a few interesting carvings, including a 16th-century one of the overworked St Florian dousing yet another conflagration. The smallish 16th-century Gothic chapel contains paintings of castle donor Henry II and his wife Kunigunda on either side of the main altar.

You can reach the castle on foot via one of three trails signposted 'Grad'. The first trail starts from the car park behind the Bledec Hostel; the second is a tortuous path up from the Castle Baths; and the third starts just north of the neo-Gothic Parish Church of St Martin (Farna Cerkev Sv Martina; Riklijeva cesta) designed by Friedrich von Schmidt in 1905.

Bled Island   ISLAND
(Blejski Otok; www.blejskiotok.si) Tiny, tear-shaped Bled Island beckons from the shore. There's a church and small museum, but the real thrill is the ride out by *pletna* (gondola). The boat sets you down on the south side at the monu-

mental South Staircase (Južno Stopnišče), built in 1655. As you walk up you pass the **Chaplain's House** and the Provost's House.

Church of the Assumption   CHURCH
(Cerkev Marijinega Vnebovzetja; www.blejskiotok.si; Bled Island; admission with Provost's House museum €3; ◷9am-7pm May-Sep, 9am-6pm Apr & Oct, 9am-4pm Nov-Mar) The baroque Church of the Assumption dates from the 17th century, though there's been a church here since the 9th century. Go inside to see some fresco fragments from the 14th century, a large gold altar and part of the apse of a pre-Romanesque chapel. The 15th-century belfry contains a 'wishing bell' you can ring to ask a special favour.

Provost's House Museum   MUSEUM
(Stavba Proštije; www.blejskiotok.si; Bled Island; admission incl Church of the Assumption €3; ◷9am-7pm May-Sep, 9am-6pm Apr & Oct, 9am-4pm Nov-Mar) This small museum has an interesting display of traditional costumes from across the country.

WORTH A TRIP

VINTGAR GORGE

One of the easiest and most satisfying day trips from Bled is to **Vintgar Gorge** (Soteska Vintgar; adult/child/student €4/2/3; ⊗8am-7pm late Apr–Oct), some 4km to the northwest.

The highlight is a 1600m wooden walkway, built in 1893 and continually rebuilt since. It criss-crosses the swirling Radovna River four times over rapids, waterfalls and pools before reaching 13m-high Šum Waterfall.

The entire walk is spectacular, although it can get pretty wet and slippery. There are little snack bars at the beginning and the end of the walkway and picnic tables at several locations along the way.

It's an easy walk to the gorge from Bled. Head northwest on Prešernova cesta then north on Partizanska cesta to Cesta Vintgar. This will take you to Podhom, where signs show the way to the gorge entrance. To return, you can either retrace your steps or, from Šum Waterfall, walk eastward over Hom (834m) to the ancient pilgrimage Church of St Catherine, which retains some 15th-century fortifications. From there it's due south through Zasip to Bled. Count on about three hours all up.

From May to September, a **tourist bus** (☑578 04 20; www.alpetour.si; one way €3.50) leaves Bled bus station daily at 10am and heads for Vintgar, stopping at the Krim and Grand Toplice hotels, Mlino, the far end of the lake and Bled Castle, arriving at 10.30am. It returns from Vintgar at 12.30pm.

🏃 Activities

Adventure Sports

Several local outfits organise a wide range of outdoor activities in and around Bled, including trekking, mountaineering, rock climbing, ski touring, cross-country skiing, mountain biking, rafting, kayaking, canyoning, caving, horse riding and paragliding.

3glav Adventures   ADVENTURE SPORTS
(☑041 683 184; www.3glav-adventures.com; Ljubljanska cesta 1; ⊗9am-7pm Apr-Oct) The number-one adventure-sport specialists in Bled for warm-weather activities from 15 April to 15 October. The 3glav Adventures agency's most popular trip is the Emerald River Adventure (€65), an 11-hour hiking and swimming foray into Triglav National Park and along the Soča River. A two-day guided ascent of Mt Triglav from Pokljuka, the Vrata Valley or Kot Valley costs around €200. If you don't fancy scaling mountains, a day-long trek through the Alpine meadows of the Triglav Lakes Valley costs around €80.

A 2½-hour rafting trip down the Sava Bohinjka/Soča River costs €35, and a three-hour canyoning descent is €55. Kayak trips lasting three hours cost €49. Paragliding is €95 and skydiving €190. Horseback riding starts at €50 for a two-hour outing.

The agency also rents bikes (half-day/full day €8/15), conduct hot-air balloon flights (€150) and lead diving expeditions of Lake Bled (€70).

Adventure Rafting Bled   ADVENTURE SPORTS
(☑051 676 008; www.adventure-rafting.si; Grajska cesta 21; ⊗Apr-Oct) Specialises in rafting and canyoning outings.

Life Trek   ADVENTURE SPORTS
(☑201 48 75; www.lifetrek-slovenia.com; Grajska cesta 4; ⊗8am-8pm Jun–mid-Sep, 9am-4pm mid-Sep–May) Offers a wide range of adventure outings, including a two-day ascent of Mt Triglav for €185.

Boating

Lake Bled is open to **rowboats**, though motorboats are banned. You can rent rowboats for around €15 per hour from the **Castle Baths** or from near the Garni Penzion Pletna in **Mlino** for getting to Bled Island or just pottering about.

Gondola   BOATING
(Pletna; ☑041 427 155; per person return €12) Riding a piloted gondola out to Bled Island is the archetypal tourist experience. There is a convenient jetty just below the **TIC** and another in **Mlino** on the south shore. You get about half an hour to explore the island. In all, the trip to the island and back takes about 1¼ hours.

Fishing

Fishing is allowed on Lake Bled, provided you have a permit. The surrounding lakes and streams are fertile ground for all manner of river fish. The TIC (p84) and Fauna can provide information.

Fauna
FISHING

(☑574 26 31; www.faunabled.com; Cesta Svobode 12; ☺8am-noon & 3-7pm Mon-Fri, 8am-noon Sat, 8-10am Sun) One-stop shopping for all your fishing needs, including organised tours, advice, map and gear rental. Sells fishing permits valid for a day on the lake (€25), the Radovna River (€50) and the Sava Bohinjka River (€59 to €69).

Flying
Lesce Alpine Flying Centre
SCENIC FLIGHTS

(Alpski Letalski Center Lesce; ☑532 01 00; www.alc-lesce.si; Begunjska cesta 10) The Lesce Alpine Flying Centre, 4km to the southeast, has panoramic flights in Cessna 172s over Bled (€75 for three people), Bohinj (€135) and even Mt Triglav (€195), or anywhere you want for €240 an hour.

Golf
Bled Golf & Country Club
GOLF

(☑537 77 11; www.golfbled.com; Mon-Fri €60, Sat & Sun €70; ☺8am-7pm Apr-Oct) The 18-hole, par-73 King's Course at the Bled Golf & Country Club, 3km to the east of the lake near Lesce, is Slovenia's best golf course and, with its dramatic mountain backdrop, one of the most beautiful in Europe. You can rent clubs and carts and there's a pro on hand for golf instruction.

Hiking
There are many short and easy signposted hikes around Bled (numbered signs correspond to numbered routes on the local hiking maps, such as the 1:30,000 GZS map *Bled*, which costs €8.50). One of the best is trail No 6 from the southwest corner of the lake to the summit of Velika Osojnica (756m). The view from the top – over the lake, island and castle, with the peaks of the Karavanke in the background – is stunning, especially toward sunset. The climb to the first summit is steep, but the round trip, returning via Ojstrica (610m), takes only three hours or so.

Skiing
Straža-Bled Ski Centre
SKIING

(☑578 05 30; www.bled.si; Rečiška cesta 2; day pass adult/child/student & senior €15/8/12; ☺mid-Dec–mid-Mar) Beginners will be content with the tiny (6-hectare) Straža-Bled ski centre, southwest of the Grand Hotel Toplice. A chairlift takes you 634m up the hill in three minutes; you'll be down the short slope in no time. Rental skis and poles are available from Life Trek (p80) and Kompas (p84).

Swimming
Bled's warm (23°C at source) and crystal-clear water – it rates a Blue Flag (a voluntary and independent eco-label awarded to beaches around the world for their cleanliness and water quality) – makes it suitable for swimming all summer, and there are decent beaches around the lake, including a big gravel one near the campground and a lovely grass one on the northern side.

Castle Baths
SWIMMING

(Grajsko Kopališče; ☑578 05 28; Veslaška promenada 11; day pass adult/child/student €7/4/5; ☺7am-8pm Jul & Aug, 7am-7pm Jun & Sep) The popular swim club offers lake swimming behind protected enclosures as well as water slides and other amusements. You can rent deckchairs, chaises longues and umbrellas (€3).

🚃 Tours
Tourist Train
SIGHTSEEING TROLLEY

(adult/child €3.50/2.50; ☺9am-9pm Jun-Oct, 9am-7pm Nov-May) This easy, family-friendly 45-minute twirl around the lake departs from just south of the TIC up to 20 times a day in season.

Horse-Drawn Carriages
HORSE-DRAWN CARRIAGE

(Fijaker; ☑041 710 970; www.fijaker-bled.si) A romantic way to experience Bled is to take a horse-drawn carriage from the stand near the Festival Hall (p81). A spin around the lake costs €40, and it's the same price to the castle; an extra 30 minutes inside costs €50. You can even get a carriage for four to Vintgar (adult/child €4/2; ☺8am-7pm mid-May–Oct); the two-hour return trip costs €90.

✨ Festivals & Events
A number of special events take place during the summer in Bled, including the **International Rowing Regatta** (www.veslaska-zveza.si) in mid-June; the **International Music Festival** (www.festivalbled.com) of violinists in early July; **Bled Days** (www.bled.si) in late July, a multimedia festival where there are fireworks and the entire lake is illuminated by candlelight; and the **Okarina Etno Festival** (www.okarina.com), a two-day international festival of folk and world music in late July/early August. For information, visit www.bled.si.

Summertime concerts take place at the **Festival Hall** (Festivalna Dvorana; Cesta Svobode 11) and the **Parish Church of St Martin** (Farna Cerkev Sv Martina; Riklijeva cesta), which houses one of the finest organs in Slovenia. In December, the Pokljuka Plateau, west of

Bled, is the venue for the **Biathlon World Cup** (www.biathlon-pokljuka.com) championship of cross-country skiing and rifle shooting.

Sleeping

Bled has a wide range of accommodation – from Slovenia's original hostel to a five-star hotel in a villa that was once Tito's summer retreat. Private rooms are offered by dozens of homes in the area. Both Kompas (p84) and the TIC have lists, with prices for singles ranging from €16 to €33 and doubles €24 to €50. Apartments for two cost from €40 to €65 and for four €60 to €110.

Hotel Triglav Bled   BOUTIQUE HOTEL €€€

(☎575 26 10; www.hoteltriglavbled.si; Kolodvorska cesta 33; s €89-159, d €119-179, ste €139-209; P✿@☎≋) This 22-room boutique hotel, in a painstakingly restored caravanserai that opened in 1906, raises the bar of accommodation standards in Bled. The rooms have hardwood floors and oriental carpets, and are furnished with antiques. There's an enormous sloped garden that grows the vegetables served in the terrace restaurants. The location is opposite Bled Jezero train station.

Garni Penzion Berc   PENSION €€

(☎574 18 38; www.berc-sp.si; Želeška cesta 15; s €35-45, d €60-70; P@☎) Try to book well in advance to snag a room in this delightful 19th-century farmhouse that's been retrofitted to serve as a peaceful, high-end pension. The rooms are simple but comfortable; the location is just a few minutes' walk from the centre of town.

Penzion Mayer   PENSION €€

(☎576 57 40; www.mayer-sp.si; Želeška cesta 7; s €57, d €77-82, apt €120-150; P@☎) This flower-bedecked 12-room inn in a renovated 19th-century house is in a quiet location above the lake. The larger apartment is in a delightful wooden cabin and the in-house restaurant is excellent.

Hotel Lovec   HOTEL €€€

(☎620 41 00; www.lovechotel.com; Ljubljanska cesta 6; s €100-120, d €120-180, ste from €180; P✿☎≋) A favourite of ours, this Best Western–member hotel boasts 60 of some of the most attractive rooms in Bled. We love the rooms (such as 402 and 403) with blond-wood walls, red carpet, and bath with Jacuzzi in front of a massive window facing the lake.

Camping Bled   CAMPGROUND €

(☎575 20 00; www.camping-bled.com; Kidričeva cesta 10c; adult €10.90-12.90, child €7.60-9, glamping huts €60-80; ☺Apr–mid-Oct; P@☎) Bled's upscale campground is one of the nicest in the country and one of the few places around in which to try 'glamping' – aka glamorous camping – in this case, ecofriendly, all-natural A-frame huts, some equipped with hot tubs. The campground setting is a well-tended rural valley at the western end of the lake, about 2.5km from the bus station.

Traveller's Haven   HOSTEL €

(☎041 396 545; www.travellers-haven.si; Riklijeva cesta 1; dm/d €19/48; P@☎) This is arguably the nicest of several hostels clustered on a hillside on the eastern shore of the lake, about 500m north of the centre. The setting is a renovated villa, with six rooms (including one private double), a great kitchen and free laundry. Note the upstairs rooms get hot in midsummer. There are two free parking spots – a godsend in Bled, where parking is well-nigh impossible.

Garni Penzion Pletna   PENSION €€

(☎574 37 02; www.sloveniaholidays.com/sobe-pletna; Cesta Svobode 37, Mlino; s €40-45, d €50-65, tr €70-85; P☎) This friendly pension with attached shop has five pleasant rooms facing the lake. The pension is situated in the small village of Mlino, along the southern shoreline of the lake and about 2km from the centre of Bled.

Vila Gorenka   PENSION €

(☎040 958 624, 574 47 22; http://freeweb.siol.net/mz2; Želeška cesta 9; per person €20-28; P@☎) This budget establishment has 10 double rooms with washbasins in a charming old two-storey villa. Toilets and showers are shared and internet access is free. Some rooms on the 2nd floor have small balconies overlooking the lake.

Bledec Hostel   HOSTEL €

(☎574 52 50; www.youth-hostel-bledec.si; Grajska cesta 17; per person €22; P@☎) This well-organised HI-affiliated hostel in the shadow of the castle has 12 rooms of three to eight beds with attached bathrooms. It also has a bar, an inexpensive restaurant and a laundry room (per load €8.50). Internet access and use of their bikes is free.

Grand Hotel Toplice HOTEL €€€
(☎579 10 00; www.hotel-toplice.com; Cesta Svobode 12; s €120-140, d €140-200, ste €220-300; P❄@☎≋) With a history that goes back to the 19th century, the 87-room Toplice is Bled's 'olde worlde' hotel, with attractive public areas and superb views of the lake. Its two extensions – the 29-room Hotel Trst (Cesta Svobode 19), and the ivy-bedecked Jadran Hotel (Cesta Svobode 23) with 45 rooms up on the hill – are around half the price.

Penzion Mlino PENSION €€
(☎574 14 04; www.mlino.si; Cesta Svobode 45, Mlino; per person €30-35; P☎) This 13-room pension, as well known for its restaurant as its accommodation, is just about as close as you'll get to the lake at this price.

Garni Hotel Berc HOTEL €€
(☎576 56 58; www.berc-sp.si; Pod Stražo 13; s €45-50, d €70-80; P@☎) This purpose-built place, reminiscent of a Swiss chalet, has 15 rooms on two floors in a quiet location above the lake.

Garni Hotel Vila Bojana HOTEL €€
(☎576 81 70; www.bled-hotel.com; Ljubljanska cesta 12; s €45-70, d €59-109; P@☎) This welcoming 11-room hotel was purpose-built in the 1930s. It may not be lakeside but it is central to everything. Be warned, though – there's no lift.

Hotel Jelovica Bled HOTEL €€
(☎579 60 00; www.hotel-jelovica.si; Cesta Svobode 8; s €47-65, d €60-122; P@☎≋) It's one of the better-value hotels in this price category in Bled. Close to the bus station, the 100-room Jelovica fronts Spa Park above the lake and has a fully equipped health and spa centre.

Hotel Krim Bled HOTEL €€
(☎579 70 00; www.hotel-krim.si; Ljubljanska cesta 7; s €49-69, d €76-104; P@☎) This sprawling 115-room hotel charges a lot less than most for its singles and doubles, but its location – up from the lake along busy Ljubljanska cesta – is not the best. The wellness centre with three saunas and whirlpool is a draw, though. Rooms with castle views have higher prices.

Eating

Vila Ajda SLOVENIAN €€
(☎576 83 20; www.vila-ajda.si; Cesta Svobode 27; mains €9-20; ⊙11am-11pm; P☎) This attractive destination restaurant with lovely views out over the lake features traditional Slovenian cooking made from locally sourced ingredients. Eat outdoors in the garden in nice weather, or in the upscale dining room. There's a very good wine list. Book in advance on warm evenings in summer.

Oštarija Peglez'n SEAFOOD €€
(☎574 42 18; http://ostarija-peglezn.mestna-izlozba.com; Cesta Svobode 19a; mains €8-18; ⊙11am-11pm) One of the better restaurants in Bled, the Iron Inn is just opposite the landmark Grand Hotel Toplice. It has fascinating retro decor with lots of old household antiques and curios (including the eponymous iron) and serves some of the best fish dishes in town.

Gostila Murka SLOVENIAN €€
(☎574 33 40; www.gostilna-murka.com; Riklijeva cesta 9; mains €9-18; ⊙10am-10pm Mon-Fri, noon-11pm Sat & Sun) This colourful and traditional Slovenian eatery set within a generous-sized and very leafy garden may at first appear a bit theme-park-ish. But the food is authentic and the welcome very warm. Offers good-value lunch specials for around €5.

Penzion Mlino SLOVENIAN €€
(www.mlino.si; Cesta Svobode 45; mains €8-15; ⊙noon-11pm; P☎) This is a wonderful choice for lunch along a quieter strip of the lake, about 3km outside the centre. The daily four-course set lunches (around €10) usually offer a fish choice, such as the unforgettable grilled trout we enjoyed on our stop.

Pizzeria Rustika PIZZA €
(☎576 89 00; www.pizzeria-rustika.com; Riklijeva cesta 13; pizza €6-10; ⊙noon-11pm; ☎) Conveniently located on the same hill as many of Bled's hostels, Rustika serves the best pizza in town and in this part of Slovenia. The terrace is one of the prettiest in the neighbourhood.

Castle Restaurant SLOVENIAN €€
(☎579 44 24; www.blejski-grad.si/restavracija; Grajska cesta 61; mains €12-21; ⊙11am-10pm) The fabulous views are 'free' from the superbly situated terrace of the restaurant in the castle. It's run by Bled's catering and tourism school and staffed by some of its students. Book in advance to land a table with a view.

Penzion Mayer SLOVENIAN €€
(www.mayer-sp.si; Želeška cesta 7; mains €10-20; ⊙6pm-midnight Tue-Sun; ☎) The restaurant at this delightful inn serves such tasty Slovenian fare as sausage, trout, roast pork and *skutini štruklji* (cheese-curd pastries). The list of Slovenian wines is a cut above.

Okarina
INTERNATIONAL €€€

(☑574 14 58; www.okarina.com; Ljubljanska cesta 8; mains €10-24; ⊙6-11pm Mon-Fri, noon-midnight Sat & Sun; 🛜🍴) This upmarket restaurant has lots of colourful art spread over a modern dining room and serves both international favourites and decent Indian dishes like chicken masala and rogan josh. There's a good choice of vegetarian dishes and a little annex behind serves Balkan-style grilled meats.

Gostilna Pri Planincu
SLOVENIAN €€

(☑574 16 13; Grajska cesta 8; mains €8-16; ⊙10am-10pm) This traditional inn is on every traveller's radar for decent, big-portion, pub-style dishes like schnitzels and *čevapčiči* (spicy meatballs). It will do in a pinch, but the food quality is only just above average, and they don't offer daily lunch specials or wi-fi for customers. The little terrace on the side is invitingly cool on a hot day.

Peking
CHINESE €€

(☑574 17 16; Ulica Narodnih Herojev 3; mains €7-16; ⊙noon-11pm) This Chinese eatery has such favourites as *hui guo rou* (twice-cooked pork) and *ma po doufu* (spicy bean curd). They aren't exactly what you'd get in Chengdu, but this is Slovenia, after all.

🍺 Drinking

Pub Bled
PUB

(Cesta Svobode 19a; ⊙9am-2am Sun-Thu, 9am-3am Fri & Sat) This friendly pub above the Oštarija Peglez'n restaurant has great cocktails and, on some nights, a DJ.

Caffe Peglez'n
CAFE

(http://ostarija-peglezn.mestna-izlozba.com; Cesta Svobode 8a; ⊙7am-midnight Mon-Fri, 9am-midnight Sat & Sun) This place does double duty as a cute French-inspired bakery and coffeehouse with croissants and strudels by day, and a welcoming terrace bar for beers in the evenings. Offers light breakfasts (€5) from 7am.

Slaščičarna Šmon
CAFE

(http://slascicarna-smon.mestna-izlozba.com; Grajska cesta 3; ⊙7.30am-10pm; 🛜) Bled's culinary speciality is *kremna rezina* (€2.40), a layer of vanilla custard topped with whipped cream and sandwiched between two layers of flaky pastry, and while Šmon may not be its place of birth, it remains the best place in which to try it.

Kavarna Park
CAFE

(www.sava-hotels-resorts.com; Cesta Svobode 10; ⊙9am-11pm; 🛜) Opposite the Hotel Park, this cafe has a commanding position over the lake's eastern end and is said to be the birthplace of Bled's famous cream cake, *kremna rezina* (€2.80).

ℹ Information

INTERNET ACCESS Most of the hostels in Bled offer free internet access. Access at the Tourist Information Centre Bled is free for the first 15 minutes and then €2.50/4 for 30/60 minutes. **A Propos Bar** (☑574 40 44; Bled Shopping Centre, Ljubljanska cesta 4; per 15/30/60min €1.25/2.10/4.20; ⊙8am-midnight Sun-Thu, to 1am Fri & Sat; 🛜), in Bled Shopping Centre, has wireless connection as well.

MONEY Gorenjska Banka (Cesta Svobode 15) is just north of the Hotel Park. **SKB Banka** (Ljubljanska cesta 4) is in the Bled Shopping Centre.

POST Post Office (Ljubljanska cesta 10)

TOURIST INFORMATION Tourist Information Centre Bled (☑574 11 22; www.bled.si; Cesta Svobode 10; ⊙8am-7pm Mon-Sat, 11am-5pm Sun) occupies a small office behind the casino at Cesta Svobode 10. It sells maps and souvenirs, rents bikes (half-day/full day €8/11) and has a computer for checking email. **Triglav Rose Centre Bled** (☑578 02 00; www.tnp.si; Ljubljanska cesta 27; ⊙10am-6pm Tue-Sun May-Sep, noon-4pm Tue-Fri Oct & Dec-Apr) has information on Triglav National Park.

TRAVEL AGENCY Kompas (☑572 75 01; www.kompas-bled.si; Bled Shopping Centre, Ljubljanska cesta 4; ⊙8am-7pm Mon-Sat, 8am-noon & 4-7pm Sun) is a full-service travel agency offering excursions to Bohinj, Radovljica and Kropa, airport transfers and transport, and bike and ski rental. It also sells fishing licences and arranges accommodation in private homes and apartments.

ℹ Getting There & Away

BUS Bled is well connected by bus. There are buses every 30 minutes or so to Radovljica (€1.80, 15 minutes, 7km) via both Lesce and Begunje and around 20 buses daily run from Bled to Lake Bohinj (€3.60, 45 minutes) via Bohinjska Bistrica, with the first bus leaving around 5am and the last about 9pm. Buses depart at least hourly for Ljubljana (€6.50, 1¼ hours, 57km).

TRAIN Bled has two train stations, though neither one is close to the centre. Main-line trains for Ljubljana (€6.50, 55 minutes, 51km, up to 21 daily), via Škofja Loka, Kranj and Radovljica, use Lesce-Bled station, 4km to the east of town. Trains to Bohinjska Bistrica (€1.60, 20 minutes,

18km, eight daily), from where you can catch a bus to Lake Bohinj, use the smaller Bled Jezero station, which is 2km west of central Bled.

Bohinj

✒04 / POP 5225 / ELEV 525M

Many visitors to Slovenia say they've never seen a more beautiful lake than Bled...that is, until they've seen Lake Bohinj, just 26km to the southwest. We'll refrain from weighing in on the Bled vs Bohinj debate other than to say we see their point. Admittedly, Bohinj lacks Bled's glamour, but it's less crowded and in many ways more authentic. It's an ideal summer holiday destination. People come primarily to chill out or go for a swim in the crystal-clear, blue-green water. There are lots of outdoor pursuits like kayaking, cycling, climbing and horseback riding if you've got the energy, and the charming villages to the lake's northeast have, remarkably, remained faithful to traditional occupations like dairy herding and farming.

⊙ Sights

Church of St John the Baptist   CHURCH
(Cerkev Sv Janeza Krstnika; Ribčev Laz; ☺10am-noon & 4-7pm summer, by appointment other times) This church, on the northern side of the Sava Bohinjka River across the stone bridge, is what every medieval church should be: small, on a reflecting body of water, and full of exquisite frescoes. The nave is Romanesque, but the Gothic presbytery dates from about 1440. Many walls and ceilings are covered with 15th- and 16th-century frescoes.

As you face the arch from the nave, look for the frescoes on either side gorily depicting the beheading of the church's patron saint. On the opposite side of the arch, to the left, is Abel making his offering to God and, to the right, Cain with his inferior one. Upon the shoulder of history's first murderer sits a white devil – a rare symbol. Behind you on the lower walls of the presbytery are rows of angels, some with vampire-like teeth; look for the three men above them singing. They have goitres, once a common affliction in mountainous regions due to the lack of iodine in the diet. The carved wooden head of St John the Baptist on the side altar to the right dates from 1380.

Alpine Dairy Museum   MUSEUM
(Planšarski Muzej; www.bohinj.si; Stara Fužina 181; adult/child €3/2; ☺11am-7pm Tue-Sun Jul & Aug, 10am-noon & 4-6pm Tue-Sun early Jan–Jun, Sep–late Oct) This museum in Stara Fužina, 1.5km north of Ribčev Laz, has a small collection related to Alpine dairy farming. The four rooms of the museum – once a cheese dairy itself – contain a mock-up of a mid-19th-century herder's cottage, fascinating old photographs, cheese presses, wooden butter moulds, copper vats, enormous snowshoes and sledges, and wonderful hand-carved crooks.

Until the late 1950s, large quantities of cheese were still being made on 28 highland pastures, but a modern dairy in nearby Srednja Vas does it all now.

Oplen House   MUSEUM
(Oplenova Hiša; www.bohinj.si; Studor 16; adult/child €3/2; ☺11am-7pm Tue-Sun Jul & Aug, 10am-noon & 4-6pm Tue-Sun early Jan–Jun, Sep–late Oct) While you're in Stara Fužina, walk over to the village of Studor, 2km to the east. Oplen House is a typical old peasant's cottage with a chimney-less 'black kitchen' that has been turned into a museum focusing on the domestic life of peasants in the Bohinj area.

Studor's real claim to fame is its many *toplarji*, the double-linked hayracks with barns or storage areas at the top. Look for the ones at the entrance to the village; they date from the 18th and 19th centuries.

Savica Waterfall   WATERFALL
(Slap Savica; Ukanc; adult/child €2.50/1.25; ☺9am-6pm Jul & Aug, 9am-5pm Apr-Jun, Sep & Oct; ℗) The magnificent Savica Waterfall, which cuts deep into a gorge 60m below, is 4km from the Hotel Zlatorog in Ukanc and can be reached by footpath from there. Cars continue via a paved road to a car park beside the Savica restaurant, from where it's a 20-minute walk up more than 500 steps and over rapids and streams to the falls.

The falls are among the most impressive sights in the Julian Alps, especially after heavy rain, but bring something waterproof or you may be soaked by the spray.

🏃 Activities
Adventure Sports
While most people come to Bohinj to relax, there are more exhilarating pursuits available, including canyoning, caving, and paragliding from the top of Vogel (p87), among others. Two companies, Alpinsport (p86) and Perfect Adventure Choice (PAC) Sports (p86), specialise in these activities and offer broadly similar programs and prices.

Expect to pay the following: **canyoning** (from €45 to €70, depending on the length and difficulty), tandem **paraglider** flights (€90 to €120), and **caving** (€60 to €100). Check the websites for details.

Alpinsport
ADVENTURE SPORTS

(☑572 34 86; www.alpinsport.si; Ribčev Laz 53; ☺9am-8pm Jul-Sep, 9am-7pm Oct-Jun) Rents sporting equipment, canoes, kayaks and bikes; also operates guided rafting, canyoning and caving trips. Located in a kiosk at the stone bridge over the Sava Bohinjka River in Ribčev Laz.

PAC Sports
ADVENTURE SPORTS

(Perfect Adventure Choice; ☑572 34 61; www .pac-sports.com; Hostel Pod Voglom, Ribčev Laz; ☺7am-11pm Jul & Aug, 10am-6pm Sep-Jun) Popular youth-oriented sports and adventure company, located in the Hostel Pod Voglom (p89), 3km west of Ribčev Laz on the road to Ukanc. Rents bikes, canoes and kayaks, and operates guided canyoning, rafting, paragliding and caving trips. In winter, it rents sleds and offers winter rafting near Vogel (per person €15). Has a **branch** (☑041 365 521; Ribčev Laz 42; ☺3-8pm Mon-Fri, 9am-8pm Sat & Sun) at Penzion Rožič in Ribčev Laz.

Boating

Boating is a popular pastime on Lake Bohinj from June through September. Both Alpinsport and PAC Sports rent kayaks (one hour/three hours/day €5/11/19) and canoes (one hour/three hours/day €7/17/29).

Both companies also offer guided rafting and canoeing trips on Lake Bohinj and along the Sava Bohinjka River. Prices start at around €27 per person for the 7km trip to Bitnje and €37 per person for the 3½ hour, 17km trip. Prices include equipment, guide and transfers. Expect relatively mild rapids in June and a slower pace by August.

Tourist Boat
BOATING

(Turistična Ladja; ☑574 75 90; one way adult/ child €9/6.50, return €10.50/7.50; ☺half-hourly 9.30am-5.30pm Jun–mid-Sep, 10am, 11.30am, 1pm, 2.30pm, 4pm & 5.30pm early Apr–May, 11.30am, 1pm, 2.30pm & 4pm mid-Sep–Oct) An easy family-friendly sail from Ribčev Laz to Ukanc and back.

Cycling

Lake Bohinj is perfect for cyclists of all skill sets. The road along the southern shore be-

tween Ribčev Laz and Ukanc is relatively flat, as are the paths leading off to Stara Fužina and Studor, north and east of Ribčev Laz. Indeed, in nice weather cycling is the best way to get around to the various villages.

The book *Bohinj by Mountain Bike*, by Matjaž Žmitek, available at the Tourist Information Centres (p90) for €8.50, marks out 15 routes, from family-friendly to downright crazy. Route No 1 is a relaxing ride through the valleys and villages between Ribčev Laz and Bohinjska Bistrica. You can rent bikes from both Alpinsport and PAC Sports (half-day/whole day €10/14).

Fishing

Lake Bohinj is home to lake trout and char, and the jade-coloured Sava Bohinjka River, which starts at the stone bridge in front of the church in Ribčev Laz, is rich in brown trout and grayling. You can buy fishing licences (lake €25, river as far as Bitnje catch/catch & release €55/38) valid for a day from the TICs (p90) and hotels. The season runs from March to late October.

Hiking

Lake Bohinj is an ideal destination for hiking and walking. A good easy walk around the lake (12km) from Ribčev Laz should take between three and four hours. Otherwise you could just do parts of it by following the hunters' trail in the forest above the south shore of the lake to the Hotel Zlatorog and taking the bus back, or walking along the more tranquil northern shore under the cliffs of Pršivec (1761m).

Another excellent hike is the two-hour walk north from Stara Fužina through the Mostnica Gorge to the Mostnica Waterfalls (Mostniški Slapovci), which rival Savica Waterfall after heavy rain.

The **Bohinj cable car** (adult/child one way €9/7, return €13/9; ☺every 30min 8am-6pm) operates year-round, hauling skiers in winter and hikers in summer. There are several day hikes and longer treks that set out from Vogel. Experienced hikers might try the ascent up to Vogel (1922m) from the cable car's upper station. Take a map and compass. The whole trip should take about four hours.

The 1:25,000 *Bohinjsko Jezero z Okolico* (*Lake Bohinj & Surrounds*; €7) map, available at the TICs (p90), lists a dozen excellent walks.

Horse Riding

Mrcina Ranč HORSE RIDING
(☎041 790 297; www.ranc-mrcina.com; Studor; per hr €20) Mrcina Ranč in Studor, 5km from Ribčev Laz, offers a range of guided tours on horseback, lasting one hour to three days on sturdy Icelandic ponies.

Skiing

Vogel Ski Centre SKIING
(☎041 774 468; www.vogel.si; Ukanc; day pass adult/child €26/17; ⏲mid-Dec–Apr) The main station at Bohinj is Vogel ski centre, 1540m above the lake's southwestern corner and accessible by cable car. With skiing up to 1800m, the season can be long, sometimes from late November to late April or even early May. Vogel has 18km of ski slopes and 2.5km of cross-country runs served by four chairlifts and four T-bars.

Kobla Ski Centre SKIING
(☎574 71 00; www.bohinj.si/kobla; Cesta na Ravne 7, Bohinjska Bistrica; day pass adult/child €22/16) The lower (up to 1480m) Kobla ski centre is about 1km east of Bohinjska Bistrica. It has 23km of slopes and 13km of cross-country runs served by three chairlifts and three T-bars.

Swimming

Lake Bohinj's chilly waters warm to a swimmable 22°C in July and August. Swimming is not restricted and you can enter the water from any point on shore, though there are decent, small beaches on both the northern and southern shores. Some beaches on the northern shore are reserved for naturists.

Aqua Park Bohinj WATER PARK
(www.vodni-park-bohinj.si; Triglavska cesta 17, Bohinjska Bistrica; adult/child 3hr €11.50/7.50, day €13.50/9.90; ⏲9am-9pm) This lively water park is open year-round and has 380 sq metres of indoor and outdoor pools with slides, as well as saunas, steam rooms, and fitness and wellness centres. If you're travelling with kids, it can be a lifesaver in winter or a rainy-day treat in summer. It's located in Bohinjska Bistrica, next to the Bohinj Park Hotel (p88).

Festivals & Events

International Wildflower Festival CRAFTS
(Mednarodni Festival Alpskega Cvetja; www.bohinj.si; ⏲late May–early Jun) A relatively new event that is gaining in popularity is the International Wildflower Festival, held over two weeks in late May/early June. It includes guided walks and tours, traditional craft markets and concerts.

Bonfire Night CULTURAL EVENT
(Kresna Noč; www.bohinj.si; ⏲Aug) On Bonfire Night, celebrated on the weekend closest to the Feast of the Assumption (15 August), candlelit flotillas go out on the lake, and there are fireworks.

Cows' Ball FOLK TRADITIONS
(Kravji Bal; www.bohinj.si; ⏲mid-Sep) The Cows' Ball is a wacky weekend of folk dance, music, eating and drinking in mid-September to mark the return of the cows from their high pastures to the valleys

Sleeping

The Tourist Information Centres (p90) can arrange private rooms for around €12 to €18 per person and apartments from €40 to €80, depending on quality and location, in Ribčev Laz, Stara Fužina and neighbouring villages.

Penzion Gasperin PENSION €€
(☎041 540 805; www.bohinj.si/gasperin; Ribčev Laz 36a; r €48-60; P❄@🛜) This spotless chalet-style guesthouse with 23 rooms is just 350m southeast of the Ribčev Laz TIC and run by a friendly British-Slovenian couple. Most rooms have balconies. The upper-storey rooms can get hot in summer, but each is equipped with an air-conditioner. The buffet breakfast is fresh and includes a sampling of local meats and cheeses.

Hotel Stare PENSION €€
(☎040 558 669; www.bohinj-hotel.com; Ukanc 128; per person €42-50; P@🛜) This beautifully appointed 10-room pension is situated north of the Hotel Zlatorog on the Sava Bohinjka River in Ukanc and is surrounded by 3.5 hectares of lovely garden. If you really want to get away from it all without having to climb mountains, this is your place. Note that rates are half-board, including breakfast and dinner.

Hotel Kristal HOTEL €€
(☎577 82 00; www.hotel-kristal-slovenia.com; Ribčev Laz 4a; per person €48-60; P@🛜) This exceedingly friendly, family-run hotel with 30 rooms and lots of activities has a very popular restaurant. There's a small sauna available for guests. Rates are half-board, including breakfast and dinner.

ZLATOROG & HIS GOLDEN HORNS

The oft-told tale of Zlatorog, the mythical chamois (*gams* in Slovene) with the golden horns that lived on Mt Triglav and guarded its treasure, almost always involves some superhuman (or, in this case, super-antelopine) feat that drastically changed the face of the mountain. But don't let Slovenes convince you that their ancient ancestors passed on the tale.

The Zlatorog story first appeared in the *Laibacher Zeitung* (*Ljubljana Gazette*) in 1868 during a period of Romanticism and national awakening. This one tells of how the chamois created the Triglav Lakes Valley, a wilderness of tumbled rock almost in the centre of Triglav National Park.

Zlatorog roamed the valley (at that time a beautiful garden) with the White Ladies, good fairies that kept the mountain pastures green and helped humans whenever they found them in need.

Meanwhile, down in the Soča Valley near Trenta, a plot was being hatched. It seemed that an innkeeper's daughter had been given jewels by a wealthy merchant from Venice. The girl's mother demanded that her daughter's suitor, a poor but skilled hunter, match the treasure with Zlatorog's gold hidden under Mt Bogatin and guarded by a multi-headed serpent. If not, he was at least to bring back a bunch of Triglav roses to prove his fidelity. This being mid-winter, it was an impossible task.

The young hunter, seething with jealousy, climbed the mountain in search of the chamois, figuring that if he were to get even a piece of the golden horns, the treasure of Bogatin – and his beloved – would be his. At last the young man spotted Zlatorog, took aim and fired. It was a direct hit.

The blood gushing from Zlatorog's wound melted the snow, and up sprang a magical Triglav rose. The chamois nibbled on a few petals and – presto! – was instantly back on his feet. As the chamois leapt away, roses sprang up from under his hooves, luring the hunter onto higher and higher ground. But as they climbed, the sun caught Zlatorog's golden horns. The glint blinded the hunter, he lost his footing and plunged into a gorge.

The once kind and trusting Zlatorog was enraged that a mere mortal would treat him in such a manner. In his fury he gored his way through the Triglav Lakes Valley, leaving it much as it looks today. He left the area with the White Ladies, never to return.

And the fate of the others? The innkeeper's daughter waited in vain for her lover to return home. As spring approached, the snow began to melt, swelling the Soča River. One day it brought her a sad gift: the body of her young swain, his lifeless hand still clutching a Triglav rose. As for the innkeeper's rapacious wife, we know nothing. Perhaps she learned Italian and moved to Venice with the merchant.

Observant (and thirsty) travellers will see the face of Zlatorog everywhere they go in Slovenia. It's on the label of the country's most popular beer.

Hotel Jezero HOTEL €€€
(572 91 00; www.bohinj.si/alpinum/jezero; Ribčev Laz 51; s €65-75, d €120-140; P@🛜🏊) This 76-room place just across from the lake has a lovely indoor swimming pool, two saunas and a fitness centre.

Bohinj Park Hotel HOTEL €€€
(577 02 11; www.bohinj-park-hotel.si; Triglavska cesta 17, Bohinjska Bistrica; s €80-90, d €160-180; P❄@🛜🏊) We might not have chosen this modern, high-rise 109-room hotel at first glance – located in Bohinjska Bistrica, it's a full 6km from our destination: Lake Bohinj. But it's a green and very energy-efficient oasis, it has an excellent and quite intimate

in-house restaurant, there's bowling, and the Aqua Park Bohinj (p87) is at the back door and included in the price.

Pension Planšar PENSION €
(041 767 254, 572 30 95; www.plansar.com; Stara Fužina 179; r per person €16-20, apt for 2 €40-45, apt for 4 €75-80; P) This welcoming place in Stara Fužina, better known for its fabulous cheeses (p89), has two cosy rooms and an apartment for rent.

Hotel Center HOTEL €€
(572 31 70; www.hotelcenterbohinj.si; Ribčev Laz 50; s €30-49, d €60-98; P@🛜) This 15-room place above a popular pizzeria is more guest-house than hotel with its standard-issue fur-

nishings and views, but the name says it all –
it's about as central as you're going to find
in Ribčev Laz.

Hotel Zlatorog
HOTEL €€

(☎572 33 81; www.hoteli-bohinj.si; Ukanc 65; r
€55-75; P@🖭🛏🌊) The Zlatorog, 5km west
of Ribčev Laz in Ukanc, dates from the late
1970s and retains a whiff of the old communist days. That said, it's out of the way, quiet
and pleasant, and one of the few full-service
hotels in the immediate lake area. There's
a pool and tennis courts, and some rooms
have been refitted to accommodate guests
with disabilities.

Autokamp Zlatorog
CAMPGROUND €

(☎577 80 00; www.hoteli-bohinj.si; Ukanc 2; per
person €6-9; ☺May-Sep) This pleasant, pine-
shaded 2.5-hectare campground accommodating 500 guests is at the lake's western end,
4.5km from Ribčev Laz. Prices vary according to site location, with the most expensive
– and desirable – sites right on the lake.

Hostel Pod Voglom
HOSTEL €

(☎572 34 61; www.hostel-podvoglom.com; Ribčev
Laz 60; dm €18, r per person with bathroom €23-
26, without bathroom €20-22; P@) Bohinj's
youth hostel, some 3km west of the centre
of Ribčev Laz on the road to Ukanc, has 119
beds in 46 rooms in two buildings. The so-
called hostel building has doubles, triples
and dormitory accommodation (up to four
beds), with shared facilities; rooms in the
Rodica Annex, with between one and four
beds, are en suite.

Camp Danica Bohinj
CAMPGROUND €

(☎572 17 02; www.camp-danica.si; Triglavska cesta
60, Bohinjska Bistrica; per adult €10-12, child €7.30-
9; ☺late Apr–Sep; P) The Danica campground,
which measures 4.5 hectares and has space
for 700 campers, is located in a small wood
200m west of the bus stop in Bohinjska Bistrica. It's convenient to the train station but
is about 6km from the shores of Lake Bohinj.

🍴 Eating

Many of the better restaurants are spread
out to the north and east of Ribčev Laz,
which will require a modest hike, or car or
bike to reach. There's a **Mercator** (Ribčev
Laz 49; ☺7am-8pm Mon-Sat, 7am-5pm Sun)
supermarket next to the TIC in Ribčev Laz.

TOP
CHOICE **Gostilna Rupa**
SLOVENIAN €€

(☎572 34 01; www.apartmajikatrnjek.com/rupa;
Srednja Vas 87; mains €8-16; ☺10am-midnight

Jul & Aug, 10am-midnight Tue-Sun Sep-Jun) If
you're under your own steam, head for
this country-style restaurant in Srednja
Vas, the next village over from Studor and
about 5km from Ribčev Laz. Among the
excellent home-cooked dishes are *ajdova
krapi*, crescent-shaped dumplings made
from buckwheat and cheese, various types
of local *klobasa* (sausage) and Bohinj
trout.

Gostilna Mihovc
SLOVENIAN €

(☎572 33 90; www.gostilna-mihovc.si; Stara
Fužina 118; mains €7-10; ☺10am-midnight) This
place in Stara Fužina is popular – not least
for its homemade brandy. Try the *pasulj*
(bean soup) with sausage (€6) or the beef
golač (goulash; €5.20). Live music on Friday
and Saturday evenings. In summer book in
advance to secure a garden table.

Strud'l
SLOVENIAN €

(☎041 710 951; www.strudl.si; Triglavska cesta 23,
Bohinjska Bistrica; mains €6-9; ☺10am-9pm; 🖭)
This modern take on traditional farmhouse
cooking is a must for local foodies. Overlook the incongruous location in the centre
of Bohinska Bistrica, and enjoy local treats
like *ričet s klobaso* (barley porridge served
with sausage and beans). The *hišni krožnik*
(house plate) is a sampling of everything,
including ham, sausage, mashed beans
and sauerkraut, potato mash, and cooked
buckwheat.

Planšar
SLOVENIAN €

(☎572 30 95; Stara Fužina 179; ☺noon-8pm summer, by appointment other times) The Herder,
opposite the Alpine Dairy Museum (p85) in
Stara Fužina, specialises in homemade dairy
products: hard Bohinj cheese, a soft cheese
called *mohant*, curd pie and sour milk. You
can taste a variety for €8 or make a meal
of cheese and different types of grain dishes
such as buckwheat (*žganci*; €8) and barley
(*ješprenj*; €9).

Rožič
INTERNATIONAL €

(☎572 33 93; www.pensionrozic-bohinj.com; Ribčev
Laz 42; mains €6-10; ☺7am-midnight) Decent
first-night choice if you arrive late and don't
have the energy to go further afield. There
are actually two restaurants: a street-level
pizzeria geared more toward walk-ins, and
an upper level for pension guests. The menu
features pizza, pasta, salads and grilled
meats. There's good homemade *štruklji*
(sweet dumplings stuffed with curd cheese,
€4) for dessert.

Hotel Center Restaurant INTERNATIONAL €
(☎041 710 952; www.hotelcenterbohinj.si; Ribčev Laz 50; €8-12; ☺9am-10pm Dec-Oct) This jack-of-all-trades below the Hotel Center (p88) just down from the TIC is the only eatery in the very centre of Ribčev Laz. It can satisfy all tastes (except very demanding ones).

🛍 Shopping

The traditional craft of Bohinj is the *gorjuška čedra*, a small hand-carved wooden pipe with a silver cover for smoking tobacco or whatever. The TIC in Ribčev Laz sells the real thing and can tell you which masters are still making them in the area.

ℹ Information

MONEY There's an ATM in Ribčev Laz, next to the TIC. **Gorenjska Banka** (Trg Svobode 2b, Bohinjska Bistrica; ☺9-11.30am & 2-5pm Mon-Fri, 8-11am Sat) is in Bohinjska Bistrica next to the post office.

POST Ribčev Laz Post Office (Ribčev Laz 47; ☺8-9.30am, 10am-3.30pm & 4-6pm Mon-Fri, 8am-noon Sat) **Bohinjska Bistrica Post Office** (Trg Svobode 2, Bohinjska Bistrica)

TOURIST INFORMATION There are two main tourist information centres in the Bohinj area: **Tourist Information Centre Ribčev Laz** (TIC; ☎574 60 10; www.bohinj-info.com; Ribčev Laz 48; parking first 30min free, per hr €1; ☺8am-7pm Mon-Sat, 8am-6pm Sun Jul & Aug, 8am-6pm Mon-Sat, 9am-3pm Sun Sep & Jun) and **Tourist Information Centre Bohinjska Bistrica** (TIC; ☎574 75 90; www.bohinj.si; Triglavska cesta 30, Bohinjska Bistrica; ☺7am-3pm Mon-Fri, 9am-1pm Sat Sep-Nov, Feb-May). The office in Ribčev Laz is closer to the lake and handier for most visitors. Both have a wealth of free material, sell souvenirs and local food products, book rooms in private homes, and offer free internet for 15 minutes. Both offices sell the **Bohinj Guest Card** (www.bohinj.si; adult/family €10/13), which entitles the holder to free parking in the lake area, along with discounts to some museums, activities, accommodation and restaurants.

ℹ Getting There & Around

BUS The easiest way to get to Bohinj from Bled or Ljubljana is by bus. Buses run regularly from Ljubljana (€9, two hours, 90km, hourly) to Bohinj Jezero and Ukanc – marked 'Bohinj Zlatorog' – via Bled and Bohinjska Bistrica. Around 20 buses daily run from Bled (€3.60, 45 minutes) to Bohinj Jezero (via Bohinjska Bistrica) and return, with the first bus leaving around 5am and the last about 9pm. In addition, from the end of June through August, **Alpetour**

(☎532 04 45; www.alpetour.si) runs special tourist buses that leave from near the post office in Ribčev Laz to Bohinjska Bistrica in one direction and to the cable car at Vogel (15 minutes) and the Savica Waterfall (23 minutes) in the other. A timetable is posted at the small bus stop or ask at the TICs.

TRAIN Several trains daily make the run to Bohinjska Bistrica from Ljubljana (€6.70, two hours), though this route requires a change in Jesenice. There are also frequent trains between Bled's small Bled Jezero station (€1.60, 20 minutes, 18km, eight daily) and Bohinjska Bistrica. From Bohinjska Bistrica, passenger trains to Novo Gorica (€5.50, 1½ hours, 61km, up to nine a day) make use of a century-old, 6.3km tunnel under the mountains that provides the only direct option for reaching the Soča Valley. In addition there are at least six daily auto trains to Podbrdo (€8, 10 minutes, 7km) and three that carry on to Most na Soči (€11.80, 35 minutes, 28km).

Kranjska Gora

☑04 / POP 5500 / ELEV 803M

Nestling in the Sava Dolinka Valley some 40km northwest of Bled, Kranjska Gora (Carniolan Mountain) is Slovenia's largest and best-equipped ski resort. It's at its most perfect under a blanket of snow, but its surroundings are wonderful to explore at other times as well. There are endless possibilities for hiking, cycling and mountaineering in Triglav National Park, which is right on the town's doorstep to the south, and few travellers will be unimpressed by a trip over Vršič Pass (1611m), the gateway to the Soča Valley.

◉ Sights

Liznjek House MUSEUM
(Liznjekova Domačija; www.gornjesavskimuzej.si; Borovška 63; adult/child €2.50/1.70; ☺10am-6pm Tue-Sat, 10am-5pm Sun) The endearing late-18th-century Liznjek House contains a good collection of traditional household objects and furnishings peculiar to this area of Gorenjska. Among the various exhibits here are some excellent examples of trousseau chests covered in folk paintings, some 19th-century icons painted on glass and a collection of linen tablecloths (the valley was famed for its flax and its weaving).

Antique carriages and a sled are kept in the massive barn out the back, which once housed food stores as well as pigs and sheep. The stable reserved for cows below the main building now contains a memorial room dedicated to the life and work of Josip Vandot (1884–1944). Vandot was a writer born in Kranjska Gora who penned the saga of Kekec, the do-gooder shepherd boy who, together with his little playmate Mojca and his trusty dog Volkec, battles the evil poacher and kidnapper Bedanec. It's still a favourite story among Slovenian kids and has been made into several popular films.

🏃 Activities

Skiing

Skiiing is Kranjska Gora's bread and butter and the resort can get very crowded in January and February. The season usually lasts from mid-December to early March.

Kranjska Gora Ski Centre   SKIING
(RTC Žičnice; ☎580 94 00; www.kr-gora.si; Borovška cesta 103a; half-day pass adult/child/senior & student €25/16/21, day pass €29/19/25; ☺9am-4pm Dec-Mar) Kranjska Gora's main ski area is just five minutes' walk from the centre of town. The slopes of the Sava Dolinka Valley run for several kilometres to Rateče and Planica, making effectively one big piste. There are lifts in the nearby village of Podkoren, 2km west of town, as well. Together Kranjska Gora and Podkoren have five chairlifts and 15 tows.

Planica Ski-Jumping Centre   SKI JUMPING
(www.planica.si; Planica) The nearby village of Planica, 6km west of Kranjska Gora and across the motorway from Rateče, is Slovenia's leading ski-jumping centre and hosts frequent competitions open to the public, including the annual Ski Jumping World Championships held in mid-March. Ask at the Kranjska Gora TIC if there's a competition scheduled during your visit.

EQUIPMENT RENTAL & INSTRUCTION

ASK Kranjska Gora Ski School   SKI SCHOOL
(☎588 53 02; www.ask-kg.com; Borovška cesta 99a; ☺9am-4pm Mon-Sat, 10am-6pm Sun mid-Dec–mid-Mar, 9am-3pm Mon-Fri mid-Mar–mid-Dec) The leading ski school in town offers a wide selection of instruction in alpine skiing and snowboarding. Offers several instruction packages, some combined with ski passes. See the website for details.

Intersport   SKI SCHOOL, EQUIPMENT RENTAL
(www.intersport-bernik.com; Borovška cesta 88a; ☺8am-8pm mid-Dec–mid-Mar, 8am-8pm Mon-Sat, 8am-1pm Sun mid-Mar–mid-Dec) This reputable outlet offers both skiing and snowboarding instruction and rents equipment, ranging from basic skis and poles to the best gear on the market.

Skipass Travel   SKI SCHOOL, EQUIPMENT RENTAL
(www.skipasstravel.si; Borovška cesta 95; ☺8am-4pm mid-Dec–mid-Mar, 9am-3pm Mon-Fri mid-Mar–mid-Dec) A full-service travel agency that offers ski instruction and equipment as well as airport transfers and special skiing excursions to nearby Italy and Austria. Consult the website for details.

Hiking

The area around Kranjska Gora and into Triglav National Park is excellent for hikes and walks, ranging from the very easy to the difficult. One of the best references available is *The Julian Alps of Slovenia* (Cicerone) by Justi Carey and Roy Clark, available at some bookshops and over the internet, with 50 walking routes and short treks. Before heading out, be sure to buy the 1:30,000-scale *Kranjska Gora* hiking map published by LTO Kranjska Gora and available at the TIC for €9.

Between the villages of Podkoren and Planica, just a couple kilometres west of Kranjska Gora, is an idyllic 15-hectare nature reserve called **Zelenci** (837m), with a turquoise-coloured lake that is the source of the Sava River. You can easily walk here in about two hours on a path from Kranjska Gora via Podkoren and on to Rateče. These attractive Alpine villages are notable for their medieval churches, rustic wooden houses and traditional hayracks. If you want to continue on your journey, there's a well-marked trail via Planica to the Category II 128-bed hut **Dom v Tamarju** (☎587 60 55; http://www.pzs.si; Tamar Valley; per person €15) at 1108m in the Tamar Valley, 6km to the south. The walk is spectacular, and lies in the shadow of **Mojstrovka** (2366m) to the east and **Jalovec** (2645m) to the south. From here, the **Vršič Pass** is less than three hours away on foot.

Cycling

In recent years, Kranjska Gora has evolved into one of the country's leading centres for mountain biking and alpine downhilling, the kind of extreme riding where you take your bike up on a chairlift and race downhill. In summer, the Kranjska Gora Ski Centre operates a chairlift for downhilling (per ride €7, whole day €21) and also rents freeride and mountain bikes (half-/full day €23/33).

CROSSING THE VRŠIČ PASS

Just a couple of kilometres from Kranjska Gora is one of the road-engineering marvels of the 20th century: a breakneck, Alpine highway that connects Kranjska Gora with Bovec, 50km to the southwest. The trip involves no fewer than 50 pulse-quickening hairpin turns and dramatic vistas as you cross the Vršič Pass at 1611m.

Commissioned during WWI by Germany and Austria-Hungary in their epic struggle with Italy, much of the hard labour was done by Russian prisoners of war, and for that reason, the highway is now called the Ruska cesta (Russian Road).

The road is open from May to October and is easiest to navigate by car or bus (in summer, buses from Kranjska Gora to Bovec use this road), though it is possible by bike. Though the following are not stops on the bus route, let the driver know when you board where you want to get off and they will usually oblige.

From Kranjska Gora, the first stop is **Jasna Lake** (Jezero Jasna). It's a beautiful blue glacial lake with white sand around its rim and the little Pivnica River flowing alongside. Standing guard is a bronze statue of that irascible old goat Zlatorog and a decent *gostišče* (inn with restaurant).

As you zig-zag up to just over 1100m, you come to the **Russian chapel**, erected on the site where more than 400 Russian POWs were buried in an avalanche in March 1916.

The climb then begins in earnest as the road meanders past a couple of huts and corkscrews up the next few kilometres to **Vršič Pass** (1611m), about 13km from Kranjska Gora. From here, to the west is Mojstrovka (2366m), to the east Prisojnik/Prisank (2547m), and to the south the valley of the **Soča River** points the way to Primorska. A hair-raising descent of about 10km ends just short of a monument to **Dr Julius Kugy** (1858–1944), a pioneer climber and writer whose books eulogise the beauty of the Julian Alps.

From here you can take a side trip along the first part of the **Soča Trail** (Soška Pot) to the source of the Soča River (Izvir Soče), about 2.5km to the northwest. Fed by an underground lake, the infant river bursts from a dark cave before dropping 15m to the rocky bed from where it begins its long journey to the Adriatic.

Not long after joining the main road again, you'll pass the entrance to the **Alpinum Juliana** (www2.pms-lj.si; Trenta; adult/child €3/2; ☉8.30am-6.30pm May-Sep), a botanical garden established in 1926 that showcases the flora of all of Slovenia's Alps (Julian, Kamnik-Savinja and Karavanke) as well as the Karst.

There are plenty of easier, family-friendly rides as well. The 1:30,000-scale *Kranjska Gora* hiking map (€9), available at the TIC, marks out 15 cycling routes of varying difficulty. Most of the ski-rental outfits hire out bikes in summer, including Intersport (p91). Expect to pay around €10 for a full-day rental and helmet.

🛏 Sleeping

Accommodation costs in Kranjska Gora peak from December to March and in midsummer.

The Kranjska Gora Tourist Information Centre (p94) books private rooms (per person €15 to €25) and apartments (for two €45 to €70, for four €70 to €100), with prices depending on the category and the time of year.

Hotel Kotnik HOTEL €€
(✆588 15 64; www.hotel-kotnik.si; Borovška cesta 75; s €50-60, d €72-80; 🅿@🛜) If you're not into big high-rise hotels with hundreds of rooms, choose this charming, bright yellow, low-rise property. It has 15 cosy rooms, a great restaurant and pizzeria, and it couldn't be more central.

Hotel Miklič HOTEL €€€
(✆588 16 35; www.hotelmiklic.com; Vitranška ulica 13; s €60-80, d €80-130; 🅿@🛜) This pristine 15-room small hotel south of the centre is surrounded by luxurious lawns and flower beds and boasts an excellent restaurant and a small fitness room with sauna (€12 per hour). It's definitely a cut above most other accommodation in Kranjska Gora.

Hotel Kompas HOTEL €€€
(✆589 21 00; www.hitholidays-kg.si; Borovška cesta 100; r €80-140; 🅿@🛜❄) With 149 rooms, the four-star Kompas is Kranjska Gora's biggest hotel. It's a pleasant-enough place, with recently renovated public areas, and is set back in its own grounds. It boasts an

The elongated mountain village of **Trenta** (elevation 620m) is just south. The lower section, **Spodnja Trenta** (Lower Trenta), is home to the **Triglav National Park Information Centre. (**Dom Trenta; ✆05-388 93 30; www.tnp.si; Trenta 31; ⊙10am-6pm late Apr–Oct, 10am-2pm mid-Jan–late Apr; 🖥) You'll also find here the **Trenta Museum** (Trentarski Muzej; ✆05-388 93 30; www.tnp.si; Trenta 31; adult/child €5/3.50; ⊙10am-6pm late Apr–Oct, 10am-2pm mid-Jan–late Apr), which focuses on the park's geology and natural history as well as the Trenta guides and pioneers of Slovenian alpinism.

The village of **Soča** is another 8km downstream. **Bovec**, the recreational centre of the Upper Soča Valley (Gornje Posočje), is 12km west of Soča.

There are several mountain huts en route where you can grab a bite or stay the night. Expect to pay €15 to €20 per person for a bunk, depending on availability. Most are open from May through September. Huts include **Koča na Gozdu** (✆051 626 641; info@prezlc. si; elev 1226m, Vršiška cesta 86; ⊙daily late Apr–Sep, Thu-Sun Oct–late Apr); **Erjačeva Koča na Vršiču** (✆051 399 226; plan.drustvo@siol.net; elev 1525m, Vršiška cesta 90; ⊙Sat & Sun May-Dec); and **Tičarjev Dom na Vršiču** (✆051 634 571; plan.drustvo@siol.net; elev 1600m, Trenta 85; ⊙May–mid-Oct).

For something fancier, the **Kekec Homestead** (Kekčeva Domačija; ✆05-381 10 88; www. kekceva-domacija.si; Trenta 76; per person €59; ➰), about 2.5km off the main road heading for the source of the Soča, has eight upmarket rooms and a small pool.

There are abundant camping opportunities. In Trenta, there's **Camping Trenta** (✆041 615 966; www.sloveniaholidays.com/camping-trenta; Trenta 60a; per person €10; ⊙Apr-Oct) and the smaller **Kamp Triglav** (✆05-388 93 11; www.sloveniaholidays.com/kamp-triglav-soca; Trenta 18a; per person €9; ⊙Apr-Oct). Further toward Soča, there's **Kamp Korita** (✆051 645 677; www.camp-korita.com; Soča 38; per person €10; ⊙May-Oct) and the more adventure-oriented **Eko Camp** (✆051 266 812; www.camp-korita.com; Soča 38; per person €9; ⊙May-Oct), standing side by side.

From June through September, several buses daily make the trip over the pass from Kranjska Gora. **Alpetour** (✆04-201 31 30; www.alpetour.si) runs three to four buses daily from Kranjska Gora to Trenta (€4.70, 70 minutes, 30km) and Bovec (€6.70, two hours, 46km). Check the website for a timetable.

indoor pool (though you'll get free access to the Aqua Larix Wellness Centre and the chairlifts to the slopes are just over the road.

Hotel Larix
HOTEL €€€

(✆588 41 00; www.hitholidays-kg.si; Borovška cesta 99; r €80-140; P@🖥➰) Close to the lifts, and in the same stable as Kompas, is the 118-room Larix. It boasts the wonderful **Aqua Larix Wellness Centre** (✆588 45 00; www. hitholidays-kg.si; Borovška cesta 99; nonguests pool €8-9, pool & sauna €13-16), with sauna, steam and a pool that seems to go on forever.

Penzion Lipa
PENSION €€

(✆582 00 00; www.penzion-lipa.si; Koroška cesta 14; s €35-50, d €70-100; P🖥) This guesthouse, with a very popular family-style restaurant and 10 attractive rooms and apartments, offers excellent value. It's right by where the buses stop.

Natura Eco Camp Kranjska Gora
CAMPGROUND €

(✆064 121 966; www.naturacamp-kranjskagora .com; Borovška cesta 62; adult €8-10, child €5-7, cabin & tree tent €25-30) This wonderful site – some 300m from the main road on an isolated horse ranch in a forest clearing – is as close to paradise as we've been for a while. Pitch a tent or stay in one of the little wooden cabins or the unique tree tents, great pouches with air mattresses suspended from the branches.

Hostel Pr' Tatko
HOSTEL €

(✆031 479 087; www.prtatko.com; Podkoren 72; dm €15, q €68; P@🖥) One of Slovenia's more unusual hostels is in Podkoren, 3km west of Kranjska Gora. It's a three-room affair in a traditional farmhouse with a decent-sized kitchen and common room. It's ideally suited to skiers who want to be close to the Podkoren lifts or hikers who see the relatively remote location as an advantage.

Hostel Nika
HOSTEL €

(☑588 10 00; www.porentov-dom.si; Bezje 16, Čičare; dm €15, s €20, d €34-40; P@) This atmospheric old 66-bed place on the Sava Dolinka River in Čičare is about 800m northeast of the centre and just across the main road from the TGC Shopping Centre.

Camping Kamne
CAMPGROUND €

(☑589 11 05; http://campingkamne.com; Dovje 9; per person €6-7, bungalows for 2 €22-26, bungalows for 4 €44-50; ☼year-round; P☳) This typical 1.2-hectare campground for 120 guests is at Dovje near Mojstrana, about 14km east of Kranjska Gora. It has a small outdoor swimming pool in the grounds.

✖ Eating

Hotel Kotnik
SLOVENIAN €€

(☑588 15 64; www.hotel-kotnik.si; Borovška cesta 75; mains €8-18; ☎) One of Kranjska Gora's better eateries, the restaurant in this stylish inn, with bits of painted dowry chests on the walls, serves grilled meats – pepper steak is a speciality – that should keep you going for a while. The adjoining **pizzeria** (pizza €6-9; ☼noon-10.30pm), with a wood-burning stove, is a great choice for something quicker.

Gostilna Pri Martinu
SLOVENIAN €€

(☑582 03 00; Borovška cesta 61; mains €7-14; ☼10am-11pm; ☎) This atmospheric tavern-restaurant in an old house opposite the fire station is one of the best places in town to try local specialities, such as *ješprenj* (barley soup), *telečja obara* (veal stew) and *ričet* (barley stew with smoked pork ribs). One of the few places to offer a full three-course luncheon menu (€7).

Penzion Lipa
SLOVENIAN €€€

(www.penzion-lipa.si; Koroška cesta 14; mains €8-20; ☼11am-11pm) This attractive, family-style restaurant below a popular guesthouse also does decent pizzas and pasta dishes. There's an enclosed terrace for summer dining.

Šang Hai
CHINESE €

(www.sanghai-restavracija.com; Naselje Slavka Černeta 34; mains €8-12; ☼noon-midnight) This Chinese restaurant in a depressing location on the ground floor of the TGC Shopping Centre offers practically the only alternative in town to Slovenian food and pizza. The menu is particularly strong on fish dishes. You'll find it facing the car park on the north side of the shopping centre.

☕ Drinking

Sport Point Café
CAFE

(www.sport-point.si; Borovška cesta 93/a; ☼7.30am-9pm Mon-Fri, 7.30am-10pm Sat & Sun; ☎) This convenient spot next to the TIC is a good place to relax over coffee and plan the day's events.

Vopa Pub
PUB

(☑041 840 806; Borovška cesta 92; ☼7am-1am Sun-Thu, 7am-5am Sat & Sun; ☎) This bar near the post office is practically the only place in town with a pulse after 10pm. The ground-floor pub operates year-round, while a club of the same name downstairs is the place to go during the ski season. Count on DJs and a pretty lively aprés-ski scene on weekends.

ⓘ Information

The **Kranjska Gora Tourist Information Centre** (TIC; ☑580 94 40; www.kranjska-gora.si; Tičarjeva cesta 2; ☼8am-7pm Mon-Sat, 9am-6pm Sun Jun-Sep & mid-Dec–Mar, 8am-3pm Mon-Sat Apr, May & Oct–mid-Dec) is centrally located. Most of the other facilities for visitors are just a short walk away, including branches of **Gorenjska Banka** (Borovška cesta 95) and **SKB Banka** (Borovška cesta 99a), and the **post office** (Borovška cesta 92).

ⓘ Getting There & Away

Buses run hourly to Ljubljana (€8.70, two hours, 91km) via Jesenice (€3.10, 30 minutes, 24km), where you should change for Bled (€2.70, 20 minutes, 19km). There's just one direct departure to Bled (€4.80, one hour, 40km) on weekdays at 9.15am and at 9.50am on weekends.

Alpetour (☑201 31 30; www.alpetour.si) runs regular buses to Trenta (€4.70, 70 minutes, 30km) and Bovec (€6.70, two hours, 46km) from June through September via the Vršič Pass. Check the website for a timetable. There are normally about four departures daily (more at the weekend). Buy tickets from the driver.

Triglav National Park

☑04 & 05 / ELEV TO 2864M

Triglav National Park (Triglavski Narodni Park), abbreviated TNP everywhere in Slovenia, with an area of 83,800 hectares (just over 4% of Slovenian territory), is one of the largest national reserves in Europe. It is a pristine, visually spectacular world of rocky mountains – the centrepiece of which is Mt Triglav (2864m), the country's highest peak – as well as river gorges,

Julian Alps & Triglav National Park

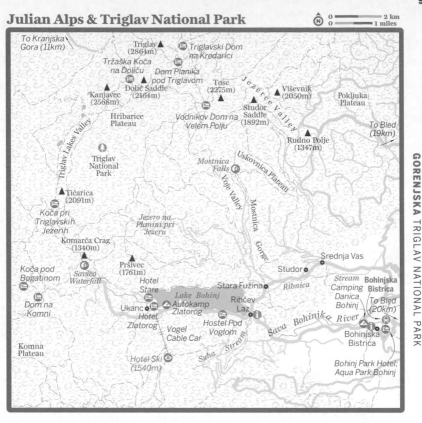

ravines, canyons, caves, rivers, streams, forests and Alpine meadows.

Although Slovenia counts three large regional parks and 44 much smaller country (or 'landscape') parks, this is the country's only gazetted national park, and it includes almost all of the Alps lying within Slovenia. The idea of a park was first mooted in 1908 and realised in 1924, when 1600 hectares of the Triglav Lakes Valley were put under temporary protection.

The area was renamed Triglav National Park in 1961 and expanded 20 years later to include most of the eastern Julian Alps. Today the park stretches from Kranjska Gora in the north to Tolmin in the south and from the Italian border in the west almost to Bled in the east. The bulk of the park lies in Gorenjska, but once you've crossed the awesome Vršič Pass – at 1611m, Slovenia's highest – and begun the descent into the Soča Valley, you've entered Primorska.

It is a popular weekend destination for all manner of activity, from hiking and mountain biking to fishing and rafting. And there are approaches from Bohinj, Kranjska Gora and, in Primorska, Trenta – to name just a few gateways.

Marked trails in the park lead to countless peaks and summits besides Mt Triglav. Favourite climbs include Mangart (2679m) on the Italian border (the 12km road that descends to the Predel Pass is the highest road in Slovenia), the needlepoint of Jalovec (2645m) in the north, and the sharp ridge of Razor (2601m) southeast of Vršič.

Triglav National Park is not only about climbing mountains. There are easy hikes through beautiful valleys, forests and meadows, too. Two excellent maps for this purpose are the PZS 1:50,000-scale *Triglavski Narodni Park* (*Triglav National Park*; €8.50) and Freytag & Berndt's 1:50,000 *Julische Alpen* for €9.

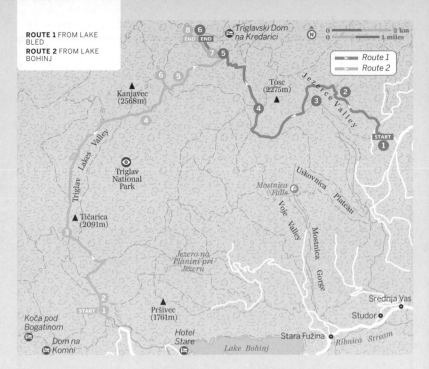

ROUTE 1 FROM LAKE BLED
ROUTE 2 FROM LAKE BOHINJ

Walking Tour
Mt Triglav: Reaching the Summit

❯ There are at least 20 different ways to reach the summit of Mt Triglav at 2864m. We've mapped out two popular approaches, one starts from near Lake Bled, the other from near Lake Bohinj.

Route 1: From Lake Bled

The shortest way to reach the peak starts from ❶ **Rudno Polje** (1347m) on the Pokljuka Plateau, 18km southwest of Bled. An experienced climber could do this in under 12 hours out and back, but most mortals choose to stay overnight. The route follows a well-marked trail under ❷ **Viševnik** (2050m) and over the ❸ **Studor Saddle** (1892m), before contouring around the slopes of Tosc (2275m). Three hours of hiking brings you to the ❹ **Vodnikov Dom na Velem Polju** mountain hut, at 1817m. You can sleep here, or continue another two hours to the ❺ **Dom Planika pod Triglavom** at 2401m. From here, it's an hour of scrambling along the ridge, grabbing hold of metal spikes and grips, to the ❻ **top of Mt Triglav**.

Route 2: From Lake Bohinj

This longer walk starts from near the ❶ **Savica Waterfall**, on the western end of Lake Bohinj, and normally requires two overnights. The path zig-zags up the steep ❷ **Komarča Crag** (1340m), with an excellent view of the lake. Four hours north of the falls is ❸ **Koča pri Triglavskih Jezerih**, at 1685m, where you spend the first night. On the second day, hike north along the valley, then northeast to the desert-like ❹ **Hribarice Plateau** (2358m). Then descend to the ❺ **Dolič Saddle** (2164m) and the ❻ **Tržaška Koča na Doliču** hut, at 2151m. You could well carry on to ❼ **Dom Planika pod Triglavom** about 1½ hours to the northeast, but this is often packed. It's better to stay where you're sure there's a bed unless you've booked ahead. From Dom Planika it's just over an hour to the ❽ **Triglav summit.**

CLIMBING MT TRIGLAV

The 2864m limestone peak called Triglav (Three Heads) has been a source of inspiration and an object of devotion for Slovenes for more than a millennium. The early Slavs believed the mountain to be the home of a three-headed deity who ruled the sky, the earth and the underworld. No one managed to reach the summit until 1778, when an Austrian mountaineer and his three Slovenian guides climbed it from Bohinj. For Slovenes under the Habsburgs in the 19th century, the 'pilgrimage' to Triglav became, in effect, a confirmation of one's ethnic identity, and this tradition continues to this day: a Slovene is expected to climb Triglav at least once in his or her life.

You can climb Slovenia's highest peak too, but despite the fact that on a good summer's day hundreds of people will reach the summit, Triglav is not for the unfit or faint-hearted. In fact, its popularity is one of the main sources of danger. On the final approach to the top, there are often scores of people clambering along a rocky, knife-edge ridge in both directions, trying to pass each other.

If you are relatively fit and confident, and have a good head for heights, then by all means go for it. We strongly recommend, though, hiring a guide for the ascent, even if you have some mountain-climbing experience under your belt. A local guide will know the trails and conditions, and can prove invaluable in helping to arrange sleeping space in mountain huts and providing transport. Guides can be hired through 3glav Adventures (p80) in Bled or Alpinsport (p86) in Bohinj, or book in advance through the **Alpine Association of Slovenia** (PZS; www.pzs.si).

The list of items to take along reflects common sense but bears repeating here: good hiking boots, warm clothes (even in summer), hat, gloves, rain gear, map, compass, whistle, head torch, first-aid kit, and emergency food and drink.

Note that Mt Triglav is inaccessible from mid to late October to early June. June and the first half of July are the rainiest times in the summer months, so late July, August and particularly September and early October are the best times to make the climb. Patches of snow and ice can linger in the higher gullies until late July, and the weather can be unpredictable at altitudes above 1500m, with temperatures varying by as much as 20°C and violent storms appearing out of nowhere.

There are many ways to reach the top, with the most popular approaches coming from the south, either starting from Pokljuka, near Bled, or from the Savica Waterfall, near Lake Bohinj. We've mapped out two of the most popular approaches in our walking tour. You can also climb Mt Triglav from the north and the east (Mojstrana and the Vrata Valley). All of the approaches offer varying degrees of difficulty and have their pluses and minuses. Note that treks normally require one or two overnight stays in the mountains.

Several good hiking maps are available from tourist information centres. Kartografija (www.kartografija.si) publishes a good and widely available 1:50,000-scale *Tourist Map of the Triglav National Park* for €9.50. The Alpine Association of Slovenia has excellent maps as well.

GORENJSKA TRIGLAV NATIONAL PARK

Primorska & Notranjska

Includes »

Best Places to Eat

» Hiša Franko (p104)

» Restaurant Neptune (p127)

» Pri Mari (p127)

» Topli Val (p104)

» Gostilna Istria (p122)

Best Places to Stay

» Kaki Plac (p129)

» Old Schoolhouse Korte (p121)

» Dobra Vila (p101)

» Miracolo di Mare (p127)

» Hotel Rakov Škocjan (p136)

Why Go?

Primorska is one of Slovenia's most diverse regions. There is mountain climbing and rafting in the Soča Valley, wine tasting near Nova Gorica, caverns at Škocjan and white stallions to ride at Lipica. On the coast, the old Venetian ports of Piran and Koper will keep even the most indefatigable of sightseers busy.

Primorska has a climate and flora that are distinctly Mediterranean right up to the foothills of the Alps. There are four distinct regions: the Soča Valley; the rolling hills of central Primorska; the Karst, with its wonderful *pršut* (dry-cured ham), olives and wine; and the coast itself (sometimes called Slovenian Istria).

Notranjska is mostly wooded, making it one of the best places in the country for outdoor activities. It's also peppered with caves and castles – Predjama even has a castle wedged in a cave. Postojna cave is one of Slovenia's most popular tourist sites, but don't miss isolated Snežnik Castle or exploring Križna cave by boat.

When to Go

Postojna

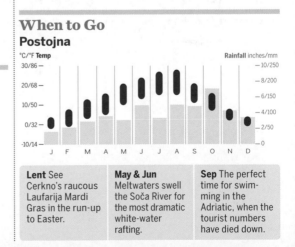

Lent See Cerkno's raucous Laufarija Mardi Gras in the run-up to Easter.

May & Jun Meltwaters swell the Soča River for the most dramatic white-water rafting.

Sep The perfect time for swimming in the Adriatic, when the tourist numbers have died down.

Primorska & Notranjska Highlights

① Dare the devil himself by **canyoning** or **rafting** on the Soča River (p100) from Bovec

② Descend into the nether world with a tour of the **Škocjan Caves** (p112)

③ Enjoy the catch of the day amid the glorious Venetian architecture of **Piran** (p122)

④ Discover many of the 270 types of feathered friends passing through in the still and very salty **Sečovlje Salina Nature Park** (p130)

⑤ Be reminded of where you come from (and where you certainly are going to) at the **Church of the Holy Trinity** (p115) in Hrastovlje

⑥ Follow Lueger's lead and throw cherries from Erazem's Nook in **Predjama Castle** (p134)

PRIMORSKA

Soča Valley

The Soča Valley region (Posočje) stretches from Triglav National Park to Nova Gorica, including the outdoor activity centres of Bovec and Kobarid. Threading through it is the magically aquamarine Soča River. Most people come here for the rafting, hiking and skiing though there are plenty of historical sights and locations, particularly relating to WWI, when millions of troops fought on the mountainous battlefront here. Between the wars, Primorska and the Soča Valley fell under Italian jurisdiction.

BOVEC
05 / POP 1631 / ELEV 470M

Soča Valley's de facto capital, Bovec offers plenty for adventure-sports enthusiasts. With the Julian Alps above, the Soča River below and Triglav National Park all around, you could spend a week here hiking, kayaking, mountain biking and, in winter, skiing at Kanin, Slovenia's highest ski station, without ever doing the same thing twice.

The centre is Trg Golobarskih Žrtev, one of the few named streets in town. Actually, it's a long square that forms the main east–west drag and runs northward to the neo-Romanesque church of St Urh. Buses stop down the side street next to Mercator super-maket in Mala Vas.

History

The area around Bovec is first mentioned in documents dating back to the 11th century, but in the modern era it has seen a lot of destruction. On two occasions Napoléon's army attacked Austria from here, and much of the town was destroyed in the fighting around the Soča Valley during WWI. It was rebuilt in the 1920s, but then suffered again as a result of severe earthquakes in 1976 and 1998.

◉ Sights

Kluže Fortress   CASTLE
(Trdnjava Kluže; ☏384 19 00; www.kluze.net; adult/child/student €3/1/2; ◐9am-8pm Jul & Aug, 10am-5pm Sun-Fri Jun & Oct, 10am-6pm Sat & Sun May & Sep) Built by the Austrians in 1882 on the site of a 17th-century fortress above a 70m ravine on the Koritnica River, Kluže Fortress is 4km northeast of Bovec and worth the trip just for its location. Even more awesome is the upper fortress (**Fort Herman**) built halfway up Mt Rombon to the west in 1900

when Kluže proved to be obsolete. There's a permanent exhibition on the ecology of the region and the history of the fortress.

Ostan Cheese Dairy   DAIRY
(☏041 589 877, 389 61 77; Trg Golobarskih Žrtev 54) The Bovec Basin abounds in family-run dairies, such as the in-town Ostan Cheese Dairy, which produces traditional sheep's cheese. Ask the TIC for a copy of the pamphlet *Along the Bovška Ovca Sheep Trail* and track down your own favourite.

⚐ Activities
ADVENTURE SPORTS

There are nearly a dozen adrenalin-raising adventure-sports companies in Bovec.

Avantura   ADVENTURE SPORTS
(☏041 718 317; www.avantura.org; Trg Golobarskih Žrtev 19; ◐9am-7pm Jun-Aug)

Aktivni Planet   ADVENTURE SPORTS
(☏031 653 417; www.aktivniplanet.si; Mala Vas 106)

Soča Rafting   ADVENTURE SPORTS
(☏041 724 472, 389 62 00; www.socarafting.si; Trg Golobarskih Žrtev 14; ◐9am-7pm year-round)

Top Extreme   ADVENTURE SPORTS
(☏041 620 636; www.top.si; Trg Golobarskih Žrtev 19; ◐9am-7pm May-Sep)

CYCLING

Ask the TIC for the *Biking Trails* pamphlet, which lists 16 trips of various degrees of difficulty. Most sports agencies rent bicycles and mountain bikes from €7.50/€18 per hour/day to €39/85 for three days/one week.

Kanin Mountain Bike Park   MOUNTAIN BIKING
(www.mtbparkkanin.com) The Kanin Mountain Bike Park is just 2km from the Bovec Kanin Ski Centre cable car's station B (one way €5); its 4.5km trail is divided into three degrees of difficulty and is open all year.

HIKING & WALKING

The 1:25,000-scale *Bovec z Okolico* (*Bovec with Surroundings*; €7.60) map lists a number of walks, from two-hour strolls to the ascent of **Mt Rombon** (2208m), a good five hours one way.

The most popular walk in the area is to the 106m **Boka Waterfall**, 5.5km to the southwest of Bovec (an especially impressive sight during the spring snow melt). To get there on foot, follow the relatively easy B2 marked path or the more difficult S1 on the *Bovec z Okolico* map; mountain-bike track No 1 on the *Biking Trails* pamphlet map will also take you there. The trip up to the falls (850m) and back takes about 1½ hours, but the path is steep in places and can be very slippery.

From the uppermost stop (station D) of the cable car more ambitious walkers and hikers could make the difficult three-hour climb of **Kanin** (2587m), or reach the **Prestreljenik Window** (2498m) in about an hour.

PARAGLIDING

Soča's best views can be had by tandem paraglider flight from the top of the Bovec Kanin cable car or the Mangart Saddle, each over 2000m above the valley floor. The cost is around €125; ask the Avantura agency for details.

SKIING

Bovec Kanin Ski Centre   SKIING
(☑389 60 03; www.boveckanin.si; day pass adult/ child/senior & student €28/18/23) Bovec Kanin Ski Centre northwest of Bovec has skiing up to 2300m – the only real altitude alpine skiing in Slovenia, with good spring skiing in April and even May. The 17km of pistes and 15km of cross-country runs (served by three chairlifts and three T-bars) is reached by a cable car in three stages. The bottom station is 600m southwest of the centre of Bovec on the main road. The ski centre links up with the Sella Nevea Ski Centre on the other side of Kanin in Italy, adding up to 30km in total. There's an **information centre** (☑389 60 03; www.boveckanin.si; Trg Golobarskih Žrtev 47; ☺7.30am-9pm Jul & Aug, 8am-noon & 1-4.30pm Sep-Jun) in central Bovec.

Kanin Cable Car   CABLE CAR
(adult/child one way €14/9, return €17/12) Kanin cable car runs continuously during the ski season; in July and August it runs hourly from 7am to 4pm (last down at 5pm) and every hour from 8am to 3pm (last down at 4pm) at the weekend in June and September. Several walks lead from the upper station.

WATER SPORTS

Rafting, kayaking and canoeing on the beautiful Soča River (10% to 40% gradient; Grades I to VI) is a major draw. The season lasts from April to October. Almost every agency sells trips.

Rafting trips of two to eight people on the Soča over a distance of 8km to 10km (1½ hours) cost from €36 to €46; 21km (2½ hours) costs from €48 to €55, including neo-

prene long johns, windcheater, life jacket, helmet and paddle. Bring a swimsuit, T-shirt and towel. Canoes for two are €45 for the day; single kayaks €30. A number of beginners kayaking courses are also on offer (eg a one-/two-day trip from €55/100). Longer guided kayak trips (up to 10km) are also available.

A 3km **canyoning** trip near the Soča, in which you descend through gorges and jump over falls attached to a rope, costs around €42.

🛏 Sleeping

The TIC has hundreds of private rooms (per person €15 to €30) on its lists.

TOP CHOICE **Dobra Vila**   BOUTIQUE HOTEL €€€
(☑389 64 00; www.dobra-vila-bovec.si; Mala Vas 112; d €120-145, tr €160-180; P✲⊛) This absolute stunner of a 10-room boutique hotel is housed in an erstwhile telephone-exchange building dating to 1932. Peppered with interesting artefacts and objets d'art, it has its own library and wine cellar, and a fabulous restaurant with a winter garden and outdoor terrace.

Martinov Hram   GUESTHOUSE €€
(☑388 62 14; www.martinov-hram.si; Trg Golobarskih Žrtev 27; s/d €33/54; P⊛) This lovely and very friendly guesthouse just 100m east of the centre has 14 beautifully furnished rooms and an excellent restaurant with an emphasis on specialities from the Bovec region.

Hotel Mangart   HOTEL €€
(☑388 42 50; www.hotel-mangart.com; Mala vas 107; s/d €55/90) A good option on the outskirts of Bovec is this clean modern hotel shaped like a giant triangular wedge of cheese.

Kamp Polovnik   CAMPGROUND €
(☑388 60 07; www.kamp-polovnik.com; Ledina 8; adult €6.50-7.50, child €5-5.75; ☺Apr–mid-Oct; P) The closest camp ground to Bovec is small (just over a hectare with 70 sites) but located in an attractive setting.

Alp Hotel   HOTEL €€
(☑388 40 00; www.alp-hotel.si; Trg Golobarskih Žrtev 48; s €58-65, d €76-90; P@⊛) This 103-room hotel, with a bit of landscaped garden around it, is fairly good value and is as central as you are going to find in Bovec. There are three saunas and guests get to use the swimming pool at the nearby Hotel Kanin.

Hotel Kanin
HOTEL €€

(☎389 68 82; www.hotel-kanin.com; Ledina 6; s €58-74, d €86-118; P@⊇) This 124-room property is set in quiet surrounds and has a large indoor swimming pool and a new wellness centre. The rooms are average to good, with some renovated and having balconies looking onto a quiet back garden.

✖ Eating & Drinking
Martinov Hram
SLOVENIAN €

(starters €5.90-9, mains €7.90-13.50, pizza €6.50-8.90; ☉10am-10pm Tue-Fri, 10am-midnight Sat & Sun) This traditional restaurant in an attractive inn specialises in game, Soča trout and mushroom dishes. During the winter, pizza rears its ugly head. There is a lovely roadside terrace in front. Set lunch is €13.

Gostišče Stari Kovač
PIZZA €

(☎388 66 99; Rupa 3; starters €6.50-7, mains €8-11, pizza €5-7.50; ☉noon-10pm Tue-Sun) The Old Blacksmith, just west of the Alp Hotel, is a good choice for pizza cooked in a wood-burning stove.

Letni Vrt
SLOVENIAN €€

(☎041 775 127, 389 63 83; Trg Golobarskih Žrtev 1; meals from €15; ☉11am-10pm Wed-Mon) Opposite the Alp Hotel, the Summer Garden has pizza, grilled dishes and trout at affordable prices. Its garden is lovely in summer – as it should be, given the name.

Plec Caffe
CAFE

(☎041 775 127; Trg Golobarskih Žrtev 18; ☉8am-1am Jul & Aug, 5pm-1am Sep Jun) This pleasant cafe in the heart of town attracts punters till the wee (for Bovec) hours year-round.

❶ Information
Bar Kavarna (☎388 63 35; Trg Golobarskih Žrtev 25; 30min €1.50; ☉7am-11pm Mon-Thu, 7am-midnight Fri & Sat, 8am-8pm Sun)
Nova KBM Banka (Trg Golobarskih Žrtev 47)
Post Office (Trg Golobarskih Žrtev 8; ☉8-9.30am, 10am-3.30pm & 4-6pm Mon-Fri, 8am-noon Sat)
Tourist Information Centre Bovec (TIC; ☎388 19 19; www.bovec.si; Trg Golobarskih Žrtev 8; ☉8.30am-8.30pm summer, 9am-6pm winter) Has an ATM next door.

❶ Getting There & Away
Buses to Kobarid (€3.10, 30 minutes) depart up to six times a day. There are also buses to Ljubljana (€13.60, 3½ hours) via Kobarid and Idrija, and to Nova Gorica (€7.50, two hours). From late June to August a service to Kranjska Gora

(€6.70, two hours) via the Vršič Pass departs four times daily, continuing to Ljubljana.

KOBARID
☑05 / POP 1250 / ELEV 234M

The charming town of Kobarid is quainter than nearby Bovec, and despite being surrounded by mountain peaks, it feels more Mediterranean than Alpine, with an Italianate look (the border at Robič is only 9km to the west).

On the surface not a whole lot has changed since Ernest Hemingway described Kobarid (then Caporetto) in *A Farewell to Arms* (1929) as 'a little white town with a campanile in a valley', with 'a fine fountain in the square'. The bell in the tower still rings on the hour, but the fountain has sadly disappeared.

Kobarid was a military settlement during Roman times, was hotly contested in the Middle Ages and was hit by a devastating earthquake in 1976, but the world will always remember Kobarid as the site of the decisive battle of 1917 in which the combined forces of the Central Powers defeated the Italian army.

Kobarid lies in a broad valley on the west bank of the Soča River. The centre of town is Trg Svobode, dominated by the Gothic Church of the Assumption and that famous bell tower. Buses stop in front of the Cinca Marinca bar-cafe on the eastern side at Trg Svobode 10.

◉ Sights & Activities
Kobarid Museum
MUSEUM

(☎389 00 00; www.kobariski-muzej.si; Gregorčičeva ulica 10; adult/child €5/2.50; ☉9am-6pm Mon-Fri, 9am-7pm Sat & Sun summer, 10am-5pm Mon-Fri, 9am-6pm Sat & Sun winter) This museum is devoted almost entirely to the Soča Front and the 'war to end all wars'. Themed rooms describe powerfully the 29 months of fighting. The **Krn Room** looks at the initial assaults along the Soča River after Italy's entry into the war in May 1915. The **White Room** describes the harsh conditions of war in the snowbound mountains. The **Hinterland Room** describes life pauses in the fighting – a sharp contrast to the **Black Room's** horrific photographs of the dead and dying. Finally, the **Battle of Kobarid Room** details the final offensive launched by the Austrian and German forces that defeated the Italian army.

There are many photographs documenting the horrors of the front, military charts,

THE SOČA (ISONZO) FRONT

The breakthrough in the Soča Front (more commonly known to historians as the Isonzo Front) by the combined Austro-Hungarian and German forces near Caporetto (Kobarid) in October 1917 was one of history's greatest and bloodiest military campaigns fought on mountainous terrain. By the time the fighting had stopped 17 days later, hundreds of thousands of soldiers lay dead or wounded, gassed or mutilated beyond recognition.

In May 1915, Italy declared war on the Central Powers and their allies and sent its army to the strategically important Soča Valley; from there, they hoped to move on the heart of Austria-Hungary. However, the Austrians had fortified the lines with trenches and bunkers for 80km from the Adriatic to the mountain peaks overlooking the Upper Soča Valley. While the Italian's First Offensive was initially successful – including the occupation of Kobarid – the attack stalled after the first month.

The Italians launched 11 offensives over the next 2½ years, but the difficult mountain terrain meant a war of attrition between the two entrenched armies. The fighting in the mountains and the limestone plateau to the south was horrific, but the territorial gains were minimal. With the stalemate, much of the fighting shifted to Gorica (Gorizia) on the edge of the Karst.

On 24 October 1917 the stalemate was broken when the Austro-Hungarians and Germans moved hundreds of thousands of troops, arms and materiel (including seven German divisions) into the area between Bovec and Tolmin, with Kobarid as the first target. The surprise 12th Offensive – the Austrians' first – began with heavy bombardment.

The 'miracle of Kobarid' routed the Italian army and pushed the fighting back deep into Italian territory. The sketches of one Lieutenant Erwin Rommel (later the 'Desert Fox' commander of Germany's North African offensive in WWII) are invaluable for understanding the battle, but no account is more vivid than the description of the Italian retreat in Hemingway's *A Farewell to Arms*. The novelist himself was wounded on the Gorica battlefield in the spring of 1917 while driving an Italian ambulance.

The 12th Offensive was the greatest breakthrough in WWI, and it employed some elements of what would later be called 'lightning war' (*blitzkrieg*). The Italians alone lost 500,000 soldiers, and another 300,000 were taken prisoner. Casualties on the Soča Front for the entire 1915–17 period, including soldiers and civilians behind the lines, number almost a million.

diaries and maps, and two large relief displays showing the front lines and offensives through the Krn Mountains and the positions in the Upper Soča Valley. Don't miss the 20-minute multimedia presentation.

GUIDED WALKS

Walk of Peace in the Soča Region Foundation
GUIDED WALK

(✆389 01 67; www.potimiruvposocju.si; Gregorčičeva ulica 8) Based opposite the museum, this organisation runs a number of guided walks along sections of the 100km-long Walk of Peace (Pot Miru), a trail following the Soča (Isonzo) Front from Tolmin in the south to Log pod Mangrtom in the north. Most guided walks are for groups, but there's a three-hour walk to the **Kolovrat Outdoor Museum** (Kolovrat Muzej na Prostem) costing €10 on Wednesday and Sunday mornings.

Kobarid Historical Walk
WALKING TOUR

(Kobariška Zgodovinska Pot) The TIC offers a free brochure describing the 5km-long Kobarid Historical Walk. From the Kobarid Museum walk to the north side of Trg Svobode, a winding road lined with the Stations of the Cross, to the **Italian Charnel House** (Italijanska Kostnica), which contains the bones of more than 7000 Italian soldiers killed on the Soča Front. It's topped with the 17th-century **Parish Church of St Anthony**.

From here, a path leads north (bearing left) for just over 1km to the ancient fortified hill of **Tonočov Grad**, then descends through the remains of the **Italian Defence Line** (Italijanska Obrambna Črta), past cleared trenches, gun emplacements and observation posts, before crossing the Soča over a 52m **footbridge**. A path leads up a side valley to a series of walkways that take you to the foot of the spectacular **Kozjak Stream Waterfalls** (Slapovi Potoka

Kozjak). The return path leads to **Napoleon Bridge** (Napoleonov Most), a replica of a bridge built by the French in the early 19th century and destroyed in 1915.

ADVENTURE SPORTS

Kobarid gives Bovec a run for its money in adventure sports, and you'll find several outfits on or off the town's main square that can organise rafting (from €34), canyoning (from €45), kayaking (€40) and paragliding (€110) between April and October.

X Point ADVENTURE SPORTS
(041 692 290, 388 53 08; www.xpoint.si; Trg Svobode 6)

Positive Sport ADVENTURE SPORTS
(040 654 475; www.positive-sport.com; Markova ulica 2)

Sleeping

Hiša Franko GUESTHOUSE €€€
(389 41 20; www.hisafranko.com; Staro Selo 1; r €80-135; P🖸) This guesthouse in an old farmhouse 3km west of Kobarid in Staro Selo, halfway to the Italian border, has 10 themed rooms – we love the Moja Afrika (My Africa) and Soba Zelenega Čaja (Green Tea Room) – some of which have terraces and Jacuzzis. Eat in their excellent restaurant.

Hotel Hvala HOTEL €€€
(389 93 00; wwww.hotelhvala.si; Trg Svobode 1; s €72-76, d €104-112; P🖷🖸) The delightful Hotel Thanks (actually it's the family's name) has 31 rooms. The snazzy lift takes you on a vertical tour of Kobarid (don't miss both the Soča trout and Papa Hemingway at work); there's a bar, a Mediterranean-style cafe in the garden and a superb restaurant.

Apartma-Ra APARTMENTS €
(041 641 899; apartma-ra@siol.net; Gregorčičeva ulica 6c; r €40-45; P🖷🖸) This welcoming little place between the museum and Trg Svobode (enter via the driveway from Volaričeva ulica) has five rooms and apartments, some with terraces.

Kamp Koren CAMPGROUND €
(389 13 11; www.kamp-koren.si; Drežniške Ravne 33; site per person €11.50, chalets d/tr from €55/60; P🖸) The oldest camp ground in the valley, this 2-hectare site with 70 pitches is about 500m northeast of Kobarid on the left bank of the Soča River and just before the turn to Drežniške Ravne, a lovely village

with traditional farmhouses. In full view is the Napoleon Bridge.

Postive Sport Hostel HOSTEL €
(Markova ulica 2; dm €16; 🖸) Compact but bright and friendly 16-bed hostel run by (and above) the adventure-sports agency of the same name.

Eating

Hiša Franko SLOVENIAN €€
(389 41 20; www.hisafranko.com; Staro Selo 1; mains €22-24; ⌚noon-3pm & 6-11pm Tue-Sun) Foodies will love this superb gourmet restaurant in the Hiša Franko guesthouse in Staro Selo, just west of town. Impeccable tasting menus, which change according to the season, are strong on locally sourced ingredients and cost €50/75 for five/eight courses. It closes on Tuesday in winter.

Topli Val SEAFOOD €€€
(Trg Svobode 1; starters €8-10, mains €9.50-25; ⌚noon-10pm) Seafood is the speciality here, and it's excellent – from the carpaccio of sea bass to the Soča trout and signature lobster with pasta. Expect to pay about €30 to €60 per person with a decent bottle of wine. There's a lovely front terrace and back garden open in warmer months.

Pizza Bar Pri Vitku PIZZA €
(389 13 34; Pri Malnih ulica 41; pizza & pasta €5.50-7.50; ⌚11am-midnight Mon-Fri, noon-midnight Sat & Sun) This upbeat little pub-restaurant is about 500m south of the town centre and serves decent pizza and pasta as well as more ambitious grilled dishes.

Drinking

Cinca Marinca BAR
(389 13 03; Trg Svobode 10; ⌚7am-11pm Mon-Fri, 7am-late Sat & Sun) This cafe-bar is just the place to cool your heels and slake your thirst while waiting for the bus to stop outside. It's open late when the rest of Kobarid has gone to bed early.

Pri Gotarju PUB
(388 57 43; Krilanova ulica 3; ⌚7am-11pm Sun-Thu, 7am-midnight Fri & Sat) This cafe-pub in a shady garden is a pleasant place for a drink. There's a rusting WWI 150mm Krupp howitzer opposite the entrance.

Information

Abanka (Markova ulica 16)
Nova KBM Banka (Trg Svobode 2)

Post Office (Trg Svobode 2; ⊘8-9.30am, 10am-3.30pm & 4-6pm Mon-Fri, 8am-noon Sat)
Tourist Information Centre Kobarid (TIC; ⌖380 04 90; www.dolina-soce.com; Trg Svobode 16; ⊘9am-1pm & 2-7pm Mon-Fri, 10am-1pm & 4-7pm Sat & Sun) Free internet.

❶ Getting There & Away

There are half a dozen buses a day to Bovec (€3.10, 30 minutes). Other destinations include Ljubljana (€11.40, three hours) via Most na Soči train station (good for Bled and Bohinj), Cerkno and Idrija (€7.20, two hours) and Nova Gorica (€6, 1¼ hours, four a day). Daily in July and August, buses cross the spectacular Vršič Pass to Kranjska Gora (€6.70, three hours).

NOVA GORICA

⌖05 / POP 13,178 / ELEV 92M

Nova Gorica is a university city straddling the Italian border, with tree-lined boulevards and a couple of lovely parks and gardens. Slovenian, Venetian and Austrian influences can be felt everywhere in the hinterland. It also straddles two important wine-growing areas: Goriška Brda to the northwest and the wide Vipava Valley to the southeast, and is a decent springboard for the Soča Valley, and the beautiful Karst region leading to the coast.

Nova Gorica is an unusually long town, running about 5km from crossing with Italy at Rožna Dolina (Casa Rossa) in the south to Solkan in the north. The bus station is in the centre of town at Kidričeva ulica 22. The train station is at Kolodvorska ulica 6, about 1.5km to the west.

History

When the town of Gorica was awarded to the Italians under the Treaty of Paris in 1947 and became Gorizia, the Yugoslav government set itself to building a model town on the eastern side of the border 'following the principles of Le Corbusier'. Appropriately enough they called it 'New Gorica' and erected a chain-link barrier between the two towns.

This 'mini Berlin Wall' was finally pulled down to great fanfare in 2004 after Slovenia joined the EU, leaving Piazza Transalpina (Trg z Mozaikom) straddling the now-existent border right behind Nova Gorica train station.

◎ Sights

Kostanjevica Monastery　　　　　MONASTERY
(Samostan Kostanjevica; ⌖330 77 50; Škrabčeva ulica 1; library admission €1; ⊘9am-noon & 3-5pm Mon-Sat, 3-5pm Sun) On a 143m hill 800m

south of the train station, this monastery was founded by the Capuchin Franciscans in the early 17th century and has a wonderful **library** with 10,000 volumes and 30 incunabula.

The **Church of the Annunciation** (Cerkev Marijinega Oznanenja; tomb of the Bourbons admission €1.50) has interesting stuccos. In the spooky crypt is the **tomb of the Bourbons** (as per library, above), which contains the mortal remains of the last members of the French house of Bourbon, including Charles X (1757–1836), who died of cholera while on holiday on the coast in Gorizia and was buried here.

Kromberk Castle　　　　　　　　CASTLE
(Grad Kromberk; Grajska ulica 1) Three kilometres east of the town, fabulous Kromberk Castle, dating from the 17th century, houses the **Goriško Museum** (Goriški Muzej; ⌖335 98 11; www.goriskimuzej.si; adult/child €2/1; ⊘8am-7pm Mon-Fri, 1-7pm Sun Jun-Sep, 8am-3pm Mon-Fri, 1-5pm Sun Oct-May). It features important archaeological, ethnological and fine-arts collections. You'll also find the fabulous Grajska Klet (p106) restaurant located here.

🏃 Activities

Ask the TIC for the pamphlet *Peš Poti na Goriškem (Footpaths in Goriška)*, which outlines a dozen **hiking trails** of between 3km and 20km around Nova Gorica. Its *Kolesarimo po Novi Gorici (Let's Cycle across Nova Gorica)* map traces paths for **cycling** around town and Kromberk Castle.

Top Extreme　　　　　ADVENTURE SPORTS
(⌖031 620 636; www.top.si; Vojkova ulica 9) Top Extreme in Solkan, north of the centre, has **bungee jumping** (jump €45; ⊘11am-4pm Sat or Sun May-Oct) from the 55m-high Solkan Bridge over the Soča. It's available at the weekend in season, but make sure you book ahead. It also organises rafting, kayaking and canyoning on the river.

🛏 Sleeping

HIT Hotel Sabotin　　　　　　　HOTEL €€
(⌖336 50 00; www.hit.si; Cesta IX Korpusa 35; s €50-81, d €76-118, tr €102-144; P🖸) This 68-room hotel in an old baroque manor house in Solkan, about 2km north of the bus station, is good value and atmospheric. Rates depend on the season and the age of the room.

Prenočišče Pertout　　　　　　HOSTEL €
(⌖041 624 452, 330 75 50; www.prenocisceper tout.com; Ulica 25 Maja 23; s/d €24/34; P🖸) This

Nova Gorica

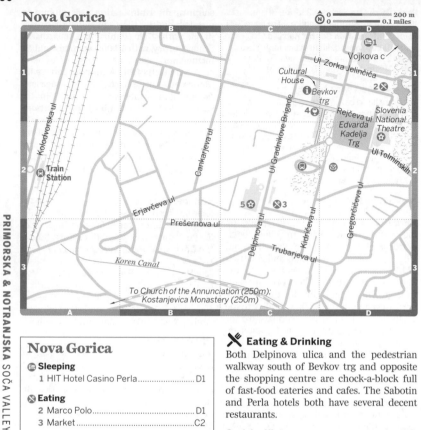

Nova Gorica

🛏 Sleeping
1 HIT Hotel Casino Perla..........................D1

✴ Eating
2 Marco Polo...D1
3 Market..C2

🍷 Drinking
4 Tokio Bar..C1

✦ Entertainment
5 HIT Casino Park C2
HIT Casino Perla ....(see 1)

five-room hostelry with singles, doubles and triples in Rožna Dolina, south of the centre, is scarcely 200m from the Italian crossing at Casa Rossa.

HIT Hotel Casino Perla   HOTEL €€€
(☑336 30 00; www.hit.si; Kidričeva ulica 7; s €102-169, d €169-224; P✴🐾🕿) This flashy place is a favourite with Italians, who can't get enough of the casino. It's in a big glass-and-steel structure with a modern extension that could be anywhere – Hong Kong, Las Vegas, Disneyland.

✘ Eating & Drinking

Both Delpinova ulica and the pedestrian walkway south of Bevkov trg and opposite the shopping centre are chock-a-block full of fast-food eateries and cafes. The Sabotin and Perla hotels both have several decent restaurants.

Grajska Klet   SLOVENIAN €€€
(☑302 71 60; Grajska ulica 1; per person from €35; ⏱noon-10pm Fri-Tue; ✎) If you've won big at the casino or just want to treat yourself, the Castle Cellar on the ground floor of Kromberk Castle is the place to go – it's one of the best restaurants in the region. There is plenty of Adriatic seafood and Soča trout; vegetarians are also catered for. There's a lovely terrace.

Marco Polo   ITALIAN €
(☑302 97 29; Kidričeva ulica 13; mains €6-17; ⏱11am-midnight) This Italian eatery with a delightful back terrace, 250m east of the TIC, is one of the town's best places to eat, serving pizza, pasta and more ambitious dishes.

Market   MARKET
(Delpinova ulica; ⏱7am-2pm Mon-Sat) The outdoor market is east of the Hotel Casino Park.

Tokio Bar   BAR
(Bevkov trg 1; ◷8am-midnight Sun-Thu, 9am-2am Fri & Sat) This uber-decorated bar is very central and popular with students.

☆ Entertainment

HIT Casino Perla (☏336 30 81; Kidričeva ulica 7; admission Mon-Fri free, Sat & Sun €5; ◷24hr)and **HIT Casino Park** (☏336 26 38; Delpinova ulica 5; admission Mon-Fri free, Sat & Sun €5; ◷24hr) are the company stores – drawing Italians from across the border who can't gamble at home. There are almost 1500 slot machines between them and all the gambling tables you could wish for.

❶ Information

Nova KBM Banka (Kidričeva ulica 11) Just south of the Hotel Casino Perla.

Nova Ljubljanska Banka (Bevkov trg 3) In the central square next to the TIC.

Post Office (Kidričeva ulica 19) Opposite the bus station.

Tourist Information Centre Nova Gorica (☏330 46 00; www.novagorica-turizem.com; Bevkov trg 4; ◷8am-8pm Mon-Fri, 9am-1pm Sat & Sun summer, 8am-6pm Mon-Fri, 9am-1pm winter) In the lobby of the Kulturni Dom (Cultural House), with free internet access.

❶ Getting There & Away

BUS Expect buses every two hours or so to Ljubljana (€10.70, 2½ hours) via Postojna (€6.70, 1½ hours). Other destinations include Bovec (€7.50, two hours) via Kobarid (€6, 1¼ hours), Idrija (€6.30, 1½ hours) and Piran (€10.70, three hours, daily) via Koper. Between June and September, a daily bus crosses the Vršič Pass to Kranjska Gora (€10.70, three hours).

Nova Gorica is an easy way to get to/from Italy; Italian bus 1 (€1) will whisk you from Via G Caprin opposite the Nova Gorica train station to its counterpart in Gorizia.

TRAIN About a half-dozen trains head north-east each day for Jesenice (€6.60, two hours) via Most na Soči, and Bled Jezero (€6.20, 1¾ hours) – arguably Slovenia's most beautiful train journey. In the other direction, an equal number of trains go to Sežana (€3.25, one hour); change here for Ljubljana, or Trieste in Italy.

GORIŠKA BRDA
☏05 / ELEV UP TO 800M

Goriška Brda, the hilly wine region, starts in **Dobrovo**, 13km to the northwest of Nova Gorica. The Renaissance-style **Dobrovo Castle** (Grad Dobrovo; ☏395 95 86; Grajska cesta 9; adult/child €2/1; ◷8am-4pm Tue-Fri, 10am-3pm Sat & Sun), dating from 1606, has a dozen rooms spread over three floors filled with elegant period furnishings and exhibits on the wine industry. In the cellar there is a **vinoteka** (☏395 92 10; ◷11.30am-9pm Tue-Sun)where you can sample the local vintages (white rebula and chardonnay or the pinot and merlot reds), with cheese and *pršut* (dry-cured ham).

More than 100 wineries offer tastings in Goriška Brda (always call ahead). The enormous **Vinska Klet Goriška Brda** (☏331 01 02; www.klet-brda.si; Zadružna cesta 9; tasting €10; ◷8am-7pm Mon-Fri, 8am-1pm Sat Apr–mid-Nov, short weekday hrs mid-Nov–Mar), which is just down the hill from the castle, has the largest wine cellar in Slovenia. Another recommended winery is **Erzetič** (☏395 94 60; www.vina-erzetic.com; Višnjevik 25a), 4km to the north.

This area has been under the influence of northern and central Italy since time immemorial. One good example is **Šmartno** (San Martino; population 220), a pretty little fortified village with stone walls and a 16th-century tower, which now contains a **gallery** (☏031 715 861; Šmartno 13). Visit **Brda House** (Briška Hiša; Šmartno 48; ◷10am-3pm Thu & Fri, 2-6pm Sat & Sun) for an idea of what life was like in medieval Brda.

Central Primorska

Central Primorska is a land of steep slopes, deep valleys and innumerable ravines, with plenty of good hiking, the magical Idrijca River and a couple of interesting towns. The region is dominated by the Cerkno and Idrija Hills, foothills of the Julian Alps.

Nowhere else in Slovenia are fields found on such steep slopes and houses found in such remote locations as in the regions around Idrija and Cerkno. The ravines and valleys were very useful to the Partisans during WWII, and the region is dotted with monuments testifying to their presence.

IDRIJA
☏05 / POP 5955 / ELEV 325M

Idrija means three things: *žlikrofi* (ravioli of cheese, bacon and chives), lace and mercury. The women of Idrija have been taking care of the first two for centuries, while the men went underground to extract the latter that made Idrija one of the richest towns in Europe during the Middle Ages.

History

The first mine opened at Idrija in 1500; within three centuries Idrija produced 13%

Idrija

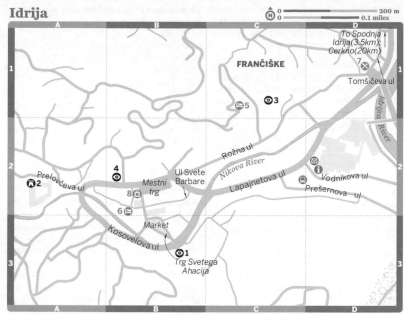

Idrija

◉ Sights
1 Anthony Mine Shaft	B3
2 Gewerkenegg Castle	A2
Idrija Lace-Making School	(see 4)
3 Miner's House	C1
Municipal Museum	(see 2)
4 Old School	B2

🛏 Sleeping
5 Dijaški Dom Nikolaj Pirnat	C1

6 Gostilna Pri Škafarju	B2
Hotel Kendov Dvorec	(see 1)

✗ Eating
7 Gostilna Kos	D1
Gostilna Pri Škafarju	(see 6)
Gostišče Barbara Restaurant	(see 1)

🛍 Shopping
8 Studio Koder	B2

of the world's quality mercury. Miners faced many health hazards, but the relatively high wages attracted workers from all over the Habsburg Empire – and because of the toxic effects of mercury, doctors and lawyers flocked as well.

The mines are no longer in operation – the price of mercury collapsed in the 1970s and in 2011 exports of mercury from the EU were banned. But an expensive legacy remains. Idrija sits on 700km of shafts that descend 15 levels. The first four have now been filled with water and more have to be loaded with hard core and concrete to stabilise the place. Otherwise, they say, the town will sink.

◉ Sights

Municipal Museum MUSEUM
(Mestni Muzej; ☑372 66 00; www.muzej-idrija
-cerkno.si; Prelovčeva ulica 9; adult/child/student €3/1.70/2.50; ◷9am-6pm) This award-winning museum is housed in the hilltop **Gewerkenegg Castle**. The collections, which deal with mercury, lace and local history (but, sadly, not *žlikrofi*) are exhibited in three wings centred around a courtyard.

Part of the **ethnographical collection** shows rooms in a typical miner's house at various times in history. Miners earned more than double the average wage in this part of Slovenia, but paid for it in short lifespans. At the bottom of the **Mercury Tower** at the start of the south wing is a plexiglas cube filled with drops of mercury and 15 halogen lights on tracks, representing the number of levels in the mercury mine here.

One large room is given over entirely to the **bobbin lace** (*klekljana čipka*) woven here in broad rings with distinctive patterns. Check out the tablecloth that measures 3m by 1.8m. It was designed for Madame Tito and took 5000 hours to make.

An exhibition on the 2nd floor of the south wing traces Idrija history in the 20th century. Take a look at the enormous, bright-red hammer and sickle in the last room; it once adorned the entrance to the mercury mine.

Anthony Mine Shaft   MINE
(Antonijev Rov; ☑031 810 194, 377 11 42; www.rzs -idrija.si; Kosovelova ulica 3; adult/child €6/4; ☺tour 10am & 3pm Mon-Fri, 10am, 3pm & 4pm Sat & Sun) The mine, a 'living museum' in the Šelštev building south of Trg Svetega Ahacija, allows you to get a feeling for the working conditions of mercury miners in Idrija. The entrance is the Anthony Shaft, built in 1500, which led to the first mine: 1.5km long, 600m wide and 400m deep.

The tour, lasting about 1¼ hours, begins in the 'call room' of an 18th-century building where miners were selected each morning and assigned their duties. There's an excellent 20-minute video in several languages (including English) describing the history of Idrija and the mine.

Before entering the shaft, you must don green overcoats and helmets with the miners' insignia and wish each other '*Srečno!*' (Good luck!), the traditional miners' farewell.

As you follow the circular tour, you'll see samples of live mercury on the walls that the miners painstakingly scraped to a depth of about 5cm, as well as some cinnabar ore. The 18th-century **Chapel of the Holy Trinity** (Cerkev Sv Trojice) in the shaft contains statues of St Barbara, the patroness of miners, and St Ahacius, on whose feast day (22 June) rich deposits of cinnabar were discovered.

Idrija Lace-Making School   NOTABLE BUILDING
(Čipkarska Šola Idrija; ☑373 45 70; Prelovčeva ulica 2; adult/student €2.50/2; ☺10am-1pm & 3-6pm Mon-Fri by appointment) To the west of the square is the Idrija Lace-Making School in the **Stara Šola** (Old School), built in 1876. Lace-making is still a popular elective course of study in elementary schools in Idrija.

Miner's House   NOTABLE BUILDINGS
(Frančiška Cesta; adult/child €1.70/1.30; ☺9am-4pm by appointment) Laid out across the slopes encircling the valley are Idrija's distinctive miners' houses. Large wooden A-frames with cladding and dozens of windows, they usually had four storeys with living quarters for three or four families. You can visit a traditional miner's house above the centre of town accompanied by a guide from the museum.

🏃 Activities

A 3km trail called **Pot ob Rakah** follows the Idrijca River Canal from the **Kamšt** (an 18th-century waterwheel used by the mines) to **Wild Lake** (Divje Jezero), a tiny, impossibly green lake fed by a karst spring. After heavy rains, water gushes up from the tunnel like a geyser and the lake appears to be boiling. The lake was declared a natural monument in 1967.

The area of the Idrijca River near the footbridge is good for **swimming** in summer, when the water averages about 20°C.

🎊 Festivals & Events

Lace-Making Festival   CULTURAL FESTIVAL
(Festival Idrijske Čipke; www.idrija-turizem.si; ☺late Jun) The big event in Idrija is the four-day Lace-Making Festival, which includes a children's competition with up to a hundred taking part.

🛏 Sleeping

The TIC has a list of private rooms available from €21 per person.

Hotel Kendov Dvorec   HOTEL €€€
(☑372 51 00; www.kendov-dvorec.com; s €130-230, d €180-300, tr €330; ℗@) If you're looking for somewhere romantic in the area, this 'castle hotel' in Spodnja Idrija, 4km north of Idrija, has 11 rooms in a converted mansion, the oldest part of which dates from the 14th century. It's fitted with 19th-century antique furniture and enjoys stunning views along the Idrijca Valley.

Gostilna Pri Škafarju   GUESTHOUSE €
(☑041 698 093, 377 32 40; www.skafar.si; Ulica Svete Barbare 9; per person €25; ℗) In addition to food, this popular *gostilna* (inn-like restaurant) offers accommodation in four smallish but well-appointed mansard rooms. You sure can't beat the location.

STONE AGE MUSIC

Despite our preconceptions, our pre-historic forebears were a sophisticated bunch. In 1995, palaeontologists looking for Stone Age tools were directed to Divje Babe, a cave some 200m above the main road linking Cerkno with the Tolmin–Idrija highway. After careful digging they found a piece of cave-bear femur measuring 10cm long and perforated with four aligned holes (two intact, two incomplete) at either end. It looked exactly like, well, a flute.

The flute was dated using electron spin resonance techniques and is believed to be around 43,000 years old. Although dubbed the 'Neanderthal flute' in Slovenia, some debate persists about whether or not it was made by that species or by Cro-Magnons – modern humans. Either way, Slovenia can claim the oldest known musical instrument on earth. And – in case you were wondering – it still plays a tune.

Dijaški Dom Nikolaj Pirnat HOSTEL €
(☎373 40 70; Ulica IX Korpusa 17; dm €11-13; ☺Jul & Aug; P@) This student dormitory 300m northeast of Mestni trg has 44 beds available in multi-bed rooms available in summer, and a limited number of doubles, triples and quads the rest of the year.

✖ Eating

Gostilna Kos SLOVENIAN €
(☎372 20 30; Tomšičeva ulica 4; starters €3-7.50, mains €7-12; ☺7am-3pm Mon, 7am-10pm Tue-Sat) The best place in town to have *žlikrofi* (€6 to €9.50), especially the mushroom ones, is here at the 'Blackbird'.

Gostišče Barbara Restaurant SLOVENIAN €
(Kosovelova ulica 3; starters €4-7.10, mains €7.10-11.30; ☺4-10pm Mon-Fri) This restaurant serves 'slow food' and many consider it to be the best eatery in town. There's a set menu for €12.

Gostilna Pri Škafarju SLOVENIAN €
(Ulica Svete Barbare 9; mains €7.70-15.50; ☺11am-10pm Wed-Sun) Pizza (€5.20 to €7.60) baked in a beautiful wood-burning tile stove is why most people come to this friendly *gostilna*, but there are plenty of other things on the menu such as *žlikrofi* (€6.90 to €11).

🛍 Shopping

Idrija lace is among the finest in the world, and a small piece makes a great gift or souvenir. There are several shops; we like the superior **Studio Koder** (☎377 13 59; www.idrija-lace.si; Mestni trg 3; ☺10am-noon & 4-7pm Mon-Fri, 10am-noon Sat), a very stylish shop run by a helpful couple across from the town hall.

ℹ Information

Abanka (Lapajnetova ulica 47)
Nova KBM Banka (Lapajnetova ulica 43)
Post Office (Vodnikova ulica 1)
Tourist Information Centre Idrija (TIC; ☎374 39 16; www.idrija-turizem.si; Vodnikova ulica 3; ☺9am-6pm Mon-Fri, 10am-4pm Sat & Sun Jul & Aug, 9am-4pm Mon-Fri, 10am-4pm Sep-Jun) On the 1st floor behind the modern post office, with free internet access.

ℹ Getting There & Away

There are hourly buses to Cerkno (€3.10, 30 minutes) and Ljubljana (€6.30, 1½ hours), and less frequently to Bovec (€9.20, 2½ hours) and Nova Gorica (€6.30, 1½ hours).

CERKNO
☎05 / POP 1596 / ELEV 324M

A quiet town in the Cerknica River Valley, Cerkno is an important destination for ethnologists and partygoers alike when the Laufarija, the ancient Shrovetide celebration, takes place. Nearby are the remains of a secret Partisan hospital from WWII.

Glavni trg, where the buses stop, is the main square and the centre of Cerkno.

◉ Sights

Cerkno Museum MUSEUM
(Cerkljanski Muzej; ☎372 31 80; www.muzej-idrija-cerkno.si; Bevkova ulica 12; adult/child €2.10/1.30; ☺9am-3pm Mon-Fri, 10am-1pm & 2-6pm Sat & Sun) The museum is about 150m southwest of Glavni trg. Its main displays trace the development of the region from earliest times to the modern period, but it's biggest draw is the collection of Laufarija masks contained in the exhibit 'The Pust Is to Blame'.

Franja Partisan Hospital MEMORIAL
(Partizanska Bolnišnica Franja; ☎372 31 80; www.muzej-idrija-cerkno.si) This hospital, hidden in a canyon near Dolenji Novaki, about 5km northeast of Cerkno, treated wounded Partisan soldiers from Yugoslavia and other countries from late 1943 until the end of WWII. A memorial to humanity and self-sacrifice, it had more than a dozen buildings, including treatment sheds, operating theatres, X-ray rooms and bunkers for convalescence. More

than 500 wounded were treated here, and the mortality rate was only about 10%.

The complex, hidden in a ravine by the Pasica Stream, had an abundance of fresh water, which was also used to power a hydroelectric generator. Local farmers and Partisan groups provided food, which was lowered down the steep cliffs by rope; medical supplies were diverted from hospitals in occupied areas or later air-dropped by the Allies. The hospital came under attack by the Germans twice – once in April 1944 and again in March 1945 – but it was never taken.

🏃 Activities

The English-language *Cerkno Map of Local Walks,* available from the TIC and Hotel Cerkno, lists eight walks in the Cerkno Hills (Cerkljansko Hribovje), most of them pretty easy and lasting between 1½ and five hours return. Walk No 7 goes to the **Franja Partisan Hospital** (3½ hours) and back.

🎉 Festivals & Events

Laufarija   CULTURAL FESTIVAL
(www.laufarija-cerkno.si; ☺late Feb–early Mar) The biggest annual event in these parts unfolds in Glavni trg.

🛏 Sleeping & Eating

Gačnk v Logu   B&B €
(☎041 753 524, 372 40 05; www.cerkno.com; per person €27-29) This B&B and restaurant in Dolenji Novaki (house No 1), not far from the Franja Partisan Hospital, has nine rooms. The restaurant (open from 9am to 11pm) is very popular with local people, particularly for lunch at the weekend.

Hotel Cerkno   HOTEL €€
(☎374 34 00; www.hotel-cerkno.si; Sedejev trg 8; s €52-59, d €76-92; 🅿@🛜🏊) This 75-room partially renovated hotel is in a modern building just south of Glavni trg. It's a comfortable-enough place with a large indoor pool, sauna, gym and three clay tennis courts.

Okrepčevalnica Pr' Padkejc   SNACK BAR €
(☎377 57 54; Platiševa ulica 70; dishes €6.50-12; ☺7.30am-10pm Mon-Thu, 7.30am-midnight Fri, 8am-1am Sat, 7am-midnight Sun) Unduly humble, this 'snack bar' is actually more like a comfortable *gostilna* about 800m north of the centre. It's famed for its cold cuts and other prepared meets like *pršut* (air-dried ham) and horse-meat sausages.

ℹ Information

Nova KMB Banka (Glavni trg 5)

Post Office (Bevkova ulica 9) In the *občina hiša* (council house) diagonally opposite Cerkno Museum.

Tourist Information Centre Cerkno (TIC; ☎373 46 45; www.cerkno.si/turizem; Močnikova ulica 2; ☺8am-4pm Mon-Fri, 8am-1pm Sat, 8am-noon Sun) Faces Glavni trg to the east, with free internet access.

ℹ Getting There & Away

There are hourly bus departures to Idrija (€3.10, 30 minutes) on weekdays (fewer at weekends), up to four a day to Ljubljana (€7.50, 1¾ hours) and a couple to Bovec (€7.20, 1¾ hours), via Tolmin (change for Nova Gorica) and Kobarid.

THE LAUFARIJA TRADITION

Ethnologists believe that the Laufarija tradition and its distinctive masks came from Austria's South Tyrol. *Lauferei* means 'running about' in German, and that's just what the crazily masked participants do as they nab their victim.

Special (and mostly male) Laufarji societies organise the annual event. Those aged 15 and over are allowed to enter, after proving themselves as apprentices by sewing costumes. Outfits are made fresh every year, with leaves, pine branches, straw or moss stitched onto a hessian backing. They take quite a beating during the festivities.

The action takes place on the Sunday before Ash Wednesday and again on Shrove Tuesday. The main character is the Pust, with a horned mask and heavy costume of moss. He's the symbol of winter and the old year – and he *must* die.

The Pust is charged with many grievances – a bad harvest, inclement weather, lousy roads – and always found guilty. Other Laufarji characters represent crafts and trades – Baker, Thatcher, Woodsman – with the rest including the Drunk and his Wife, the Bad Boy, Sneezy and the accordion-playing Sick Man. The Old Man, wearing Slovenian-style lederhosen and a wide-brimmed hat, executes the Pust with a wooden mallet, and the body is rolled away on a caisson.

Karst Region

The Karst region (www.kras-carso.com) is a limestone plateau stretching from Nova Gorica southeast to the Croatian border, west to the Gulf of Trieste and east to the Vipava Valley. Rivers, ponds and lakes can disappear and then resurface in the Karst's porous limestone through sinkholes and funnels, often resulting in underground caverns like the caves at Škocjan. Along with caves, the Karst is rich in olives, ruby-red Teran wine, *pršut*, old stone churches and red-tiled roofs.

VIPAVA VALLEY
📍05 / ELEV UP TO 180M

This fertile, wine-rich valley stretches southeast from Nova Gorica into the Karst. Some of the red wines produced here are world class, and Vipava merlot is among the best wines of Central Europe. It's an excellent place to tour by car or bike; ask the TIC in Nova Gorica for the brochure *Wine Road of the Lower Vipava Valley*. The valley's mild climate also encourages the cultivation of stone fruits such as peaches and apricots and in autumn, when the red sumac tree changes colour, the valley can look like it is in flames.

The town of **Vipava**, in the centre of the valley, some 33km southeast of Nova Gorica, is full of stone churches below **Mt Nanos**, a karst plateau from which the Vipava River springs. You can make a side trip 2km north to Dornbeck and **Zemono Manor** (Dvorec Zemono; www.zemono.si; Prešernova ulica 6), a mansion built as a summer hunting lodge in 1680. Built in the shape of a cross, with arcaded hallways and a raised central area, the main hall is covered in wonderful frescoes. The manor's wine cellar now houses the **Gostilna Pri Lojzetu** (📞040 777 726, 368 70 07; mains €18-27, 2-/3-course menus €20/40; ⊙5-10pm Wed & Thu, noon-10pm Fri-Sun), a luxurious restaurant. Have a peek at the baroque murals near the entrance; they portray a phoenix and a subterranean cave, symbols of fire and water. In Vipava, a winery worth visiting is **Vipava 1894** (📞367 12 00; www.vipava1894.si; Vinarska cesta 5), the largest in the valley.

In **Branik**, look up for a glimpse of **Rihemberk Castle** (Cesta IX Korpusa 46), which dates back to the 13th century and has a dominant cylindrical tower in the centre, but is not open to the public. Some 6km to the southeast is the walled village of **Štanjel,** with its own castle containing a restaurant and a gallery. There are also the magnificent Ferrari Gardens to the north. Just west of the centre you'll find the **Tourist Information Centre Štanjel** (TIC; 📞041 383 986, 769 00 56; tic.stanjel@komen.si; ⊙10am-6pm Tue-Sat, 2-5pm Sun May-Oct, 10am-4pm Tue-Sat Nov-Apr), but the areas with the most to see and do are to the south.

About 10km southwest of Štanjel and 12.5km northwest of Sežana is the fabulous **Mladinski Hotel Pliskovica** (📞041 947 327, 764 02 50; www.hostelkras.com; Pliskovica 11; dm €14-16, d €36; @), a hostel with six rooms and 45 beds purpose-built into a 400-year-old Karst house. It has a kitchen, laundry room, free use of bicycles and is open year-round.

ℹ Getting There & Away

Buses departing from Nova Gorica for Postojna every two hours or so pass through Vipava (€4.10, 50 minutes, 34km). Three buses a day at 10.40am, 2.18pm and 3.30pm link Sežana (€2.70, 30 minutes, 18km) with the Mladinski Hotel Pliskovica.

Trains between Nova Gorica and Sežana serve Štanjel (€2.20, 40 minutes, 24km) and Dutovlje (€2.90, 50 minutes, 31km), 4.5km east of Pliskovica, six times a day on weekdays and twice at the weekend.

ŠKOCJAN CAVES
📍05 / ELEV 424M

The immense system of karst caves at Škocjan, a Unesco World Heritage site, easily rival those at Postojna, and for many travellers, a visit here will be a highlight of their trip to Slovenia – a page right out of Jules Verne's *A Journey to the Centre of the Earth*.

The Škocjan Caves, 5.8km long and 250m deep, were carved out by the Reka River, which enters in a gorge below the village of Škocjan and eventually flows into the Dead Lake, a sump at the end of the cave where it disappears. It surfaces again – this time as the Timavo River – at Duino in Italy, 40km to the northwest, before emptying into the Gulf of Trieste.

◉ Sights

Škocjan Caves   CAVES
(Škocjanske Jame; 📞708 21 10; www.park-skocjanske-jame.si; Škocjan 2; adult/child €15/7; ⊙10am-5pm) Visitors walk in guided groups from the ticket office for about 500m down a gravel path to the main entrance in the Globočak Valley. Through a 116m-long tunnel built in 1933, you soon reach the head of the so-called **Silent Cave**, a dry branch of

the underground canyon that stretches for 500m. The first section, called **Paradise**, is filled with beautiful stalactites, stalagmites and flowstones that look like snowdrifts; the second part (called **Calvary**) was once the riverbed. The Silent Cave ends at the **Great Hall**, 120m wide and 30m high. It is a jungle of exotic dripstones and deposits; keep an eye out for the mighty stalagmites called the Giants and the Organ.

The sound of the Reka River heralds your entry into the **Murmuring Cave** (Šumeča Jama), with walls 100m high. To get over the Reka and into **Müller Hall**, you must cross **Cerkevnik Bridge**, some 45m high and surely the highlight of the trip. Only experienced speleologists are allowed to explore the 5km of caves and halls that extend to the northwest of the bridge.

Schmidl Hall, the final section, emerges into the Velika Dolina (Big Valley). From here you walk past **Tominč Cave**, where finds from a prehistoric settlement have been unearthed, and over a walkway near the **Natural Bridge**. The tour ends at a funicular lift that takes you back to the entrance.

The Škocjan Caves are home to an incredible amount of flora and fauna: 250 varieties of plants and 15 different types of bats; your guide will point out mounds of bat guano. The temperature in the caves is constant at 12°C so bring along a light jacket or sweater. Good walking shoes, for the sometimes slippery paths, are recommended.

If you have time before your tour, follow the path leading north and down some steps from the reception area for 200m to the lookout (signposted 'Razgledišče/ Belvedere'). Extending before you is a superb vista of the Velika Dolina and the gorge where the Reka starts its subterranean journey.

Vilenica Cave
CAVE

(Jama Vilenica; ☑051 648 711, 734 42 59; www .vilenica.com; adult/child €5/3.35; ☺10am, 3pm & 5pm Sun May-Sep, 3pm Sun Oct-Apr) Vilenica Cave is 2km northwest of Lokev, halfway between Divača and Lipica. It was the first karst cave to open to the public in the early 19th century and still welcomes guests every Sunday year-round.

Divača Cave
CAVE

(Divaška Jama; ☑041 498 103, 031 522 785; www .divaska-jama.info; adult/child €5/3.35; ☺3pm Sun May-Oct) Divača Cave, about 3km northeast

on the road to Divača, is only 672m long but has excellent dripstones and rock formations.

🛏 Sleeping & Eating

TOP **Pr' Vncki Tamara**
CHOICE GUESTHOUSE €

(☑040 697 827, 763 30 73; pr.vnck.tamarai@gmail .com; Matavun 10; per person €23-26) This welcoming spot in Matavun is just steps south of the entrance to the caves and as close as you are going to get. It has four traditionally styled rooms, with a total of 10 beds, in a charming old farmhouse. We love the old kitchen with the open fire.

Gostilna Malovec
GUESTHOUSE €

(☑763 12 25; Kraška 30a; s/d €32/48) The Malovec, in Divača, has a half-dozen basic, but comfortable, renovated rooms in a building beside its butcher's (!) and popular restaurant (mains €5 to €15, open 8am to 10pm daily), which serves Slovenian favourites (including first-rate *gibanica* – a rich dessert) to an appreciative crowd.

Orient Express
ITALIAN €

(☑763 30 10; pizza €4.60-14; ☺11am-11pm Sun-Fri, 11am-2am Sat) For something a bit more, well, 21st century, try this large and lively pizzeria and pub in Divača with great salads and a large back terrace.

ℹ Information

Banka Koper (Kolodvorska ulica 2/a) In Divača, just west of the petrol station.

Post Office (Kraška cesta 77; ☺8-9.30am, 10am-3.30pm, 4-6pm Mon-Fri, 8am-noon Sat) In Divača, opposite the petrol station.

ℹ Getting There & Around

Buses from Ljubljana to Koper and the coast stop at Divača (€7.90, 1½ hours, half-hourly). Other destinations include Postojna (€3.60, 30 minutes) and Murska Sobota (€23.20, six hours) via Maribor and Celje. For Croatia, there are daily buses to Poreč and Rovinj (€14.40, four hours) from June to September. The bus stop is next to the train station.

Divača is on the rail line to Ljubljana (€7.30, 1½ hours, hourly) , with up to five trains a day to Koper (€4.05, 50 minutes) via Hrpelje-Kozina.

The Škocjan Caves are about 5km by road southeast of the Divača train station – the route is signed. A courtesy van normally meets incoming Ljubljana trains several times a day, but wasn't running when we most recently visited.

LIPICA
☑05 / POP 100 / ELEV 403M

The impact of Lipica, some 9km southwest of Divača and 2km from the Italian border, has been far greater than its tiny size would

DANCING HORSES OF LIPICA

Lipizzaners are the finest riding horses in the world. Intelligent, sociable, robust and graceful, they are much sought after for *haute école* dressage.

Breeding is paramount. Just four equine families with 16 ancestors can be traced back to the early 18th century, and their pedigrees read like medieval royalty. When you walk around the stables at Lipica you'll see charts on each horse stall with complicated names and dates tracing their lineage.

Lipizzaners foal between January and May, and the foals remain in the herd for about three years. They are then separated for four years of training.

Lipizzaners are born grey, bay or even chestnut. The celebrated 'imperial white' comes about when their hair loses its pigment between five and 10 years old. Their skin remains grey, however, so when they are ridden hard enough to sweat, they become mottled.

A mature Lipizzaner measures about 15 hands (approximately 153cm). They have long backs, short, thick necks, silky manes and expressive eyes. Like most horses they are somewhat near-sighted and they will nuzzle you out of curiosity if you approach them while they graze.

suggest. This tiny village lives for and on its snow-white Lipizzaner horses, which were first bred here for the Spanish Riding School in Vienna in the late 16th century.

History

In 1580 Austrian Archduke Charles founded a stud farm here for the imperial court in Vienna. Andalusian horses from Spain were coupled with the local Karst breed that the Romans had once used to pull chariots – and the Lipizzaner was born. But they weren't quite the sparkling white horses we know today. Those didn't come about for another 200 years when white Arabian horses got into the act.

The breed has subsequently become scattered – moved to Hungary and Austria after WWI, to the Sudetenland in Bohemia by the Germans during WWII, and then shipped off to Italy (along with the studbooks) by the American army in 1945. Only 11 horses returned when operations resumed at Lipica in 1947.

Today some 400 Lipizzaners remain at the original stud farm while others are bred in various locations around the world, including Piber in Austria, which breeds the horses for the Spanish Riding School. Everyone claims theirs is the genuine article – patriotic Slovenia even has a pair of Lipizzaners on the reverse side of its €0.20 coin.

◉ Sights

Lipica Stud Farm   STUD FARM
(☑739 15 80; www.lipica.org; Lipica 5; tour adult/child €11/5.50; training/classical performance €13/18; ⊘training & classical performance Tue, Fri & Sun Apr-Oct) The 311-hectare stud farm can be visited on a **guided tour**. The tours begin opposite the information and ticket office; a visit covers the stables and the riding halls, giving you an idea of what it's like to learn dressage and control a very large animal.

A highlight is the daily afternoon **exhibition performance** of these elegant horses as they go through their complicated paces pirouetting and dancing to Viennese waltzes with riders *en costume*. There's a lower-key training performance in the mornings.

If you miss the performances, try to be around when the horses are moved from the stables to pasture (usually between 9am and 10am) and again in the afternoon (around 5.30pm to 6pm).

🏃 Activities

You can get on a Lipizzaner by signing up for a **riding course** of three/six 30-minute lessons (from €135/210) for beginners, novices and advanced riders. Three-day trail rides (€399) are also available, as are short horse-drawn carriage jaunts (30/60 minutes €20/40).

🛏 Sleeping & Eating

Hotel Maestoso   HOTEL €€€
(☑739 15 80; s/d €80/120; ⓟ🛜🏊) This 59-room hotel is managed by the Lipica Stud Farm. It has most of the usual amenities, including a restaurant, swimming pool, a sauna and nearby tennis courts. Rates depend on the season and are heavily discounted for stays of a week or more if you are taking a riding course.

Letni Vrt CAFE €

(☎739 15 80; dishes €5-15.50; ⊙11am-7pm Apr-Oct) The Summer Garden is an open-air cafe with a terrace serving simple meals and Balkan grills. It is open in the warmer months only.

❶ Getting There & Around

Most people visit Lipica as a day trip from Sežana, 4km to the north, or Divača, 13km to the northeast, both of which are on the Ljubljana–Koper rail line. There is no public transport from the train stations in Sežana and Divača to Lipica; a taxi from either will cost between €10 and €20.

Bicycles are available for hire from the fitness centre at the Hotel Klub for €5/10/14 per hour/three hours/day.

The Coast

Slovenia has just 47km of coastline on the Adriatic Sea. Three seaside towns – Koper, Izola and glorious Piran – are full of impor-tant Venetian Gothic architecture and art, and have clean beaches, boats for rent and rollicking clubs. It's overbuilt, and jammed from May to September, so if you want soli-tude, head for the hinterland to the south or east where 'Slovenian Istria' still goes about its daily life.

Many of the hotels, camping grounds, tourist offices and restaurants here close or severely curtail their opening times during the November to March/April off-season.

KOPER
🖉05 / POP 24,996

Coastal Slovenia's largest town, Koper (Capodistria in Italian) at first glance appears to be a workaday port city that scarcely gives tourism a second thought. Yet its central core is delightfully medieval and far less overrun than its ritzy cousin Piran. Koper is the centre of the Italian ethnic community of Slovenia and the street signs are in two languages.

> **WORTH A TRIP**
>
> ### HRASTOVLJE
>
> The Romanesque church in this tiny Karst village is the Istrian equivalent of St John the Baptist's Church in Bohinj. OK, so it's not on a lake. But it is small, surrounded by medieval walls with corner towers and covered inside with extraordinary 15th-century frescoes. This is the reason to make the trip here – as difficult as it can be.
>
> The **Church of the Holy Trinity** (Cerkev Sv Trojica; 🖉031 432 231; adult/student & child €2/1; ⊙8am-noon & 1-5pm) was built between the 12th and 14th centuries in the southern Romanesque style, with fortifications added in 1581 in advance of the Otto-mans. Its sombre exterior is disarming in the extreme.
>
> The interior of the church is completely festooned with **narrative frescoes** painted by John of Kastav around 1490. The paintings helped the illiterate understand the Old Testament stories, the Passion of Christ and the lives of the saints. Spare the 20 min-utes it takes to listen to the taped commentary (in four languages, including English) that will guide you around the little church.
>
> Facing you as you enter the church is the 17th-century altar, the central apse with scenes from the Crucifixion on the ceiling, and portraits of the Trinity and the Apostles. On the arch, Mary is crowned Queen of Heaven. To the right are episodes from the seven days of Creation, with Adam and Eve, and Cain and Abel on the right.
>
> On the ceilings of the north and south aisles are scenes from daily life as well as the liturgical year and its seasonal duties. Christ's Passion is depicted at the top of the southernmost wall, including His descent into Hell, where devils attack him with blazing cannons.
>
> Below the scenes of the Passion is what attracts most people to this little church: the famous **Dance of Death** or Danse Macabre, a fresco that shows 11 skeletons leading the same number of people forward to a freshly dug grave. A twelfth holds open a coffin. The doomed line-up includes peasants, kings, cardinals, and even a money lender (who attempts to bribe his skeletal escort with a purse): all are equal in the eyes of God.
>
> Hrastovlje is 24km southwest of Divača off the main highway to the coast; Koper is 18km to the northwest. Without a car or bicycle the only sure way of making it to Hras-tovlje is by the daily early-morning trains from Divača (€2.90, 35 minutes) or Koper (€1.75, 20 minutes); the church is about 1km to the northwest of the station.

PRIMORSKA & NOTRANJSKA THE COAST

Koper

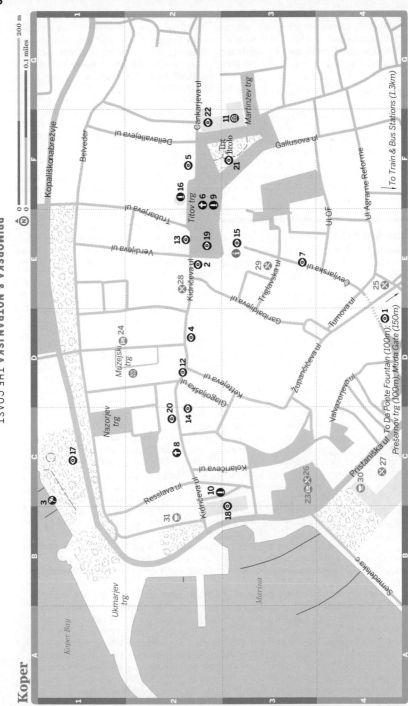

Koper Bay

Ukmarjev trg

Marina

Semedelska c

200 m
0.1 miles

To Train & Bus Stations (1.3km)

To Da Ponte Fountain (100m);
To Preševov trg (100m), Muda Gate (150m)

Koper

PRIMORSKA & NOTRANJSKA THE COAST

History

Koper has been known by many names during its long history – as Aegida to ancient Greeks, Capris to the Romans and Justinopolis to the Byzantines. In the 13th century it became Caput Histriae – Capital of Istria – from which its Italian name Capodistria is derived. Its golden age was during the 15th and 16th centuries under the Venetian Republic, when the town monopolised the salt trade. But when Trieste, 20km to the northeast, was proclaimed a free port in the early 18th century, Koper lost much of its importance.

Between the World Wars Koper was controlled by the Italians. After WWII the disputed Adriatic coast area – the so-called Free Territory of Trieste – was divided into two zones, with Koper going to Yugoslavia and Trieste to Italy.

◉ Sights & Activities

The easiest way to see Koper's Old Town is to walk from the marina on Ukmarjev trg east along Kidričeva ulica to Titov trg and then south down Čevljarska ulica, taking various detours along the way.

Kidričeva Ulica   STREET

One of the most colourful streets in Koper, Kidričeva ulica starts at Carpacciov trg, where the **Column of St Justina** (Steber Sv Justine; Kidričeva ulica) commemorates Koper's contribution – a galley – to the Battle of Lepanto in which Turkey was defeated by the European powers in 1571. Just north is a large Roman covered basin that now serves as a fountain. At the western end of the square is the large arched **Taverna** (Carpacciov trg, Kidričeva ulica), a one-time salt warehouse dating from the 15th century.

On the north side of Kidričeva ulica there are several churches from the 16th century, including the **Church of St Nicholas** (Cerkev Sv Nikolaja; Kidričeva ulica 30), some restored **Venetian houses** and the 18th-century baroque **Totto Palace** (Palača Totto; Kidričeva ulica 22/a), with winged lion relief. Opposite the palace are some wonderful medieval **town houses** (Kidričeva ulica 33), with protruding upper storeys painted in a checked red, yellow and green pattern.

The 17th-century **Belgramoni-Tacco Palace** (Palača Belgramoni-Tacco; Kidričeva ulica 19) houses the **Koper Regional Museum** (☑663 35 70; www.pmk-kp.si; Kidričeva ulica 19; adult/child €2/1.50; ◷9am-7pm Tue-Fri, to 1pm Sat & Sun), which has displays of old maps and photos, Italianate sculptures and paintings dating from the 16th to 18th centuries, copies of medieval frescoes and a garden with Roman remains. The museum's **ethnological collection** (Etnološka Zbirka; ☑663 35 86; Gramšijev trg 4; ◷8am-1pm & 6-9pm Tue-Sun Jul & Aug, 8am-3pm Tue-Fri, 9am-1pm Sat & Sun Sep-Jun) is in a 17th-century building in the eastern section of the Old Town.

Titov Trg   SQUARE

In almost the exact centre of old Koper, Titov trg is a beautiful square full of interesting buildings; mercifully, like much of the Old Town's core, it is closed to traffic. On the north side is the arcaded Venetian Gothic **Loggia** (Loža; Titov trg 1) built in 1463; attached is the **Loggia Gallery** (Loža Galerija; ☑627 41 71; www.obalne-galerije.si; adult/child €2/1; ☉10am-1pm & 6-9pm Tue-Sat, 10am-noon Sun Jul & Aug, 10am-1pm & 4-7pm Tue-Sat, 10am-noon Sun Sep-Jun).

To the south, directly opposite, is the gleaming white **Praetorian Palace** (Titov trg 3; admission free; ☉9am-8pm), a mixture of Venetian Gothic and Renaissance styles dating from the 15th century and the very symbol of Koper. It contains the town hall, with a reconstructed old pharmacy and the TIC on the ground floor, and exhibits on the history of Koper and a ceremonial hall for weddings on the 1st floor. The facade of the palace, once the residence of Koper's mayor who was appointed by the doge in Venice, is festooned with medallions, reliefs and coats of arms.

On the square's western side, the **Armoury** (Armeria; Titov trg 4) was a munitions dump four centuries ago. Opposite is the **Cathedral of the Assumption** (Stolnica Marijinega Vnebovzetja; ☉7am-9pm) and its 36m-tall belfry, now called the **City Tower** (adult/child €2/1.50; ☉9am-2pm & 4-9pm), with 204 climbable stairs. The cathedral, partly Romanesque and Gothic but mostly dating from the mid-18th century, has a white classical interior with a feeling of space and light that belies the sombre exterior.

Behind the cathedral to the north is a circular Romanesque **Rotunda of John the Baptist** (Rotunda Janeza Krstnika; Titov trg), a baptistery dating from the second half of the 12th century with a ceiling fresco.

Trg Brolo   SQUARE

Linked to Titov trg to the east, Trg Brolo is a wide and leafy square of fine old buildings, including the late-18th-century baroque **Brutti Palace** (Palača Brutti; Trg Brolo 1), now the central library, to the north. On the eastern side is the 17th-century **Vissich-Nardi Palace** (Palača Vissich-Nardi; Trg Brolo 3) containing government offices and the **Fontico** (Fontiko; Trg Brolo 4), a granary (1416) where the town's wheat was once stored, with wonderful medallions and reliefs. Just south is the disused **Church of St James** (Cerkew Sv Jakoba) dating to the 14th century.

Čevljarska Ulica   STREET

Historic Čevljarska ulica (Cobbler Street), a narrow commercial street for pedestrians, runs south from Titov trg. As you walk under the arch of the Praetorian Palace, have a look to the right. The little hole in the wall with the Italian inscription *'Denontie'* was where anonymous denunciations of officials and others could be made.

At the end of Čevljarska ulica is the **Almerigogna Palace** (Palača Almerigogna; Gortanov trg 13), a painted 15th-century Venetian Gothic palace (now a pub) and arguably the most beautiful building in Koper.

Prešernov Trg   SQUARE

The 17th-century Italian family that erected the fountain in Prešernov trg, 200m to the southeast, was named Da Ponte; thus it is shaped like a bridge (*ponte* in Italian). At the southern end is the **Muda Gate** (Vrata Muda). Erected in 1516, it's the last of a dozen such entrances to remain standing. On the south side of the archway you'll see the city symbol: the face of a youth in a sunburst.

FREE Beach   BEACH

(Kopališko nabrežje 1; ☉8am-7pm May-Sep) Koper's tiny beach, on the northwest edge of the Old Town, has a small bathhouse with toilets and showers, grassy areas for lying in the sun, and a bar and cafe.

✯ Festivals & Events

Primorska Summer Festival   CULTURAL FESTIVAL

(www.portoroz.si; ☉late Jul–mid Aug) Concerts, theatre and dance events take place during the Primorska Summer in Koper and Ankaran as well as Izola, Pian and Portorož over four weeks in late July and the first half of August.

🛏 Sleeping

Kompas Travel Agency can arrange private rooms (single €21 to €32), most of which are in the new town beyond the train station.

Hotel Koper   HOTEL €€€

(☑610 05 00; www.terme-catez.si; Pristaniška ulica 3; s €76-92, d €120-150; ✲@☀) This pleasant, 65-room property on the edge of the historic Old Town is the only really central hotel in town. Rates include entry to the **Aquapark** (☑610 03 00; www.terme-catez.si/en/obala/aqua park; day pass adult/child Mon-Fri €13/9, Sat & Sun €17/12; ☉8am-8pm). Choose a harbour-facing room such as No 303.

Museum Hostel

APARTMENTS €

(☑041 504 466, 626 18 70; bozic.doris@siol.
net; Muzejski trg 6; per person €20-25; ☎) This
place is more a series of apartments with
kitchens and bathrooms than a hostel.
Reception is at Museum Bife, a cafe-bar
on Muzejski trg; the rooms are scattered
nearby. Always double-confirm bookings.

Camp Adria Ankaran

CAMPGROUND €

(☑663 73 50; www.adria-ankaran.si; Jadranska
cesta 25; adult €11-13.50, child €5-6.50; ☉late Apr–
mid-Oct; P@☀) This enormous camping
ground in Ankaran, 10km to the north and
the closest site to Koper, has 400 sites for
1200 guests over 7 hectares. There is any
number of sporting facilities, and the camping charge includes use of the two seawater
swimming pools (nonguests pay €15/10 per
adult/child).

Hotel Vodišek

HOTEL €€

(☑639 24 68; www.hotel-vodisek.com; Kolodvorska cesta 2; s €48-60, d €72-90; P✻@☎) This
small hotel with 35 reasonably priced rooms
is in a shopping centre halfway between the
Old Town and the train and bus stations.
Guests get to use the hotel's bicycles for free.

✖ Eating

Istrska Klet Slavček

SLOVENIAN €

(☑627 67 29; Županičeva ulica 39; dishes €3-12;
☉7am-10pm Mon-Fri) The Istrian Cellar, situated below the 18th-century Carli Palace, is
one of the most colourful places for a meal
in Koper's Old Town. Filling set lunches go
for less than €8, and there's local Malvazija
and Teran wines from the barrel.

Pizzeria Atrij

PIZZA €

(☑627 22 55; Čevljarska ulica 8, enter from Triglavska ulica 2; pizza €3-6.50; ☉9am-9pm Mon-Fri,
10am-10pm Sat) This deservedly popular
pizzeria (down a very narrow alleyway) has a
small covered garden out back and a salad bar.

La Storia

ITALIAN €€

(☑626 20 18; www.lastoria.si; Pristaniška ulica 3;
mains €8.50-25) This Italian-style trattoria
with sky-view ceiling frescoes focuses on salads, pasta and fish dishes and has outside
seating in the warmer months.

Okrepčevalnica Bife Burek

SLOVENIAN €

(Kidričeva ulica 8; snacks & light bites €1.80-2.50;
☉7am-10pm) This place serves good-value
burek (pastry stuffed with cheese, meat or
even apple), which you can carry to Titov trg
and eat there.

Market

MARKET €

(Pristaniška ulica; ☉7am-2pm Mon-Sat) There's
an outdoor market in the open courtyard of
the shopping centre.

🍺 Drinking

The Slovenian Istria (Slovenska Istra)
wine-producing area is known for its white
Malvazija and chardonnay and red Refošk.

Forum

CAFE, BAR

(Pristaniška ulica 2; ☉7am-11pm; ☎) This cafe-
bar, at the northern side of the market
facing a little park and the sea, is a popular
local hangout.

Kavarna Kapitanija

CAFE

(☑040 799 000; Ukmarjev trg 8; ☉7am-midnight
Mon-Fri, 8am-midnight Sat & Sun) This attractive
space, with its wide, open terrace and comfortable wicker lounges, would be even more
inviting if the tacky souvenir kiosks and
parked cars across the grassy strip didn't
block the harbour view.

ℹ Information

INTERNET ACCESS Internet access at the TIC
is free for the first hour, then €1 per hour. Koper
is a free wireless zone; get tickets from **Pina
Internet Cafe** (☑627 80 72; Kidričeva ulica 43;
per hr adult/student €4.20/1.20; ☉noon-10pm
Mon-Fri, from 4pm Sat & Sun).

MONEY Banka Koper (Kidričeva ulica 14)
Nova Ljubljanska Banka (Pristaniška ulica 45;
☉8.30am-1pm & 3.30-5pm Mon-Fri)

POST Post Office (Muzejski trg 3)

**TOURIST INFORMATION Tourist Information
Centre Koper** (TIC; ☑664 64 03; www.koper.si;
Praetorian Palace, Titov trg 3; ☉9am-8pm Jul &
Aug, 9am-5pm Sep-Jun) On the ground floor of the
Praetorian Palace.

TRAVEL AGENCIES Kompas (☑663 05 82;
Pristaniška ulica 17; ☉8am-7.30pm Mon-Fri,
8am-1pm Sat)

ℹ Getting There & Away

BUS Buses go to Izola (€1.80), Strunjan, Piran
(€3.10, 30 minutes) and Portorož every half-hour
on weekdays. There's a handy bus stop at the corner of Piranška ulica. Some five daily buses daily
make the run to Ljubljana (€11.10, 1¾ to 2½ hours).

Buses to Trieste (€3, one hour) run along the
coast via Ankaran and from Muggia Monday
to Saturday. Destinations in Croatia include
Rijeka (€11.20, two hours) and Rovinj (€12, three
hours) via Poreč (€10, two hours).

TRAIN Half a dozen trains a day link Koper to
Ljubljana (€10.70, 2½ hours, 153km) via Postojna
and Divača. To get to Buzet and Pula in Croatia
from Koper, you must change at Hrpelje-Kozina

(€2.90 to €5.90, 30 minutes, 37km, five daily) for any of three trains a day.

❶ Getting Around

BUS Local buses 1 and 2 link the bus and train stations to the eastern edge of Cankarjeva ulica in the Old Town, with a stop near Muda Gate.

PARKING Parking in much of the Old Town is severely restricted – or banned altogether – between 6am and 3pm. Leave your vehicle in the pay car parks along Pristaniška ulica.

TAXI To order a taxi in Koper ring ☎051 671 271, ☎040 222 272 or ☎041 737 083.

IZOLA

☎05 / POP 11,223

Izola, a somewhat scruffy fishing port 7km southwest of Koper, is the poor relation among the historical towns on the Slovenian coast, especially compared with genteel Piran. As a result, it is often bypassed by foreign visitors. But Izola does have a certain Venetian charm, a few narrow old streets, and some nice waterfront bars and restaurants where you might linger.

Almost everything of a practical nature is located around central Trg Republike. Buses stop in front of the Bela Skale travel agency at Cankarjev drevored 2 on the square's southeastern edge. To reach the Old Town and its main square, Veliki trg, walk north along Sončno nabrežje, the waterfront promenade.

History

The Romans built a port called Haliaetum at Simon's Bay (Simonov Zaliv) southwest of the Old Town, and you can still see parts of the original landing when the tide is very low. While under the control of Venice in the Middle Ages, Izola – at that time an island (*isola* is Italian for 'island') – flourished, particularly in the trading of such commodities as olives, fish and wine. But a devastating plague in the 16th century and the ascendancy of Trieste as the premier port in the northern Adriatic destroyed the town's economic base. During the period of the Illyrian Provinces in the early 19th century, the French pulled down the town walls and used them to fill the channel separating the island from the mainland. Today, Izola is the country's foremost fishing port.

◉ Sights

Izola isn't overly endowed with important historical sights; Napoléon and his lot took care of that. Those that did survive include the renovated salmon-coloured 16th-century

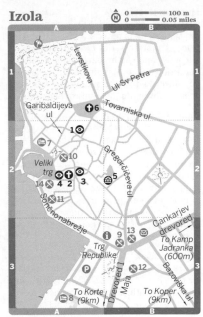

Izola

N 0 — 100 m
0 — 0.05 miles

Izola

◉ Sights
1 Besenghi degli Ughi Palace A2
2 Church of St Mary of Haliaetum A2
3 Manzioli House A2
4 Municipal Palace A2
5 Parenzana Museum B2
6 Parish Church of St Maurus A1

◉ Sleeping
7 Hotel Marina A2
8 Riviera Hostel A3

◉ Eating
9 Gostilna Istria B3
10 Gostilna Ribič A2
11 Gostilna Sidro A2
12 Gušt B3
13 Mercator B3
14 Mercator A2

Parish Church of St Maurus (Župnijska Cerkev Sv Mavra; Garibaldijeva ulica) and its detached bell tower on the hill above the town, the **Municipal Palace** (Mestna Palača; Veliki trg), which now houses offices of the local council and, behind it, the lovingly restored **Church of St Mary of Haliaetum** (Cerkev Sv Marije Alietske; Veliki trg).

Manzioli House   NOTABLE BUILDING
(Manziolijev trg) Opposite the Mary of Haliae-tum church is the renovated Venetian Gothic Manzioli House, which was built in 1470 and was the residence of an Istrian chronicler in the 16th century. Today it houses the bureau looking after the interests of the *communità italiana* (Italian community) in Izola.

Besenghi degli Ughi Palace   NOTABLE BUILDING
(cnr Gregorčičeva ulica & Ulica Giordano Bruno) Izola's most beautiful building is the rococo Besenghi degli Ughi Palace below the Parish Church of St Maurus. Built between 1775 and 1781, the mansion has windows and balconies adorned with stuccos and wonderful wrought-iron grilles painted light blue. It is now a music school.

Parenzana Museum   MUSEUM
(☑640 10 50; 1st fl, Ulica Alme Vivode 3; adult/child €2.10/1.50; ☺9am-3pm Mon-Fri) Izola Museum can now make its superlative claim to fame with the Parenzana, a branch of the Pomorski Museum Sergej Mašera in Piran. It has train models – the largest such collection in the world – and ship models too.

🏃 Activities
There are pebble **beaches** to the north and southeast of the Old Town, but the best one is at **Simon's Bay** about 1.5km to the southwest. It has a grassy area for sunbathing.

The *Prince of Venice* is a 39.6m high-speed catamaran that makes day trips between Izola and Venice. A number of boats offer sailing excursions lasting 2½ to three hours from the main port just off Veliki trg. They include **Delfin II** (☑041 675 781, 641 45 38; adult/child €12/8; ☺10am Tue & Thu) and **Meduza** (☑041 675 781; adult/child €12/8; ☺10am & 5pm daily). You can rent sailing boats (from €60 per day) and speedboats (from €95 a day) from **Adriarent** (☑041 300 050, 663 24 60; ☺8-10am & 6-8pm) at the marina a short distance from the Hotel Delfin.

🛏 Sleeping
The Laguna Travel Agency has private rooms (singles €18 to €26, doubles €26 to €36) and apartments (for two €38 to €56, for four €51 to €82).

TOP CHOICE Old Schoolhouse Korte   HOSTEL €
(Stara Šola Korte; ☑031 375 889, 642 11 14; www.hostel-starasola.si; Korte 74; dm €17-19, s & d €20-24; P✹@) This renovated old school in the idyllic hilltop Slovenian Istrian village of Korte, 8km south of Izola, opened its doors

as a hostel in late 2006 and has become a winner among the *cognoscenti*. It's got 17 modern rooms with between two and four beds and a couple of apartments with two bedrooms and a living room. You could do your own cooking but the food at the nearby **Gostilna Korte** (☑041 607 863, 642 02 00; Korte 44), celebrated far and wide, is hard to resist.

Hotel Marina   HOTEL €€€
(☑660 41 00; www.hotelmarina.si; Veliki trg 11; s €59-126, d €79-156; P✹@☎) The 52-room Hotel Marina, faced with chocolate-coloured glazed brick, couldn't be any more central: it's right on the main square and fronting the harbour. Rates depend on the season and whether your room faces the water and has a balcony. There's a very attractive spa and wellness centre here.

Riviera Hostel   HOSTEL €€
(☑662 17 45; www.s-sgtsi.kp.edus.si; Prekomorskih Brigad ulica 7; s/d/tr €28/52/69; ☺Jul & Aug) This 174-bed hostel in the Srednja Gostinska in Turistična Šola (Middle School of Catering and Tourism) overlooks the marina and welcomes foreign guests in summer.

Kamp Belvedere Izola   CAMPGROUND €
(☑660 51 00; www.belvedere.si; Dobrava ulica 1/a; adult €9-12, child €6-9; ☺Apr-Aug; P✹) This 2.5-hectare campground on a bluff 3km west of Izola has wonderful views of the town and the Adriatic, a large swimming pool and sites for 500 campers.

Kamp Jadranka   CAMPGROUND €
(☑640 23 00; freetimedoo@siol.net; Polje cesta 8; per person €10; ☺year-round; P) This small site on the waterfront 1km east of the Old Town is just off the busy coastal road and fills up quickly in summer.

Hotel Delfin   HOTEL €€
(☑660 70 00; www.hotel-delfin.si; Tomažičeva ulica 10; s €45-58, d €76-102; P✹☎) By Izola's marina complex, the Delfin is a bit out of the centre but still near the water. It's a pleasant-enough place on a hill about 1km southwest of Trg Republike and has its own swimming pool. But it's huge, with 219 rooms, and caters largely to tour groups.

🍴 Eating
Izola is the best place on the coast to enjoy a seafood meal. Be careful when you order, however, and ask the exact price of the fish. As seafood is sold by decagram (usually abbreviated as *dag* on menus), you might end up eating (and paying) a lot more than

you expected. And be sure to have a glass of low-alcohol Malvazija, the pale-yellow local white that is light and reasonably dry.

Gostilna Sidro
SLOVENIAN €€

(☑641 47 11; Sončno nabrežje 24; starters €4.50-9.50, mains €8-22; ⊗8am-10pm) One of Izola's best restaurants, Sidro is an old standby on the waterfront, strong on seafood and Slovenian favourites, just up from the TIC.

Gostilna Ribič
SLOVENIAN €€

(☑641 83 13; Veliki trg 3; starters €6-15, mains €9-25; ⊗noon-1am) Another of the town's top restaurants, this eatery on the inner harbour is much loved by locals and specialises in turbot fish. Set lunch is €8.

Gostilna Istria
SLOVENIAN €

(☑031 384 243, 641 80 50; Trg Republike 1; dishes €7.50-16, pizza €5.20-6.50; ⊗7am-midnight Mon-Sat, 8am-midnight Sun) An old favourite, this relatively simple eatery on the main road into the Old Town has good-value set lunches (€7) and stays open throughout the day. Try the gnocchi with *pršut* in a red Refošk wine sauce.

Gušt
ITALIAN €

(☑041 650 333; Drevored 1 Maja 3; pizza & pasta €4.60-10.90; ⊗10am-midnight) This *picerija* and *špageterija* opposite the Banka Koper has decent pizza, pasta and salads.

Mercator
SUPERMARKET €

(Trg Republike 4; ⊗7am-8pm Mon-Fri, 7am-5pm Sat, 8am-noon Sun) There's a supermarket opposite the bus stops and a more central Mercator (Veliki trg; ⊗7am-8pm Mon-Sat, 8am-noon Sun) near the inner port.

☆ Entertainment

Ambasada Gavioli
CLUB

(☑641 82 12, 041 353 722; www.myspace.com/ambasadagavioli; Industrijska cesta 10; ⊗11pm-6am Fri & Sat) In the industrial area southeast of the port, the Ambasada Gavioli holds the crown as queen of Slovenia's electronic clubs, showcasing a procession of international and local DJs.

❶ Information

Banka Koper (Drevored 1 Maja 5)

Laguna Travel Agency (☑041 412 611, 641 86 30; Istrska vrata 7; ⊗9am-1pm & 4-7pm Mon-Sat, 9am-noon Sun)

Nova Ljubljanska Banka (Trg Republike 3) Opposite the bus stops.

Post Office (Cankarjev drevored 1)

Tourist Information Centre Izola (TIC; ☑640 10 50; www.izola.eu; Sončno nabrežje 4; ⊗9am-9pm Jun-Sep, 9am-5pm Mon-Fri, 10am-5pm Sat Oct-May)

❶ Getting There & Away

Frequent buses between Koper (€1.80, 15 minutes, 8km), Piran (€1.80, 20 minutes, 10km) and Portorož go via Izola. Other destinations from Izola (via Koper) include Ljubljana (€11.40, 2½ hours, 130km, five a day, with up to nine in July and August) and Nova Gorica (€9.60, 2½ hours, 103km, one or two a day).

International routes include six buses a day (five on Saturday) to Trieste (€3.10, 40 minutes, 23km) in Italy; and Umag (€5.20, 1¼ hours, 45km, five daily), Pula (€8.70, 2½ hours, 94km, 7.45am and 2.12pm daily) and Rovinj (€11.10, three hours, 4.07pm June to September) in Croatia.

❶ Getting Around

MINIBUS From June to August a minibus does a continuous loop from the Belvedere Izola holiday village west of the Old Town to Simon's Bay, Izola Marina, Trg Republike, the Jadranka campground and back.

TAXI Order a taxi in Izola on ☑040 602 602 or ☑041 706 777.

BICYCLE You can rent bicycles from **Ritosa** (☑640 12 41, 641 53 37; Kajuhova ulica 28; per day €15; ⊗8am-7pm Mon-Fri, 8am-noon Sat). You can also rent them from the Hotel Marina (p121) for €5/8/10 per two/five/12 hours.

PIRAN
☑05 / POP 4192 / ELEV 23M

Picturesque Piran (Pirano in Italian), sitting at the tip of a narrow peninsula, is everyone's favourite town on the Slovenian coast. Its Old Town – one of the best-preserved historical towns anywhere on the Adriatic – is a gem of Venetian Gothic architecture, but it can be a mob scene at the height of summer. In April or October, though, it's hard not to fall in love with the winding Venetian Gothic alleyways and tempting seafood restaurants.

History

It's thought that Piran's name comes from the Greek word for the fires *(pyr)* lit at the very tip of the peninsula, to guide ships to the port at Aegida (now Koper). The Romans established a settlement here called Piranum, and were followed by the early Slavs, Byzantines, Franks and the Patriarchs of Aquileia.

Five centuries of Venetian rule began in the late 13th century, and Piran was a major salt supplier for its rulers. The Venetian period was the town's most fruitful, and many of its beautiful buildings and its fortifications were erected then.

◉ Sights

Sergej Mašera Maritime Museum   MUSEUM
(☎671 00 40; www.pommuz-pi.si; Cankarjevo nabrežje 3; adult/student & senior/child €3.50/2.50/2.10; ⊙9am-noon & 5-9pm Tue-Sun summer, 9am-5pm Tue-Sun winter) Located in the lovely 19th-century **Gabrielli Palace** on the waterfront, this museum's focus is the sea, sailing and salt-making – three things that have been crucial to Piran's development over the centuries. There are some old photographs showing salt workers going about their duties in coolie-like straw hats, as well as a wind-powered salt pump and little wooden weights in the form of circles and diamonds that were used to weigh salt during the Venetian Republic. The 2000-year-old Roman amphorae beneath the glass floor here are impressive.

The antique model ships upstairs are very fine; other rooms are filled with old figureheads and weapons, including some lethal-looking blunderbusses. The folk paintings are offerings placed by sailors on the altar of the pilgrimage church at Strunjan for protection against shipwreck.

Museum of Underwater Activities   MUSEUM
(Muzej Podvodnih Dejavnosti; ☎041 685 379; www.muzejpodvodnihdejavnosti.si; Župančičeva ulica 24; adult/student & child €3/2; ⊙9.30am-10pm Jun-Sep) The Museum of Underwater Activities makes much of Piran's close association with the sea and diving.

Tartinijev Trg   SQUARE
The **statue** of the nattily dressed gentleman in Tartinijev trg, an oval-shaped, marble-paved square that was the inner harbour until it was filled in 1894, is that of local boy-cum-composer and violinist Giuseppe Tartini (1692–1770). To the east is the 1818 **Church of St Peter** (Cerkev Sv Petra; Tartinijev trg), which contains the wonderful 14th-century **Piran Crucifix**. Across from the church is **Tartini House** (Tartinijeva Hiša; ☎663 35 70; Kajuhova ulica 12; adult/child €1.50/1; ⊙9am-noon & 6-9pm Tue-Sun Jul & Aug, 11am-noon & 5-6pm Tue-Sun Sep-Jun), the composer's birthplace and a popular concert venue.

The **Court House** (Sodnijska Palača; Tartinijev trg 1), which has two 17th-century doors, and the porticoed 19th-century **Municipal Hall** (Občinska Palača; Tartinijev trg 2) housing the TIC are to the south. The two 15th-century **flagpoles** at the entrance to the square bear Latin inscriptions praising Piran, the town's coat of arms, a relief of St George (the patron) to the left and one of St Mark with the lion symbol on the right.

Venetian House   HISTORIC BUILDING
(Benečanka; Tartinijev trg 4) One of Piran's most eye-catching structures is the red 15th-century Gothic Venetian House, with its tracery windows and balcony, in the northeast of the square. There is a story attached to the stone relief between the two windows of a lion with a banner in its mouth and the Latin inscription *Lassa pur dir* above it. A wealthy merchant from Venice fell in love with a beautiful local girl, but she soon became the butt of local gossips. To shut them up (and keep his lover happy), the merchant built her this little palace complete with a reminder for his loose-lipped neighbours: 'Let them talk.'

Cathedral of St George   CATHEDRAL
(Stolna Cerkev Sv Jurija; Adamičeva ulica 2) This Renaissance and baroque cathedral stands on a ridge north of Tartinijev trg above the sea. To the east runs a 200m stretch of the 15th-century **town walls** complete with loopholes. The walls once ran from the sea all the way to the harbour, and seven crenellated towers are still intact.

The church was founded in 1344 and was rebuilt in baroque style in 1637. If time weighs heavily on your hands, visit the attached **Parish Museum of St George** (☎673 34 40; admission €1; ⊙10am-1pm & 5-7pm Mon-Fri, 11am-7pm Sat & Sun), which contains church plate, paintings and a lapidary in the crypt.

The cathedral's freestanding, 47m-high **bell tower** (Zvonik; admission €2; ⊙10am-2pm & 5-8pm), built in 1609, was clearly modelled on the campanile of San Marco in Venice and its 146 stairs can be climbed for excellent views of the town and harbour. Next to it, the octagonal **baptistery** (*krstilnica*) from 1650 contains altars, paintings and a Roman sarcophagus from the 2nd century recycled as a baptismal font.

Minorite Monastery   MONASTERY
(☎673 44 17; Bolniška ulica 20) On your way up to Tartinijev trg are the Minorite Monastery with a wonderful cloister and the **Church of St Francis Assisi**, built originally in the early 14th century but enlarged and renovated over the centuries. Inside are ceiling

Piran

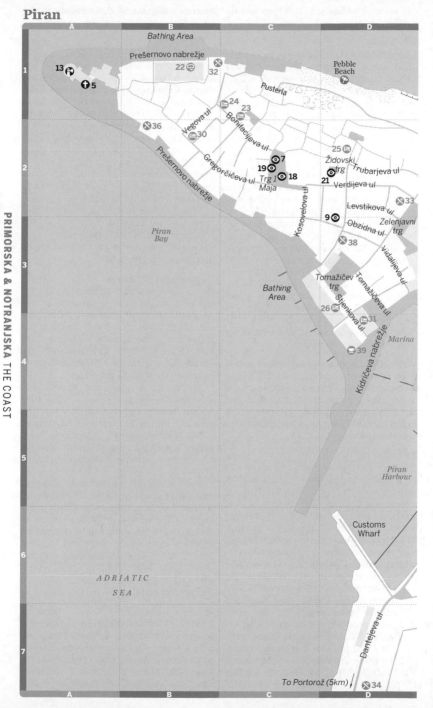

frescoes, a giant clamshell for donations and the Tartini family's burial plot.

Church of Our Lady of the Snows CHURCH
(Cerkev Marije Snežne; Bolniška ulica) Almost opposite the Minorite Monastery is the Church of Our Lady of the Snows, with a superb 15th-century arch painting of the Crucifixion.

Obzidna Ulica STREET
Behind the market north of Tartinijev trg, **medieval homes** have been built into an ancient defensive wall along Obzidna ulica, which passes under the 15th-century **Dolphin Gate** (Dolfinova Vrata; Obzidna ulica), with a plaque showing three of our smiling friends. **Židovski trg**, the centre of Jewish life in Piran in the Middle Ages, is about 100m to the northwest of here.

Trg 1 Maja & Punta SQUARE
(1st May Sq) This square may sound like a socialist parade ground, but it was the centre of Piran until the Middle Ages, when it was called Stari trg (Old Sq). The surrounding streets are a maze of pastel-coloured overhanging houses, vaulted passages and arcaded courtyards. The square is surrounded by interesting baroque buildings, including the former town **pharmacy** (Lekarna; Trg 1 Maja 2) on the north side (now the Fontana restaurant). In the centre of the square is a large baroque **cistern** *(vodnjak)* that was built in the late 18th century to store fresh water; rainwater from the surrounding roofs flowed into it through the fish borne by the stone *putti* cherubs in two corners.

Punta, the historical 'point' of Piran, still has a **lighthouse**, but today's is small and modern. Attached to it out back, however, the round, serrated tower of the **Church of St Clement** (Prešernovo), originally built in the 13th century but altered 500 years later, evokes the ancient beacon from which Piran got its name. It has a lovely (though decrepit) stuccoed ceiling.

🏃 Activities
BOATING & CRUISES
The Maona Tourist Agency (p128) and several other agencies in Piran and Portorož can book you on any number of cruises – from a loop that takes in the towns along the coast to day-long excursions to Brioni National Park and Rovinj in Croatia, or Venice and Trieste in Italy.

Piran

⊙ Sights

1	Baptistery	E2
2	Bell Tower	E2
3	Cathedral of St George	E2
4	Church of Our Lady of the Snows	F3
5	Church of St Clement	A1
6	Church of St Peter	E3
7	Cistern	C2
8	Court House	E3
9	Dolphin Gate	D3
10	Minorite Monastery	F3
11	Municipal Hall	E3
12	Museum of Underwater Activities	E6
	Parish Museum of St George	(see 3)
13	Punta Lighthouse	A1
14	Sergej Mašera Maritime Museum	E4
15	Statue of Giuseppe Tartini	E3
16	Tartini House	E3
17	Tartinijev Trg	E3
18	Trg 1 Maja	C2
19	Trg 1 Maja & Punta	C2
20	Venetian House	E2
21	Židovski trg	D2

⊙ Activities, Courses & Tours

22	Noriksub	B1

⊙ Sleeping

23	Alibi B11	C1
24	Alibi B14	C1
25	Alibi T60	D2
26	Hotel Piran	D3
27	Hotel Tartini	E4
28	Max Piran	F2
29	Miracolo di Mare	E6
30	Val Hostel	B2
31	Vila Piranesi	D4

⊗ Eating

32	Flora	B1
33	Market	D2
34	Pri Mari	D7
35	Restaurant Neptune	E5
36	Riva Piran	B2
37	Skarabej	E6
38	Stara Gostilna	D3

⊙ Drinking

39	Cafe Teater	D4
40	Caffe Tartini	E2
41	Žižola Kantina	E3

⊙ Shopping

	Piranske Soline	(see 20)

DIVING

Noriksub
DIVING
(☑041 590 746, 673 22 18; www.skupinanorik sub.si; Prešernovo nabrežje 24; shore/boat dive €30/40; ☉10am-noon & 2-6pm Tue-Sun summer, 10am-4pm Sat & Sun winter) Organises shore and boat-guided dives, runs PADI open-water courses (beginners €240) and hires equipment.

SWIMMING

Piran has several 'beaches' – rocky areas along Prešernovo nabrežje – where you might get your feet wet. They are a little better on the north side near Punta, but as long as you've come this far keep walking eastward on the paved path for just under 1km to Fiesa, which has a small but clean beach.

⋆⋆ Festivals & Events

Tartini Festival
MUSIC FESTIVAL
(www.tartinifestival.org; ☉late Aug–mid-Sep) The Tartini Festival of classical music takes place in venues throughout Piran, including the vaulted cloister of the Minorite Monastery, from late August to mid-September.

🛏 Sleeping

Private rooms (single €16 to €30, double €23 to €42) and apartments (for two €38 to €50, for four €60 to €84) are available through the Maona Tourist Agency (p128) and Turist Biro (p128).

Max Piran
TOP CHOICE
B&B €€
(☑041 692 928, 673 34 36; www.maxpiran.com; Ulica IX Korpusa 26; d €60-70; ✴@☎) Piran's most romantic accommodation has just six rooms, each bearing a woman's name rather than a number, in a delightful coral-coloured 18th-century town house. It's just down from the Cathedral of St George.

Val Hostel
HOSTEL €
(☑673 25 55; www.hostel-val.com; Gregorčičeva ulica 38a; per person €22-27; @☎) This excellent central hostel on the corner of Vegova ulica has 22 rooms (including a few singles) with shared shower, kitchen and washing machine. It's a deserved favourite with backpackers, and prices include breakfast.

Miracolo di Mare
B&B €€

(☑051 445 511, 921 76 60; www.miracolodimare.si; Tomšičeva ulica 23; s €50-55, d €60-70; @ ☎) A lovely B&B on the coast, the Wonder of the Sea has a dozen charming (though small-ish) rooms, some of which (like No 3 and the breakfast room) give on to the loveliest raised back garden in Piran. Floors and stairs are wooden (and original) and beds metal framed.

Hotel Tartini
HOTEL €€€

(☑671 10 00; www.hotel-tartini-piran.com; Tartinijev trg 15; s €62-88, d €84-124; P ✳ ☎) This attractive, 45-room property faces Tartinijev trg and manages to catch a few sea views from the upper floors. The staff are especially friendly and helpful. If you've got the dosh, splash out on suite No 40/a; we're suckers for eyrie-like round rooms with million-dollar views.

Hotel Piran
HOTEL €€€

(☑676 21 00; www.hoteli-piran.si; Stjenkova ulica 1; s €72-102, d €84-144, ste €152-198; P ✳ @) Hotel Piran has 80 renovated rooms and 10 suites, and is right on the water. Its latest addition is **Vila Piranesi** (☑676 21 00; www.hoteli-piran.si; Kidričevo nabrežje 4; apt for 2 €76-116, with harbour view €98-142), with 17 super-modern and large self-contained apartments above the aquarium.

Kamp Fiesa
CAMPGROUND €

(☑674 62 30; autocamp.fiesa@siol.net; adult/ child €12/4; ☺May-Sep; P) The closest campground to Piran is at Fiesa, 4km by road but less than 1km if you follow the coastal path (obalna pešpot) east from the Cathedral of St George. It's tiny and becomes very crowded in summer, but it's in a quiet valley by two small protected ponds and right by the beach.

Alibi B11
HOSTEL €

(☑031 363 666; www.alibi.si; Bonifacijeva ulica 11; per person €20-22; ☺Apr-Dec; @ ☎) The flagship of the Alibi stable is not its nicest property but reception for all three hostels is here. It has five doubles and three rooms with three to four beds over four floors in an ancient (and rather frayed) town house on a narrow street. Diagonally opposite is **Alibi B14** (Bonifacijeva ulica 14; per person €20-22), a more upbeat four-floor party place with seven rooms, each with two to four beds and bath. There's also a washing machine. More subdued is **Alibi T60** (Trubarjeva ulica 60; per person €25; ✳) to the east

with fully equipped doubles (TV, fridge and bathroom) on each of five floors served by a vintage wooden staircase.

🍴 Eating

One of Piran's attractions is its plethora of fish restaurants, especially along Prešernovo nabrežje. Most cater to the tourist trade and are rather overpriced.

TOP CHOICE Pri Mari
MEDITERRANEAN, SLOVENIAN €€

(☑041 616 488, 673 47 35; Dantejeva ulica 17; mains €8.50-16; ☺noon-11pm Tue-Sun summer, noon-10pm Tue-Sat, noon-6pm Sun winter) This stylish and welcoming restaurant run by an Italian-Slovenian couple serves the most inventive Mediterranean and Slovenian dishes in town. Be sure to book ahead.

Riva Piran
SEAFOOD €€

(☑673 22 25; Gregorčičeva ulica 46; mains €8-28; ☺11.30am-midnight) Classy Riva Piran is the best waterfront seafood restaurant and is worth patronising. It has the strip's best decor and sea views.

Restaurant Neptune
SEAFOOD €

(☑673 41 11; Župančičeva 7; mains €6-12; ☺noon-4pm, 6pm-midnight) It's no bad thing to be more popular with locals than tourists, and this family-run place hits all the buttons – a friendly welcome, big seafood platters (as well as meat dishes and salads), and a good-value daily two-course set lunch (you might want to wrap up with mama's dessert though).

Stara Gostilna
BISTRO €

(☑040 640 240, 673 31 65; Savudrijska ulica 2; starters €5-9, mains €7.50-17; ☺9am-11pm) This delightful bistro in the Old Town serves both meat and fish dishes and has some of the best service in town.

Skarabej
ITALIAN €

(☑040 522 271; Župančičeva ulica 21; starters €5-9, mains €6-13.50; ☺9am-11pm) This very welcoming and attractive place – note the fantastic mosaic of the namesake 'scarab' on the back wall – serves excellent pizza and pasta as well as more ambitious dishes.

Flora
PIZZA €

(☑673 12 58; Prešernovo nabrežje 26; pizza €4-8; ☺10am-1am summer, 10am-10pm winter) The terrace of this simple pizzeria east of the Punta lighthouse has uninterrupted views of the Adriatic.

Market
MARKET €

(Zelenjavni trg; ☉7am-2pm Mon-Sat) There's an outdoor market in the small square behind the Municipal Hall.

🍷 Drinking & Entertainment

Caffe Tartini
CAFE

(☑051 694 100; Tartinijev trg 3; ☉7am-3am) This cafe, in a classical building opposite the Venetian House, is a wonderful place for a drink and people-watching on the square.

Žižola Kantina
BAR

(Tartinijev trg 10; ☉9am-2am) This simple, nautically themed bar – named after the jujube (Chinese date) that grows prolifically along the Adriatic – has tables right on the main square and serves 15 different flavours of *žganje* (Slovenian fruit brandy).

Cafe Teater
CAFE, BAR

(☑051 694 100; Stjenkova ulica 1; ☉8am-3am) With a waterfront terrace and faux antique furnishings, this is where anyone who's anyone in Piran can be found.

🛍 Shopping

Piranske Soline
GIFTS

(☑673 31 10; Tartinijev trg 4; ☉9am-1pm & 5-9pm Jul & Aug, 10am-5pm Sep-Jun) In the Venetian House, this place sells bath sea salts and other products from Sečovlje.

ℹ Information

INTERNET ACCESS Caffe Neptun (☑041 724 237; www.caffeneptun.com; Dantejeva ulica 4; per 20min €1; ☉7am-1am; 🖥) Modern cafe next to the bus station with free wi-fi.

MONEY Banka Koper (Tartinijev trg 12)

POST OFFICE Post Office (Cankarjevo nabrežje 5)

TOURIST INFORMATION Tourist Information Centre Piran (TIC; ☑673 44 40, 673 02 20; www.portoroz.si; Tartinijev trg 2; ☉9am-8pm summer, 9am-5pm winter) In the impressive Municipal Hall.

TRAVEL AGENCIES Maona Tourist Agency (☑673 45 20; www.maona.si; Cankarjevo nabrežje 7; ☉9am-8pm Mon-Sat, 10am-1pm & 5-7pm Sun) Helpful travel agency organising everything from private rooms to activities and cruises.

Turist Biro (☑673 25 09; www.turistbiro-ag.si; Tomažičeva ulica 3; ☉9am-1pm & 4-7pm Mon-Sat, 10am-1pm Sun) Opposite Hotel Piran.

ℹ Getting There & Around

BUS From the bus station, buses run every 20 to 30 minutes to Koper (€2.70, 30 minutes) via Izola. Other destinations include Ljubljana (€12, three hours) via Divača and Postojna, and Nova Gorica (€10.30, 2¾ hours). Sečovlje (€1.80, 15 minutes) is served by up to eight buses a day and Strunjan (€1, 10 minutes) by between four and seven. There's also a long-distance bus to Murska Sobota (€28, 7½ hours) via Maribor and Celje.

Some five buses go to Trieste (€10, 1¾ hours, Monday to Saturday) in Italy. One bus a day heads south for Croatian Istria from June to September, stopping at the coastal towns of Umag, Poreč and Rovinj (€10.30, 2¾ hours).

MINIBUS From Tartinijev trg, minibuses (€1 on board, €0.40 in advance from newsagencies, €6 for 20 rides) shuttle to Portorož and the campgrounds at Lucija every half-hour from 5.40am to 11pm year-round.

CATAMARAN There are catamarans from the harbour to Trieste (adult/child €8.30/4.75, 30 minutes, Thursday to Tuesday) in Italy, departing around 7pm.

PARKING Traffic is understandably restricted here – park your car at the Fornače car park and walk or take a free shuttle bus into the centre.

PORTOROŽ
☑05 / POP 2947

Every country with a coast has got to have a honky-tonk beach resort and Portorož (Portorose in Italian) is Slovenia's. But the 'Port of Roses' is making a big effort to scrub itself up. Portorož's sandy beaches are relatively clean, and there are pleasant spas and wellness centres where you can take the waters or cover yourself in curative mud. The vast array of accommodation options makes Portorož a useful fallback if everything's full in Piran.

Portorož's main development looks on to the bay from Obala, but there are satellite resorts and hotel complexes to the northwest at Bernardin and south near the Portorož Marina at Lucija. Buses stop opposite the main beach on Postajališka pot.

◉ Sights

Forma Viva
GARDEN

(☑671 20 80; www.obalne-galerije.si) Perched atop the Seča Peninsula, Forma Viva is an outdoor sculpture garden with some 130 works of art carved in stone. The real reason for coming is the fantastic view of Portorož and Piran Bays. The salt pans at Sečovlje (p130) are a short walk to the south.

🏃 Activities
BOATING & CRUISES

A couple of boats make the run between the main pier in Portorož and Izola in summer on trips lasting four hours. They include the **Meja** (☑041 664 132; adult/child €10/7; ☉9.15am Tue & Fri) and the **Svetko** (☑041 623 191; adult/

child €15/10.50; ⊗2.30pm daily). The **Solinarka** (⍜031 653 682; www.solinarka.com; adult/child €12.50/6.25; ⊗varies) tour boat sails from Portorož to Piran and Strunjan and back.

Kompas (⍜617 80 00; Obala 41; ⊗9am-7pm Mon-Fri, 9am-1pm & 5-8pm Sat & Sun Jul & Aug, 9am-7pm Mon-Fri, 9am-1pm Sat & Sun Sep-Jun) and Atlas Express (p131) can book day trips to Venice aboard the *Prince of Venice* and with Venezia Lines.

Adrenaline Check
SAILING

(⍜040 476 123; www.adrenaline-check/sea; Lucija; ⊗Apr-Nov) This activity campsite in Lucija can take you sailing (€60, fours hours, minimum group four), sea kayaking (€30, two to three hours) and even organises scuba diving.

Watersport Centre Portorož
WATER SPORTS

(Center Vodnih Športov Portorož; ⍜041 617 999) You can hire kayaks, pedal boats, wakeboards and various other seagoing paraphernalia at the Watersport Centre Portorož on the grassy beach area west of the Grand Metropol Hotel.

Spinaker
SAILING

(⍜041 281 133; www.spinaker.si; Obala 7; 2/3/4hr €79/113/139; ⊗10am-6pm May-Sep) Spinaker can take five of you sailing along the coast to Piran and beyond from the main pier in Portorož. It also rents Zero 22 sailing boats (from €149 a day) and runs day-long sailing courses.

PANORAMIC FLIGHTS & SKYDIVING

Sightseeing by ultra-light plane is available at the **Portorož airport** (⍜041 719 260, 617 51 40; info@portoroz-airport.si; Sečovlje 19; ⊗8am-8pm Apr-Sep, 3-5pm Oct-Mar). Eight-minute flights for three people over Portorož and Piran cost €55, 15-minute flights over the whole coast cost €80. Skydiving costs from €170 for a tandem jump.

SPAS

Terme & Wellness Centre Portorož
SPA

(⍜692 80 60; www.lifeclass.net; Obala 43; swimming pool 2/4hr pass Mon-Fri €8/12, Sat & Sun €10/15; ⊗8am-9pm Jun-Sep, 7am-7pm Oct-May, swimming pool 1-8pm Mon-Wed & Fri-Sun, 2-8pm Thu) Terme & Wellness Centre Portorož, a large spa connected with the Grand Hotel Portorož that you can also enter from K Stari cesti, is famous for thalassotherapy (treatment using seawater and by-products like mud from the salt flats). The spa offers various types of warm seawater and brine baths (€36 to €44), Sečovlje mud baths (€23), massage (€30 for 20 minutes) and

a host of other therapies and beauty treatments. There is also a palatial indoor swimming pool.

SWIMMING

The lifeguard-patrolled **beaches** (⊗8am-8pm Apr-Sep), including the main one, which accommodates 6000 fried and bronzed bodies, have water slides and outside showers. Beach chairs (€4.10) and umbrellas (€4.10) are available for rent. Beaches are off-limits between 11pm and 6am and camping is strictly forbidden.

The large outdoor **swimming pool** (adult/child €4/3; ⊗9am-7pm May-Sep), south of the Grand Hotel Metropol, is open in the warmer months.

🛏 Sleeping

Portorož counts upwards of two dozen hotels, and very few of them fit into the budget category. Rates at hotels in Portorož can be very high during the summer months; many close for the winter in October or November and do not reopen until April or even May.

The Maona Tourist Agency has **private rooms** (s €18-21, d €26-40, tr €36-52) and **apartments** (apt for 2 €40-50, apt for 4 €65-75), with prices varying widely and depending on both the category and the season. Some of the cheapest rooms are up on the hillside, quite a walk from the beach. Getting a room for fewer than three nights (for which you must pay a supplement of 30% to 50%) or a single any time can be difficult, and in winter many owners don't rent at all.

🖥 Kaki Plac
CAMPGROUND €

(⍜040 476 123; www.adrenaline-check/sea; Lucija; own tent €13, pitched tent €15, lean-to €20; ⊗Apr-Nov; ℗) A small new eco-friendly campsite tucked into the woods just outside Lucija on the outskirts of Portorož. Tents come with mattresses and linen, some sit snugly under thatched Istrian lean-tos, so you can sleep like a traditional shepherd (sort of). There's a wood-hewn communal eating area, free bike hire, and staff can arrange activities from horse riding and sea kayaking to sailing.

Kempinski Palace Portorož
HOTEL €€€

(⍜692 70 00; www.kempinski.com/portoroz; Obala 45; s/d from €135/185; ℗✳@⩗⛱) This 19th-century grande dame is a 181-room, five-star masterpiece in the Kempinski stable, with a new and an old wing. The Palace has been renovated to within an inch of its life – you'll

WORTH A TRIP

SALT OF THE SEA

Salt-making is a centuries-old business along the Slovenian coast. The best place to get a briny taste is at the old salt pans of the **Sečovlje Salina Nature Park** (Krajinski Park Sečoveljske Soline; ☑672 13 30; www.kpss.soline.si; adult/child/family €5/3/10; ☺9am-8pm Jun-Sep, 9am-5pm Oct-May), on the Croatian border. The 721-hectare area, criss-crossed with dykes, channels, pools and canals, was once a hive of activity and was one of the biggest money-spinners on the coast in the Middle Ages. Nowadays its wealth is in birdlife – some 270 species have been recorded here.

In the centre of the reserve is the wonderful **Saltworks Museum** (Muzej Solinarstva; ☑671 00 40; www.pommuz-pi.si; adult/child/senior & student incl Maritime Museum in Piran €3.50/2.10/2.50; ☺9am-8pm Jun-Aug, 9am-6pm Apr, May, Sep & Oct). The exhibits relate to all aspects of salt-making and the lives of salt workers and their families. Some 2000 tonnes of salt are still made here every year in the traditional way.

The seawater canals lead into shallow ponds, and were then dammed with small wooden paddles. Wind-powered pumps removed some of the water, and the rest evaporated in the sun and the wind as the salt crystallised from the remaining brine. The salt was collected, drained, washed and, if necessary, ground and iodised.

Salt-harvesting was dry-weather, seasonal work, lasting from 24 April (St George's Day) to 24 August (St Bartholomew's Day). During that time most of the workers lived in houses lining the canals, often paying their rent in salt. In September the workers returned to their villages to tend their crops and vines. Because they lived both on the land and 'at sea', Slovenian salt-workers were said to 'sit on two chairs'.

The main entrance to the park is at Lera just south of Seča and off the main road from Portorož. The other entrance, which is at Fontanigge and leads to the museum, is not connected by land with the Lera section. It is right on the border with Croatia; to reach it you must pass through Slovenian immigration and customs first, so don't forget your passport. Just before you cross the Croatian checkpoint, take a sharp turn to the east and continue along a sealed road for just under 3km. The two museum buildings stand out along one of the canals.

look high and low for any original features (stone staircase, chandeliers in the Crystal Hall). Keep your eyes instead on things like the rose-themed rooms, the faux-baroque trendy furniture, the enormous front balconies with stunning sea views, and the interconnecting indoor and outdoor pools.

Hotel Riviera & Hotel Slovenija   HOTEL €€€
(☑692 00 00; www.lifeclass.net; Obala 33; s €142-185, d €184-250; P✳@☒) These four-star sister properties are joined at the hip and are good choices if you want to stay someplace central. The Riviera has 160 rooms, three fabulous swimming pools and an excellent wellness centre. The Slovenija is somewhat bigger with 183 rooms.

Camp Lucija   CAMPGROUND €
(☑690 60 00; www.metropol-hotels.com; Seča 204; adult €10-16, child €6-7; ☺early Apr–early Oct; P✳@☒) This 5.5-hectare campground is below the Seča Peninsula and south of the marina about 2km from the bus station. It

offers all sorts of sporting facilities and can (and often does) accommodate 1000 guests.

✗ Eating

Staro Sidro   SEAFOOD €
(☑674 50 74; Obala 55; mains €8-19; ☺noon-11pm Tue-Sun) A tried-and-true favourite in Portorož, the Old Anchor is next to the lovely (and landmark) Vila San Marco. It specialises in seafood and has both a garden and a lovely terrace overlooking Obala and Portorož Bay.

San Lorenzo   MEDITERRANEAN €€
(☑690 10 00; Obala 77; mains €9.50-25; ☺noon-11pm) Located on the ground floor of the Grand Hotel Metropol, this Italian/Mediterranean restaurant is very fancy-schmancy and among the finest Portorož has to offer. The wine selection is superb.

Pizzeria Figarola   PIZZA €
(☑031 313 415; Obala 18; pizza €5.50-8.90) There must be a dozen pizzerias along Obala but Figarola, with a huge terrace just up from the main pier, is the place of choice.

Papa Chico
MEXICAN €

(☎677 93 10; Obala 26; mains €5.90-16.30; ◷10am-2am) This pleasant cantina serves 'Mexican fun food' (go figure), including hysterical fajitas.

Stara Oljka
BALKAN €€

(☎674 85 55; Obala 20; starters €5-9.60, mains €8.60-24; ◷10am-midnight) The Old Olive Tree specialises in grills (Balkan, steaks etc), which you can watch being prepared in the open kitchen. There's a large and very enticing sea-facing terrace.

▼ Drinking & Entertainment

Kavarna Cacao
BAR

(☎674 10 35; Obala 14; ◷8am-1am Sun-Thu, to 3am Fri & Sat) This place wins the award as the most stylish cafe-bar on the coast and boasts a fabulous waterfront terrace.

Kanela Bar
BAR

(☎674 61 81; Obala 14; ◷11am-3am) Secreted between the beach and the Cacao, the 'Cinnamon' is a workhorse of a rock-'n'-roll bar up late (and early) with frequent live concerts.

Portorož Auditorium
AUDITORIUM

(Portorož Avditorij; ☎676 67 00; www.avditorij.si; Senčna pot 12; ◷box office 8am-2pm Mon-Fri) The main cultural venue in Portorož has two main indoor theatres and a huge open-air amphitheatre, and is 200m behind where the buses stop. Some of the events of the Primorska Summer Festival (p118) in July and part of August take place here.

❶ Information

Atlas Express (☎674 67 72; atlas.portoroz@ siol.net; Obala 55; ◷9am-4pm Mon-Fri, 10am-1pm Sat) Local rep for American Express.

Banka Koper (Obala 33) Beside the Hotel Slovenija.

Maona Tourist Agency (☎674 03 63; Obala 14/b; ◷9am-8pm Mon-Sat, 10am-1pm & 5-8pm Sun Jul & Aug, 9am-7pm Mon-Fri, 10am-7pm Sat, 10am-1pm Sun Sep-Jun) Branch of the excellent travel agency in Piran.

Post Office (K Stari cesti 1)

Tourist Information Centre Portorož (TIC; ☎674 22 20; www.portoroz.si; Obala 16; ◷9am-8pm summer, 9am-5pm winter)

❶ Getting There & Away

BOAT There is a daily service from Portorož to Trieste from May to September.

BUS Buses leave Portorož for Koper (€2.30, 25 minutes) and Izola (€1.80, 15 minutes) about every 30 minutes throughout the year. Other destinations include Ljubljana (€13.20, 3¼ hours), Nova Gorica (€10.30, three hours) and a long distance bus to Murska Sobota (€30, eight hours) via Maribor and Celje. There are plentiful local buses to Sečovlje (€2, 25 minutes) and Strunjan (€1.30, 15 minutes) throughout the day.

Minibuses make the loop from the Lucija campgrounds through central Portorož to Piran throughout the year.

NOTRANJSKA

Postojna

☎05 / POP 8870 / ELEV 555M

The karst cave at Postojna, one of the largest in the world, is among Slovenia's most popular attractions and its stalagmite and stalactite formations are unequalled anywhere. It's a busy destination and claims that it is visited by a third of all tourists coming to Slovenia – the amazing thing is how the large crowds at the entrance seem to get swallowed whole by the size of the caves.

The cave has been known – and visited – by residents of the area for centuries; you need only look at the graffiti dating back seven centuries in the Gallery of Old Signatures by the entrance. But people in the Middle Ages knew only the entrances; the inner parts were not explored until April 1818, just days before Habsburg Emperor Franz I (r 1792–1835) came to visit. The following year the Cave Commission accepted its first organised tour group, including Archduke Ferdinand, and Postojna's future as a tourist destination was sealed. Since then more than 32 million people have visited the cave.

The town of Postojna lies in the Pivka Valley at the foot of Sovič Hill (677m). The Pivka River and the entrance to the cave are about 1.5km northwest of Titov trg in the town centre.

Postojna's bus station is at Titova cesta 36, about 250m southwest of Titov trg. The train station is on Kolodvorska cesta about 600m southeast of the square.

◉ Sights & Activities

Postojna Cave
CAVE

(Postojnska Jama; ☎700 01 00; www.postojnska-jama.eu; Jamska cesta 30; adult/child/student €22.90/13.70/18.30; ◷tours hourly 9am-6pm summer, 3 or 4 times from 10am daily winter) The Postojna Cave system, a series of caverns, halls and passages some 20.6km long and two million years old, was hollowed out by

THE HUMAN FISH

Postojna is home to the blind, eel-like *Proteus anguinus*, or olm. A kind of salamander, it lives hidden in the pitch black for up to a century and can go a decade without food.

The chronicler Valvasor wrote about the fear and astonishment of local people when an immature 'dragon' was found in a karst spring near Vrhnika in the late 17th century. Several other reports about this four-legged 'human fish' (*človeška ribica* as it's called in Slovene) were made before a Viennese doctor described it for science in 1786, naming it for the protector of Poseidon's sea creatures in Greek mythology and the Latin word for 'snake'.

Proteus reaches 30cm long, with a swimming tail and stubby legs. Although blind, with atrophied eyes, *Proteus* has an excellent sense of smell and is sensitive to weak electric fields in the water, which it uses to move around in the dark, locate prey and communicate. It breathes through frilly, bright-red gills. The skin entirely lacks pigmentation but looks pink in the light due to blood circulation.

Cool pitch-black caves slow down life cycles – the gills are a strange evolutionary throwback to the animals' tadpole stage, which it never fully outgrows, instead reaching sexual maturity at 14 years. No wonder it's always been a creature of local fascination.

the Pivka River, which enters a subterranean tunnel near the cave's entrance. The river continues its deep passage underground, carving out several series of caves, and emerges again as the Unica River.

Visitors get to see about 5.7km of the cave on 1½-hour tours; some 4km of this is covered by an electric train, which takes you to the **Big Mountain** (Velika Gora) cavern, on a trip that's like entering the secret lair of a James Bond villain. From here a guide escorts you through halls, galleries and caverns in one of four languages (audio guides are available in a further dozen languages).

These are dry galleries, decorated with a vast array of white stalactites shaped like needles, enormous icicles and even fragile spaghetti. The stalagmites take familiar shapes – pears, cauliflower and sand castles – but there are also bizarre columns, pillars and translucent curtains that look like rashers of bacon.

From the Velika Gora cavern you continue across the **Russian Bridge**, built by prisoners of war in 1916, through the 500m-long **Beautiful Caves** (Lepe Jame) that are filled with wonderful ribbon-shaped stalactites and stalagmites two million years old (it takes 30 years to produce 1mm of stalactite). The halls of the Beautiful Caves are the furthest point you'll reach; from here a tunnel stretches to the Black Cave (Črna Jama) and Pivka Cave.

The tour continues south through the Winter Hall (Zimska Dvorana), past the Diamond Stalagmite and the Pillar Column, which have become symbols of the cave.

You then enter the **Conference Hall** (Kongresna Dvorana), which is the largest in the cave system and can accommodate 10,000 people for musical performances. In the week between Christmas and New Year, the Live Christmas Crib (Jaslice) – the Nativity performed by miming actors – takes place in the cave. Visitors reboard the train by the Conference Hall and return to the entrance.

Postojna Cave has a constant temperature of 8°C to 10°C with a humidity of 95%, so a waterproof jacket and decent shoes are essential. Green felt capes can be hired at the entrance for around €2.50. Check the website for package deals, including combination tickets that include Proteus Vivarium and Predjama Castle.

Proteus Vivarium   MUSEUM
(www.turizem-kras.si; adult/child €8/4.80, with cave €27/16.20; ⊗9am-5.30pm May-Sep, 10.30am-3.30pm Oct-Apr) Two hundred species of fauna (including cave beetles, bats, hedgehogs and the 'human fish' found in the cave are studied at the Proteus Vivarium, which is part of a speleobiological research station located in the cave. It's open to visitors and has a video introduction to underground zoology. A 45-minute tour then leads you into a small, darkened cave to peep at some of the shy creatures you've just learned about.

Planina Cave   CAVE
(Planinska Jama; ☑041 338 696, 756 52 42; www.planina.si; adult/child €6.50/3.50; ⊗tours 5pm Mon-Fri Jun-Aug, 3pm & 5pm Sat, 11am, 3pm & 5pm Sun Apr-Sep) Planina Cave, 12km to the north-

east of Postojna Cave, near the unpredictable Lake Planina, is the largest water cave in Slovenia and a treasure trove of fauna (including *Proteus anguinus*). The cave's entrance is at the foot of a 100m rock wall. It's 6.5km long, and you are able to visit about 900m of it in an hour. There are no lights so take a torch.

Caving treks (€30 to €60) lasting three to six hours and visiting Planina and other caves in the area can be organised through the Sport Hotel.

Other Caves

For information about other caves north of Postojna, ask at the TIC at Postojna Cave or at Kompas Postojna agency in town. **Pivka Cave** (Pivka Jama) and **Black Cave** (Črna Jama; adult/child/student €7/4/6; ☉9am & 3pm Jun-Aug), the most popular caves in the area after Postojna, are about 5km to the north, with the entrance in the Pivka Jama campground. You reach the 4km-long system by descending more than 300 steps. A walkway has been cut into the wall of a canyon in Pivka Cave, with its two siphon lakes and a tunnel; a bridge leads to Black Cave. This is a dry cavern and, as the name implies, its dripstones are not white. A tour of both caves takes about two hours.

🛏 Sleeping

Kompas Postojna (☎721 14 80; www.kompas-postojna.si; Titov trg 2a; r per person €18-24; ☉8am-7pm Mon-Fri, 9am-1pm Sat summer, 8am-5pm Mon-Fri, 9am-1pm Sat winter) organises private rooms (per person from €18) in town and farmhouse stays (per person from €20) further afield in Narin (15km southwest) and Razdrto (11km west). The most central rooms are at Jamska cesta 21 and Kajuhova ulica 20.

Hotel Kras   HOTEL €€
(☎700 23 00; www.hotel-kras.si; Tržaška cesta 1; s €68-74, d €84-96, apt €100-120; ⓟ☎) This rather flash hotel has risen, phoenix-like, from the ashes of a decrepit old caravanserai in the heart of town and now boasts 27 comfortable rooms with all the mod-cons. If you've got the dosh, choose one of the apartments on the top (5th) floor, with enormous terraces.

Sport Hotel   HOTEL €€
(☎720 22 44; www.sport-hotel.si; Kolodvorska cesta 1; dm €25-35, s €55-75, d €70-80, tr €96-101; ⓟ@) A hotel of some sort or another since 1880,

the Sport offers reasonable value for money, with 32 spic-and-span and very comfortable rooms, including five rooms with nine hostel beds each. There's a kitchen with small eating area, a restaurant with set menus from €8 to €20, and laundry costs €10. It's just 300m north of the centre of Postojna.

Camping Pivka Jama   CAMPGROUND €
(☎720 39 93; www.venus-trade.si; Veliki Otok 50; adult €9.90-11.40, child €7.90-8.90, 4-bed bungalow €74-84, 4-bed bungalow with kitchen €89-99; ☉Apr-Oct; ⓟ☎) This 7-hectare site is hidden in a deep pine forest near the entrance to Pivka and Black Caves. Some of the little stone-and-wood bungalows have kitchens, and there's a swimming pool.

Hotel Jama   HOTEL €€
(☎728 24 00; www.turizem-kras.si; Jamska cesta 30; s €51-56, d €82-92, tr €113-128; ⓟ) This 150-room property 200m southeast of the entrance to Postojna Cave was under renovation when we visited, and expected to re-open in mid-2013.

🍴 Eating

Čuk   PIZZA €
(☎720 13 00; Pot k Pivki 4; starters €5-7.50, pizza & pasta €6-9.50; ☉10am-11pm Mon-Fri, 11am-midnight Sat, noon-11pm Sun) A large, excellent restaurant southwest of Titov trg just off Tržaška cesta, Čuk takes its pizza seriously but offers a wide range of Slovenian mains too.

Pizzeria Minutka   PIZZA €
(☎720 36 25; Ljubljanska cesta 14; starters €4.65-7.50, pizza €5.60-7.20, mains €7.50-13.50) A pizzeria with a terrace, Minutka is a favourite with locals and also does more ambitious main courses. It's rolling distance from the Sport Hotel.

Jamski Dvorec   INTERNATIONAL €€
(☎700 01 81; starters €6.50-10, mains €13.50-22; ☉9am-6pm) Housed in a stunning 1920s-style building next to the entrance to the Postojna Cave, the Cave Manor has fairly average international dishes but its set menus at €11 and €12 are a big attraction.

Macao   CHINESE €
(☎757 28 88; Tržaška cesta 11a; starters €1.60-3.20, mains €4-9.20) Don't expect the real McCoy at this hole-in-the-wall Chinese eatery just north of the bus station but it's there if you need a fix of rice or noodles.

PRIMORSKA & NOTRANJSKA POSTOJNA

PREDJAMA CASTLE

Predjama Castle (⏹700 01 03; www.postojnska-jama.eu; Predjama 1; adult/child/student €9/5.40/7.20; ⏲9am-7pm summer, 10am-4pm winter) is a short hop from Postojna and is one of the world's most dramatic castles. It teaches a clear lesson: if you want to build an impregnable redoubt, put it in the gaping mouth of a cavern halfway up a 123m cliff. Its four storeys were built piecemeal over the years from 1202, but most of what you see today is from the 16th century. It looks simply unconquerable.

The castle holds great features for kids of any age – a drawbridge over a raging river, holes in the ceiling of the entrance tower for pouring boiling oil on intruders, a very dank dungeon, a 16th-century chest full of treasure (unearthed in the cellar in 1991), and an eyrie-like hiding place at the top called **Erazem's Nook**, named for Erazem Lueger.

Lueger was a 15th-century robber-baron who, like Robin Hood, stole from the rich to give to the poor. During the wars between the Hungarians and the Austrians, Erazem supported the former. He holed up in Predjama Castle and continued his daring deeds with the help of a secret passage that led out from behind the rock wall. In 1484 the Austrian army beseiged the castle, but it proved impregnable. Erazem mocked his attackers, even showering them with fresh cherries to prove his comfortable situation. But the Austrians had the last laugh – finally hitting him with a cannonball as he sat on the toilet. An ignoble fate for a dashing character.

In mid-July, the castle hosts the **Erasmus Tournament**, a day of medieval duelling, jousting and archery.

The **cave** below Predjama Castle is a 6km network of galleries spread over four levels. Casual visitors can see about 900m of this; longer tours are available by prior arrangement only. **Gostilna Požar** (⏹751 52 52; Predjama 2; meals from €11; ⏲10am-10pm Thu-Tue, daily Aug) is a simple restaurant next to the ticket kiosk and in heart-stopping view of the castle.

Joint tickets can be bought for the castle and Postojna Caves.

🍷 Drinking

Two places worth heading for if the whistle is dry include the **Boem Bar** (⏹726 13 11; Ljubljanska cesta 11; ⏲7am-11pm Mon-Thu, 7am-midnight Fri & Sat, 10am-11pm Sun), a comfortable place near the Sport Hotel, and the lively **Sport Bar** (⏹700 23 00; Tržaška cesta 1; ⏲8am-11pm Sun-Thu, 8am-2am Fri & Sat) at the Hotel Kras.

ℹ Information

Banka Koper (Tržaška cesta 1)

Kompas Postojna (⏹721 14 80; www.kompas-postojna.si; Titov trg 2a; ⏲9am-1pm Sat year-round, 8am-7pm Mon-Fri Jun-Aug, 8am-6pm Mon-Fri May, Sep & Oct, 8am-5pm Mon-Fri Nov-Apr) This travel agency is the best source of information in town. It also has private rooms and changes money.

Post Office (Ulica 1 Maja 2a)

Tourist Information Centre Postojna (TIC; ⏹720 16 10; www.tdpostojna.si; Jamska cesta 28; ⏲8am-4pm Mon-Fri) In a kiosk just south of the Postojna Cave entrance.

ℹ Getting There & Away

BUS Buses from Ljubljana to the coast as well as Ajdovščina stop in Postojna (€6, one hour, 53km, hourly). Other destinations include Cerknica (€3.10, 30 minutes, 24km, six on weekdays), Koper (€6.90, 1¼ hours, 68km, four to seven daily), Nova Gorica (€6.70, 1½ hours, 63km, five to eight a day), Piran (€8.30, 1½ hours, 86km, three or four a day), and Snežnik and Stari Trg pri Ložu (€8, two hours, 88km, 2.10pm weekdays).

International bus destinations include Trieste (€5.70, 1¼ hours, 52km, 6.50am Monday to Friday and 7.40am Monday to Saturday) in northern Italy, Rijeka (€11, 1½ hours, 82km) and Split (€37.50, 9½ hours, 474km) in Croatia at 8.35pm daily, and Banja Luka (€29.90, six hours, 378km, 3.04pm Tuesday and Thursday) in Bosnia-Hercegovina.

TRAIN Postojna is on the main train line linking Ljubljana (€4.90, one hour, 67km) with Sežana and Trieste via Divača (€2.90 to €4.45, 40 minutes, 37km), and is an easy day trip from the capital. As many as 20 trains a day make the run from Ljubljana to Postojna and back. You can also reach Koper (€5.90 to €10.30, 1½ hours, 86km) on one of up to seven trains a day.

❶ Getting Around

BUS Buses bound for Postojna Cave and Pred-jama Castle leave Postojna's train station at 10.30am, noon, 2.30pm and 4.10pm. The bus is free but those with train tickets take precedent. The last bus from the castle is at 4.40pm and from the cave at 5.05pm.

TAXI If you need a taxi in Postojna, call ☑031 777 974 or ☑041 752 751.

BICYCLE The Sport Hotel (p133) rents mountain bikes (€9/15 per half-/full day).

Cerknica & Around

☑01 / POP 3890 / ELEV 559M

Cerknica is the largest town on a lake that isn't always a lake – one of Slovenia's most unusual natural phenomena. It's an excellent springboard for the gorge at Rakov Škocjan and Notranjska Regional Park as a whole.

Cerknica lies about 3km north of Lake Cerknica. Cesta 4 Maja is the main street in the centre of town. The bus station is on Čabranska ulica about 100m to the south-west and behind the post office.

◉ Sights

Lake Cerknica LAKE
Since ancient times periodic Lake Cerknica (Cerniško Jezero) has baffled and perplexed people, appearing and disappearing with the seasons.

Cerknica is a *polje*, a field above a collapsed karst cavern riddled with holes like a Swiss cheese. The *polje* is fed by a disappearing river, the Stržen, and also collects water underground from the Bloke Plateau and the Javornik Mountains. During rainy periods, usually in the autumn and spring, all this water comes rushing into the *polje*. As the water percolates between the rocks, the sink-holes and siphons can't handle the outflow underground, and the *polje* becomes Lake Cerknica – sometimes in less than a day.

The surface area of Lake Cerknica can reach 29 sq km, but it is never more than a few metres deep. When full it is an important wetland, attracting some 250 species of birds each year. During dry periods (usually July to September or later), farmers drive cattle down to the *polje* to graze.

The lake really begins at the village of Do-lenje Jezero, 2.5km south of Cerknica, where you'll find the **Lake House Museum** (Muzej Jezerski Hram; ☑041 561 870, 709 40 53; www.jez erski-hram.si; Dolenje Jezero 1e; adult/child €6/5;

⊙demonstration 3pm Sat Apr-Oct), with a 5m by 3m 1:2500-scale working model of Lake Cerknica. It shows how the underground hydrological system actually works in a 45-minute-long demonstration and video about the lake in the four seasons. There's also ethnological exhibits about local fishing and boat building.

Rakov Škocjan GORGE
Protected Rakov Škocjan is a 6km-long gorge lying some 5km west of Cerknica. The Rak River, en route to join the Pivka River at Planina Cave, has sculpted 2.5km of hollows, caves, springs and **Veliki** and **Mali Naravni Most**, the Big and Little Natural Bridges. There are lots of hiking and biking trails through and around the gorge and it is surrounded by Notranjska Regional Park. To the south lies the Snežnik-Javornik Massif, including its tallest peak, **Veliki Javornik** (1268m).

🏃 Activities

The **Kontrabantar farmhouse** (☑709 22 53; Dolenja Vas 72; per hr €10; ⊙noon-10pm Thu-Sun) in Dolenja Vas, 2km southwest of Cerknica, has horses, riding lessons and riding gear for rent.

The Hotel Rakov Škocjan (p136) can organise any number of activities from guided **hiking** (from €20 per person) and **caving** (from €23) to **cycling** and **fly-fishing** in the surrounding Notranjska Regional Park. It offers packages such as one that includes accommodation, half-board, a bicycle and a trip to Križna Cave for €38 per person per day in a double room. Ask for the booklet *Rakov Škocjan and the Nature Trail*.

The **Cerknica Mountain Trail** heads southwest from Cerknica to thickly forested Veliki Javornik. From here you can take a side trip of about two hours to the gorge at Rakov Škocjan. Otherwise the trail skirts the southern shore of Lake Cerknica and carries on northeast to **Križna Gora** (857m) and its nearby **cave**. It continues northwest to **Slivnica** (1114m), where you will find the Dom na Slivnici (p136) mountaintop guest-house. The next day you walk north-north-west to **Stražišče** (955m) and then south along the main road for 3km to Cerknica.

🎭 Festivals & Events

Pustni Karneval RELIGIOUS FESTIVAL
(www.cerknica.net/pust; ⊙late-Feb–early Mar) Cerknica is famous for its pre-Lenten carnival called Pustni Karneval, which takes

PRIMORSKA & NOTRANJSKA CERKNICA & AROUND

TALES FROM A DARK PROVINCE

Slovenian folk tales are rife with fairies, witches and things that go bump in the night, but among the most common stories are those describing the derring-do of 'super-heroes', whose strong wills and unusual strength enabled them to overcome evil and conquer their brutish enemies.

Some of the most popular stories revolve around the feats of one Martin Krpan, the hero of the Bloke Plateau in Notranjska. Krpan's traits and characteristics are familiar: he was an outlaw with a big heart, hunted by the imperial guard for smuggling salt. When he was arrested, Martin Krpan proved his super-human strength to the emperor in Vienna by picking up and carrying his own horse. (Portrayed in a statue in the centre of Cerknica.)

Realising his fortune at having such a powerful giant under his control, the emperor set Martin Krpan on Berdavs, the local scourge and personification of the marauding Turk. Martin Krpan defeated Berdavs and chopped off his head with a magic axe – complete with a handle made of Slovenian linden wood. For his pains the imperial court allowed him to freely transport and sell salt.

place for four days over the weekend before Ash Wednesday (late February/early March). Mask-wearing merrymakers parade up and down while being provoked by upstarts with pitchforks.

🛏 Sleeping & Eating

TOP CHOICE Hotel Rakov Škocjan GUESTHOUSE €€
(☎051 310 477, 709 74 70; www.h-rakovskocjan.com; Rakov Škocjan 1; s/d/tr €45/76/106; ℗@) In the heart of Notranjska Regional Park (7km west of Cerknica), this 13-room guesthouse is the ideal spot for an active holiday. It has a sauna and an excellent restaurant (mains €7.70 to €15) specialising in game dishes, with outdoor grill and terrace seating in the warmer months.

Dom na Slivnici GUESTHOUSE €
(☎041 518 108, 709 41 40; s/d €28.60/44; ⊙daily May-Sep, Sat & Sun Oct-Apr; ℗) This splendidly positioned guesthouse at 1075m, just below Mt Slivnica, is accessible by foot or by road about 8km east of Cerknica. There are 12 beds in five rooms; there's a popular restaurant here too.

Valvasorjev Hram SLOVENIAN €
(☎709 37 88; Partizanska cesta 1; mains €6-10; ⊙8am-11pm Mon-Sat, 3-10pm Sun) This simple eatery opposite the TIC serves hearty dishes like *jota* (bean soup) and *klobasa* (sausage) as well as pizza. It has its own wine cellar and outside seating in summer.

ℹ Information

Notranjska Regional Park (Notranjski Regijski Park; ☎059 091 612; www.notranjski-park.si; Tabor 42; ⊙by appointment) Headquarters of the 22,282-hectare regional park, 100m north of the TIC.

Nova Ljubljanska Banka (Cesta 4 Maja 64) In the Imam shopping centre.

Post Office (Cesta 4 Maja 52) Next door to the TIC.

SKB Banka (Partizanska cesta 1) Next door to Valvasorjev Hram.

Tourist Information Centre Cerknica (TIC; ☎031 465 707, 709 36 36; tdrustvo@volja.net; Cesta 4 Maja 51; ⊙8am-3.30pm Mon-Fri, 8.30am-1pm Sat)

ℹ Getting There & Around

Half a dozen daily buses run between Cerknica and Ljubljana (€6, 1¼ hours) and Postojna (€2.70, 30 minutes). Up to half a dozen go to the train station in Rakek (€1.80, 10 minutes) and to Stari Trg pri Ložu (€2.70, 30 minutes). Two buses a day cross the Croatian border to Prezid (€4.10, one hour).

Hotel Rakov Škocjan rents bicycles and mountain bikes for €3/15 per hour/day.

Lož Valley

☎01 / ELEV 593M

The secluded Lož Valley southeast of Cerknica is home to the recently restored 16th-century Renaissance **Snežnik Castle** (Grad Snežnik; ☎705 78 14; www.nms.si; Kozarišče 67; adult/child €4/3; ⊙tours hourly 10am-7pm Tue-Sun Apr-Sep, 10am-4pm Tue-Sun Oct-Mar), one of the loveliest and best-situated fortresses in Slovenia, and surrounded by attractive parkland.

Entrance is through a double barbican with drawbridge and moat. The four floors are richly decorated with period furniture and portraits – the household inventory of the Schönburg-Waldenburg family, which bought the castle in 1853 and used it as a summer residence and hunting lodge until WWII.

The castle's isolation means you really need your own wheels to visit. Otherwise, take a bus from Cerknica to Stari Trg pri Ložu (up to six a day) and face a 4km walk.

You can explore plenty of Slovenia's caves on foot, but only at **Križna** (☏041 632 153; www.krizna-jama.si; adult/child €7/4.50; ⊘tours 11am, 1pm, 3pm & 5pm Jul & Aug, 11am, 1pm & 3pm Sep, 3pm Sat & Sun Apr-Jun) can you take a subterranean boat ride. About 7km north of Snežnik Castle and a kilometre or so after you turn off the main road from Cerknica, Križna Cave is one of the most magnificent water caves in the world – it's 8.8km long and counts 22 underground lakes filled with green and blue water as well as a unique 'forest' of ice stalagmites near the entrance. The dry part of the cave, which includes a short boat ride, can be toured without booking in advance.

With advance booking, you can go as far as the Kalvarija chamber by rubber raft via 13 lakes (€45 to €65 according to group size). It's a four-hour tour if you elect to do the entire cave, and the price includes all equipment.

Dolenjska & Bela Krajina

Includes »

Best Places to Eat

» Gostilna Kmečki Hram (p154)

» Grad (p156)

» Oštarija Debeluh (p156)

» Hotel Bela Krajina (p158)

Best Places to Stay

» Hotel Balnea (p146)

» Hostel Situla (p149)

» Gostilna Kmečki Hram (p154)

» Šeruga Farmhouse (p151)

Why Go?

'Lower Carniola' is a gentle area of rolling hills topped with red-roofed churches, vineyards and forests, all bisected by the Krka River. It's a place to experience the great Slovenian outdoors – the E6 and E7 European Hiking Trails pass through Dolenjska, and there are lots of chances to do some kayaking or canoeing on the Krka. The province is also the cycling centre of Slovenia and famous for its thermal spas.

Bela Krajina, the 'White March', is separated from Dolenjska by the scenic Gorjanci Mountains. The province, which takes its name from the countless stands of birch trees here, is a treasure trove of Slovenian folklore, and, you'll find more traditional dance music here than anywhere else.

When to Go

Novo Mesto

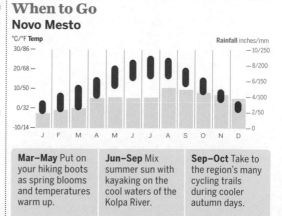

Mar–May Put on your hiking boots as spring blooms and temperatures warm up.

Jun–Sep Mix summer sun with kayaking on the cool waters of the Kolpa River.

Sep–Oct Take to the region's many cycling trails during cooler autumn days.

DOLENJSKA

The many castles and monasteries along the Krka River in Dolenjska are some of the best preserved in Slovenia, and you will see Dolenjska's distinctive *toplarji* (double hayracks) everywhere.

Dolenjska was settled early on and is well known for its Hallstatt (early Iron Age) ruins, especially near Stična, Šmarjeta and Novo Mesto. The Romans made the area part of the province of Upper Pannonia (Pannonia Superior) and crossed it with roads. In the Middle Ages, the population clustered around the many castles along the river, such as those at Žužemberk and Otočec, while monasteries sprung up at Stična, Kostanjevica na Krki and near Šentjernej. Dolenjska declined after the Middle Ages and progress only came in the late 19th century when a railway line linked Novo Mesto with Ljubljana.

Ribnica & Around

📱01 / POP 9333 / ELEV 492M

Ribnica is the oldest and most important settlement of western Dolenjska. It sits in the area known locally as Kočevsko – all woods, underground rivers and brown bears. It is an excellent springboard for the unspoiled forests of the Kočevski Rog.

Ribnica's main street, Škrabčev trg, lies on the east bank of the tiny Bistrica River and runs parallel to it. Buses stop in front of the Parish Church of St Stephen.

Sights

Ribnica Castle CASTLE
(Ribniški Grad; Gallusovo nabrežje 1) Ribnica Castle was originally built in the 11th century and was expanded over the centuries. Only a small section – a Renaissance wall and two towers – survived bombings during WWII. Today the castle houses a small ethnographic collection (📱041 390 057, 835 03 76; www.miklovahisa.si/muzej; adult/child & student/senior €2.50/1.70/2.10; ⊙10am-1pm & 4-7pm Tue-Sun) showcasing the traditional crafts of the area.

Parish Church of St Stephen CHURCH
(Župnijska Cerkev Sv Štefana; Škrabčev trg) Built in 1868 on the site of earlier churches, this parish church would not be of much interest were it not for the two striking towers added by Jože Plečnik in the form of his signature pyramids in 1960 to replace the ones toppled during WWII.

Štekliček House HISTORIC BUILDING
(Štekličkova Hiša; Škrabčev trg 16) Opposite the parish church is Štekliček House, where the 19th-century poet and patriot France Prešeren spent two years (1810–12) in what was then the region's best-known school.

Mikel House GALLERY
(Miklova Hiša; 📱835 03 76; Škrabčev trg 21; ⊙8am-4pm Mon-Fri) The gallery at Mikel House, a lovely cream-and-white building dating from 1858, has exhibitions of contemporary art and does double duty as the town's library.

Activities

Ribnica is the base for many excellent walks. A well-marked trail leads north of the town for about 4.5km to the summit of **Stene Sv Ana** (963m), with fantastic views over the Ribnica Valley; ask the TIC for a copy of the *Natural Heritage of Ribnica* pamphlet.

From the Jasnica recreational centre (on the way to Kočevje), a more difficult path leads north about 6km to the junction with the Ribnica Alpine Trail. This joins up with the E7 European Hiking Trail about 5km west of Velike Lašče.

Festivals & Events

Dry Goods and Pottery Fair CRAFT FAIR
(Ribniški Semenj Suhe Robe, in Lončarstva; www.ribnica.si; ⊙Sep) Ribnica's main event is the Dry Goods and Pottery Fair held on the first Sunday in September.

Sleeping

Pri Boltetnih GUESTHOUSE €
(📱836 02 08, 041 898 034; bernarda.arko@gmail.com; Dane 9; per person €24; 🅿@) This engaging farmhouse at Dane, an 'end-of-the-line' village 4km west of Ribnica, offers accommodation in three rooms and is about the best place to stay in the area.

Izlaty INN €
(📱041 373 550, 836 45 15; lauryka_1@gmail.com; Prigorica 115; s/d from €20/30; 🅿) This small *gostilna* (inn-like restaurant), 4km southeast of Ribnica on the road to Kočevje, has basic but comfortable accommodation.

Eating & Drinking

Gostilna Mihelič BALKAN €
(📱836 31 31; Škrabčev trg 22; starters €4.50-8.50, mains €7.50-16.50; ⊙9am-10pm Tue-Fri, 9am-11pm Sat, 8am-5pm Sun) This old place with brick vaulted ceilings opposite the Church of

Dolenjska & Bela Krajina Highlights

1 Cycle the back roads of the picturesque **Krka River valley** (p144)

2 Visit the haunt of the Partisans at **Base 20** (p146) in the virgin forests of **Kočevski Rog**

3 Walk back in time at **Bogenšperk Castle** (p143), especially in the study of the late, great Janez Vajkard Valvasor

4 Enjoy the almost-medieval merrymaking of the **Jurjevanje** (p161) festival in Črnomelj in mid-June

5 Kayak the rapid-water run on the **Kolpa River** (p162) from Stari Trg to Vinica

6 Cock your ear to Bela Krajina folk music, especially around **Adlešiči** (p162)

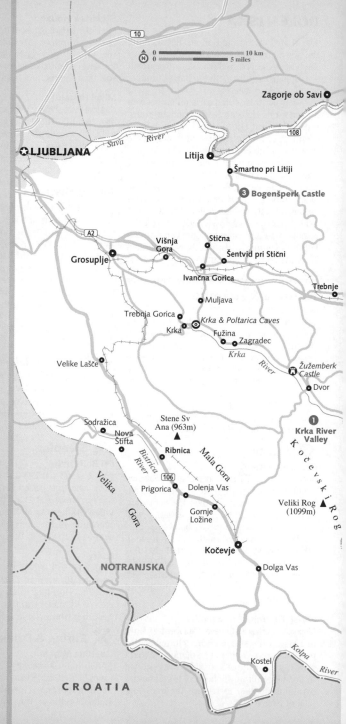

St Stephen is one of the very few central places for a proper meal in Ribnica. It serves excellent Balkan-style grills (€5 to €7.50).

Pizzerija Harlekin PIZZA €
(☑836 15 32; Gorenjska cesta 4; pizzas €4-6; ☺10am-11am Mon-Sat, 10am-10pm Sun) North of the centre, this convenient place serves pizzas and salads.

Amadeus Pub PUB
(☑051 341 042; Škrabčev trg 25; ☺7am-11pm Mon-Thu, 7am-midnight Fri & Sat, 9am-11pm Sun) This convivial cafe-pub next door to the TIC is a popular hang-out for young Ribničani.

❶ Information

Nova Ljubljanska Banka (Škrabčev trg 11) Southeast of the Church of St Stephen.
Post Office (Kolodvorska ulica 2)
Tourist Information Centre Ribnica (TIC; ☑051 415 429, 836 93 35; www.miklovahisa .si/tic; Škrabčev trg 23; ☺9am-7pm Mon-Fri, 8am-noon Sat, 10am-2pm Sun Jul & Aug only) Has a shop selling local *suha roba* (wooden products) and pottery.

❶ Getting There & Around

Buses run at least hourly north to Ljubljana (€5.60, one hour), and south to Kočevje (€2.70, 30 minutes). The infrequent bus to Sodražica (€1.80, 15 minutes) is good for Nova Štifta.

Nova Štifta

☑01 / ELEV 625M

The **Church of the Assumption of Mary** (Cerkev Marije Vnebovzete; ☑041 747 188, 836 99 43; Nova Štifta 3; ☺10am-noon & 2-6pm) at Nova Štifta, in the foothills of the Velika Gora 6km west of Ribnica, is one of the most important pilgrimage sites in Slovenia. Completed in 1671, the baroque church is unusual for its octagonal shape.

The interior of the church, with its golden altars and pulpit, is blindingly ornate. In the courtyard opposite the Franciscan monastery (where the church key is kept) stands a wonderful old Dolenjska *toplarji* and a linden tree, planted in the mid-17th century, complete with a tree house that has been there for over a century.

Dom na Travni Gori (☑836 63 33; travna .gora@gmail.com; Ravni Dol 43; per person €18), a guesthouse 905m up, with restaurant and 19 beds, can be reached in less than an hour on a marked trail heading southwest from just opposite the monastery.

Stična

☑01 / POP 780 / ELEV 357M

The abbey at Stična is the oldest monastery in Slovenia and one of the country's most important religious and cultural monuments. Only 35km from Ljubljana, it's an easy day trip from the capital.

Stična is about 2.5km north of Ivančna Gorica, where you'll find the train station on Sokolska ulica. Long-distance buses stop in front of the station.

◉ Sights

Stična Cistercian Abbey ABBEY
(Cistercijanska Opatija Stična; ☑041 689 994, 787 78 63; www.mks-sticna.si; Stična 17; adult/student/senior/family €4.50/2/3/7; ☺tours 8.30am, 10am, 2pm & 4pm Tue-Sat, 2pm & 4pm Sun) Established in 1136 by the Cistercians (famous for their vows of silence), this abbey was for centuries the most important religious, economic, educational and cultural centre in Dolenjska. There are currently some 15 priests and monks in residence.

The entrance to the walled monastery, an incredible combination of Romanesque, Gothic, Renaissance and baroque architecture, is on the east side across a small stream. On the north side of the central courtyard is the Old Prelature, a 17th-century Renaissance building, which contains the **Museum of Christianity in Slovenia** (Muzej Krščanstva na Slovenskem), a hotchpotch mix of antique clocks, furniture, icons and old documents (though note, the medieval ones are facsimiles).

On the west side of the courtyard is the **Abbey Church** (1156), a buttressed, three-nave Romanesque cathedral, rebuilt in the baroque style in the 17th and 18th centuries. Look inside for the Renaissance red-marble tombstone of Abbot Jakob Reinprecht in the north transept and the blue organ cupboard with eight angels (1747) in the choir loft. The greatest treasures here are the Stations of the Cross painted in 1766 by Fortunat Bergant.

South of the church is Stična's vaulted cloister, mixing Romanesque and early Gothic styles. The arches and vaults are adorned with frescoes of the prophets and Old Testament stories and allegorical subjects. The carved stone faces on the west side were meant to show human emotions and vices.

On the south side of the cloister is a typically baroque monastic refectory, with an 18th-century pink ceiling with white stucco decoration. **Neff's Abbey**, built in the mid-16th century by Abbot Volbenk Neff, runs to the west. The arches in the vestibule on the ground floor are painted with a dense network of leaves, blossoms, berries and birds.

The Cistercians sell their own products (honey, wine, herbal teas, liqueurs) in a small shop at the abbey entrance.

🛏 Sleeping & Eating

Grofija　　　　　　　　　　GUESTHOUSE €
(☑787 81 41; www.grofija.com; Vir pri Stični 30; per person €28-32; P) This 19th-century farmhouse called 'County' has four charming rooms and is 2km along a circuitous route southeast of the Cistercian Abbey. Of historical note: a Hallstatt settlement dating from 800 BC once stood near the farmhouse's tennis court.

Krjavelj　　　　　　　　　　PIZZA €
(☑051 367 330, 787 71 10; Ljubljanska cesta 38; pizza €5.60-6.40, mains €4.80-12; ⊙10am-11pm Jun-Sep, 9am-10pm Mon-Sat, 11am-9pm Sun Oct-May) This little place in Ivančna Gorica, about 150m northeast of the train station and just off the road to the Cistercian Abbey, serves local favourites and decent pizza.

ℹ Getting There & Away

BUS Stična is served by up to a dozen buses a day from Ljubljana (€4.70, one hour) on weekdays, with fewer on weekends.

TRAIN Ivančna Gorica is on the rail line linking Ljubljana with Novo Mesto, Črnomelj and Metlika. Up to 14 trains a day arrive from the capital (€2.90, one hour) with as many heading for Novo Mesto (€2.90, 50 minutes).

Bogenšperk Castle

☑01 / ELEV 412M

The 16th-century **Bogenšperk Castle** (Grad Bogenšperk; ☑041 703 992, 898 76 64; www.bogensperk.si; Bogenšperk 5; adult/child & student/senior €3.50/2.50/2.70; ⊙tours hourly 10am-6pm Tue-Sat, 10am-7pm Sun Jul & Aug, shorter hrs Sep-Jun) is in many respects the secular equivalent of the Cistercian Abbey at Stična. Here the celebrated polymath Janez Vajkard Valvasor spent the most productive two decades of his life.

Valvasor bought the Renaissance-style castle from the aristocratic Wagen family in 1672 and installed his printing press, engraving workshop and extensive library here. But due to the enormous debts incurred in getting his magnum opus published, he was forced to sell up 20 years later.

The castle, with its rectangular courtyard and three towers (the fourth burned down in the 19th century), houses a museum devoted to the great man, his work and Slovenian culture. Valvasor's library is now used as a wedding hall, but his study, with its beautiful parquetry, black limestone columns and painted ceiling, is pretty much the way he left it when he performed his last alchemical experiments here. Other rooms contain examples of Valvasor's original cartography and etching, an original

---

VALVASOR, SLOVENIA'S RENAISSANCE MAN

Most of our knowledge of Slovenian history, geography, culture and folklore before the 17th century comes from the writings of one man, Janez Vajkard Valvasor, and more specifically his book *The Glory of the Duchy of Carniola*.

Valvasor was born to a noble family from Bergamo in 1641, in Ljubljana's Old Town. After a Jesuit education there and in Germany, he joined Miklós Zrínyi, the Hungarian count and poet, in the wars against the Turks and travelled widely, visiting Germany, Italy, North Africa, France and Switzerland. He collected data on natural phenomena and local customs as well as books, drawings, mineral specimens and coins.

In 1672 Valvasor installed himself, his books and his precious collections at Bogenšperk Castle, where he conducted scientific experiments (including alchemy) and wrote. In 1689 he completed his most important work, *The Glory of the Duchy of Carniola*. It ran to four volumes, comprising 3500 pages with 535 maps and copper engravings and remains one of the most comprehensive works published in Europe before the Enlightenment – such a wealth of information on the Slovenian patrimony that is still explored and studied to this day.

Valvasor never enjoyed the success of his labours. Publishing such a large work at his own expense ruined him financially and he was forced to leave Bogenšperk in 1692 and died a year later at Krško, 65km to the east on the Sava River.

four-volume set of his famous work, a working printing press and a collection of hunting trophies, including a 360kg brown bear. The most interesting exhibits, however, are the ones that deal with folk dress, superstition and folk medicine.

Bogenšperk is accessible from Ivančna Gorica only by car or bicycle. Trains link Ljubljana with Litija (€2.90 to €4.50, 30 minutes, up to two dozen a day), but it's still another 7km south to Bogenšperk – much of it uphill.

Krka Valley

The Krka River springs from a karst cave southwest of Stična, near the village of Trebnja Gorica, and runs to the southeast and east until it joins the mightier Sava near Brežice. At 94km it is Dolenjska's longest waterway and one of the cleanest rivers in Slovenia.

KRKA RIVER CAVES
📍 01 / ELEV 268M

Two kilometres from the main road and just southeast of the village of Trebnja Gorica, **Krka Cave** (Krška Jama; ☎041 276 252; www.tdkrka.si; ticket office Krka 4; adult/child €2.50/1.60; ☺tours hourly 2-5pm Sat & Sun Apr-Sep) isn't in the same league as Postojna or Škocjan Caves, but along the 1.9km route (a bit more than half the total length) you get to see some stalactites shaped like ribbons and fragile-looking 'spaghetti', a century-old specimen of *Proteus anguinus* (p132) and a lake that's the source of the Krka River. The usual depth of the lake is 17m, but in winter – depending on the rain and the snowfall – the lake can rise almost as high as the ceiling. The cave temperature is 8°C to 9°C. **Poltarica Cave** (Jama Poltarica; ☎031 766 555; ☺by appointment) is a cave 400m before the entrance to Krka Cave.

ŽUŽEMBERK
📍 07 / POP 4536 / ELEV 240M

About 17km from Muljava is the site of the mighty, 13th-century **Žužemberk Castle** (☎388 51 80, 041 324 710; www.zuzemberk.si; Grajski trg 1; ☺by arrangement), perched on a cliff overlooking the Krka River. It was refortified in the 16th century, only to be all but flattened during air raids in WWII. Its towers have been partially reconstructed, and renovations continue apace. Annual events at the castle include the June-to-September **Summer Castle Performances** (Poletne Grajske Prireditve), a series of concerts, and **Medieval Day** (Srednjeveški dan) in early July.

The fast-flowing Krka offers excellent **kayaking** and **canoeing**, and Žužemberk is a good spot from which to set out. **Carpe Diem** (☎041 739 771, 780 60 11; www.kayak.si; Krka 27) and **Žužemberk Kayak & Raft Club** (☎031 556 641, 308 70 55; Prapreče 1), 1km

WORTH A TRIP

KRKA CRUISING

If you have your own transport, you can make a maze-like trip through Dolenjska by following Route No 216 along the Krka River, which cuts a deep and picturesque valley along its upper course. Along the way you'll chance upon historical churches, mighty castles and even a couple of caves worth visiting. A few buses from Ljubljana to Novo Mesto via Dolenjske Toplice follow this route but they are very infrequent.

The journey begins about 9km south of **Ivančna Gorica**, in the village of **Krka**, where you can find a pair of **caves**, one of which is the source of the Krka River. Carry on for another 13km or so and you'll reach **Žužemberk**, a town dominated at street level by a multi-turreted castle but watched from on high by the mammoth **Parish Church of Sts Mohor and Fortunat** (Župnijska Cerkev Sv Mohorja in Fortunata), built over six decades in the 18th century. Nine kilometres to the south of Žužemberk at **Soteska** are the ruins of **Soteska Castle**, a fortress admired by Valvasor but more or less razed during WWII. Nearby is the irresistibly sweet **Garden Pavilion**, a cylindrical structure from the late 17th century with trompe l'oeil frescoes.

At Soteska you can elect to carry on south on the No 216 to the spa town of **Dolenjske Toplice** or turn east on to Route No 419 and continue following the Krka River. If you choose the latter, within 6km you'll reach **Straža**, which boasts the massive **Church of the Assumption of Mary** (Cerkev Marije Vnebovzete), built at the very end of the 18th century and featuring some impressive illusionist paintings. Then it's onto Dolenjska's main city, **Novo Mesto**.

northwest of Žužemberk, charge €20 to €25 for adults and €15 to €20 for children.

Koren (☑308 72 60; Dolga Vas 5; per person €20, apt €40-50), a farmhouse in Dolga Vas near Žužemberk, has accommodation for 13 people in five rooms and one apartment. **Gostilna Pri Gradu** (☑308 72 90; Grajski trg 4; mains €6.90-18; ☺6am-11pm Sun-Thu, 2pm-midnight Fri & Sat), an old-style eatery under a linden in front of Žužemberk Castle, has a terrace open in the warmer months. Fare is pretty standard but it's the only game in town.

The bus stop is in front of the post office at Grajski trg 28. Up to four buses a day go to Ljubljana (€6, one hour, 5km) on weekdays, with just one on Saturday and Sunday. From Monday to Friday one bus a day departs at 8.14am for Novo Mesto (€4.10, 45 minutes, 31km) via Dolenjske Toplice.

Dolenjske Toplice

☑07 / POP 795 / ELEV 179M

Within striking distance of Novo Mesto, this thermal resort is Slovenia's oldest spa town. Located in the karst valley of the Sušica (a tributary of the Krka River), and surrounded by the wooded slopes of Kočevski Rog, it's an excellent place in which to hike, cycle or simply relax.

History

The first spa was built here in 1658. The Kopališki Dom (Bathers' House), complete with three pools, was built in the 18th century. Despite getting its own guidebook, tourism didn't really take off until 1899, with the opening of the Zdraviliški Dom (Health Resort House). Strascha Töplitz, as it was then called, was a great favourite of Austrians from around the turn of the 20th century up to WWI.

🏃 Activities

Thermal Spas

Hotel Vital SPA
(Zdraviliški trg 11; adult €9-12, child €7.50-9.50; ☺7am-8pm) Taking the waters is the *sine qua non* of Dolenjske Toplice: the 36°C mineral water, gushing from 1000m below the three covered thermal pools at the Hotel Vital, is perfect for therapeutic purposes. Detox and beauty treatments are also available.

Balnea Wellness Centre SPA
(☑391 97 50) The large Balnea Wellness Centre, 200m north of the hotels and reached via a lovely park or walkway, is composed of three parts. The park-like **Laguna complex** (day pass adult/child Mon-Fri €9.20/7.20, Sat & Sun €12.20/10.20; ☺9am-9pm Sun-Thu, 9am-11pm Fri & Sat) counts four pools (three outdoor and one inside) with thermal water of between 27°C and 32°C. In the **Oaza section** (day pass Mon-Fri €16.20, Sat & Sun €18.20; ☺11am-9pm Mon, Wed & Thu, 9am-9pm Tue & Sun, 11am-11pm Fri, 9am-11pm Sat) are a host of indoor and outdoor saunas and steam baths over two floors, including a rooftop naturist sauna with excellent, err, views. The **Aura section** (☺11am-9pm) has treatments and massages, including the rather sticky-sounding honey massage (€60). Hotel Balnea guests get into Laguna for free but pay €9.20/11.20 per adult/child at Oaza. There are a number of combination tickets and packages available.

Hiking

Paths listed on the free *Dolenjske Toplice Municipal Tourist Trails* include four hiking and six cycling trails. In addition the TIC distributes some two dozen separate sheets with themed hikes, walks and cycle routes. One is a 2.5km **archaeological walk** west to Cvinger (263m), where Hallstatt tombs and iron foundries have been unearthed. Nature lovers may be interested in the 8km **herbalist trail**, a loop south to Sela and Podturn and back via forest roads, which takes in a herbalist farm and the 15th-century Church of the Holy Trinity at Cerovec. Further afield is the 2km **Dormouse Trail**, which makes a loop from Kočevske Poljane, about 4.5km southwest of Dolenjske Toplice, and could be combined with a hike to Base 20 (p146).

Other Activities

Horse riding is available at the **Urbančič farmhouse** (☑040 608 969, 306 53 36; Kočevske Poljane 13; per hr €10-15) in Kočevske Poljane, 4km to the southwest, but be sure to book ahead.

Travel agency K2M (p146) can organise kayak, canoe and rafting trips on the Krka for between €14 and €20 per person.

The **Bela Ski Centre** (Smučarski Center Bela; ☑384 94 35; nada.frankovic@iskra-semic.si; day pass adult/child/student & senior €22/17/18.70) is on the edge of the Kočevje forest, 16km south of Dolenjske Toplice. It has 6km of slopes and 7km of cross-country trails on Mt Gače at altitudes between 700m and 965m, served by a chairlift and five T-bar tows.

🛏 Sleeping

TOP CHOICE **Hotel Balnea** RESORT
(☑391 94 00; www.terme-krka.si; Zdraviliški trg 11;
s/d €86/142; **P**@**🛜🏊**) Few newly-built hotels
in Slovenia can compare with this 63-room,
four-star (plus) palace in terms of design
and facilities. The child-like drawings in
the public areas are fetching, the aphorisms
etched into the walls of the lift are infec-
tious, and we love the back-facing rooms
with balconies looking on to the park.

Tomlje Farmhouse GUESTHOUSE €
(☑306 50 23, 031 643 345; Zdraviliški trg 24; s/d/
tr €19/32/48; **P**) This attractive and very
welcoming farmhouse above the Balnea spa
complex has rooms with a total of 15 beds as
well as three apartments sleeping between
two and four people.

Gostišče Rečka GUESTHOUSE €€
(☑041 210 486, 306 55 10; www.gostisce-racka.si;
Ulica Maksa Henigmana 15; s/d €30/56; **P**) This
modernised and attractive village house to
the east of the town centre has six rooms as
well as apartments for up to six people.

Kamp Dolenjske Toplice CAMPGROUND €
(☑391 94 00; www.terme-krka.si; per person €2.90-
9.60, incl 3hr pool pass €9.40-16.40; ⊙year-round;
P) This 3-hectare camping ground accommodating 100 people is just off the northern
end of Zdraviliški trg, more or less opposite
the Balnea spa complex.

🍴 Eating

Gostišče Rečka PIZZA €
(Ulica Maksa Henigmana 15; pizza & pasta €3-6;
⊙8am-11pm Sun-Thu, 8am-midnight Fri & Sat Jul &
Aug, shorter hrs Sep-Jun) This guesthouse does
double duty as a restaurant and is a popular
place for pizza and pasta.

Gostilna Lovec SLOVENIAN €
(☑040 225 135; Pionirska cesta 2; starters €4.50-6,
mains €6-12; ⊙7am-11pm Mon-Thu, 7am-midnight
Fri & Sat, 8am-11pm Sun) About as central as
you'll find, this lively *gostilna* with an outside terrace along the narrow Sušica offers
Slovenian favourites like grilled *klobasa*
(sausage; €5) and some decent fish dishes,
including trout (about €5.50).

Gostilna Rog SLOVENIAN €
(☑391 94 12; Zdraviliški trg 22; meals from €10;
⊙9am-10pm Sun-Thu, 9am-11pm Fri, 9am-midnight
Sat) On the edge of the central park, the
Horn serves traditional Slovenian dishes

and has folk music from 8pm on Friday and
Saturday.

ℹ Information

K2M (☑041 887 362, 306 68 30; www.k2m.si;
Pionirska cesta 3; ⊙9am-6pm Mon-Fri, 9am-
noon Sat) Travel agency with private rooms,
guides, excursions and bike rentals.
Nova Ljubljanska Banka (Zdraviliški trg 8)
There's a branch on Zdraviliški trg and an ATM
at Zdraviliški trg 10a, south of the Church of
St Anne.
Post Office (Zdraviliški trg 3)
Terme Krka Dolenjske Toplice (☑391 94 00;
www.terme-krka.si) Central contact for book-
ings at the three main hotels and camping
ground, beauty and medical treatments etc.
Tourist Information Centre Dolenjske Toplice
(TIC; ☑384 51 88; www.kkc-dolenjske
.si; Sokolski trg 4; ⊙9am-6pm Mon-Fri, 9am-
3pm Sat, 9am-noon Sun May-Sep, shorter hrs
Oct-Apr)

ℹ Getting There & Around

There are frequent weekday buses to Novo
Mesto (€2.20, 20 minutes) but few at the weekend. Two weekday morning buses go to Ljubljana
(€7.20, 1½ hours) via Žužemberk (€2.70, 30
minutes).

Kočevski Rog

☑07 / ELEV TO 1098M

One of the most pristine areas in Slovenia,
Kočevski Rog's virgin forests have been a
protected nature area for over a century. As
many as 500 brown bears are believed to
live amid its 200 hectares – the largest bear
population in Europe.

During the early days of WWII the Partisans, under the command of Marshal
Tito, headquartered here amid the region's
limestone caves operating hospitals, schools
and even printing presses. The nerve centre
was the so-called **Base 20** (Baza 20; ☑306 60
25; www.dolmuzej.com/en/muzej/baza20), about
10km southwest of Dolenjske Toplice at 711m,
reconstructed and turned into a national
monument after the war.

Once a favourite 'pilgrimage' spot for
Slovenes and Yugoslavs, Base 20 is now just
a shadow of its former self, its 26 wooden
buildings slowly being consumed by the forest, though two barracks exhibits are open
to the public. A plaque erected near the
site in 1995 diplomatically pays homage to
everyone involved in the 'national liberation
war', presumably including the thousands of

Domobranci (Home Guards) executed here by the Partisans in 1945. The site is always open, but a tourist guide at **Lukov Dom** (☑041 315 165; 1½hr tour adult/child & student €4.50/2.50, film €1; ☺8am-4pm Mon-Fri Apr-Oct), the building at the start of the trail, is on hand in season. **Okrepčevalnica Pri Bazi 20** (☑041 959 109; ☺10am-9pm Tue-Fri, 9am-9pm Sat & Sun) is a simple eatery near the main car park.

There's no scheduled bus service, but Base 20 is easily reached by sealed road on foot or bicycle from Podturn, 7km to the north.

Novo Mesto

☑07 / POP 22,940 / ELEV 189M

Situated on a sharp bend of the Krka River, the inappropriately named New Town – it's actually pretty old – is the capital of Dolenjska and one of its prettiest towns. It is an important gateway to the historical towns and castles along the lower Krka, the karst forests of the Gorjanci Hills to the southeast, Bela Krajina and Croatia (Zagreb is a mere 75km away).

Today's Novo Mesto shows two faces to the world: the Old Town (with the cobbled square of Glavni trg) on a rocky promontory above the left bank of the Krka; and a new town to the north and south, thriving on the pharmaceutical, chemical and car manufacturing of the Krka.

History

Novo Mesto was settled during the late Bronze Age around 1000 BC, and helmets and decorated burial urns unearthed in surrounding areas suggest that Marof Hill, northwest of the Old Town, was the seat of Hallstatt princes during the early Iron Age. The Illyrians and Celts came later, and the Romans maintained a settlement here until the 4th century AD.

During the early Middle Ages, Novo Mesto flourished as a marketplace at the centre of the estates owned by Stična abbey. But by the 16th century plague, fires, and raids by the Turks on their way to Vienna took their toll on the city.

Prosperity returned in the 18th and 19th centuries: a college was established in 1746, Slovenia's first National Hall (Narodni Dom) opened here in 1875, and a railway line linked the city with Ljubljana in the 1890s. Heavy bombardments during WWII severely damaged the city.

◉ Sights

Cathedral of St Nicholas   CATHEDRAL
(Stolna Cerkev Sv Nikolaja; Kapiteljska ulica) Perched above the Old Town, this Gothic cathedral is Novo Mesto's most important historical monument. It has a 15th-century vaulted (and very floral) presbytery and crypt, wall frescoes, a belfry that had once been a medieval defence tower, and an altar painting of the church's eponymous saint supposedly painted by the Venetian master Jacopo Tintoretto (1518–94).

If the church is locked, you'll find the key at the **Provost's House** (Proštija; Kapiteljska ulica 1), the yellow building to the northwest of the cathedral built in 1623. Just south of this is a section of the **medieval town walls** erected in the 14th century.

Dolenjska Museum   MUSEUM
(Dolenjski Muzej; ☑373 11 30; www.dolmuzej. com; Muzejska ulica 7; incl Jakac House adult/student & child €5/3; ☺9am-5pm Tue-Sat, 9am-1pm Sun) About 100m to the southeast of the Cathedral of St Nicholas is the enormous Dolenjska Museum. The oldest building, which once belonged to the Knights of the Teutonic Order, houses a valuable collection of archaeological finds unearthed in the southern suburb of Kandija in the late 1960s. Don't miss the Hallstatt helmet dating from the 4th century BC with two enormous axe blows on top, the fine bronze *situla* (or pail) from the 3rd or 4th century BC embossed with battle and hunting scenes, and the Celtic ceramics and jewellery (particularly the bangles of turquoise and dark blue glass).

Other collections in the complex include one devoted to recent history, and an excellent ethnographic collection with farm implements, commemorative jugs presented at weddings, decorated heart-shaped honey cakes, and icons painted on glass.

The museum also administers **Jakac House** (Jakčev Dom; ☑373 11 31; Sokolska ulica 1; adult/child €2.50/1.80; ☺9am-5pm Tue-Sat, 9am-1pm last Sun of month), which exhibits some of its 830-odd works by the prolific painter and local boy Božidar Jakac (1899–1989). The artist visited dozens of countries in the 1920s and '30s, painting and sketching such diverse subjects as Parisian dance halls, Scandinavian port towns, African villages and American city skylines. But his best works are of Novo Mesto's markets, people, churches and rumble-tumble wooden riverside houses. The Dolenjska Museum's permanent collection of

Novo Mesto

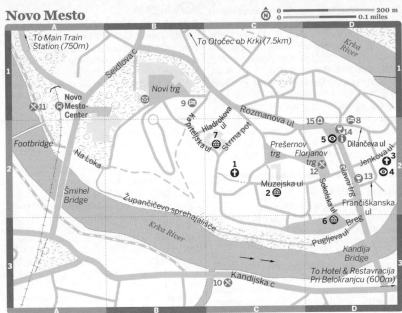

Novo Mesto

⊙ Sights
1	Cathedral of St Nicholas	C2
2	Dolenjska Museum	C2
3	Franciscan Church of St Leonard	D2
4	Franciscan Monastery	D2
5	Glavni Trg	D2
6	Jakac House	D3
7	Provost's House	C2

🛏 Sleeping
8	Hostel Situla	D2
9	Hotel Krka	B1

🍴 Eating
10	Don Bobi	C3
11	Gostišče Loka	A1
12	Market	D2

🍷 Drinking
13	Lokal Patriot	D2
14	Pub Pri Vodnjaku	D2

🛍 Shopping
15	Trgovina Žefran	D2

paintings from the 17th to 20th centuries is also exhibited here.

Glavni Trg
SQUARE

The neo-Renaissance **town hall** (rotovž; Glavni trg 7), out of step with the square's other arcaded buildings, ostentatiously calls attention to itself with its bells and unusual facade. The coat of arms on the front is that of Archduke Rudolf IV, the town's 14th-century founder.

Southeast of the town hall is the bright yellow **Franciscan Church of St Leonard** (Frančiškanska Cerkev Sv Lenarta; Frančiškanska ulica), which was originally built by monks

fleeing the Turks in Bosnia in 1472, and the attached **Franciscan monastery** (Frančiškanski samostan; Frančiškanska ulica 1), whose library contains some 12,000 volumes, including 12th-century incunabula.

🏃 Activities

The Hostel Situla rents **kayaks** and **canoes** for €7 per hour on weekdays and €9 per hour on weekends.

Novo Mesto Sport Equestrian Centre
HORSE RIDING

(☎041 554 265, 337 30 40; www.konji-cescavas .si; per hr €10-15; ☺by appointment) About 3km south of Prečna, the Novo Mesto Sport Equestrian Centre has Holsteiner and Arabian breeds for riders of all levels. You can ride on any day, but should book first.

Sleeping

The TIC has a list of private rooms (from €25 per person). The closest camping grounds are at Otočec ob Krki, 7.5km to the northeast, and Dolenjske Toplice, 12km to the southwest.

TOP CHOICE Hostel Situla   HOSTEL €

(☑394 20 00; www.situla.si; Dilančeva ulica 1; dm €13.50-19, d €35-60, s/tr/q €25/57/76; P@🅿️@🛜) One Slovenia's nicest hostels, partially built within the walls of an 18th-century town house with rooms deposited willy-nilly over five 'I'm-lost-again' floors. Iron Age–style art sets off the cosy rooms (we love the attic room under the mansard roof). There are kitchens for guests, and a bar-restaurant has a set lunch from €4 daily and à la carte dinner at the weekend.

Ravbar Apartmaji-Sobe   GUESTHOUSE €

(☑041 738 309, 373 06 80; www.ravbar.net; Smrečnikova ulica 15-17; s €20-30, d €30-40, apt for 2 €40-60, apt for 4 €65-75; P@) This family-run guesthouse has seven rooms and nine modern, spotlessly clean apartments in a leafy and quiet suburban area south of the river.

Hotel Krka   HOTEL €€€

(☑394 21 00; www.terme-krka.si; Novi trg 1; s €77-82, d €114-124, ste from €157; P❄🛜) This four-star business hotel in the centre of town has 53 modern, comfortable rooms, some adapted for travellers with disabilities. Guests get complimentary use of the thermal pools at Šmarješke Toplice, 15km away.

Hotel Pri Belokranjcu   HOTEL €€

(☑302 84 44; www.hotel.pribelokranjcu.si; Kandijska cesta 63; s/d/tr €38/55/72; P❄@🛜) About 1.5km from the Old Town, this rather boxy place behind a popular restaurant on a busy road has 19 comfortable rooms with some restful countryside views in the back.

✖ Eating

Don Bobi   PIZZA €

(☑338 24 00; Kandijska cesta 14; pizza €4.90-8.20; ⊙10am-11pm Mon-Fri, noon-midnight Sat) This simple eatery on the south side of the river is said to serve the best pizza and pasta in town.

Restavracija Pri Belokranjcu   SLOVENIAN €

(Kandijska cesta 63; starters €4.50-9, mains €7-17; ⊙8am-11pm Mon-Sat; ✍) This popular restaurant in an inn a short distance from the Old Town serves hearty Slovenian favourites and has good-value set menus (€11 and €12), including a very un-Slovenian vegetarian one.

Gostišče Loka   INTERNATIONAL €€

(☑332 11 08; Župančičevo sprehajališče 2; starters €5-6.40, mains €6.60-19.80; ⊙9am-10pm Mon-Thu, 11am-midnight Fri & Sat, 11am-10pm Sun) Located right on the Krka River, just beyond the small footbridge linking the two banks, the Meadow Inn serves fish dishes and pizza and pasta (€4.90 to €10.20), and is the spot to try Cviček, the uniquely Slovenian light (10% alcohol) red wine from Dolenjska.

Market   MARKET

(Florjanov trg; ⊙6am-5pm Mon, Wed & Fri) There is an outdoor market selling fruit and vegetables in the centre of the Old Town.

🍷 Drinking

Lokal Patriot   BAR

(☑337 45 10; www.lokalpatriot.si; Glavni trg 11; ⊙7am-11pm Mon-Wed, 7am-midnight Thu, 9am-2am Fri & Sat, 11am-10pm Sun) The venue of choice among Novo Mesto's movers and boppers, this bar and club below a large cafe has programs throughout the week and DJs (and sometimes live music) at the weekend.

Pub Pri Vodnjaku   PUB

(☑041 616 882; Glavni trg 3; ⊙6.30am-midnight Sun-Thu, 6.30am-2am Fri & Sat) Novo Mesto's favourite boozer is as central as you'll find – just 'by the fountain' at the northern end of Glavni trg.

Čajarna Pri Starem Mostu   TEAHOUSE

(☑337 01 60; Glavni trg 17; ⊙7am-10pm Mon-Thu, 7am-midnight Fri, 9am-midnight Sat, 9am-9pm Sun) The Teahouse by the Old Bridge is on the picturesque Krka and serves many varieties of lovely tea (with a nice line of teapots and assorted paraphernalia for sale) as well as drinks, snacks and cakes.

🔒 Shopping

Trgovina Žefran   SOUVENIRS

(☑041 350 424; Glavni trg 1; ⊙8am-noon & 3.30-7pm Mon-Fri, 9am-noon Sat) This hole-in-the-wall in the back of a courtyard at the start of Glavni trg does a lovely line of local souvenirs and handicrafts, including comestibles like local honey and Cviček.

ℹ Information

BANK Abanka (Rozmanova ulica 40)

SKB Banka (Novi trg 3)

BOOKSHOP Knjigarna Goga (🖉393 08 01; Glavni trg 6; ⊗9am-7pm Mon-Fri, 9am-1pm Sat) Lovely arcade bookshop with regional maps, guides and cafe.

POST OFFICE Post Office (Novi trg 7)

TOURIST INFORMATION Tourist Information Centre Novo Mesto (TIC; 🖉393 92 63; www. novomesto.si; Glavni trg 6; ⊗9am-7pm Mon-Fri, 9am-4pm Sat, 9am-noon Sun Apr-Oct, shorter hrs Nov-Mar) Next door to the town hall.

TRAVEL AGENCY Kompas Novo Mesto (🖉393 15 20; www.robinson-sp.si; Novi trg 10; ⊗8am-6pm Mon-Thu, 8am-4pm Fri, 9am-noon Sat) Organises excursions and adventure sports in Dolenjska.

ℹ Getting There & Away

BUS There are frequent departures to Dolenjske Toplice (€2.20, 20 minutes), Otočec ob Krki (€1.80, 10 minutes), Šentjernej (€2.70, 30 minutes) and Šmarješke Toplice (€2.30, 20 minutes). Up to 10 buses a day go to Brežice (€5.20, 70 minutes) and Kostanjevica na Krki (€3.10, 40 minutes), with four to Ljubljana (€7.20, one hour). One or two daily buses go to Črnomelj (€5.20, one hour).

TRAIN Up to 14 trains a day serve Novo Mesto from Ljubljana (€5.50, 1½ hours) via Ivančna Gorica and Trebnje Gorica. Ten of these continue on to Črnomelj (€2.90, 45 minutes) and Metlika (€3.60, one hour), where there are connections to Karlovac in Croatia. There are two train stations – the smaller Novo Mesto-Centro is more convenient for the town centre than Novo Mesto station.

ℹ Getting Around

Book taxis by calling 🖉332 57 77 or 🖉041 625 108. The TIC rents bicycles.

Otočec ob Krki

🖉07 / POP 700 / ELEV 173M

The castle at Otočec, on a tiny island in the middle of the Krka River, 7.5km northeast of Novo Mesto, is one of Slovenia's loveliest and most complete fortresses. The first castle here stood on the right bank of the river, but during the Mongol onslaught in the mid-13th century, a canal was dug on the south side, creating an artificial island. The present castle, which dates from the 16th century, now houses a five-star hotel. The area around Otočec, the gateway to the lower Krka and the Posavje region, has become something of a recreational (especially cycling) centre.

◉ Sights

Otočec Castle CASTLE
(Otoški Grad) Even if you're not staying at the hotel, there's no harm in having a look around Otočec Castle and, if the weather is warm, enjoying a drink or a coffee at the terrace cafe in the courtyard. The castle, with elements of late Gothic and Renaissance architecture, consists of two wings and an entrance block connected by a pentagonal wall. There are four squat, rounded towers with very thick walls, narrow windows and conical roofs at each end.

The castle is 1km east of Otočec village on a secondary road running parallel to the river. You reach the castle via a wooden bridge.

🏃 Activities

The **sport centre** just east of the Hotel Šport can organise **horse riding** and **hot-air ballooning**.

The best areas for boating on the Krka are downstream from Struga; rent canoes from **Kamp Otočec** (🖉040 466 589; per hr €2).

The Krka River around Otočec is a popular **fishing spot** for pike, perch and carp, and fishing permits (per day €15) are available from the Hotel Grad Otočec in the castle.

Tennis Centre TENNIS
(per hr indoor courts €20-24, for guests €18-20, outdoor courts €6-8, for guests €5-7; ⊗8am-11pm) The tennis centre has three indoor courts and six outdoor courts. There's also a sauna and steam room (€8 to €10), and fitness centre (per hour €6), which guests of the Hotel Šport get to use for free.

Golf Grad Otočec GOLF
(🖉041 304 444, 307 56 27; www.terme-krka.si; 9/18 holes Mon-Fri €25/45, Sat & Sun €30/50 Mar-Oct) Along the Krka, about 800m from the castle, the Golf Grad Otočec is Slovenia's newest 18-hole golf course (par 72). Hiring a set of clubs costs €10 and a pull car/electric cart is €4/25.

🛏 Sleeping

Hotel Grad Otočec HOTEL €€€
(🖉384 89 00; www.terme-krka.si; s/d €180/260, ste from €300; P@) The five-star Otočec Castle Hotel is one of the most atmospheric places to stay in Slovenia, but since its epic 2008 renovation (in which they grafted an unsightly lift onto a castle tower) is now off limits to all but the very well-heeled and

gloved. The 10 rooms, with polished parquet floors, oriental carpets, marble-topped tables and large baths, are of a uniform size, though you could lose yourself in one of the half-dozen suites. There are lots of themed packages (golf, cycling, wellness) on offer and guests get to use the thermal pools at Šmarješke Toplice and Dolenjske Toplice free of charge.

Šeruga Farmhouse
GUESTHOUSE €€

(☏334 69 00; turist.kmetija.seruga@siol.net; s/d €32/54) If you want something a bit more rural, this farmhouse in an idyllic valley in Sela pri Ratežu (house No 15), a hamlet about 4km south of Otočec village, has nine double rooms (some with kitchen), a self-catering apartment for four and a recommended restaurant open for lunch and dinner and specialising in trout and *štruklji* (dumplings made with cheese).

Hotel Šport
HOTEL €€

(☏384 86 00; www.terme-krka.si; s €62-66, d €84-96; P@) This hotel, housed in a concrete-and-glass box opposite the castle, has 88 rooms, as well as 38 rooms in attractive detached bungalows (singles €33 to €36, doubles €50 to €56) in the adjacent holiday centre.

Kamp Otočec
CAMPGROUND €

(☏040 466 589; www.sloveniaholidays.com/camp-otocec; adult €7-8.50, child €3.50-4.25; ☺Apr-mid-Oct; P) This camping ground, with 40 sites accommodating 160 guests, is on a 2-hectare strip of land running along the south bank of the Krka with its own grassy 'beach'. To reach it from the castle, cross the second bridge, turn left (east) and walk for 300m.

✗ Eating

Grad
SLOVENIAN €€

(☏384 87 00; starters €6-23, mains €14-25; ☺6am-11pm) At the Hotel Grad Otočec, this restaurant seats 45 people while the smaller Hunter's Room accommodates another 16. With ancient stone walls, stained glass and locally made artisan furniture, it's loaded with atmosphere (check out the plexiglas 'trophies' in the Hunter's Room). Specialities are game and fish; try the unusual beech-leaf soup followed by the red trout with a glass of Dolenjska Cviček and blueberry strudel. The four-course set menus, one of them for vegetarians, are excellent value at €35.

Tango
SLOVENIAN €

(☏384 86 00; meals from €10; ☺noon-11pm Sun-Thu, noon-1am Fri & Sat) Diagonally opposite the Hotel Šport building, the Tango should be a distant second choice to the Grad, but given how fast the Grad fills up with non-guests and wedding parties, you may have no choice.

Gostilna Vovko
SLOVENIAN €

(☏308 56 03; www.gostilna-vovkoi.si; Ratež 48; starters €3.50-6, mains €7-16.50; ☺11am-10pm Tue-Sat, 11am-4pm Sun) If you happen to be under your own steam (of two or four wheels), head south from Otočec for a couple of kilometres to the village of Ratež and try this excellent local *gostilna* serving barbecued meats and such local specialities as pumpkin gnocchi and Dolenjska's own take on *žlikrofi* ('raviolis' stuffed with millet porridge and topped with crackling).

❶ Information

You can change money at the reception of the Hotel Šport or at the post office in Otočec village. There's an ATM at the petrol station next to the Hotel Šport.

❶ Getting There & Around

BUS The buses linking Novo Mesto (€1.70, 15 minutes, 7.5km, five a day to 5pm) and Šmarješke Toplice (€1.80, 15 minutes, 7km, 11 a day to 10.15pm) stop at the bridge leading to the castle.

BICYCLE The sport centre rents bicycles and mountain bikes (per hour/four hours €6/10).

TAXI You can book a taxi on ☏041 708 733 or ☏041 466 330.

Around Otočec ob Krki

The vineyards of **Trška Gora** (428m) can be reached by road and trail from Mačkovec, about 5km southwest of Otočec. From there follow the road north for 1km to Sevno and then continue along the winding track for 2km until you reach Trška Gora and the **Church of St Mary**. From here there are wonderful views of the Gorjanci Hills, Kočevski Rog and the Krka Valley.

Approximately 13km southeast of Otočec, in the shadow of **Trdinov Vrh** (1178m), the highest peak in the Gorjanci and right on the Croatian border, is **Gospodična** (828m) and **Planinski Dom pri Gospodični na Gorjancih** (☏051 661 903, 041 682 469; ☺Wed-Sun mid-Apr–mid-Oct, Sat & Sun mid-Oct–mid-Apr), a Category III mountain lodge containing a restaurant and 49 beds. The route from Otočec goes for 5km southeast to Velike Brusnice, famous for its cherries (and cherry festival in mid-June), then to Gabrje (4.5km) and to Gospodična (3.5km).

Kostanjevica na Krki

07 / POP 720 / ELEV 50M

Situated on an islet just 500m long and 200m wide in a loop of the Krka River, sleepy Kostanjevica is Slovenia's smallest town. And with a charter that dates back to 1252, it is also one of its oldest. Though it's dubbed 'the Venice of Dolenjska' by the tourist industry, as well as being under full protection as a cultural monument, many of its buildings are in poor condition. Still, it remains an important art centre and its location is magical. It's best seen from on high but if you can't afford a ride in a hot-air balloon, have a look at the photographs of the town in *Slovenia from the Air*.

Although most of Kostanjevica's historical sights are on the island, amenities are on the mainland to the northwest or southeast.

◉ Sights

Kostanjevica Castle CASTLE
(Kostanjeviški Grad; ☎498 61 20, 498 70 08; www .galerija-bj.si; Grajska cesta 45; adult/student & child/family €3/1.50/5, Cviček Wine Cellar admission with tasting €7.50; ⏱9am-6pm Tue-Sun Apr-Oct, 9am-4pm Tue-Sun Nov-Mar) About 1.5km southwest of town, this former Cistercian monastery was a very wealthy institution in the Middle Ages, but abandoned in 1785 when monastic orders were dissolved. Today it houses a large and important art collection.

The beautifully painted main entrance through two squat painted towers leads to an enormous courtyard enclosed by a cloister with 230 arcades across three floors. To the west stands the **Church of the Virgin Mary** containing elements from the 13th to 18th centuries; it is now used as exhibition space.

The **Božidar Jakac Gallery** upstairs in the castle contains 16th-century frescoes taken from the church, and also works by such Slovenian artists as the impressionist Božidar Jakac (1899–1989) and brothers France (1895–1960) and Tone Kralj (1900–75), who painted expressionist and-cum-socialist realist canvases

respectively. There's also a permanent collection of Old Masters from the Carthusian monastery at Pleterje.

Also in the castle is the **Cviček Wine Cellar**, all ancient casks and mould a-blooming in the vaulted ceiling. Ask the TIC for the brochure *The Land of Cviček: Podgorjanska Wine Tourist Road*.

Kostanjevica Cave CAVE
(Kostanjeviška Jama; ☎041 97 001, 498 70 88; www.kostanjeviska-jama.com; adult/child/student €6/3/4; ⏱tours 10am, noon, 2pm, 4pm & 6pm daily Jul & Aug, Sat & Sun mid-Apr–Jun, Sep & Oct) This tiny cave, on a partly unsealed road about 1.5km southeast of town, has half-hour tours in spring, summer and autumn. The guide will lead you 300m in (only 750m of the cave has been fully explored), past a small lake and several galleries full of stalactites and stalagmites. The temperature is a constant 12°C. The cave is home to several species of bat.

Old Town NEIGHBOURHOOD
No one's going to get lost or tired touring Kostanjevica – walk 400m up Oražnova ulica and 400m down Talcev ulica and you've seen the lot.

On Kambičev trg, across the small bridge from the bus stop (but enter from Oražnova ulica), stands the Church of St Nicholas (Cerkev Sv Miklavža), a tiny late-Gothic structure. The presbytery contains brightly coloured frescoes of scenes from the Old and New Testaments painted in 1931.

About 200m northwest along Oražnova ulica is a 15th-century manor house containing the **Lamut Art Salon** (Lamutov Likovni Salon; ☎498 81 52; www.galerija-bj.si/arazstav; Oražnova ulica 5; admission €2; ⏱9am-6pm Tue-Sun), a branch of the Božidar Jakac Gallery.

Continue along Oražnova ulica, passing a decrepit fin-de-siècle house (No 24), to the **Parish Church of St James** (Župnijska Cerkev Sv Jakoba), a 13th-century Romanesque building with a mostly baroque interior. Above the carved stone portal on the western side are geometric designs and decorative plants and trees. On the south side is a 15th-century depiction of Jesus rising from the tomb, as well as ancient grave markers embedded in the wall.

Talcev ulica, the island's other street, is lined with attractive 'folk baroque' houses, including the 200-year-old **St Nicholas Pharmacy** at No 20.

PLETERJE MONASTERY

Located 10km southwest of Kostanjevica na Krki, the enormous **Pleterje Monastery** (Samostan Pleterje; ☎308 12 29; www.kartuzija-pleterje.si; Drča 1; admission free; ⊙7.30am-6pm) belongs to the Carthusians, the strictest of all monastic orders. The Gothic **Holy Trinity Church** (also called the Old Gothic Church or Stara Gotska Cerkev), 250m up a linden-lined path from the car park, is the only part of the complex open to the general public. There is a **multimedia display** (€4, including admission to the *skanzen* – an open-air museum displaying village architecture) in a side chapel on Sunday. But the monastery's location in a narrow valley between slopes of the Gorjanci Hills is so attractive and peaceful that it's worth a visit in any case. The **Pleterje Trail** (Pleterski Pot) is a 1½-hour walk in the hills around the complex.

Pleterje was built in 1407 by the Counts of Celje. It was fortified with ramparts, towers and a moat during the Turkish invasions, and all but abandoned during the Protestant Reformation in the 16th century. The Carthusian order, like all monastic communities in the Habsburg Empire, was abolished in 1784. When French Carthusian monks returned in 1899, they rebuilt to the plans of the order's charterhouse at Nancy in France.

You may catch a glimpse of some of the white-hooded monks quietly going about their chores – they take a strict vow of silence – or hear them singing their offices in the Gothic church at various times of the day. But the ubiquitous signs reading *Klavzura – Vstop Prepovedan* (Seclusion – No Entry) and *Območnje Tišine* (Area of Silence) remind visitors that everything apart from the church is off limits.

Above the ribbed main portal of the austere church (1420) is a fresco depicting Mary being crowned and the Trinity. Inside, the rib-vaulted ceiling with its heraldic bosses and the carved stone niches by the simple stone altar are worth a look, as is the medieval rood screen, the low wall across the aisle that separated members of the order from laypeople.

There's a monastery **shop** (⊙7.30am-5.30pm Mon-Sat), where the monks sell some of their own products, including packs of beeswax candles, honey, Cviček wine (€2.80 a litre) and various fruit brandies, including *hruška* (pear) which comes with a pear grown inside each bottle and then picked when ripe.

To the west of the monastery car park is the **Pleterje Open-Air Museum** (Muzej na Prostem; ☎041 639 191, 308 10 50; www.skansen.si; Drča 1; adult/child/family €2.50/1.90/7; ⊙10am-6pm Wed-Sun Apr-Oct, 10am-4pm Tue-Sat Nov-Mar), with thatched peasant houses, a pigsty, hayracks and even an outhouse – moved here from the areas around Šentjernej. The *skanzen* also rents **bicycles** (per hour/day €3/10).

🏃 Activities

Kanu Safari
CANOEING

(☎031 531 069; www.kanusafari.com; ⊙8am-8pm mid-Apr–mid-Oct) Based at the grassy 'beach' along the Krka in front of Bar Štravs, Kanu Safari rents canoes for €10 per hour and can drop you upriver for €30 so you can lazily paddle back.

Hosta Stud Farm
HORSE RIDING

(Kobilarna Hosta; ☎041 690 066, 031 220 059; http://hosta-lipizzans.eu) In the village of Sela pri Šentjerneju, 7km west of Kostanjevica, this is the second-largest stud in Slovenia, after the one at Lipica in Primorska, and has 60 horses. It has riding tours of two hours, a full day and two days and boasts a riding school too.

Kostanjevica na Krki
Balloon Club
HOT-AIR BALLOONING

(☎040 883 007, 489 73 62; www.balonarstvo .net; per person €100) Has 'flightseeing' trips in a hot-air balloon over Kostanjevica and surrounds.

🛏 Sleeping & Eating

Gostilna Žolnir
INN €

(☎041 626 717, 498 71 33; www.zolnir-sp.si; Krška cesta 4; s/d/tr €30/48/60, apt €50-56; P) This comfortable *gostilna*, about 700m northwest of the island, has 12 double rooms and an apartment as well as a wonderful **restaurant** (mains €8.30-11.90; ⊙7am-10pm daily). The owners are very serious about the food and wine they serve. A speciality of Kostanjevica is duck served with *mlinci* (thin dried flatbread) and, of course, Cviček wine.

TOP CHOICE Gostilna Kmečki Hram SLOVENIAN €€
(☏031 369 750, 498 70 78; www.gkh.si; Oražnova ulica 11; starters €5.50-6.50, mains €9.90-18; ⊗noon-10pm Tue-Thu, noon-3am Fri, 9am-3am Sat, 9am-9pm Sun) This wonderful old-style inn with retro decor really looks like the Peasant House it calls itself and offers excellent home-cooking – among the best grilled dishes and roast lamb in Slovenia, locals say. Note the old wine press outside.

🍷 Drinking

Rock Cafe CAFE
(☏041 233 312; Talcev ulica 28; ⊗6am-midnight Mon-Fri & Sun, 6am-2am Sat; 🐾) At the northeastern end of the island, the Rock attracts a relatively raucous (for a comatose town) crowd.

Bar Štravs BAR
(☏041 520 960; Talcev ulica 31; ⊗5.15am-midnight Mon-Thu, 5.15am-1am Fri & Sat, 6am-midnight Sun) Fronting the Krka, this pleasant little bar and cafe is the ideal spot in which to while away a warm and lazy afternoon in Kostanjevica.

ⓘ Information

Nova Ljubljanska Banka (Ljubljanska cesta 6) Southwest of the bus stops on the main road into town.

Post Office (Kambičev trg 5; ⊗8-9.30am & 10am-5pm Mon-Fri, 8am-noon Sat)

Tourist Information Centre Kostanjevica (☏498 81 50; tic-gbj@galerija-bj.si; ⊗9am-6pm Tue-Sun Apr-Oct, 9am-4pm Tue-Sun Nov-Mar) On the ground floor of an old mill just beyond the entrance to Kostanjevica Castle.

ⓘ Getting There & Away

There are daily departures from Kostanjevica to Novo Mesto (€3.10, 40 minutes), Brežice (€2.70, 30 minutes), Ljubljana (€9.20, 1½ hours) and Krško (€2.70, 20 minutes).

Posavje Region

Posavje, the area 'on the river' is rich in archaeological finds from the Hallstatt, Celtic and especially Roman periods. Its large number of fortified castles date from the Turkish invasions from the 15th century, and a century later it took centre stage during the peasant uprisings and the Protestant Reformation. The 19th-century railway brought prosperity.

During WWII, the occupying German forces engaged in a brutal program of 'ethnic cleansing' and expelled more than 15,000 Slovenes. Many were deported to Serbia, Croatia or Germany.

BREŽICE
☏07 / POP 6490 / ELEV 158M

From a traveller's perspective, Brežice is the most interesting town in Posavje. One of the best museums in provincial Slovenia is here, and a popular spa and water-park complex is just down the road.

History

Situated near where the Krka flows into the Sava, Brežice was an important trading centre in the Middle Ages. Its most dominant feature has always been its castle, mentioned in documents as early as 1249. In the 16th century the original castle was replaced with a Renaissance fortress to strengthen the town's defences against the Turks and, later, marauding peasants who, during one uprising, beheaded nobles at the castle and impaled their heads on poles. Today the castle houses the Posavje Museum.

🅞 Sights

Posavje Museum CASTLE MUSEUM
(Posavski Muzej; ☏466 05 17; www.posavski-muzej .si; Cesta Prvih Borcev 1; adult/student & child €2.5/1; ⊗8am-2.30pm Mon-Fri, 10am-2pm Sat & Sun) Housed in Posavje Castle, the Posavje Museum is one of provincial Slovenia's richest museums, particularly for its archaeological and ethnographic collections.

From the courtyard with arcades on the west side you ascend a staircase whose walls and ceiling are illustrated with Greek gods, the four Evangelists and the Attems family coat of arms. Rooms on the 2nd floor are archaeological; look out for the skeletons from the 9th century BC unearthed near Dobova, the 5th-century BC bronze horse bridle and the Celtic and Roman jewellery. In the ethnographic rooms, along with the carved wooden bowls, decorated chests and plaited loaves of bread, there is a strange beehive in the shape of a soldier from the early 1800s.

Rooms on the 1st floor cover life in the Posavje region in the 16th century and during the two world wars, with special emphasis on the deportation of Slovenes by the Germans during WWII. The museum's real crowd-pleaser is the Knights' Hall (Viteška Dvorana), an Italian baroque masterpiece where everything except for the floor is painted with landscapes, and classical gods, heroes, allegories and muses.

🏃 Activities

The thermal spring near Čatež ob Savi, situated 3km southeast of Brežice, has attracted rheumatics since the late 18th century. Today, the huge **Terme Čatež** (⏰493 50 00, 493 67 00; www.terme-catez.si; Topliška cesta 35) complex is every bit as much a recreational area. The spa counts 10 thermal-water (27°C to 36°C) outdoor pools at the **Poletna Termalna Riviera** (Summer Thermal Riviera; day pass adult/child Mon-Fri €10.50/9, Sat & Sun €13/11; ⏰8am-8pm Jun-Aug, 9am-7pm Apr, May & Sep), with massive slides, fountains and artificial waves. The indoor **Zimska Termalna Riviera** (Winter Thermal Riviera; day pass adult/child Mon-Fri €12/10, Sat & Sun €15/12; ⏰9am-9pm year-round) complex has a water temperature of about 32°C. The spa's **Sauna Park** boasts eight different saunas, a steam room, Roman bath, solarium, gym, a jogging track along the river, tennis courts and a naturists' terrace.

You can rent a **bicycle** (per two hour/five hour/day €4/6/8.50) from the Terme Čatež TIC. Ask at the TIC for a free copy of its *Cycling & Hiking Brežice Map*.

🎉 Festivals & Events

Seviqc Brežice MUSIC FESTIVAL
(www.seviqc-brezice.si; ⏰ Jun-Jul) This month-long series of concerts, featuring ancient music, is held in various venues around the region, including the Knights' Halls in the castles at Brežice, Bizeljsko and Mokrice, and at the Hotel Toplice at Čatež ob Savi.

🛌 Sleeping

Camping Terme Čatež CAMPGROUND €
(⏰493 50 100; www.terme-catez.si; Topliška cesta 35; per person €16-17.50; ⏰year-round; P🏊) This five-star, 3.6-hectare camping ground accommodates 550 guests at the Terme Čatež spa complex. The daily rate includes two day-long entrances to the outdoor swimming pools or one three-hour pass to the Zimska Termalna Riviera.

Terme Čatež Spa Complex HOTEL €€
(⏰493 67 00, 493 50 00; www.terme-catez.si; Topliška cesta 35; apt 1-3 people €71-93, 4-5 people €85-147) The Terme Čatež spa complex has some 15 apartments and three hotels. **Hotel Toplice** (s €107-114, d €170-184; P❄🏊) has 139 rooms and four stars in both a new and an old (1925) wing. The nicest of the three properties, the four-star **Hotel Terme** (s €114-122, d €184-200; P❄🏊) in a somewhat isolated section of the complex and has 149 rooms.

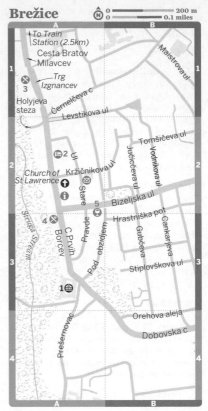

Brežice

Hotel Splavar HOTEL €€
(⏰041 428 362, 499 06 30; www.splavar.si; Cesta Prvih Borcev 40a; s/d €50/75; P@) The Raftman, with 16 rooms on Brežice's main street, is above the Gostilna Splavar and popular

Rafter's Pub. The rooms are in the back and are dark, but the staff are welcoming and friendly.

✕ Eating

TOP CHOICE Oštarija Debeluh   SLOVENIAN €€
(☑496 10 70; Trg Izgnancev 7; mains €18-22; ⊘noon-4pm Mon-Sat) This attractive eatery, whose name roughly translates as Fatty's Inn, serves the best and most inventive Slovenian and international dishes in Brežice, including horse pâté with carpaccio (€6.50). The all-Slovenian wine list is admirable and the advice sage.

Gostilna Splavar   SLOVENIAN €
(Cesta Prvih Borcev 40a; mains €7-17; ⊘7am-10pm Mon-Fri, noon-10pm Sun) A popular B&B, this *gostilna* is also a fine restaurant with a winter garden and summer terrace. The Laški Rizling, a slightly fruity, medium-dry wine from Bizeljsko, is not a bad accompaniment to the fish dishes on offer. It's also celebrated for its homemade ice cream.

Santa Lucia   PIZZA €
(☑041 624 596, 499 25 00; Cesta Prvih Borcev 15; starters €4-5, pizza €5.50-7.80, mains €7-11; ⊘11am-11pm) This pizzeria with an over-the-top ceiling fresco does a roaring trade in takeaway and eat-in pizza. There's both a front and back terrace.

🍺 Drinking

Rafter's Pub   BAR
(Cesta Prvih Borcev 40a; ⊘6am-10pm Mon-Fri, 6am-11pm Sat, 8am-11pm Sun) This popular English-style pub has tables spilling out on to the main street.

Aquarius Café Bar   BAR
(☑499 25 05; Bizeljska ulica 4; ⊘7am-11pm Sun-Thu, 7am-1am Fri & Sat) Housed on three levels of Brežice's unmistakeable pink and half-timbered water tower (1914), this cafe-bar is decorated with old photos of the town and faux antiques.

ℹ Information
Nova Ljubljanska Banka (Cesta Prvih Borcev 42)

Post Office (Ulica Stare Pravde 34) In a new building behind the Church of St Lawrence.

SKB Banka (Cesta Prvih Borcev 39)

Terme Čatež Tourist Information Centre (TIC; ☑493 67 57, 041 530 427; Topliška cesta 35; ⊘8am-7pm Mon-Fri, 9am-4pm Sat, 9am-2pm Sun Jun-Aug, shorter hrs Sep-May)

Tourist Information Centre Brežice (TIC; ☑496 69 95; www.visitbrezice.com; Cesta Prvih Borcev 22; ⊘8am-4pm Mon-Fri)

ℹ Getting There & Around
BUS Buses make the run to Terme Čatež (€1.30, five minutes) at least half-hourly Monday to Saturday. There are two regular daily buses to Bizeljsko (€2.70, 30 minutes), as well as up to four to Ljubljana (€10.70, 2¼ hours), Kostanjevica (€2.70, 30 minutes) and Novo Mesto (€5.20, 70 minutes).

TRAIN As many as 16 trains a day serve Brežice from Ljubljana (€7.30, two hours) via Zidani Most, Sevnica and Krško. Many of these trains carry on to Zagreb in Croatia.

TAXI You can order a taxi on ☑041 611 391.

AROUND BREŽICE

MOKRICE CASTLE
☑07 / ELEV 200M

Mokrice Castle, about 10km southeast of Brežice, is the loveliest fortress in the Posavje region and is also a luxury hotel. With grounds including pear orchards and a 20-hectare 'English park' full of rare plants, it's worth an excursion from Brežice.

The castle today dates from the 16th century, but there are bits and pieces going back to Roman times built into the structure. It's supposedly haunted by the ghost of the 17th-century countess Barbara, who committed suicide here after her lover failed to return from sea. She's particularly active on her name day (4 December) when she spends the night rolling cannonballs around the joint.

The 29 rooms at the **Golf Hotel Mokrice Castle** (☑457 42 40; www.terme-catez.si; s €120-128, d €190-206, ste from €250; @🏊) have beamed ceilings and period furniture, and the huge suites have fireplaces. The **Grad** (mains €8.50-20; ⊘7am-11pm) restaurant is a gorgeous venue with fancy game and fish dishes, and classical music. The cellar has dozens of different Slovenian wines available. Try some *viljamovka*, Mokrice's famous pear brandy.

You can reach Mokrice from Brežice on the infrequent bus to the border town of Obrežje (€1.80, 15 minutes). Better is by bicycle from Čatež – ask the TIC in Brežice for their *Cycling Booklet* with four itineraries.

BIZELJSKO-SREMIČ WINE DISTRICT
☑07 / ELEV TO 175M

Cycling the 18km from Brežice to **Bizeljsko** is a great way to see the Bizeljsko-Sremič wine country, stopping off whenever you see a *gostilna*, *vinska klet* (wine cellar) or *repnica* (flint-stone cave for storing wine) that takes your fancy. In Bizeljsko, try some of the local medium-dry whites and reds at the **Vinska Klet Pinterič** (☑041 520 481, 495 12 66; Bizeljska cesta 115; ☉10am-7pm) or at **Gostilna Šekoranja** (☑495 13 10; Bizeljska cesta 72; ☉8am-11pm Tue-Sun). In the nearby village of Stara Vas, visit the **Vinoteka Pri Peču** (☑452 01 03; ☉10am-midnight Wed-Mon) or **Repnica Pudvoi** (☑031 484 003, 495 12 28; ☉11am-7pm Sat or by appointment) cellars at house No 58 and No 89 respectively.

BELA KRAJINA

Bela Krajina has countless opportunities for active pursuits and relaxing stops along the heritage trails and wine roads. Ask the TIC in Metlika or Črnomelj for the excellent brochure-map *Kolesarske Poti Bela Krajina* (Bela Krajina Bike Trails), with 15 itineraries – some of them circular – outlined. Bela Krajina contains two important parks: the 259-hectare Lahinja Country Park and a large part of the 4332-hectare Kolpa Country Park.

Like Dolenjska, Bela Krajina is famous for its Hallstatt and Roman sites; a 3rd-century shrine to the god Mithra near the village of Rožanec is one of the best preserved in Europe. In the Middle Ages, Bela Krajina was the most remote part of Slovenia, and in some ways it still feels like that. Many of the peasant uprisings of the 15th and 16th centuries started here or just across the border in Croatia.

Metlika

☑07 / POP 3273 / ELEV 167M

Metlika lies in a valley at the foot of the Gorjanci Hills and is an excellent springboard for hiking and cycling in the area. It is surrounded by Croatia on three sides; the Kolpa River and its 'beaches' lie about 1km to the south. There was a major Hallstatt settlement here during the early Iron Age, and the Romans established an outpost in Metlika on the road leading to the important river port of Sisak in Croatia. During the Turkish onslaught of the 15th and 16th centuries, Metlika was attacked 17 times and occupied in 1578.

◉ Sights

Trg Svobode   SQUARE
Located in **Metlika Castle** (Metliški Grad; Trg Svobode 4) with its splendid courtyard, the **Bela Krajina Museum** (Belokranjski Muzej; ☑305 81 77, 306 33 70; www.belokranjski-muzej.si;

adult/child/student & senior €3.50/2.50/3; ☉9am-5pm Mon-Sat, 10am-2pm Sun) houses a collection of local archaeological finds. There's Hallstatt metalwork from Pusti and Roman displays, as well as items relating to the area's ethnology and agriculture. A 20-minute film introduces the collection in four different languages.

Metlika was the first town in Slovenia to have its own fire brigade (1869), commemorated by the **Slovenian Firefighters' Museum** (Slovenski Gasilski Muzej; ☑305 86 97; Trg Svobode 5; admission €1; ☉9am-2pm Tue-Sat, 9am-noon Sun). There are old fire trucks with enormous wheels, ladders and buckets.

Mestni Trg   SQUARE
This colourful, leafy square, where a dry-goods and produce market is held every first and third Tuesday of the month, contains stunning 18th- and 19th-century buildings, including the neo-Gothic **town hall** (Mestni trg 24). At the southern end of the square is the so-called **Commandery** (Komenda; Mestni trg 2), which once belonged to the Knights of the Teutonic Order. Note the Maltese cross above the entrance. To the northwest is the **Parish Church of St Nicholas** (Farna Cerkev Sv Nikolaja). On the ceiling are sobering contemporary frescoes of the Day of Judgment, with devils leading sinners to damnation.

Kambič Gallery   GALLERY
(Galerija Kambič; ☑305 83 32; Cesta Bratstva in Enotnosti 51; ☉10am-4pm Tue-Sat, 10am-1pm Sun) This suprisingly good gallery has 200 artworks donated by a university professor and stages cutting-edge temporary exhibits. Metlika-born Alojzij Gangl (1859–1935) has pride of place.

✇ Activities

The Kolpa River is clean and very warm (up to 30°C in summer), so you might want to go **swimming** at the Primostek or Podzemelj camping grounds.

There are a lot of **hikes** and **walks** in the surrounding areas, including the 6.5km-long **St Urban's Trail** (Urbanova Pot) to Grabrovec and back via **Veselica**, a 233m-high small hill less than 1km north of Metlika, with great views over the town. Another is the **Učna Pot Zdence Vidovec** from the village of Božakovo, just east of Rosalnice, to the Zdence and Vidovec karst caves. Ask the TIC for brochures outlining the walks. It also has the *Kolesarske Poti Bela Krajina* (Bela Krajina Bike Trails) brochure-map.

DOLENJSKA & BELA KRAJINA METLIKA

Metlika

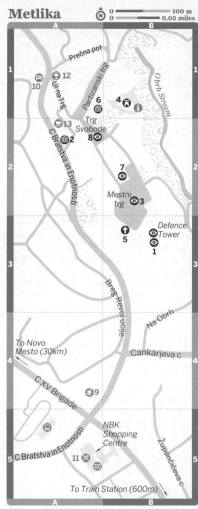

N 0 ——— 100 m
0 ——— 0.05 miles

Metlika

◉ Sights
Bela Krajina Museum .... (see 4)
1 Commandery B3
2 Kambič Gallery.....................................A2
3 Mestni Trg..B2
4 Metlika Castle.. B1
5 Parish Church of St Nicholas B3
6 Slovenian Firefighters' Museum......... A1
7 Town Hall B2
8 Trg Svobode A2

◎ Activities, Courses & Tours
9 Vinska Klet...A4

◎ Sleeping
10 Hotel Bela Krajina A1

◎ Eating
Hotel Bela Krajina .... (see 10)
11 Julija Pizzeria......................................A5

◎ Drinking
12 Bar Na Draga A1
Grajska Klet .... (see 4)
13 Slaščičarna Murn................................A2

Ask the TIC about organised wine tastings at the **Vinska Klet** (☑363 70 52; www.kz-metlika.si; Cesta XV Brigade 2; per person €2.50-8.50; ☺8am-3pm Mon-Fri, 8am-noon Sat or by appointment), the 'Wine Cellar' run by the local wine cooperative, which usually requires a minimum 'group' of 10 people.

🎉 Festivals & Events

Vinska Vigred   WINE FESTIVAL
(www.metlika-turizem.si; ☺May) Metlika's main event is the Vinska Vigred wine festival held on the third weekend of May.

🛏 Sleeping

Hotel Bela Krajina   HOTEL €€
(☑040 327 492, 305 81 23; www.hotel-belakrajina.si; Cesta Bratstva in Enotnosti 28; s/d/tr €53/87/105; P🌬@🛜) A former Slovenian socialist holdover pulled into the 21st century with air-conditioning and upgraded furnishings.

Kamp Podzemelj ob Kolpi   CAMPGROUND €
(☑363 52 81, 306 95 72; www.kamp-podzemelj.si; Podzemelj 16b; campsite adult/child €7.80/5.50, caravans for 4 €33-74; ☺May–mid-Sep; P🏊) A large and well-equipped camping ground with a 'beach' on the Kolpa River, 7km southwest of Metlika. It accommodates 70 tents and 250 guests. Without wheels, the only way to reach it is by train from Metlika and it's a 2km walk from the station at Gradac.

🍴 Eating

Hotel Bela Krajina   SLOVENIAN €
(Cesta Bratstva in Enotnosti 28; starters €5.20-9.50, mains €6.90-13.20; ☺8am-10pm) This convivial place, which starts you off with a giant loaf of *belokranjska pogača* (local flatbread), is the best place for a meal in Metlika. Try the Bela Krajina–style *žlikrofi* (raviolis; €6) and the excellent trout in white wine.

Gostilna Budački
SLOVENIAN €€

(☎363 52 00; Ulica Belokranjskega Odreda 14; meals from €15; ☺8am-10pm Mon-Fri, 8am-11pm Sat & Sun) One of the very few 'real' places to eat in the city limits, this *gostilna* 450m south of the centre gets good reviews for its home-style cooking.

Julija Pizzeria
PIZZA €

(☎305 94 87; NBK 9; pizza €4.50-7.20; ☺7am-midnight Sun-Thu, 7am-1am Fri & Sat) This pizzeria, with a popular bar (open from 9am to 11pm daily) just opposite, is in the large shopping centre across from the bus station.

⚑ Drinking

Slaščičarna Murn
CAFE

(☎041 952 058; Ulica na Trg 3; ☺8am-noon Tue, 9am-noon & 3-5pm Wed-Fri, 8am-1pm Sat, 8-10am Sun) This little cafe with the bankers' hours serves the best cakes and ice cream in town.

Grajska Klet
WINE TASTING

(☎031 632 470, 305 89 99; ☺7am-11pm Mon-Thu, 7am-midnight Fri, 8am-midnight Sat, 8am-noon Sun) If you want to try some Bela Krajina wine but don't have the time to get out into the countryside, head for this *vinoteka* (wine-tasting cellar) in the castle courtyard. You can sample pinot blanc, chardonnay, rieslings and sweet *rumeni muškat* (yellow muscatel).

Bar Na Draga
BAR

(☎040 309 970; Ulica na Trg; ☺7am-11pm Mon-Thu, 7am-1.30am Fri & Sat) Opposite Hotel Bela Krajina, this large pub is popular among Metlika's youngbloods and stays open late.

❶ Information

Metlika Public Library (Ljudska Knjižnica Metlika; ☎305 83 70, 369 15 20; Cesta Bratstva in Enotnosti 23; ☺11am-6pm Mon, 9am-3pm Tue-Fri Jul & Aug, 10am-6pm Mon, Wed & Fri, 7am-3pm Tue & Thu, 7.30am-12.30pm Sat Sep-Jun) Free internet access.

Nova Ljubljanska Banka (NBK 2)
Nova Ljubljanska Banka (Trg Svobode 7)
Post Office (NBK 2)
Tourist Information Centre (TIC; ☎363 54 70; www.metlika-turizem.si; Trg Svobode 4; ☺8am-5pm Mon-Fri, 9am-1pm Sat Jun-Aug, 8am-4pm Mon-Fri, 9am-noon Sat Sep-May)

❶ Getting There & Around

BUS Destinations served by bus from Metlika include Črnomelj (€2.70, 30 minutes, seven daily during the week), Novo Mesto (€3.60, one

hour, 30km) and Vinica (€5.60, 1½ hours, 46km, three daily during the week).

TRAIN Metlika has up to eight trains daily from Ljubljana (€7.20, 2¾ hours) via Novo Mesto and Črnomelj (€1.60, 20 minutes). Three to five trains a day head for Karlovac in Croatia.

TAXI Book a taxi on ☎041 708 733.

Metlika Wine Area

☎07 / ELEV TO 235M

The hills to the north and northeast of Metlika are some of the Bela Krajina wine district's most important areas and produce such distinctive wines as Metliška Črnina (the ruby-red 'Metlika Black') and a late-maturing sweet 'ice wine' called Kolednik Ledeno Vino. They're also superb areas for easy walking.

On the way to **Vinomer** and **Drašiči**, two important wine towns about 4km and 6km respectively from Metlika, you'll walk through *steljniki*, stands of birch trees growing among ferns in clay soil – the very symbol of Bela Krajina.

Drašiči is famous for its folk architecture, and you can sample local wines at several places, including the **Simonič farmhouse** (☎041 572 596, 305 81 85; Drašiči 56) and the **Prus farmhouse** (☎041 690 112, 305 90 98; Krmačina 6). Be sure to phone ahead. Ask the TIC in Metlika about wine tastings at the 250-year-old **Soseska Zidanica** (☎041 788 938; Drašiči 46; ☺by appointment), a vineyard cottage next to the Church of St Peter in the centre of Drašiči.

Črnomelj

☎07 / POP 14,717 / ELEV 163M

The capital of Bela Krajina and its largest town, Črnomelj (pronounced cher-*no*-ml) is on a promontory in a loop where the Lahinja and Dobličica Rivers meet. This relaxed town is the 'folk heart' of Bela Krajina, and its popular Jurjevanje festival attracts hundreds of dancers and singers from the region.

Črnomelj's Roman presence is evident from the Mithraic shrine at Rožanec, about 4km northwest of the town. During the Turkish invasions in the 15th and 16th centuries the town was attacked incessantly, but due to its strong fortifications and excellent hilltop lookouts it was never taken. After Italy's surrender in 1943, the town functioned for a time as Slovenia's capital.

Črnomelj

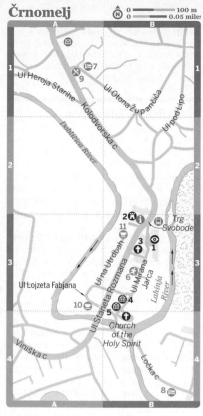

Legend has it that Črnomelj (a corruption of the words for 'black miller') got its name when a beggar, dissatisfied with the quality of the flour she'd been given, put a curse on the local miller. The town's symbol today is a smiling baker holding a pretzel.

◉ Sights & Activities

Črnomelj Castle   CASTLE

(Črnomeljski Grad; Trg Svobode 3) The castle, parts of which date from the mid-12th century, houses the **Town Museum Collection** (Mestna Muzejska Zbirka; ☎306 11 00, 305 65 30; www.belokranjski-muzej.si; adult/child €1/0.50; ◷8am-4pm Mon-Fri, 9am-noon Sat) on the 1st floor, with items and documents related to the history of Črnomelj and Bela Krajina.

Commandery   LANDMARK

(Komenda; Trg Svobode 1) The Commandery of the Teutonic Knights, the grey building with stone reliefs across the square to the south-east of the castle, was originally built in the mid-17th century. Opposite are the foundations of Črnomelj's original castle.

Parish Church of St Peter   CHURCH

(Cerkev Sv Petra; Ulica Staneta Rozmana) The church dates to the 13th century but what you'll see today is a standard-issue baroque structure with a single spire. There are Roman tombstones built into the walls, and on the western exterior above the main entrance, is a fresco of St Christopher.

Špelič House   GALLERY

(Špeličeva Hiša; ☎306 11 90, 040 238 714; Ulica Mirana Jarca 20; ◷8am-noon Mon, Wed & Fri) Hosts a gallery of Bela Krajina art. Next door, **Primožič House** (Primožičeva Hiša; Ulica Mirana Jarca 18; ◷8am-4pm Mon-Fri, 9am-noon Sat) has local arts and crafts on display and for sale.

Črnomelj Wine Cellar   WINE TASTING

(Črnomaljska Klet; ☎305 65 30; Ulica Mirana Jarca) The wine cellar, in the basement of the beautifully renovated music school, offers tastings from the Bela Krajina wine-growing district with *belokranjska pogača* (local flatbread) and cheese for €7 (though you might have to join a group).

Hiking

A popular hike starts at the northern end of Ulica 21 Oktobra; it goes for 18km northwest to Mirna Gora (1047m), where you can stay

1000m high at Category III **Planinski Dom na Mirni Gori** (☑041 910 357, 306 85 73; ☺Tue-Sun), with nine rooms and three dorms.

✪ Festivals & Events

Jurjevanje   CULTURAL FESTIVAL
(www.jurjevanje.si; ☺mid-Jun) One of the most important and oldest festivals of Slovenian folklore, Jurjevanje is five days of music, dance and bonfires at the fairground near the train station and other locations around town in mid-June. It's based on the Zeleni Jurij (Green George), an early Slavic deity of vegetation, fertility and spring.

⊨ Sleeping

Camping grounds in the region of Črnomelj include those at Podzemelj, 9km northeast of Črnomelj; Adlešiči, 12km to the southeast; and Vinica, 19km to the south.

Gostilna Müller   B&B €
(☑041 689 056, 356 72 00; Ločka cesta 6; r per person €25; P) This B&B across the river to the south of the Old Town is pretty decent. The four rooms are bright and attractive, and it's an easy walk into central Črnomelj.

Dijaški Dom Črnomelj   HOSTEL €
(☑040 734 230, 306 21 60; www.dd-crnomelj.si; Ulica Otona Župančiča 7; dm per person €15; ☺year-round; P@) This HI-affiliated hostel has 60 beds in 10 doubles and as many triples open to visitors in summer. A third of those are available year-round.

✕ Eating

Pri Klepcu   PIZZA €
(☑356 74 70; Kolodvorska cesta 24; pizza €3.20-6.50; ☺9am-10pm Mon-Thu, 9am-11pm Fri, noon-11pm Sat, 4-10pm Sun) For pizza, try this place just southeast of the bank and post office. It's not the most authentic but it's cheap and central. Enter from Ulica Otona Župančiča.

Gostilna Müller   SLOVENIAN €
(Ločka cesta 6; starters €5-7.50, mains €7-12; ☺8am-10pm Tue-Fri, 11am-11pm Sat, 11am-10pm Sun) This guesthouse restaurant is just so-so, but is one of the few real options in Črnomelj. Try the cold-meat platter.

☕ Drinking

Odeon Café   CAFE
(☑305 22 86; Ulica na Utrdbah 2; ☺7am-11pm Sun-Thu, 7am-midnight Fri & Sat; 🛜) This wonderful little place in a renovated old building just west of Črnomelj Castle overlooks the Dobličica River and has outside seating in the warmer months.

Črnomaljska Kavarna   CAFE
(☑040 741 006; Ulica Lojzeta Fabjana 7; ☺7am-10pm Mon-Thu, 7am-midnight Fri-Sun) Known locally as 'the mayor's place' (his wife owns it), the Črnomelj Cafe is an upmarket pub-cafe serving hot and cold drinks just below the bridge over the Lahinja River.

❶ Information

Nova Ljubljanska Banka (Kolodvorska cesta 32b)
Nova Ljubljanska Banka (Trg Svobode 2)
Post Office (Kolodvorska cesta 30)
Tourist Information Centre Črnomelj (TIC; ☑040 883 162, 305 65 30; www.belakrajina.si; Trg Svobode 3; ☺8am-4pm Mon-Fri, 9am-noon Sat) On the ground floor of Črnomelj Castle.

❶ Getting There & Around

BUS Črnomelj's bus connections are poor, although there are up to nine daily departures to Vinica (€2.70, 30 minutes) depending on the season; two daily buses to Adlešiči (€2.30, 30 minutes); a couple to Novo Mesto (€5.20, one hour); and weekday departure to Ljubljana (€9.60, 2½ hours).

TRAIN Črnomelj is served by up to nine trains a day from Ljubljana (€6.50, 2½ hours) via Novo Mesto. There are also trains for Karlovac in Croatia.

BICYCLE You can hire bicycles from **L Šport** (☑040 657 657, 305 24 81; Kolodvorska cesta 13; per day €10; ☺8am-7pm Mon-Fri, 8am-noon Sat).

Around Črnomelj

SEMIČ
POP 2050

A **wine road** *(vinska cesta)* runs from Tanča Gora, 5km southwest of Črnomelj, northward through Dobliička Gora, Stražnji Vrh and Ručetna Vas to Semič. This attractive little town, 9km north of Črnomelj, has the ruins of a 13th-century **castle** and **church**.

ROŽANEC
☑07 / POP 65 / ELEV 195M

About 4km northwest of Črnomelj is the village of Rožanec; to reach it, turn west just after Lokve. From the village centre a sign points along a trail leading about 400m to the **Mithraeum** (Mitrej), a temple in a cavern dedicated to the god Mithra (p162), dating from the 2nd century AD. One of the

MITHRA & THE GREAT SACRIFICE

Mithraism, the worship of the god Mithra, originated in Persia. As Roman rule extended west, the religion became extremely popular with traders, imperial slaves and mercenaries of the Roman army, and spread rapidly throughout the empire in the 1st and 2nd centuries AD. In fact, Mithraism was the principal rival of Christianity until Constantine, a Christian convert, came to the throne in the 4th century.

Mithraism's devotees guarded its secrets well. What little is known of Mithra, the god of justice and social contract, has been deduced from reliefs and icons found in temples, such as the ones at Rožanec near Črnomelj and at Ptuj in Štajerska. Mithra is portrayed in Persian dress sacrificing a white bull in front of Sol, the sun god. From the bull's blood sprout grain and grapes, and from its semen animals grow. Sol's wife Luna, the moon, begins her cycle and time is born.

Mithraism and Christianity shared many ritual aspects and competed strongly. Both religions involved the birth of a deity on winter solstice, shepherds, death and resurrection, and a form of baptism. Devotees of Mithraism knelt when they worshipped and a common meal – a 'communion' of bread and water – was a feature of the liturgy.

exposed limestone faces is a 1.5m-high carved relief of Mithra sacrificing the sacred bull, watched by the sun and moon with a dog, serpent and scorpion at his feet.

LAHINJA COUNTRY PARK
07 / ELEV TO 242M

This 259-hectare park, about 9km south of Črnomelj, is a protected karst area rich in birdlife and is the source of the Lahinja River. Trails criss-cross the area. The areas around **Pusti Gradac** and **Veliki Nerajec** are treasure troves of prehistoric finds and caves. The **Lahinja Park Information Centre** (031 705 519, 305 74 28) is in Veliki Nerajec at house No 18a. There's also a shop here selling local folk art and crafts including distinctive 'kingfisher' whistles.

Kolpa Valley
07 / ELEV TO 264M

The 118km-long Kolpa River marks the border with Croatia, and is the warmest and one of the cleanest rivers in the country. As a result, it has become a popular recreational area for swimming, fishing and boating, especially around the village of **Vinica** and to the northeast (and downstream) **Adlešiči**.

◉ Sights

Žuniči   VILLAGE
In the village of Žuniči, about 10km northeast of Vinica, keep your eyes open for traditional rural architecture, especially the farmsteads at Nos 2 and 5, which are sometimes open to the public.

Čebelar Adlešič   FARM
(Adlešič Beekeepers; 307 02 37; Purga 5) While passing through the village of **Purga** just north of Adlešiči, visit the Čebelar Adlešič. The family will be happy to show you their hives, explain all things apiarian, and sell you their honey and *domača medica* (homemade mead).

Pobrežje Castle   CASTLE
The ruins of 16th-century Pobrežje Castle, on a steep rock above the Kolpa River about 1km northeast of Purga, are worth exploring.

🏃 Activities

Much of the Slovenian riverbank from Fučkovci, just north of Adlešiči, as far southwest as Stari Trg ob Kolpi forms the **Kolpa Country Park** (Kolpa Krajinski Park; 356 52 40; www.kp-kolpa.si; information centre Adlešiči 15), a protected area of natural wonders and cultural monuments. The **Žagar farmhouse** (306 44 41, 041 609 920; zvonko.zagar@volja .net) in Damelj (house No 11), southwest of Vinica, rents canoes and minirafts (per day €15 or €18) and organises river excursions. There's rapid-water kayaking from Stari Trg, 20km upriver, to Vinica costing €20, organised by **Grand Kolpa** (305 51 01, 041 740 798; www.grandkolpa-sp.si; Stari Trg ob Kolpi 15). It also rents canoes and rafts.

From Adlešiči two easy **hikes** to nearby hills afford great views of the surrounding countryside. To get to **Mala Plešivica** (341m), walk south along a marked trail for about half an hour. A short distance to the west is a sinkhole with a water source called Vodenica; steps lead down to the source, where you'll find a large stone vault. **Velika Plešivica** (363m), topped with a 12th-century church, is about an hour's walk northwest of Adlešiči. The *Tourist Destination Bela Krajina* brochure, available from the TICs in Metlika and Črnomelj, includes suggested itineraries.

🛏 Sleeping & Eating

Grabrijanovi Farmhouse GUESTHOUSE €
(☑040 391 286, 307 00 70; Adlešiči 5; r per person €24; ◷Mar–mid-Jan; P) This farmhouse, with five rooms and one apartment on the main road 500m from the Kolpa in Adlešiči, is one of the better choices in the area and the food gets rave reviews. Bikes are available for free to guests.

Camping Kolpa Vinica CAMPGROUND €
(☑031 513 060; www.kamp-kolpa.si; Vinica 19a; per adult €6-7.50, child €4.50-5.50, chalets €48-60; ◷May-Sep; P) This camping ground by the Kolpa River has 60 tent and caravan sites, as well as chalets for four people.

Pri Štefaniču Farmhouse GUESTHOUSE €
(☑041 689 057, 305 73 47; Dragatuš 22; d per person from €20; P) This farmhouse, with a popular restaurant that serves produce almost uniquely grown here (including buckwheat ground at the nearby Klepčev mill), has accommodation in four double rooms

and is an excellent starting point for walks in Lahinja Country Park.

Gostilna Balkovec SLOVENIAN €
(☑305 76 32; starters €4.80-6.50, mains €7.20-9.50; ◷8am-11pm) This little *gostilna* in Mali Nerajec (house No 3), on the edge of Lahinja Country Park, specialises in *pečenka* (roast meat), especially *jagenjček* (roast lamb).

Gostilna Milič SLOVENIAN €
(☑307 00 19; Adlešiči 15; meals from €12; ◷11am-midnight Tue-Thu, 11am-1am Fri & Sat, 9am-10pm Sun) In the centre of Adlešiči, Milič's drawcard is a large baker's oven that produces anything and everything from pizza to roast suckling pig.

🛍 Shopping

The Lahinja Park Information Centre in Veliki Nerajec has a wide range of locally produced quality handicrafts for sale.

At Čebelar Adlešič you can buy honey, mead, beeswax, pollen and propolis, the sticky substance collected from certain trees by bees to cement their hives, which is considered an elixir.

❶ Getting There & Around

Depending on the season, up to nine buses a day link Vinica with Črnomelj (€2.60, 30 minutes) via Dragatuš. There are a couple of buses a day from Adlešiči to Črnomelj (€2.20, 30 minutes).

Štajerska & Koroška

Includes »

Why Go?

Štajerska (Styria in English), far and away Slovenia's largest province, gets a bum rap from other Slovenes. They dismiss the province as one huge industrial farm and tease the locals for being country bumpkins. It's true that Štajerska has more big agricultural land than any other part of Slovenia, but it also has the Savinja Alps, to the west, and the Pohorje Massif, an adventure-land of outdoor activities, to the north. Those in search of culture will be drawn to three of the country's most fascinating historical centres: Maribor, Celje and that little gem, Ptuj.

In stark contrast is tiny Koroška, a mere shadow of what it was before being truncated after WWI. Basically just three valleys, Koroška is a region of forests, mountains and highland meadows and is tailor-made for outdoor activities, including skiing, mountain biking, horse riding and hiking.

Best Places to Eat

» Gostilna Ribič (p177)
» Pri Florjanu (p181)
» Lastoria (p189)
» Gril Ranca (p180)

Best Places to Stay

» MCC Hostel (p189)
» MuziKafe (p176)
» Hotel Mitra (p176)
» Hostel Pekarna (p179)

When to Go

Maribor

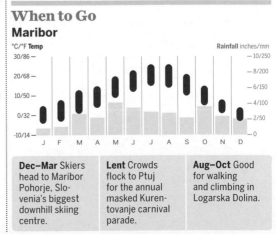

Dec–Mar Skiers head to Maribor Pohorje, Slovenia's biggest downhill skiing centre.

Lent Crowds flock to Ptuj for the annual masked Kurentovanje carnival parade.

Aug–Oct Good for walking and climbing in Logarska Dolina.

ŠTAJERSKA

Štajerska has long been the crossroads of Slovenia and virtually everyone has 'slept here' – Celts, Romans, early Slavs, Habsburgs and the Nazi occupiers. In the 14th century the German-speaking Counts of Celje were among the richest and most powerful feudal dynasties in Central Europe and they challenged the Austrian monarchy's rule for a century. Štajerska suffered more than most of the rest of Slovenia during WWII, when many of its inhabitants were murdered, deported or sent to Nazi labour camps.

Kozjansko Region

Kozjansko is a remote region along the eastern side of the Posavje Mountains and the 90km-long Sotla River, which forms part of the eastern border with Croatia. It is an area of forests, rolling hills, vineyards, scattered farms and the site of one of Slovenia's three regional parks, with much to offer visitors in the way of spas, two important castles, hiking, cycling and excellent wine.

PODČETRTEK & AROUND
⏱03 / POP 565 / ELEV 211M

Most people make their way to this village, on a little bump of land extending into Croatia, to relax at the Terme Olimia thermal spa. Looming overhead are the remains of a castle originally built in the 11th century and an important fortification during the wars with the Hungarians 300 years later.

The town's seemingly unpronounceable name comes from the Slovene word for 'Thursday' – the day the market took place and the district court sat.

The centre of Podčetrtek is at the junction of four roads. All buses stop at the crossroads as well as at the spa and the campground. There are three train stations. For the village centre and the castle, get off at Podčetrtek. Atomske Toplice is good for Terme Olimia and the spa hotels. Podčetrtek Toplice is the correct stop for the campground.

◉ Sights

Podčetrtek Castle   CASTLE
(Grad Podčetrtek) The enormous Renaissance-style Podčetrtek Castle, atop a 355m-high hill to the northwest of town, went up sometime in the mid-16th century but was badly damaged by an earthquake in 1974. The castle (not open to the public but offering views) can be easily reached by walking

north along Trška cesta and then west on Cesta na Grad for about 1.5km.

Olimje Minorite Monastery   MONASTERY
(Minoritski Samostan Olimje; ⏱582 91 61; www.ol imje.com; Olimje 82; pharmacy adult/child €1/0.50; ⏲pharmacy 10am-noon & 1-7pm Mon-Sat) The Olimje Minorite Monastery, 3km southwest of Podčetrtek, was built as a Renaissance-style castle in about 1550. Its **Church of the Assumption**, boasts 17th-century ceiling paintings in the presbytery, one of the largest baroque altars in the country and the unbelievably ornate **Chapel of St Francis Xavier**. On the ground floor of one of the four corner towers is the monastery's greatest treasure: a 17th-century **pharmacy** painted with religious and medical scenes. The Franciscan monks here grow their own herbs and medicinal plants.

Čokoladnica Olimje   CHOCOLATE FACTORY
(Olimje Chocolate Boutique; ⏱810 90 36; www .syncerus.si; Olimje 61; ⏲10am-7pm Jun-Aug, 10am-5pm Sep-May) Čokoladnica Olimje is a short distance from the Olimje Minorite Monastery and makes and sells the most famous chocolate in Slovenia.

✦ Activities

Terme Olimia   SPA
(⏱829 70 00; www.terme-olimia.com; Zdraviliška cesta 24) Formerly known as Atomske Toplice (thus the train station name, Atomske Toplice), Terme Olimia, about 1.2km northeast of Podčetrtek centre, has thermal water (28°C to 35°C) full of magnesium and calcium for health. These days, however, it places most of the emphasis on recreation and beauty. The eight indoor and outdoor pools connected by an underwater passage at the **Termalija** (⏱829 78 05; nonguests adult/child Mon-Fri €10.50/8, Sat & Sun €12.50/9.50; ⏲8am-10pm Sun-Thu, 8am-midnight Fri & Sat) pool and spa complex alone cover an area of 2000 sq metres. In addition, the complex has two wellness centres: the **Spa Armonia** at the Hotel Sotelia and the luxurious **Orchidelia**.

Hiking & Biking   HIKING, BIKING
Some of the most rewarding hikes and bike trips in Slovenia can be made in this area. The free 1:26,000-scale *Podčetrtek-Terme Olimia* tourist map lists and outlines two dozen excursions for walkers, cyclists and mountain bikers. The easiest walks on marked trails take a couple of hours (though the 6.6km-long circuitous one northeast to the 18th-century Church of St Emma at 345m

Štajerska & Koroška Highlights

❶ Walk back into and through the past via the narrow backstreets of medieval **Ptuj** (p172), the jewel of Štajerska

❷ Enjoy the wonderland (and the uncrowded skiing) that is **Rogla** (p185) in winter

❸ Watch the world walk (and maybe even sail) by from a cafe or bar in the waterfront Lent district of **Maribor** (p178)

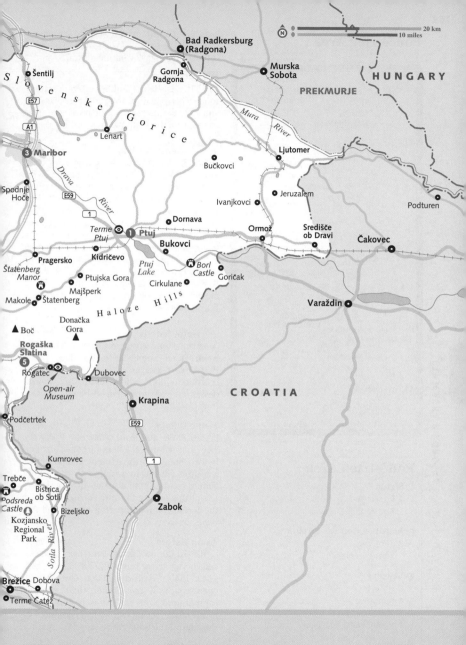

4 Stay with the locals on a farm holiday in **Logarska Dolina** (p192), the greenest of Štajerska's valleys

5 Take the waters in style at the thermal baths of **Rogaška Slatina** (p169), one of the few true spa towns in Slovenia

Podčetrtek Area

Podčetrtek Area

0 — 500 m
0 — 0.25 miles

lasts about four hours), and there are bicycle routes all the way to Kozje (37km), Podsreda (41km) and Rogaška Slatina (31km).

🛏 Sleeping

The TIC has a list of families offering private rooms (per person from €20) in Podčetrtek and Sodna Vas, 2km north of the spa complex on the main road.

TOP CHOICE **Jelenov Greben**   FARMSTAY €€
(☎041 317 093, 582 90 46; www.jelenov-greben.si; Olimje 90; s €35-40, d €60-70, apt for 4 €65-75; ◻☎) This spectacular property, set on a ridge some 500m south of Olimje at Ježovnik, has 12 cosy rooms (some with balconies), four apartments and a popular restaurant (mains €7.50 to €15) that is open daily from 7am to 10pm and celebrated for its venison and wild mushroom dishes. There is also a shop selling farm products and souvenirs. 'Deer Ridge' is a working farm and a hundred head of deer roam freely on the 8 hectares of land. It also offers balloon rides.

Hotel Sotelia   HOTEL €€€
(www.terme-olimia.com; s/d €99/170) The 145-room Hotel Sotelia is a luxurious place that does packages exclusively. It's a very ecofriendly hotel whose undulating, stylish design and colours seem to blend into the forest behind it.

Terme Olimia   SPA COMPLEX
(☎829 70 00; www.terme-olimia.com; ◻✳☎⛱) The spa complex offers accommodation in two hotels, an apartment complex and a tourist village, in addition to the Kamp Natura campground. Package deals are endless at this place and those staying at any of the Terme Olimia properties may use all the pools for free.

Kamp Natura   CAMPGROUND €
(☎829 70 00; www.terme-olimia.com; Zdraviliška cesta; campsite per person €7.70-8.80, with pools €12.30-15.40; ⊙mid-Apr–mid-Oct) Owned and operated by Terme Olimia, this 1-hectare campground with 200 sites is about 1km north of the Terme Olimia spa complex, on the edge of the Sotla River.

Youth Hostel Podčetrtek   HOSTEL €
(☎582 91 09; www.ciril-youthhostel-bc.si; Zdraviliška cesta 10; r per person €14-17; ◻@) This hostel, above the popular Gostišče Ciril on the main road just across from the entrance

to the campground, has 15 basic rooms with two and three beds. Holders of a HI card or equivalent get a 10% discount. It's pretty basic but comfortable enough and convenient to the area's recreational facilities.

✗ Eating

Gostilna Amon   SLOVENIAN €
(☑818 24 80; Olimje 24; starters €7.30-12.70, mains €8-15; ☺11am-10pm Sun-Thu, 11am-11pm Fri & Sat) This Maisons de Qualité establishment, up on the hill south of Olimje and opposite the golf course, is simply the best place for miles around. It offers high-quality food and organic wines. The set lunch from €9 to €16 is excellent value.

Gostišče Ciril   SLOVENIAN €
(Zdraviliška cesta 10; starters €4-7, mains €7-9; ☺9am-9pm Mon-Fri, 9am-10pm Sat & Sun) This grill restaurant is frequented by local Slovenes and their Croatian neighbours. The vine-covered terrace is lovely on a warm evening. It also does pizza (€4 to €7).

Mercator   SUPERMARKET €
(Cesta Slake 1; ☺7am-7pm Mon-Fri, 7am-noon Sat & Sun) There's a Mercator supermarket in Podčetrtek village.

❶ Information

Banka Celje (Zdraviliška cesta 276) In the new shopping mall between the centre and spa complex.

Post Office (Trška cesta 23; ☺8am-9.30am, 10am-5pm Mon-Fri, 8am-noon Sat) Some 200m north of the crossroads.

Tourist Information Centre Podčetrtek (TIC; ☑810 90 13; www.turizem-podcetrtek.si; Cesta Škofja Gora 1; ☺8am-3pm Mon-Fri, 8am-1pm Sat) At the crossroads.

❶ Getting There & Around

Two to five buses a day pass by Podčetrtek and Terme Olimia on their way from Celje (€4.70, one hour) to Bistrica ob Sotli (€2.30, 20 minutes) and vice versa.

Podčetrtek is on the rail line linking Celje (via Stranje) with Imeno. Up to eight trains leave the main Podčetrtek station every day for Celje (€3.25, 50 minutes)

KOZJANSKO REGIONAL PARK
☑03 / ELEV TO 685M
Established in 1999, the 20,760-hectare **Kozjansko Regional Park** (Kozjanski Regijski Park; ☑800 71 00; www.kozjanski-park.si; Podsreda 45; ☺8am-4pm Mon-Fri) stretches along the Sotla River, from the border with Dolenjska and Bizeljsko in the south to Podčetrtek in the north.

The forests and dry meadows of the park harbour a wealth of flora and fauna, notably butterflies, reptiles and birds, including corncrakes, kingfishers and storks. There are a number of trails in the park, including educational ones and the circular 32km-long **Podsreda Trail** (Pešpot Podsreda), which ends at one of the best-preserved Romanesque castles in Slovenia.

Podsreda Castle (Grad Podsreda; ☑580 61 18; adult/child €4/2.50; ☺10am-6pm Tue-Sun Apr-Oct) looks pretty much the way it did when it was built in about 1200. A barbican on the south side, with walls 3m thick and a medieval kitchen, leads to a central courtyard with a sgraffito of a knight and a dungeon hidden beneath a staircase. The rooms in the castle wings, some with beamed ceilings and ancient chandeliers, now contain a glassworks exhibit (crystal from Rogaška Slatina, vials from the Olimje pharmacy, green Pohorje glass). The fabulous wood-panelled Renaissance Hall hosts exhibitions, classical concerts and, of course, weddings. Next to it is a wonderful collection of prints of Štajerska's castles and monasteries taken from *Topographii Ducatus Stiria* (1681) by Georg Mattäus Vischer (1628–96). There are exhibition spaces of art and photographs in the east and north wings. The tiny Romanesque chapel is under protracted renovation.

A rough, winding 5km-long road leads to the castle, but you can also reach it via a relatively steep 2km footpath from Stari Trg, less than 1km southeast of the village of Podsreda. In the village there's a bar near the park headquarters called the **Pod Gradom** (☑580 61 04; Podsreda 49; ☺6.30am-10pm) and a **Tuš** (Podsreda 53; ☺7am-4pm Mon-Fri, 7am-2pm Sat, 7am-noon Sun) supermarket around the corner.

You can reach Podsreda from Podčetrtek (€4.10, 50 minutes, 33km) on just one weekday bus at 11.11am, though there's another one during school term at 4.12pm.

Rogaška Slatina
☑03 / POP 5050 / ELEV 228M
Rogaška Slatina is Slovenia's oldest and largest spa town, a veritable 'cure factory' with almost a dozen hotels and treatments and therapies. It's an attractive place set among scattered forests in the foothills of the Macelj range. Hiking and cycling in the area are particularly good.

ŠTAJERSKA & KOROŠKA ROGAŠKA SLATINA

Rogaška Slatina

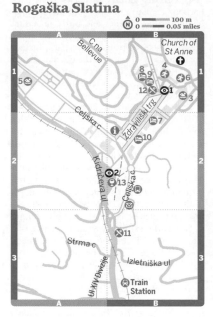

The hot spring here was known in Roman times but first made it onto the map in 1574, when the governor of Styria took the waters on the advice of his physician. A century later visitors started arriving in droves and by the early 19th century Rogaška Slatina was an established spa town.

The heart of Rogaška Slatina is the spa complex, an architecturally important group of neoclassical, Secessionist and Plečnik-style buildings surrounding a long landscaped garden called Zdravilíški trg, or Health Resort Square.

Rogaška Slatina's bus station is south of Zdravilíški trg on Celjska cesta. The train station is 300m further south on Kidričeva ulica.

🏃 Activities

Rogaška Slatina's mineral water (called Donat Mg) contains the largest amount of magnesium found in the world and is primarily for drinking, although you might find it tastes a little metallic and salty. It's said to eliminate stress, aid digestion and encourage weight loss. The magnesium alone, it is claimed, regulates 200 bodily functions.

Pivnica   DRINKING HALL
(admission €1.50, 3-/5-day pass €7/11; ⊘7am-1pm & 3-7pm Mon-Sat, 7am-1pm & 4-7pm Sun) You can engage in a 'drinking cure' of your own at the Pivnica, the round, glassed-in drinking hall where mineral water is dispensed directly from the springs. It's just beyond the oval-shaped **bandstand** where concerts are staged in the warmer months.

Terapija   SPA
(✆811 70 15; www.rogaska-medical.com; Zdravilíški trg 9; ⊘7am-8pm Mon-Fri, 8am-noon & 3-7pm Sat, by appointment Sun) The centre of spa action is the 12-storey Terapija building, where you'll find everything from pearl baths to lymph-glands drainage. Treatments start from €22.

Hotel Donat Thermal Pool   SWIMMING
(✆811 30 00; Zdravilíški trg 10; indoor thermal pool admission €7; ⊘indoor thermal pool 8am-8pm Mon-Sat, 9am-8pm Sun) At the Hotel Donat, opposite the bandstand, there's an **indoor thermal pool**, sauna, steam room and gym. A 30-minute body massage costs €24. Most of the larger hotels have their own wellness centres, including the Grand Hotel Rogaška's Vis Vita and the Lotus Terme at the Sava.

Rogaška Riviera   SWIMMING
(✆818 19 50; Celjska cesta 5; day pass adult/child Mon-Fri €9/6, Sat & Sun €10/7.50; ⊘9am-8pm Sun-Thu, 9am-11pm Fri & Sat) The so-called Rogaška Riviera at the northern end of Celjska cesta has two indoor and two out-

door swimming pools that are all connected. There's also a whirlpool and saunas. Terme Rogaška hotels include free entry to these pools in their rates.

Walking Trails   HIKING
Walking trails fanning out into the surrounding hills and meadows are marked on the 1:25,000 *Rogaška Slatina* GZS map (€2.10) available from the TIC. One leads 15km to the hilltop **Church of St Florian**, and to Ložno, from where you can continue on another 4km to **Donačka Gora**. To return, walk two hours down to Rogatec to catch a bus or train back.

The walk to **Boč** (979m), northwest of Rogaška Slatina and in the centre of the 886-hectare **Boč Country Park** (Krajinski Park Boč; www.boc.si), will take you about four hours, though you can drive as far as Category III **Dom na Boču** (☎041 609 615, 582 46 17; gt-mali@volja.net; ☺Tue-Sun year-round), a mountain hut a couple of kilometres south of the peak at 658m with 47 beds in 15 rooms.

Festivals & Events

Rogaška Musical Summer   MUSIC FESTIVAL
(☺Jun-Sep) Rogaška Musical Summer is a series of concerts, from chamber music and opera to Slovenian folk music, held around the central bandstand from June to September.

Sleeping

The TIC has a list of private rooms and apartments, for between €12 and €20 per person.

Grand Hotel Rogaška   HOTEL €€€
(☎811 20 00; www.terme-rogaska.com; Zdraviliški trg 10; s €94-119, d €116-216; P❄@) Grand Hotel Rogaška, along with its two branches, the contiguous **Hotel Styria** and **Hotel Strossmayer** (s €56-64, d €84-112), on the eastern side of Zdraviliški trg have more than 350 beds among them. The Grand, with its spectacular public areas (especially the Crystal Hall), dates from 1913, the other two were built in the mid-19th century.

Grand Hotel Sava   HOTEL €€€
(☎811 40 00; www.rogaska.si; Zdraviliški trg 6; s €62-101, d €100-202; P❄@� 🏊) The modern Grand Hotel Sava and the attached older (and cheaper) **Hotel Zagreb** (s €62-70, d €100-116; P❄🏊), each with four stars, are at the northwestern end of Zdraviliški trg and count a total of 276 rooms.

Eating & Drinking

Gostišče Jurg   SLOVENIAN €€
(☎581 47 88; Male Rodne 20a; dishes €6.50-18; ☺11am-10pm Tue-Thu, 11am-11pm Fri & Sat, 11am-8pm Sun) This very swish farmhouse restaurant about 4km southwest of the centre gets rave reviews for its excellent home-made Slovenian dishes and stylish though traditional decor.

Gostilna Bohor   SLOVENIAN €
(☎581 41 00; Kidričeva ulica 23; pizza €4.90-6.60, mains €6.90-18; ☺8am-10pm Mon-Thu, 8am-11pm Fri & Sat, 10am-10pm Sun) For hearty Slovenian fare and better-than-average pizza, try this popular local eatery. The *kmečka* pizza (farmer's pizza) has virtually everything from the barnyard on top.

Restavracija Kaiser   INTERNATIONAL €€
(☎811 47 10; Zdraviliški trg 6; mains €11-26; ☺noon-11pm) Rogaška Slatina's fanciest eatery, this international restaurant (with some Slovenian favourites thrown in for good measure) faces the main square. Look out for daily specials.

Kavarna Attems   BAR
(☎051 200 600; Zdraviliški trg 22; ☺8am-2am) Most visitors to Rogaška Slatina spend their evenings in the hotel bars and cafes; the Attems, in the renovated art-nouveau Tempel building, dating from 1904 at the southern end of Zdraviliški trg, is popular with a local crowd. We love the 'olde worlde' decor.

Shopping

Steklarska Nova   HOMEWARES
(☎818 20 27; Steklarska ulica 1; ☺8am-7pm Mon-Fri, 8am-1pm Sat) Rogaška Slatina is as celebrated for its crystal as it is for its mineral water and this outlet attached to the crystal-making school has a wide range of leaded crystal items for sale.

Information

Post Office (Kidričeva ulica 3)

SKB Banka (Kidričeva ulica 11)

Tourist Information Centre Rogaška Slatina (TIC; ☎581 44 14; www.rogaska-slatina.si; Zdraviliški trg 1; ☺8am-7pm Mon-Fri, 11am-5pm Sat & Sun Jul & Aug, 8am-4pm Mon-Fri, 8am-noon Sat Sep-Jun)

Getting There & Around

BUS Buses to Celje (€4.10, one hour) and Rogatec (€1.80, 10 minutes) leave Rogaška Slatina

THE HAYRACK: A NATIONAL ICON

Few things are as Slovenian as the *kozolec*, the hayrack seen almost everywhere in the country. Because the Alpine ground can be damp, wheat and hay are hung from racks, allowing the wind to do the drying faster and more efficiently.

Until the late 19th century, the *kozolec* was just another tool to make a farmer's work easier and the land more productive. But when artist Ivan Grohar made it the centrepiece of many of his impressionist paintings, the *kozolec* became as much a part of the cultural landscape as the physical one. Today it's virtually a national icon.

There are many different types of Slovenian hayracks: single ones standing alone or 'goat hayracks' with sloped 'lean-to' roofs, parallel and stretched ones and double *toplarji* (hayracks), often with roofs and storage areas on top – deserving subjects of an artist's eye.

Hayracks were traditionally made of hardwood (usually oak). Today, however, the hayrack's future is in concrete, and the new stretched ones seem to go on forever.

more or less hourly. There are regular buses to Maribor (€7.20, 1½ hours).

TRAIN Rogaška Slatina is on the train line linking Celje (€2.95, 50 minutes) via Rogatec (€1.10, 10 minutes) and Dobovec with Zabok in Croatia (change for Zagreb).

Rogatec

⤴03 / POP 1605 / ELEV 234M

This small town, about 7km east of (and accessible by bus and train from) Rogaška Slatina, has two important sights worth tarrying over.

Rogatec Open-Air Museum (Muzej na Prostem Rogatec; ⤴818 62 00; www.rogatec.net/muzej; adult/child/senior & student/family €3/2.30/2.60/6, with Strmol Manor €5.40/4.10/4.60/10.80; ⊙10am-6pm Tue-Sun Apr-Oct), Slovenia's largest and most ambitious *skanzen* (open-air village museum) has original structures or replicas including farmhouses, barns, a *toplarji* (double-linked hayrack) and vintner's cottage, replicating a typical Styrian farm of the 19th and early 20th centuries. There are regular displays (including participation) of activities such as weaving, stone-cutting, bread-making and so on.

The colossal, 15th-century **Strmol Manor** (Dvorec Strmol; ⤴051 322 287, 810 72 22; www.rogatec.net/strmol; adult/child/senior & student/family €5.40/4.10/4.60/10.80; ⊙10am-6pm Tue-Sun Apr-Oct) has exhibits over five floors. Don't miss the restaurant on the 1st floor, with its original open-hearth *črna kuhinjam* (black kitchen); the chapel, with its baroque and Renaissance murals; and the exhibit in the loft, which re-creates an early-20th-century country kitchen, complete with original furnishings and fittings.

Ptuj

⤴02 / POP 19,015 / ELEV 224M

Rising gently above a wide valley, Ptuj (in English sounding not unlike someone spitting) forms a symphony of red-tile roofs best viewed from across the Drava River. One of the oldest towns in Slovenia, Ptuj equals Ljubljana in terms of historical importance but the compact medieval core, with its castle, museums, monasteries and churches, can easily be seen in a day. There are so many interesting side trips and activities in the area that you may want to base yourself here for a while.

History

Ptuj began life as a Roman military outpost on the south bank of the Drava River and later grew into a civilian settlement called Poetovio on the opposite side. By the 1st century AD the largest Roman township in what is now Slovenia, Poetovio was the centre of the Mithraic cult and several complete temples have been unearthed in the area.

Ptuj received its town rights in 977 and grew rich through river trade. By the 13th century it was competing with the 'upstart' Marburg (Maribor) upriver, in both crafts and commerce. Two monastic orders – the Dominicans and the Franciscan Minorites – settled here and built important monasteries. The Magyars attacked and occupied Ptuj for most of the 15th century.

When the railroad reached eastern Slovenia from Vienna on its way to the coast in the mid-19th century, the age-old rivalry between Maribor and Ptuj turned one-sided: the former was on the line and the latter missed out altogether. The town remained essentially a provincial centre with a German majority until WWI.

◉ Sights & Activities

Ptuj's Gothic centre, with its Renaissance and baroque additions, can be viewed on a 'walking tour' taking in Minoritski trg and Mestni trg, Slovenski trg, Prešernova ulica, Muzejski trg and Ptuj Castle.

Minoritski Trg & Mestni Trg   SQUARES
On the east side of Minoritski trg, which has a **plague pillar** (1655), is the massive **Minorite monastery** (Minoritski Samostan; ✆059 073 000; Minoritski trg 1; ⊙by appointment), built in the late 13th century. Due to its teaching role, it avoided dissolution under Habsburg Emperor Joseph II in the late 18th century, and it has continued to function in Ptuj for more than seven centuries.

The arcaded monastery, which dates from the second half of the 17th century, has a **summer refectory** on the 1st floor, with beautiful stucco work and a dozen ceiling paintings of St Peter (north side) and St Paul (south side). It also contains a 5000-volume library of important manuscripts.

About 150m west of the monastery is round **Drava Tower** (Dravski Stolp; Dravska ulica 4), a Renaissance water tower built as a defence against the Turks in 1551. It houses the **Mihelič Gallery** (Miheličeva Galerija; ✆787 92 50; admission free; ⊙10am-5pm Tue-Fri, 2-6pm Sat & Sun), which hosts exhibitions of modern art.

At the end of Krempljeva ulica is Mestni trg, a rectangular square once called Florianplatz in honour of the **St Florian Column** (1745) standing in the northwest corner. To the east is the 1907 neo-Gothic **town hall** (Mestni trg 1).

A couple of hundred metres to the east, **Ptujska Vinska Klet** (Ptuj Wine Cellar; ✆041 394 896, 787 98 10; www.pullus.si; Vinarski trg 1; tours €9-12; ⊙9am-3pm Mon-Fri) is the place to go if you want to sample Štajerska wine, especially Haloze chardonnay, Šipon or Laški Rizling. It also stocks Zlata Trta, the 'Golden Vine' sweet wine, Slovenia's oldest vintage.

Slovenski Trg   SQUARE
Murkova ulica, lined with interesting old houses, leads westward from Mestni trg to funnel-shaped Slovenski trg, the heart of old Ptuj. In the centre, the **City Tower** (Mestni Stolp) was erected in the 16th century.

Roman tombstones and sacrificial altars from Poetovio were incorporated into the walls in the 1830s – check the reliefs of Medusa's head, dolphins, a man with grapes and a man on horseback.

In front of the City Tower stands the 5m-tall **Orpheus Monument** (Orfejev Spomenik), a Roman tombstone from the 2nd century with scenes from the Orpheus myth. It was used as a pillory in the Middle Ages.

Behind the City Tower is the **Church of St George** (Cerkev Sv Jurija). The church contains some lovely mid-15th-century choir chairs decorated with animals, a carved relief of the Epiphany dating from 1515 and frescoes in the middle of the south aisle, and the **Laib Altar**, a three-winged altar painting (1460). Near the entrance is a carved 14th-century statue of St George slaying the dragon.

On the northern side of the square are several interesting buildings, including the 16th-century **Provost's House** (Slovenski trg 10), the baroque **Old Town Hall** (Slovenski trg 6) and **Ljutomer House** (Slovenski trg 5), now housing the TIC, whose Mediterranean-style loge was built in 1565.

Prešernova Ulica   STREET
Pedestrian Prešernova ulica was the town's market in the Middle Ages. The arched spans above some of the narrow side streets support older buildings. The **Late Gothic House** (Prešernova ulica 1), dating from about 1400, has an unusual projection held up by a Moor's head. Opposite is the sombre **Romanesque House** (Prešernova ulica 4), the oldest building in Ptuj. The renovated yellow pile called the **Little Castle** (Mali Grad; Prešernova ulica 33-35) was the home of the Salzburg bishops and various aristocratic families over the centuries.

Muzejski Trg   SQUARE
Just past Sunny Park (Sončni Park) in Muzejski trg is the former **Dominican Monastery** (Dominikanski Samostan; Muzejski trg 1) dating from the 13th century, which contains the **lapidary and archaeological collections** of the Ptuj Regional Museum (p175). But the main attractions are the Roman tombstones, altars and wonderful mosaics unearthed in Ptuj and at the **Mithraic shrines** (✆778 87 80; adult/child €1/0.50; ⊙by appointment) at Spodnja Hajdina (key at house No 37a) and Zgornji Breg (key at Ulica K Mitreju 3), a couple of kilometres west of town.

Ptuj

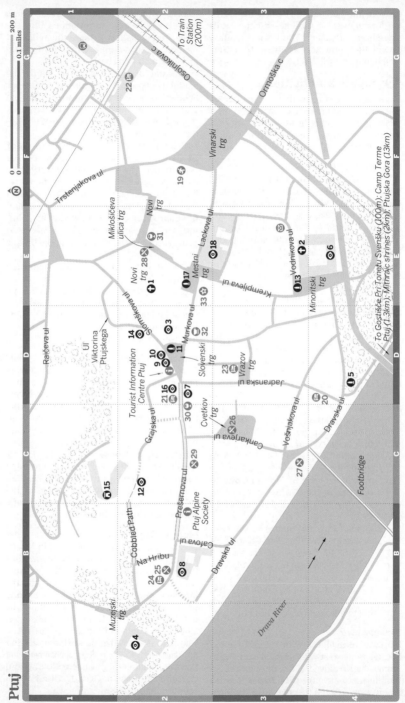

200 m
0.1 miles

To Train Station (200m)

Osojnikova c

Ormoška c

Vinarski trg

Trstenjakova ul

Miklošičeva ulica trg

Novi trg

19

Lackova ul

31

18

Mestni trg

2

Vodnikova ul

17

Kremplljeva ul

6

Minoritski trg

Novi trg 28

33

13

Slomškova ul

Murkova ul

1

3

32

Slovenski trg

Ul Viktorina Ptujskega

Raičeva ul

14

10

9

11

Vrazov trg

23

Jadranska ul

5

Tourist Information Centre Ptuj

21 16

7

30

Cvetkov trg

26

Vošnjakova ul

20

Grajska ul

29

Cankarjeva ul

27

Dravska ul

12

15

Cobbled Path

Preŝernova ul

Ptuj Alpine Society

Na Hribu

Cafova ul

Dravska ul

24 25

8

Muzejski trg

4

Drava River

Footbridge

To Gostišče Pri Tonetu Svenšku (100m); Camp Terme Ptuj (1.3km); Mitnrajc strnes (2km); Ptujska Gora (13km)

Ptuj

Ptuj Castle   CASTLE, MUSEUM
(Grad Ptuj; ☎787 92 45, 748 03 60; Na Gradu 1) Ptuj castle is an agglomeration of styles from the 14th to the 18th centuries. It houses the **Ptuj Regional Museum** (☎787 92 30; www .pok-muzej-ptuj.si; adult/child €4/2.50; ◷9am-6pm Mon-Fri, 9am-8pm Sat & Sun summer, 9am-5pm daily winter) but is worth the trip mostly for the views of Ptuj and the Drava River. The shortest way to the castle is to follow narrow Grajska ulica, east of Hotel Mitra, which leads to a covered wooden stairway and the castle's Renaissance **Peruzzi Portal** (1570).

As you enter the castle courtyard, look to the west at the red marble **tombstone of Frederick IX**, the last lord of Ptuj (he died in 1438). The ground floor of one wing is devoted to an **arms collection** of some 500 weapons. The suits of armour are particularly fine. Also here is a fascinating **musical instruments collection** from the 17th to 19th centuries.

The 1st floor is given over to period rooms – treasure-troves of original tapestries, painted wall canvases, portraits, weapons and furniture left by the castle's last owners, the Herbersteins (1873–1945).

Notice the coat of arms containing three buckles and the English motto 'Grip Fast' – it belonged to the Leslies, a Scottish-Austrian family who owned the castle from 1656 to 1802. The **Chinoiserie Room** is excellent.

Festival Hall contains Europe's largest collection of aristocratic **Turkerie portraits**, though possibly of more historical rather than artistic interest.

On the 2nd floor is a large collection of **Kurent masks** as well as various Gothic statues and oil paintings.

★ Festivals & Events

Kurentovanje   CARNIVAL
(www.kurentovanje.net; ◷Feb) Kurentovanje is a rite of spring celebrated for 10 days in February leading up to Shrove Tuesday; it's the most popular and best-known folklore event in Slovenia.

Days of Poetry and Wine   FESTIVAL
(www.versoteque.com; ◷Aug) This annual festival held in August gathers international poets, writers, storytellers and musicians for readings, concerts and good wine through the summer evenings.

ŠTAJERSKA & KOROŠKA PTUJ

KURENT: PARTY TIME IN PTUJ

Ptuj marks Shrovetide with Kurentovanje, a rite of spring and fertility that dates to the time of the early Slavs.

The main character of the rite is Kurent, Dionysian god of unrestrained pleasure and hedonism. The Kurents (there are many groups of them) are dressed in sheepskins with five cowbells dangling from their belts. On their heads they wear huge furry caps decorated with feathers, sticks or horns and coloured streamers. Their leather masks have red eyes, trunk-like noses and enormous tongues hanging down to the chest.

The Kurents process from house to house, scaring off evil spirits with their bells and *ježevke* (wooden clubs) topped with hedgehog quills. A *hudič* (devil), covered in a net to catch souls, leads each group. Young girls present the Kurents with handkerchiefs, which they then fasten to their belts, and people smash little clay pots at their feet for luck and good health.

Kurentovanje is now an organised carnival and a centrepiece of Ptuj's calendar. Festivities are spread over 11 days, culminating in the Kurent parades on the Saturday and Sunday before Shrove Tuesday, when hundreds of masked and costumed Kurents march through the town. Tens of thousands of spectators visit Ptuj for the parades (book accommodation well in advance). For more information (including event programs for the annual festivities), check out www.kurentovanje.net.

🛏 Sleeping

The TIC can arrange private rooms (per person €20 to €25) but most are on the other side of the Drava near Terme Ptuj or the nearby village of Juršinci.

TOP CHOICE MuziKafe HOTEL €€
(☑787 88 60; www.muzikafe.si; Vrazov trg 1; s/d from €40/52; 🛜) This quirky cracker of a place is tucked away off Jadranska ulica. Everything is bright, with each room idiosyncratically decorated by the hotel's artist owners. There's a terrace cafe and funky interior with old cinema chairs, plus a vaulted brick cellar that hosts musical and artistic events. A great addition to Ptuj's accommodation scene.

TOP CHOICE Hotel Mitra HOTEL €€€
(☑051 603 069, 787 74 55; www.hotel-mitra.si; Prešernova ulica 6; s €62-88, d €106; P✴@🛜) One of provincial Slovenia's more interesting hotels has 25 generous-sized guest rooms and four humongous suites, each with its own name and story, and specially commissioned paintings on the wall. There are lovely oriental carpets on the original wooden floors and a wellness centre in an old courtyard cellar. Rooms at the top have mansard ceilings.

Park Hotel Ptuj BOUTIQUE HOTEL €€
(☑749 33 00; www.parkhotel-ptuj.si; Prešernova ulica 38; s €47-69, d €88-107, ste €116-126; @) This lovely boutique hotel with 15 individually designed rooms and lots of original artwork on the walls is situated in an 18th-century town house. It's right in the thick of the action too, with cafes and bars in every direction.

Hostel Eva HOSTEL €
(☑040 226 522, 771 24 41; www.hostel-ptuj.si; Jadranska ulica 22; per person €12-20) If you're looking for budget accommodation, look no further than this welcoming, up-to-date hostel connected to a bike shop (per day bike rental €10) with six rooms containing two to six beds and a large, light-filled kitchen.

Gostišče Pri Tonetu Svenšku GUESTHOUSE €
(☑041 764 407, 788 56 83; svensek.marjeta@amis.net; Zadružni trg 13; r per person €18; P) This guesthouse, with 24 beds in nine rooms and a popular **restaurant** (🕗7am-10pm Mon-Sat, 8am-10pm Sun), is just over the footbridge on the south bank of the Drava. Ptuj's thermal baths and the golf course are nearby.

Camp Terme Ptuj CAMPGROUND €
(☑749 45 80; www.terme-ptuj.si; Pot v Toplice 9; adult €14.50-16.50, child €7.25-8.25; 🕗year-round; P🏊) This 1.5-hectare campground next to the thermal spa and water park has 110 sites. Rates include entry to the park and use of pools and other recreational facilities.

Kurent Youth Hostel HOSTEL €
(Mladinsko Prenočišče Kurent; ☑051 319 186, 771 08 14; www.csod.si; Osojnikova cesta 9; dm €17-18) This HI-affiliated dormitory situated near

the bus station has 13 rooms with between two and six beds and is open all year. HI members get a 10% discount.

✖ Eating

TOP CHOICE **Gostilna Ribič** SLOVENIAN €€
(☑749 06 35; Dravska ulica 9; mains €9.50-20; ☺10am-11pm Sun-Thu, 10am-midnight Fri & Sat) Arguably the best restaurant in Ptuj, the Angler Inn faces the river, with an enormous terrace, and the speciality here is – not surprisingly – fish, especially herbed and baked pike perch, or sander. The seafood soup served in a bread-loaf bowl is exceptional. There's live Slovenian music some nights.

Amadeus SLOVENIAN €€
(☑771 70 51; Prešernova ulica 36; mains €6.50-20; ☺noon-10pm Mon-Thu, noon-11pm Fri & Sat, noon-4pm Sun) This very pleasant *gostilna* (inn-like restaurant) above a pub and near the foot of the road to the castle serves *štruklji* (dumplings with herbs and cheese), steak and pork dishes, and fish.

Cantante Café MEXICAN €
(☑777 14 02; Cvetkov trg 6; dishes €3-9; ☺11am-midnight Sun-Thu, 11am-1am Fri & Sat) This popular place, in a quiet square south of Prešernova ulica and opposite the Kino Ptuj, attracts punters with its 150 cocktails as much as it does its Mexican dishes.

Picerija Slonček PIZZA €
(☑776 13 11; Prešernova ulica 19; pizza €4.10-5.80; ☺9am-10pm Mon-Fri, 10am-10pm Sat; ☑) The cosy Little Elephant, with an interesting marble fountain out front, serves pizza and some meatless dishes as well as grills.

Market MARKET €
(Novi trg; ☺7am-3pm) The town's open-air market sells fruit, vegetables and more.

🍺 Drinking & Entertainment

Kavarna Kipertz CAFE
(☑787 74 55; Prešernova ulica 6; ☺8am-11pm Mon-Thu, 8am-midnight Fri-Sun) Named after the very first man in Ptuj to roast coffee beans, this wonderful cafe in Hotel Mitra attracts Ptuj's boho set with its very own coffee roast and rich desserts.

Kavabar Orfej BAR
(☑772 97 61; Prešernova ulica 5; ☺6.30am-11pm Mon-Thu, 6.30am-1am Fri & Sat, 10am-11pm Sun) The Orfej is the anchor tenant of Prešernova

ulica and is usually where everyone starts (or ends) the evening.

Trajana CAFE, BAR
(Murkova ulica 5; ☺6.30am-11pm Sun-Thu, 6.30am-1am Fri & Sat) This uber-designed cafe and bar, 100m east of Prešernova ulica, has a good selection of wine and welcomes a well-heeled clientele.

Maska Caffe BAR
(☑041 708 526; Novi trg 2; ☺7am-10pm Mon-Thu, 7am-2am Fri, 8am-2am Sat, 3-10pm Sun) This very trendy redder-than-red designer bar is one of the top spots in town. The front bar just goes on and on.

Café Evropa CAFE, CLUB
(☑771 02 35; Mestni trg 2; ☺11am-10pm Mon-Thu, 11am-3am Fri & Sat, 6-10pm Sun) By day and evening a popular cafe, the Evropa turns into one of Ptuj's hottest central clubs on Friday and Saturday nights.

ℹ Information

Banka Koper (Slovenski trg 3) Directly opposite the TIC.

Ivan Potrč Library (☑771 48 11; Prešernova ulica 33-35; per hr €0.90; ☺noon-7pm Mon, 8am-1pm Tue-Fri Jul & Aug, 8am-7pm Mon-Fri, 8am-1pm Sat Sep-Jun) Ten terminals with cheap internet access.

Nova Ljubljanska Banka (Prešernova ulica 6) Next door to Hotel Mitra.

Post Office (Vodnikova ulica 2)

Ptuj Alpine Society (☑777 15 11; Prešernova ulica 27; ☺2-4pm Tue, 5-7pm Fri) Information about hiking in the area.

Tourist Information Centre Ptuj (TIC; ☑779 60 11; www.ptuj.info; Slovenski trg 5; ☺8am-8pm summer, 9am-6pm winter) Advice in the 16th-century Ljutomer House.

ℹ Getting There & Around

BUS Buses to Maribor (€3.60, 45 minutes) and Ormož (€3.60, 40 minutes) run every couple of hours, less frequently at weekends (if at all). One to two buses a day head for Stuttgart (€80, 11½ hours) via Munich in Germany.

TRAIN There are plentiful train departures to Ljubljana (€8 to €13.60) direct or via Pragersko. Up to a dozen trains go to Maribor (€2.90 to €5.90, 50 minutes). Up to eight trains a day head for Murska Sobota (€4.90 to €8.90, 1¼ hours).

TAXI Book a taxi on ☑031 842 227, ☑041 798 788 or ☑051 681 400.

Around Ptuj

WINE ROADS

Ptuj is within easy striking distance of two important wine-growing areas: the **Haloze** district and the **Jeruzalem-Ljutomer** district.

The Haloze Hills extend from Makole, 18km southwest of Ptuj, to Goričak on the border with Croatia. The footpath taking in this land of gentle hills, vines, corn and sunflowers is called the **Haloze Highlands Trail** (Haloška Planina Pot). It is accessible from near **Štatenberg** (☑041 829 854; adult/child €2/1; ⊘by appointment), an 18th-century manor with grand rooms at Makole. There's a **restaurant** (⊙10am-10pm Wed-Fri, 10am-11pm Sat, 11am-10pm Sun) here.

The **Jeruzalem-Ljutomer wine road** begins at Ormož and continues for 18km north to Ljutomer, the main seat in the area, via the hilltop village of Jeruzalem. There are many cellars, small restaurants and pensions along this gorgeous route where you can sample the local whites, including **Gostišče Taverna Jeruzalem Svetinje** (☑719 41 28; www.taverna-jeruzalem.si; Svetinje 21; s/d/tr €30/55/75). For guidance, visit the **Tourist Information Centre Jeruzalem** (TIC; ☑719 45 45; www.jeruzalem.si; Jeruzalem 8; ⊘10am-6pm), next door to the **Chateau Jeruzalem** (Dvorecc Jeruzalem; ☑719 48 05; Jeruzalem 8; s €75-95, d €130-170) with a wine cellar, romantic restaurant and flashy rooms. The TIC rents bicycles (per hour/day/week €2/10/50).

Maribor

☑02 / POP 88,350 / ELEV 275M

Despite being the nation's second-largest city, Maribor has only about a third of the population of Ljubljana and often feels more like an overgrown provincial town. It has no unmissable sights but oozes charm thanks to its delightfully patchy Old Town along the Drava River. Pedestrianised central streets buzz with cafes and student life and the riverside Lent district hosts a major summer arts festival – indeed, Maribor was European City of Culture in 2012. Maribor is the gateway to the Maribor Pohorje, a hilly recreational area to the southwest, and the Mariborske and Slovenske Gorice wine-growing regions to the north and the east.

History

Maribor rose to prominence in the Middle Ages and grew wealthy through the tim-ber and wine trade, financed largely by the town's influential Jewish community. The waterfront landing (Pristan) in the Lent district was one of the busiest river ports in the country. The town was fortified in the 14th century.

Though its fortunes declined in later centuries, the tide turned in 1846 when it became the first town in Slovenia to have train connections with Vienna. Maribor thrived again and began to industrialise.

Air raids during WWII devastated Maribor, and by 1945 two-thirds of it lay in ruin.

⊙ Sights

Grajksi Trg   SQUARE
The centre of the Old Town, this square is graced with the 17th-century **Column of St Florian**, dedicated to the patron saint of firefighters, and home to Maribor's 15th-century **castle** (Grajski trg 2). It contains a Knights' Hall (Viteška Dvorana) with a remarkable painted ceiling, the baroque Loretska Chapel and a magnificent rococo staircase. It also hosts the **Maribor Regional Museum** (☑228 35 51; www.pmuzej-mb.si; Grajski trg; adult/child €3/2; ⊘9am-4pm Tue-Sat, 9am-2pm Sun), which has one of the richest collections in Slovenia. The buiding is undergoing renovations, so be advised that some parts of the collection may be off limits.

On the ground floor there are archaeological, clothing and ethnographic exhibits, including 19th-century beehive panels painted with biblical scenes from the Mislinja and Drava Valleys, models of Štajerska-style hayracks, Kurent costumes and wax ex-voto offerings from the area around Ptuj. Upstairs there are rooms devoted to Maribor's history and its guilds and crafts, a fascinating 18th-century pharmacy, and altar paintings and sculptures from the 15th to the 18th centuries. Taking pride of place are the exquisite statues by Jožef Straub (1712–56) taken from the Church of St Joseph in Studenci.

National Liberation Museum   MUSEUM
(Muzej Narodne Osvoboditve; ☑235 26 00; www.muzejno-mb.si; Ulica Heroja Tomšiča 5; adult/child €1.50/1; ⊘8am-6pm Mon-Fri, 9am-noon Sat) Housed in a stunning 19th-century mansion, the collections here document Slovenia's struggle for freedom throughout the 20th century, with particular emphasis on the work of the Pohorje Partisans during the Nazi occupation.

City Park
PARK

City Park (Mestni Park) is a lovely arboretum with 150 species of trees and three ponds. Here you'll find the small but diverting **Maribor Aquarium-Terrarium** (Akvarij-Terarij Maribor; ☑234 96 63; www.florina.si/akvarij-terarij; Ulica Heroja Staneta 19; adult/child €4/3.20; ☺8am-7pm Mon-Fri, 9am-noon & 2-7pm Sat & Sun). To the northeast is **Piramida** (386m), where the titans of Marchburg once held sway and a chapel now takes pride of place.

Slomškov Trg
SQUARE

South of City Park is the square named after Anton Martin Slomšek (1800–62), the Slovenian bishop and politician beatified 1999, the first Slovene to earn such distinction.

Parts of the imposing **Cathedral** (Stolna Cerkev; Slomškov trg) date from the 13th century and it shows elements of virtually every architectural style from Romanesque to modern. Of special interest are the flamboyant Gothic sanctuary and the gilded choir stalls, as well as the lovely modern stained glass. The grand building across the park to the west is the **University Library** (Univerzitetna Knjižnica; ☑250 74 00; www.ukm.uni-mb.si; Gospejna ulica 10).

Maribor Fine Arts Gallery
GALLERY

(Umetnostna Galerija Maribor; ☑229 58 60; www.ugm.si; Strossmayerjeva ulica 6; adult/child/family €2/1.25/4; ☺10am-6pm Tue-Sun) The Maribor Fine Arts Gallery, southwest of Slomškov trg, has a relatively rich collection of modern works by Slovenian artists.

Lent
NEIGHBOURHOOD

South of Koroška cesta is Maribor's renovated market and the remains of the 13th-century **Minorite monastery**, used as a military barracks until 1927. Along the riverfront is the round **Judgement Tower** (Sodni Stolp), the first of four defence towers still standing, with curious friezes on the south side.

About 150m east along the Pristan embankment is the so-called **Old Vine** (Stara Trta; Vojašniška ulica 8), the world's oldest living grapevine. Four centuries old, it still produces between 35kg and 55kg of grapes – making about 25L of wine – per year. Its dark red wine, called Žametna Črnina (Black Velvet), is distributed to visiting dignitaries as 'keys' to Maribor in 0.25L bottles. Learn more about it and Slovenian viniculture at the adjacent **Old Vine House** (Hiša Stare Trta; ☑251 51 00; www.maribor-pohorje.si; admission free; ☺10am-6pm Tue-Sun).

About 300m east is the pentagonal **Water Tower** (Vodni Stolp; Usnjarska ulica 10), a 16th-century defence tower now housing a *vinoteka* (wine-tasting cellar). Just north of it a set of steps leads to **Židovska ulica** (Jewish St), the centre of the Jewish district in the Middle Ages. The 15th-century **synagogue** (☑252 78 36; Židovska ulica 4; adult/child €1/0.50; ☺8am-4pm Mon-Fri, 9am-2pm Sun) is now open to the public, and the square **Jewish Tower** (Židovski Stolp; Židovska ulica 6), dating from 1465, houses the **Tower Photo Gallery** (Fotogalerija Stolp; ☑620 97 13; www.galerijastolp.si; ☺10am-1pm & 3-7pm Mon-Fri, 10am-1pm Sat).

Glavni Trg
SQUARE

Maribor's marketplace in the Middle Ages, Glavni trg is just north of the river and the main bridge crossing it. In the centre of the square is Slovenia's most extravagant **plague pillar**, erected in 1743. Behind it is the **town hall** (Glavni trg 14) built in 1565 by Venetian craftsmen.

🎊 Festivals & Events

Maribor hosts a lot of events throughout the year.

Lent Festival
CULTURAL FESTIVAL

(http://lent.slovenija.net; ☺Jun-Jul) The biggest event on the city's calendar is the Lent Festival, a two-week celebration of folklore, culture and music from late June into July, when stages are set up throughout the Old Town.\

Festival Maribor
MUSIC FESTIVAL

(www.festivalmaribor.si; ☺Sep) A 10-day extravaganza of 20 classical music concerts.

Harvesting of the Old Vine
FOOD & WINE

(☺Oct) Among the most colourful ceremonies here is the harvesting of the Old Vine for wine in early October.

🛏 Sleeping

The TIC can organise private rooms (from €25 for singles, €40 for doubles) and apartments.

TOP CHOICE ⓒ Hostel Pekarna
HOSTEL €

(☑059 180 880; www.mkc-hostelpekarna.si; Ob železnici 16; dm/s/d €17/21/42; ☎) This bright and welcoming new hostel south of the river is a converted army bakery, hence its name ('pekarna' means bakery in Slovene). Facilities, from the dorms to the cafe, are up-to-the-minute, and there are several apartments with kitchens.

Maribor

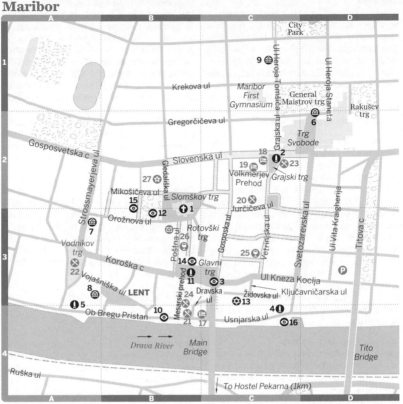

Grand Hotel Ocean BOUTIQUE HOTEL €€€
(📞234 36 73; www.hotelocean.si; Partizanska cesta 39; s/d €118/152; P🐾@) This stunning four-star boutique hotel is named after the first train to pass through Maribor city in 1846 and is the most exciting thing to happen here, well, since then. It's got 22 rooms and the breakfast room on the top floor is a sun-drenched delight.

Orel City Hotel HOTEL €€€
(Orel Mestni Hotel; 📞250 67 00; www.termemb .si; Volkmerjev prehod 7; s €79-110, d €120-168, ste €220-260; P🐾@🛜) Shiny, pretty and ready to kick ass, Maribor's most central hotel has 71 rooms and the price includes entry to the Fontana Terme Maribor.

Uni Hotel HOTEL €
(📞250 67 00; www.termemb.si; Volkmerjev prehod 7; HI member/nonmember €24/29; @) This very central, almost luxurious 53-room 'residence hotel' affiliated with Hostelling International-

al is run by, and attached to, the Orel City Hotel, where you'll find reception. Home to students during the academic year, it lets out beds in singles and doubles to visitors during holidays.

Hotel Lent HOTEL €€
(📞250 67 69; www.hotel-lent.si; Dravska ulica 9; s/d €69/89; 🐾🛜) Shiny new riverside hotel in Lent, with cafe out front. Rooms are well turned-out and comfortable, though the suites are tricked-out in unexpected gangster bling.

🍴 Eating

TOP CHOICE **Gril Ranca** BALKAN €
(📞252 55 50; Dravska ulica 10; dishes €4.80-7.50; 🕗8am-11pm Mon-Sat, noon-9pm Sun) This place serves simple but scrumptious Balkan grills like *pljeskavica* (spicy meat patties) and *čevapčiči* (spicy meatballs of beef or pork) in full view of the Drava. Cool place on a hot night.

To Maribor Aquarium-Terrarium (200m);
Pri Treh Ribnikih (720m);
Piramida (850m)

0 ——— 200 m
0 ——— 0.1 miles

Partizanska c

Maribor

Partizanska c

Ul Heroja Šlandra

Mlinska

Pilnarniška ul

Oreško nab

Pri Treh Ribnikih   SLOVENIAN €€

(☎234 41 70; Ribniška ulica 9; mains €10-17; ⊙11am-10pm Mon-Sat, 11am-9pm Sun) A great place for a meal if you want to get out of the city but don't feel like travelling is 'At the Three Fishponds' in City Park. Oddly, its specialities are cheese *štruklji* (dumplings) and stuffed pork ribs, with fish all but banished from the menu. There's quite a good wine list.

Takos   MEXICAN €

(☎252 71 50; Mesarski prehod 3; mains €6.50-12; ⊙11am-11pm Mon-Thu, 11am-2.30am Fri & Sat) This atmospheric Mexican restaurant in Lent serves excellent fajitas and enchiladas, and turns into a snappy little nightspot after the 11pm happy hour on Friday and Saturday.

Ancora   PIZZA €

(☎250 20 33; Jurčičeva ulica 7; pizza €4-7.50; ⊙9am-midnight Mon-Thu, 9am-1am Fri, 10am-1am Sat, 10.30am-10.30pm Sun) Located on the 1st floor of a very popular bar-restaurant, this place is the most beloved pizzeria in town.

Pri Florjanu   MEDITERRANEAN €€

(☎059 084 850; Grajski trg 6; starters €5.50-7, mains €9-18; ⊙11am-10pm Mon-Thu, 11am-11pm Fri & Sat; ☑) A great spot in full view of the Column of St Florian, this very stylish place has both an open front and an enclosed back terrace with a huge minimalist restaurant in between. It serves rather inspired Mediterranean food, with a good supply of vegetarian options.

Market   MARKET €

(Vodnikov trg; ⊙6.30am-3pm Mon-Sat) There's a market selling produce just north of the former Minorite monastery.

🍷 Drinking

Gledališka Kavarna   CAFE

(☎252 37 20; Slovenska ulica 27; ⊙8am-11pm Mon-Thu, 8am-midnight Fri, 10am-2pm & 7pm-midnight Sat) The very upmarket Theatre Cafe, next to the Slovenian National Theatre (enter from Slomškov trg), attracts a classy crowd.

Patrick's J&B Pub   PUB

(☎251 18 01; Poštna ulica 10; ⊙8am-midnight Mon-Thu, 8am-2am Fri & Sat, 4-11pm Sun) Someone had better tell them that Paddy doesn't drink scotch but what the heck? It's one of the liveliest places on pedestrian Poštna ulica.

Cantante Café   BAR

(☎252 53 12; Vetrinjska ulica 5; ⊙8am-1am Mon-Thu, 8am-3am Fri, 9am-3am Sat, noon-1am Sun) This popular place with its Cuban/Hemingway feel does do Mexican and South American dishes, but we come here for the mojitos and 149 other cocktails on its extensive drinks list.

☆ Entertainment

Slovenian National
Theatre Maribor   THEATRE

(Slovensko Narodno Gledališče Maribor; ☎250 61 00, box office 250 61 15; www.sng-mb.si; Slovenska ulica 27; ⊙10am-1pm & 5-7.30pm Mon-Fri, 10am-1pm Sat & 1hr before performance) This branch of the SNG in Ljubljana has one of the best reputations in the country, and its productions have received critical acclaim throughout Europe. The city's ballet and opera companies also perform here. Enter from Slomškov trg.

Maribor

ŠTAJERSKA & KOROŠKA MARIBOR POHORJE

Jazz Klub Satchmo JAZZ
(☑250 21 50; www.jazz-klub.si; Strossmayerjeva ulica 6; ☉9am-2am Mon-Thu, 9am-3am Fri, 7pm-3am Sat, 7pm-midnight Sun) Maribor's celebrated jazz club meets in a wonderful cellar in the Fine Arts Gallery building.

❶ Information

Abanka (Glavni trg 18) In the mall at the eastern end of Glavni trg.

Kit Kibla (☑252 44 40; www.kibla.org/kit; Glavni trg 14; per 30/60min €0.70/1; ☉9am-10pm Mon-Sat) City-run centre in the town hall with a dozen internet terminals.

Mladinska Knjiga (☑234 31 13; Gosposka ulica 24; ☉9am-7pm Mon-Fri, 9am-1pm Sat) Bookshop, with Lonely Planet guides and maps.

Nova KBM Bank (Trg Svobode 2) Opposite Maribor Castle.

Post Office (Slomškov trg 10)

Tourist Information Centre Maribor (TIC; ☑234 66 11; www.maribor-pohorje.si; Partinzanska cesta 6a; ☉9am-7pm Mon-Fri, 9am-6pm Sat & Sun) Very helpful TIC in kiosk opposite Franciscan church.

❶ Getting There & Away

BUS You can reach virtually any town in Slovenia (and certain international destinations) from Maribor's huge bus station.

Bus services are frequent to Celje (€6.70, 1½ hours), Murska Sobota (€6.30, 1¼ hours), Ptuj (€3.60, 45 minutes) and Ljubljana (€12.40, three hours). Other destinations include Rogaška Slatina (€7.20, two hours) and Slovenj Gradec (€7.20, two hours).

There's a daily bus to Sarajevo (€60, 9½ hours) at 9.15pm (5.15pm on Friday), as well as Munich (€46, 7½ hours) and Vienna (€29, 4½ hours).

TRAIN From Ljubljana there is the ICS express service (€15.20, 1¾ hours), or more frequent slower trains (€9, 2½ hours). Both stop at Celje. Eastbound, services run to Murska Sobota (€8.50, two hours).

International connections include Zagreb (€16, three hours), Vienna (€49, 3½ hours) and Belgrade (€49, 8½ hours).

❶ Getting Around

Maribor and its surrounds are well served by local buses. They depart from the stands south of the train station near Meljska cesta.

Maribor Bike (☑234 66 11; per 2hr/1 day €1/5; ☉8am-8pm Apr-Oct) has bikes available from outside the TIC.

For a local taxi, call ☑250 07 77 or ☑031 801 339.

Maribor Pohorje

☑02 / ELEV TO 1347M

Maribor's green lung and central playground, the eastern edge of the Pohorje Massif is known in these parts as the Maribor Pohorje (Mariborsko Pohorje). It's in easy reach of the city and has countless activities on offer – from skiing and hiking to horse riding and mountain biking.

🏃 Activities

The **Pohorje Sport Centre** (Športni Center Pohorje; ☑220 88 00; www.pohorje.org; Mladinska ulica 29) in Maribor organises most of the activities in the Maribor Pohorje. It can also offer excursions to the Pohorje Adrenaline Park.

Walking

There are heaps of easy **walks** and more difficult **hikes** in every direction from the Hotel Areh (p184). Following a stretch of the marked **Slovenian Mountain Trail**, which originates in Maribor and goes as far as Ankaran on the coast, first west and then southwest for 5km will take you to the two **Šumik waterfalls** and **Pragozd**, one of the very few virgin forests left in Europe. Another 6km to the southwest is **Black Lake** (Črno Jezero), the source of the swift-running Lobnica River, and **Osankarica**, where the Pohorje battalion of Partisans was wiped out by the Germans in January 1943. PZS and GZS each produce their own 1:50,000-scale *Pohorje* map (€8.10 to €8.50).

Adventure Parks

Pohorje Adrenaline Park ADVENTURE SPORTS
(Adrenalinski Park Pohorje; ☑031 655 665, 220 88 21; adult/child from €17/15) A recreational area with all manner of towers, high-rope courses, swings and beams near Koča Luka, midway between the two cable-car stations.

Biking

Cycling is an ideal way to explore the back roads and trails of the Maribor Pohorje. The TIC offers the 1:100,000 *Pohorje Cycling Map* and the simple but useful *Kolesarske Poti na Mariborskem Pohorju (Cycle Trails in the Maribor Pohorje)*. The sport centre rents GT DHI Pro mountain bikes (per four hours/day €40/50) from the lower cable-car station.

Bike Park Pohorje CYCLING
(☑040 645 054, 220 88 25; adult/child with bike half-day €19/14, full day €23/17) Operated by Pohorje Sport Centre, this excellent park starts at 1050m next to the upper cable-car station (p183) and wends its way down 4km through the forests, with more than 30 different obstacles such as table-tops, banks, step-downs and jumps up to 6m.

Horse Riding

You can rent horses from **Koča Koča** (☑040 216 089), a restaurant in a hut 50m from the upper cable-car station (p183), for €4 if you are content to twirl around the paddock three times, or €13/60 per hour/five hours to take one out on the trails. A trip in a horse-drawn coach will set you back €25/40 per half-hour/hour.

Skiing

Maribor Pohorje Ski Grounds SKIING
(☑603 65 53; www.pohorje.org; day pass adult/child/student & senior €28/18/24) Maribor Pohorje ski grounds stretch from Hotel Habakuk (336m) near the lower cable-car station to Žigartov Vrh (1347m) west of Hotel Areh. With 80km of slopes, 36km of cross-country runs and 20 ski lifts and tows (plus gondola), this is Slovenia's largest ski area. Ski-equipment rentals are available from the upper cable-car station, and there's a ski and snowboarding school as well.

🎉 Festivals & Events

Women's World Cup Slalom and Giant Slalom Competition SPORTS
(www.goldenfox.org; ◷Jan) The annual Women's World Cup Slalom and Giant Slalom Competition – the coveted Zlata Lisica (Golden Fox) trophy – takes place on the main piste of the Maribor Pohorje ski grounds in mid-January.

🛏 Sleeping & Eating

There are plenty of places to stay in the Maribor Pohorje, including more than a dozen mountain lodges and holiday homes, some of them run by the Pohorje Sport Centre, which can provide you with a list and basic map. Places close to main roads are the Category III hut **Ruška Koča pri Arehu** (☑041 666 552, 603 50 46; ◷year-round) with 36 beds at 1246m, and the more swish Category III lodge **Poštarski Dom pod Plešivcem** (☑875 09 06, 822 10 55; ◷Wed-Mon) with 37 beds at 805m.

There are two camping grounds at the foothills of the Maribor Pohorje near the cable car's lower station: **Camp Pohorje** (☑614 09 50; www.pohorje.org; Pot k Mlinu 57; adult/child €9/6; ◷year-round), with only 20 pitches for tents and 10 for caravans; and **Camping Centre Kekec** (☑040 225 386; www.cck.si; Pohorska ulica 35; adult/child €9/6.50), with three-dozen pitches.

Almost everyone takes their meals in their hotels in the Maribor Pohorje; there are no independent restaurants except for snack bars. Be on the lookout for dishes and drinks unique to the region, including *pohorski lonec* (Pohorje pot), a kind of goulash; *pohorska omleta*, a pancake filled with fruit; and *boroničevec*, a brandy made with forest berries.

Hotel Bellevue   HOTEL €€€
(☑607 21 00; www.termemb.si; Na Slemenu 35; s €90-140, d €130-230, ste €160-260; [P][✳][@][⊚]) A Pohorje landmark, this very stylish place has 50 rooms and apartments within tumbling distance of the upper cable-car station and is simply the poshest place in the region. Rates include entry to the hotel's fine wellness centre.

Hotel Areh   LODGE €
(☑220 88 41; www.pohorje.org; Lobnica 32; per person half-board €35-45; [P][@]) At the summit of Areh peak (1250m), about 6km southwest of the upper cable-car station, this pleasant 84-bed ski lodge has wood-panelled rooms, a pleasant restaurant and helpful staff. It rents ski equipment and mountain bikes as well.

Hotel Bolfenk   HOTEL €€
(☑603 65 05; www.pohorje.si; Hočko Pohorje 131; per person half-board €45-75; [P][@]) This well-maintained property next to Hotel Bellevue Hotel is an apartment hotel with 20 suites, some of which are quite grand and have living rooms and fireplaces.

ⓘ Getting There & Away

CAR You can drive or, if ambitious, cycle the 20km from the Old Town in Maribor south past the Renaissance-style Betnava Castle, turning west at Spodnje Hoče before reaching a fork in the road at a small waterfall. Go left and you'll reach Hotel Areh after about 5km. A right turn and less than 4km brings you to the upper cable-car station.

CABLE CAR A much easier – and more exhilarating – way to get to Hotel Bellevue and the heart of the Maribor Pohorje is to take the cable car from the station in Zgornje Radvanje, 6km southwest of Maribor's Old Town. There are clamps on the outside of each of the cable car's cabins for mountain bikes and skis.

BUS To reach the lower station from the train station in Maribor take local bus 6 (bus €1.10, 20 minutes) and get off at the terminus – the cable car station is just behind the bus stop.

Central Pohorje Region
☑03 / ELEV TO 1517M

Travellers can easily sample Pohorje's recreational offerings along its eastern edge from Maribor and its western fringes from Slovenj Gradec and Dravograd in Koroška. But the pear-shaped massif's highest and most beautiful area is in the centre. And although it's true that the Pohorje peaks can't exactly compete with those of the Julian and the Kamnik-Savinja Alps – most here barely clear the 1500m mark – hiking and trekking in the winter here is as good as it is in the summer.

Zreče, about 40km southwest of Maribor, is the springboard for the central Pohorje region; indeed, the region is also known as the Zreče Pohorje (Zreško Pohorje). Although certainly not Slovenia's most attractive town – it's dominated by the tool-manufacturing company Unior – Zreče has a modest spa and is within easy striking distance of the ski and sport centre around **Rogla** (1517m), 16km to the north, where teams – including the Slovenian Olympic one – train.

🏃 Activities
Hiking & Mountain Biking

The 1:50,000 GZS *Pohorje* (€8.10) map outlines various circular hiking trails that are as short as 2km (30 minutes) and as long as 32km (eight hours). The latter covers the Šumik waterfalls, Black Lake and Osankarica. Another good one is the 12km hike (three hours) that leads northwest to the **Lovrenc Lakes** (Lovrenska Jezera), a turf swamp with 20 small lakes that are considered a natural phenomenon. The free map/brochure *Rogla Terme Wanderwege/Footpaths* has eight hikes and walks of between 1km (15 minutes) and 32km (eight hours).

Mountain bikers should get hold of a copy of the excellent free 1:100,000 *Pohorje Cycling Map*, with a dozen trails outlined from Maribor in the east to Slovenj Gradec and Dravograd in the west. The spa's map/brochure (1:50,000) called *Rogla Terme Radfahrwege/Cycling Paths* is much more basic with nine trails linking Zreče, Rogla and Areh.

Rogla Cycling & Hiking Centre   HIKING
(Kolesarsko in Pohodriško Center; ☑757 74 68; mountain bikes 1hr/half-day/day €8/14/18; ⊙9am-7pm daily Aug, 9am-7pm Thu-Sun Jun & Jul) The Rogla Cycling & Hiking Centre, next to Pizzerija Planja, organises guided walks in season (per person €3 to €8) and rents moun-

tain bikes. You can also rent bicycles for the same price from the Dobrava 2000 Hotel.

Skiing

Rogla Ski Grounds · SKIING

(☑757 61 55, 232 92 64; www.rogla.eu; day pass adult/child/senior & student €28/18/25) The Rogla ski grounds has 12km of ski slopes (mostly intermediate) and 18km of cross-country trails served by two chairlifts and 10 tows. The season is a relatively long one – from the end of November to as late as April.

Rogla Ski School · SKI SCHOOL

(Smučarska Šola Rogla; ☑757 74 68; www.rogla.eu; ☺8.30am-4pm daily in season) At the Rogla Ski School, in a little wooden cabin at the base of the ski lift, you can also learn to snowboard.

Ski Servis · EQUIPMENT RENTAL

(☑757 74 89; skis per day adult/child €16/11; ☺8.30am-4.45pm) You can rent equipment from the Ski Servis office at the Planja Hotel.

🛏 Sleeping

The central Pohorje region abounds in farmhouses with rooms and apartments for rent, particularly along Cesta Kmečnega near Resnik, about 7km southwest of Rogla. One of the best is the four-room **Pačnik farmhouse** (☑576 22 02; Resnik 21; per person €23-28; ☺Jul–mid-Sep, mid-Dec–mid-Mar; P). There are even more farmhouses accepting guests in Skomarje to the southwest.

Garni Hotel Zvon · PENSION €€

(☑757 36 00; www.garnihotelzvon; Slomškova ulica 2, Zreče; r per person €40, apt €70-85; P🌸@) There's no particular reason to stay down in Zreče; all the fun is up in Rogla. But if you're a serious disciple of things thermal, the pension-like 'Bell' is just opposite the entrance to the spa and has 15 spotless rooms and apartments.

Planja Hotel · HOTEL €€€

(☑757 71 00; www.terme-zrece.si; Rogla; s €60-70, d €100-120; P@📶🏊) This four-star, 30-bed property, the poshest place to stay in Rogla, also has a three-star wing with 88 beds called the **Rogla Hotel** (s €55-60, d €80-100). Its rooms, frankly, are brighter and more attractive than those in the main hotel. The **Brinje Hotel** (s €45-50, d €70-80) is essentially just a poky annex of the Planja with 22 apartments. The hotel's **Jurgova Apartments** (s €40-45, d €60-70) are set off on their own.

Dobrava 2000 Hotel · HOTEL €€€

(☑757 60 00; www.terme-zrece.si; Cesta na Roglo 15, Zreče; s/d €80/130; P🌸@📶🏊) The spa's flagship hotel, this four-star place has 76 rooms at the entrance to the spa. Several rooms are adapted for guests with disabilities. Make sure you get one of the rooms with a balcony. The **Dobrava Hotel** (s/d €70/110) is a slightly cheaper extension with 35 rooms. More pleasant (and still cheaper) are the **Terme Zreče Villas** (s/d €60/100) in a small wooded area 150m from the main spa building, with 40 apartments and an equal number of double rooms.

🍴 Eating

Dom na Pesku · SLOVENIAN €

(☑757 74 45; Rogla; dishes €4.50-12.50; ☺7am-9pm Apr-Oct, 8am-7pm Nov-Mar) This mountain lodge (rooms per person €28), 3km north of Rogla on the unsealed road to Koroša, is a popular place for hearty Slovenian fare, especially its celebrated mushroom soup with buckwheat goats (*gobova kremna juha z ajdovimi žganci;* €4.50) and *pohorski lonec* (Pohorje pot; €5), a kind of goulash.

Pizzerija Planja · PIZZA €

(☑757 72 50; Rogla; pizza €4.40-6; ☺8.30am-8pm Jul & Aug, 8.30am-5pm Sep-Jun) Along with pizza, this place – just north of the Planja Hotel in Rogla and near the ski lift – does breakfasts and some Slovenian dishes.

Stara Koča · RESTAURANT €€

(☑757 74 47; Rogla; set lunch €12; ☺7am-midnight) The Old Hut is the main restaurant (and original structure) at the Planja Hotel and it retains its rustic mountain-hut vibe.

Gostilna Jurček · SLOVENIAN €

(☑041 686 725; Cesta na Roglo 4b, Zreče; starters €5-8, mains €5.20-12; ☺7am-10pm Mon-Fri, 7am-11pm Sat, 9am-10pm Sun) This *gostilna* in Zreče, on the main road to Rogla and opposite the shopping centre, is a friendly place for a quick meal.

ℹ Information

Post Office (Cesta na Roglo 13b, Zreče) To the southeast of the bank.

Rogla Unitur Ski Resort (www.rogla.si) Useful website, especially for activities.

Tourist Information Centre Zreče (TIC; ☑759 04 70; tic.zrece.lto@siol.net; Cesta na Roglo 13b, Zreče; ☺7am-3pm Mon, Tue, Thu & Fri, 7am-5pm Wed, 9am-noon Sat) In the Zreče Bazaar.

ŠTAJERSKA & KOROŠKA CENTRAL POHORJE REGION

ℹ Getting There & Away

There are regular connections from Zreče to Celje (€3.60, 45 minutes) via Slovenske Konjice. In winter two buses a day from Celje and a couple from Slovenske Konjice stop at Zreče and then carry on to Rogla. Local buses make the runs from Zreče bus station to Rogla.

In winter there are special ski buses from Zreče (five in each direction), as well as Celje and Slovenske Konjice. **Terme Zreče** (☑757 61 56; www .terme-zrece.si; Cesta na Roglo 15; swimming pools adult/child 3hr Mon-Fri €8/6, Sat & Sun €8/9, all day Mon-Fri €10/7.50, Sat & Sun €12/9; ☉swimming pools 9am-9pm) runs buses hourly from 6am to 8.30pm or 9pm up to Rogla for its

guests in winter, with up to four in each direction departing daily during the rest of the year.

Celje

☑03 / POP 36,725 / ELEV 241M

With its time-warp historical centre, fabulous architecture, excellent museums and enormous castle looming over the picturesque Savinja River, Celje might appear to have won the tourism sweepstakes. But for some reason it gets perennially overlooked in favour of Maribor and Ptuj – so making it here can feel like a bit of a discovery.

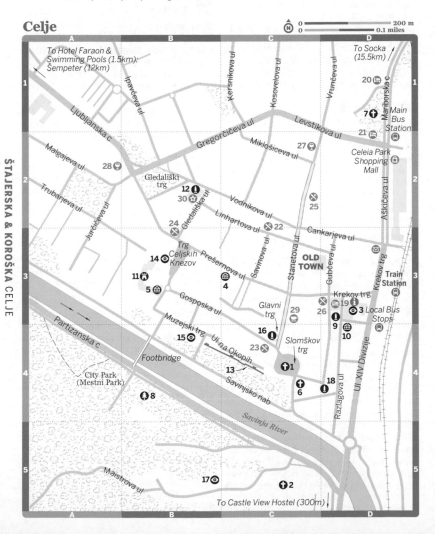

Celje

Celje's compact Old Town is bordered by Levstikova ulica and Gregorčičeva ulica to the north and northwest, the area around the Lower Castle to the west, the train tracks to the east and the Savinja River to the south.

The town has two main squares: Glavni trg, at the southern end of pedestrian Stanetova ulica, and Krekov trg, opposite the train station. The main bus station is 300m north of the train station, opposite the huge Celeia shopping mall on Aškičeva ulica. Local buses stop south of the train station on Ulica XIV Divizije.

History

Celeia was the administrative centre of the Roman province of Noricum between the 1st and 5th centuries. In fact, it flourished to such a degree that it gained the nickname 'Troia secunda', the 'second Troy'.

Celje's second Camelot came in the mid-14th century when the Counts of Celje took control of the area. The counts (later dukes), one of the richest and most powerful feudal dynasties in Central Europe, were the last on Slovenian soil to challenge the absolute rule of the Habsburgs, and they united much of Slovenia for a time. Part of the counts' emblem – three gold stars forming an inverted triangle – has been incorporated into the Slovenian national flag and seal.

Celje was more German than Slovenian until the end of WWI, when the town government passed into local hands for the first time.

◉ Sights

Celje Old Castle   CASTLE
(Stari Grad Celje; ✆031 348 296; Cesta na Grad 78; admission €2; ⊙9am-5pm Mon-Thu, 9am-7pm Fri, 11am-7pm Sat & Sun Jun-Aug, shorter hrs rest of year) The largest fortress in Slovenia, this castle is perched on a 407m-high escarpment about 2km southeast of the Old Town; the walk up via a footpath from Cesta na Grad takes about half an hour. The castle was originally built in the early 13th century and went through several transformations, especially under the Counts of Celje in the 14th and 15th centuries.

When the castle lost its strategic importance in the 15th century it was left to deteriorate, and subsequent owners used the stone blocks to build other structures, including parts of the Lower Castle and the Old County Hall. A surprisingly large portion remains intact, however, and has been restored, including the 35m-high **Frederick Tower** (Friderikov Stolp).

ŠTAJERSKA & KOROŠKA CELJE

Celje

◉ Sights

Celje Regional Museum   MUSEUM
(Pokrajinski Muzej Celje; ☑428 09 50; www.pok muz-ce; adult/child/student €3/1/2; ☻10am-6pm Tue-Sun Mar-Oct, 10am-6pm Tue-Fri, 10am-noon Sat Nov-Feb) In the 16th-century **County Hall** (Stara Grofija; Muzejski trg 1), this museum is devoted to Celeia and the Counts of Celje, even exhibiting 18 of the nobles' skulls in glass cases. The museum has a dozen rooms, many of them done up in styles from different periods (eg baroque, neoclassical, Biedemeier, Secessionist), but its main attraction is the quite astonishing **Celje Ceiling** (Celjski Strop), an enormous trompe l'oeil painting in the main hall, of columns, towers, angels frolicking skyward, noblemen and ladies looking down at you looking up. Completed in about 1600 by a Polish artist, the mural was meant to lift the ceiling up to the sky, and it does just that. Other panels represent the four seasons and show scenes from Roman and Greek mythology.

The impressive **Knežji dvorec** annexe in the 14th-century Lower Castle on Trg Celjskih Knezov offers an archaeological history of Celje in one building: its cellars house a complete 3rd-century Roman road brilliantly displayed with excavated statuary and frescoes and parts of the old city walls. On top of these are traces of the medieval buildings up to parts of air-raid shelters built to withstand the bombs of WWII.

Krekov Trg   SQUARE
Opposite the train station is the mammoth neo-Gothic **Celje Hall** (Celjski Dom; Krekov trg 3), built in 1907 and once the centre of social life for German-speaking Celjani. It now contains the year-round TIC (p190) and, in the lower ground floor, the **Children's Art Gallery** (Galerija Likovnih Del Mladih; ☑041 615 273; admission free; ☻10am-6pm Tue-Sat), devoted to art produced by those under the age of 20 and the only such museum in all of Slovenia. To the south and connected to the Hotel Evropa is the 16th-century **Defence Tower** (Obrambni Stolp), and about 150m further on, the **Water Tower** (Vodni Stolp; Razlagova ulica 19), part of the city wall and ramparts, built between 1451 and 1473.

Josip Pelikan Photo Studio   MUSEUM
(Fotografski Atelje Josipa Pelikana; ☑548 58 91; www.muzej-nz-ce.si; Razlagova ulica 5; ☻10am-2pm Tue-Fri, 9am-1pm Sat, 2-6pm Sun) Looking like an oversized greenhouse (to let in the light), the Josip Pelikan Photo Studio is the complete studio of an early-20th-century Celje photographer and part of the Museum of Recent History.

Slomškov Trg & Glavni Trg   SQUARE
The **Abbey Church of St Daniel** (Opatijska Cerkev Sv Danijela), dating from the early 14th century, has some magnificent frescoes and tombstones, but its greatest treasure is a carved wooden **pietà** dating from 1415. The chapel has carved stone walls and vaults with remnants of frescoes from the early 15th century and carved effigies of the Apostles. Parts of Celje's **medieval walls** and **ramparts** can be seen along Ulica na Okopih, west of the church. In the southeast corner of Slomškov trg is the **Chapel of St Elizabeth** (Kapela Sv Elizabete) and the 15th-century **town almshouse** (mestni špital).

Contiguous with Slomškov trg is Glavni trg, the heart of the Old Town. It is filled with lovely town houses dating from the 17th and 18th centuries and, in the warmer months, outdoor cafes. In the centre of the square is the requisite **plague pillar** (1776) dedicated to Mary.

Celje Museum of Recent History   MUSEUM
(Muzej Novejše Zgodovine Celje; ☑428 64 10; www .muzej-nz-ce.si; Prešernova ulica 17; adult/child/ senior & student/family €3/1.50/2/6; ☻10am-6pm Mon-Fri, 9am-1pm Sat, 2-6pm Sun) The museum records the story of Celje ('Living in Celje: 1900–2000') from the late 19th century onwards and includes a re-creation of an early-20th-century street complete with tailor, hairdresser, clockmaker and goldsmith.

Trg Celjskih Knezov   SQUARE
The funnel-shaped Square of the Celje Counts leads north from Muzejski trg. At the start is the **Lower Castle** (Spodnij grad) built in the 14th century for the Celje Counts and today containing the **Centre for Contemporary Arts** (Center Sodobnih Umetnosti; ☑426 51 60; Trg Celjskih Knezov 8; admission free; ☻11am-6pm Tue-Fri, 10am-noon Sat, 2-6pm Sun), which contains the rather titillating **Račka Gallery of Erotic Art** (Galerija Erotike Račka), a first for Slovenia, as well as the Roman annexe to the Regional Museum. To the north is the **National Hall** (Narodni Dom; Trg Celjskih Knezov 9), the cultural and social centre for Celje's Slovenes at the end of the 19th century and now the city hall.

Breg NEIGHBOURHOOD

On the south bank of the Savinja River a covered stairway with 90 steps at Breg 2 leads to the **Capuchin Church of St Cecilia** (Kapucinska Cerkev Sv Cecilije). The Germans used the nearby monastery (now apartments) as a prison during WWII. Between the church and **City Park** (Mestni Park; Partizanska cesta) is the reconstructed Roman **Temple of Hercules** (Heraklejev Tempelj; Maistrova ulica) dating from the 2nd century AD. Further south, you can walk up 396m-high **Nicholas Hill** (Miklavški Hrib), topped by the **Church of St Nicholas** (Cerkev Sv Miklavža), for a wonderful view of the castle, the Old Town and the Savinja.

🏃 Activities

The TIC has brochures listing a number of **walks** and **hikes** into the surrounding countryside lasting between one and four hours. The longest one (28km) leads southeast to **Mt Tovst** (834m) and the picturesque village of Svetina via the **Celjska Koča** (☏059 070 400; www.celjska-koca.si), a mountain hut at 650m that has metamorphosed into a delightfully modern three-star hotel with adjacent skiing piste. It also distributes the brochure *Poti Primerne za Kolesarjenje* (*Trails Suitable for Cycling*), with 10 routes outlined for Celje and settlements to the north.

🛏 Sleeping

TOP
CHOICE **MCC Hostel** HOSTEL €

(☏490 87 42; www.hostel-celje.com; Mariborksa cesta 2; dm €18, s/d €29/36; 🖥) A fantastic addition to Slovenia's hostel scene – private rooms and dorms are immaculately presented, but each is a unique installation, decorated by local artists to tell a story from Celje's hidden history. Who can resist the room of the Celje ninja (costume included), the giant catfish or the cop who had to arrest himself? There are regular music and social events, plus free bike hire.

Hotel Evropa HOTEL €€€

(☏426 90 00; www.hotel-evropa.si; Krekov trg 4; s €62-98, d €98-124, ste €260; P@) Located near the train station and in the centre of town, this 46-room historic hotel has been lovingly restored and is now a provincial favourite. We love the high-end cafe, the stunning new restaurant and the pleasant and helpful staff. Rooms on the 3rd and 4th floors are superior. Enter from Razlagova ulica.

Castle View Hostel HOSTEL €

(☏070 220 069; www.elfa-sp.si; Breg 21; dm with/without HI card from €17/19; @🖥) In the very shadow of the castle is the, well, Castle View, with eight beds in three rooms. It has a generous-sized kitchen and wi-fi in each room.

Hotel Faraon HOTEL €€

(☏545 20 18; www.hotel-faraon.si; Ljubljanska cesta 39; s/d/tr €42/69/89; P@🏊) The Pharaoh has 26 modern rooms about 1.5km west of the Old Town and as close as you'll get to the Savinja River. It has its own swimming pool and casino. Good value.

Hotel Štorman Celje HOTEL €€

(☏426 04 26; www.storman.si; Mariborska cesta 3; s €42-57, d €65-84, tr €90, ste from €100; P✳@) The 52-room Štorman is in a canary-yellow, nine-storey block just north of the 15th-century Church of St Maximilian. The hotel is a favourite with businesspeople but eschew any of the rooms facing Mariborska cesta – it's a major and very busy highway.

🍴 Eating

TOP
CHOICE **Lastoria** INTERNATIONAL €

(☏544 29 25; Glavni trg 12; pizza €4.70-7.20; ⏱10am-11pm Mon-Sat) This popular restaurant overlooking a pretty square is always packed, offering pasta, pizza and plenty of local dishes. Soon to expand to include jazz nights.

Restavracija Evropa INTERNATIONAL €€

(Krekov trg 4; starters €6.80-9.90, mains €12.50-18.90; ⏱11am-10pm Sun-Thu, 11am-midnight Fri & Sat) This stunning eatery in the Hotel Evropa has superb international cuisine and some very inspired decor. We love the Manet-like portraits of film and rock stars (though we don't get the connection either).

Gostilna Jež SLOVENIAN €

(Linhartova ulica 6; dishes €4.20-6; ⏱8am-5pm Mon-Sat) This very simple eatery is a great place for a cheap and filling lunch – as so many market-goers seem to think.

Country Pub SLOVENIAN €€

(☏426 04 14; Mariborska cesta 3; starters €7.50-9.20, mains €6.50-17.90; ⏱6am-midnight) It's not often that we recommend hotel outlets but this pleasant pub-restaurant on the ground floor of the Hotel Štorman (p189) is a viable option in a city with few choices. Go for one

EKO MUZEJ

Halfway between Šempeter and Celje but worth the detour, this **museum** (☎710 04 34; www.ekomuzej-hmelj.si; Aškerčeva 9a, Žalec; adult/child €2.5/1; ☺Mon/Wed/Fri 3-7pm, Tue/Thu/Sat 9am-1pm) is dedicated to the hop and the noble art of brewing – a speciality of the region. August to October are the best times to visit, when their are plenty of outdoor activities and demonstrations, from hop-picking, crowning of the hop princess and guided walks. And yes, you can do beer tastings too.

of the salads (€3.90 to €7.90) and a steak (€15.90 to €17.90).

Market   MARKET €

(cnr Gledališki trg & Trg Celjskih Knezov; ☺6am-3pm) This outdoor market has fresh fruit, vegetables and other foodstuffs.

Mercator   SUPERMARKET €

(Stanetova ulica 14; ☺7am-7pm Mon-Fri, 7am-3pm Sat, 8am-noon Sun) You'll find a large Mercator supermarket opposite the art-deco Kino Metropol (Metropol Cinema; 1929). There's also a **Mercator** (Prešernova ulica 1; ☺6am-6pm Mon-Fri, 7am-noon Sat) branch next to the Hotel Evropa.

🍷 Drinking & Entertainment

Kavarna Evropa   CAFE

(☎496 90 00; Krekov trg 4; ☺7am-11pm Mon-Sat, 8am-10pm Sun) This 'olde worlde' cafe in the Hotel Evropa – all dark wood panelling, gilt mouldings and fusty chandeliers – is a good place for a cup of coffee and a cake.

Oscar Caffe   CAFE

(Glavni trg 9; ☺8am-10pm) This ever-so-cool cafe attracts the intelligentsia of Celje – at least that's what the retro decor and lots and lots of attitude suggests.

Branibor Pub   PUB

(☎492 41 44; Stanetova ulica 27; ☺6am-1am Mon-Thu, 6am-2.30am Fri, 7am-2.30am Sat, 8am-1am Sun) This is one of the best pubs in town, with jazz and other live music some nights.

Maverick Pub   PUB

(Ljubljanska cesta 7; ☺6am-2am Mon-Thu, 6am-4am Fri & Sat, 6am-midnight Sun) One of several watering holes bunched up opposite

Gledališki trg, this is a lively place with a large outdoor terrace for people-watching in the warmer months.

Slovenian People's Theatre   THEATRE

(Slovenski Ljudsko Gledališče; ☎426 42 00, box office 426 42 08; www.slg-ce.si; Gledališki trg 5; ☺9am-noon Mon-Fri) The SLG, which encompasses part of a medieval tower once used as a dungeon on Vodnikova ulica, stages six plays between September and May.

🛈 Information

Abanka (Aškičeva ulica 10) Diagonally opposite the post office.

Banka Celje (Vodnikova ulica 2) In a building designed by Jože Plečnik in 1930.

Mladinska Knjiga (☎428 52 52; Stanetova ulica 3; ☺8am-7pm Mon-Fri, 8am-noon Sat) Sells regional maps and guides.

Post Office (Krekov trg 9) Purpose-built in 1898.

Tourist Information Centre Celje (TIC; ☎492 50 81, 428 79 36; www.celje.si; Celje Hall, Krekov trg 3; ☺9am-5pm Mon-Thu, 9am-7pm Fri, 11am-7pm Sat & Sun Jun-Aug, shorter hrs rest of year)

🛈 Getting There & Away

BUS Intercity buses run frequently to Mozirje (€4.10, 50 minutes), Rogaška Slatina (€4.10, one hour) and Rogatec and Zreče (€3.60, 40 minutes). Count on up to six buses on weekdays and two at the weekend to Ljubljana (€7.20, 1½ hours) and Maribor (€6.70, 1½ hours). Other destinations accessible by bus from Celje: Gornji Grad (€5.60, 1½ hours), Logarska Dolina (€7.20, two hours), and Murska Sobota (€11.10, 2¾ hours).

For local destinations such as Šempeter (€2.60, 20 minutes), Škofja Vas, Šentjur, Prebold and Žalec, go to the **bus stops** south of the train station on Ulica XIV Divizije.

TRAIN Celje is a good rail hub. From Ljubljana (€6.60 to €11.60, 1½ hours) you can reach Celje up to two dozen times a day by regular train and six times a day by ICS express train.

Celje is also on the line linking Zidani Most (connections to and from Ljubljana and Zagreb) with Maribor (€5.50 to €9.90, one hour, 67km, half-hourly) and the Austrian cities of Graz and Vienna.

A spur line links Celje with Šempeter up to nine times a day Monday to Saturday in each direction. A third line connects Celje with Zabok in Croatia via Rogaška Slatina (€3.25, 50 minutes), Rogatec and Dobovec. Up to seven trains arrive and depart on weekdays but only a couple at the weekend.

❶ Getting Around
For a local taxi call ☎544 22 00 or ☎031 464 646.

Šempeter
☎03 / POP 2025 / ELEV 257M

Some 12km west of Celje, Šempeter is the site of a reconstructed **Roman necropolis** (Rimska Nekropola; ☎700 20 56; www.td-sempeter .si; Ob Rimski Nekropoli 2; adult/child €4/3; ☺10am-6pm daily mid-Apr–Sep, 10am-3pm daily early Apr, 10am-4pm Sat & Sun Oct). The burial ground contains four complete tombs and scores of columns, stelae and fragments carved with portraits, mythological creatures and scenes from daily life. They have been divided into about two dozen groups linked by footpaths.

The most beautiful is the **Ennius family tomb**, with reliefs of animals and, on the front panel, the priestess Europa riding a bull. The largest is the 8m-high **Spectacius tomb**, raised in honour of a Roman official, his wife and son. (Notice the kidnapping scene on the side relief.) If you compare these with the later **Secundinus family tomb** erected in about 250 AD, it's obvious that Roman power and wealth was on the decline here in the mid-3rd century.

Upper Savinja Valley
The beautiful Upper Savinja Valley (Zgornja Savinjska Dolina) is bound by forests, ancient churches, traditional farmhouses and high Alpine peaks. There are activities here to suit every taste and inclination – from hiking, mountain biking and rock climbing to fishing, kayaking and swimming in the Savinja.

The valley has been exploited for its timber since the Middle Ages. Rafters transported the timber from Ljubno to Mozirje and Celje and some of the logs travelled as far as Romania. The trade brought wealth to the valley, evident from the many fine buildings still standing here.

The best place to get active is around Logarska Dolina. The free English-language brochure entitled *The Savinjska and Šaleška Valleys* is helpful if you intend to spend a bit of time in the area. Serious hikers should pick up a copy of the 1:50,000 *Kamniško Savinjske Alpe* map (€8.10) by PZS. Cyclists will want the *Kolesarska Karta Zgornja Savinjska Dolina (Upper Savinja Valley Cycling Map)* available everywhere for €3.

LOGARSKA DOLINA
☎03 / POP 95 / ELEV TO 1250M

Most of the glacial Forester Valley, which is 7.5km long and no more than 500m wide, has been a country park of just under 2431 hectares since 1987. This 'pearl of the Alpine region', with more than 40 natural attractions – caves, springs, peaks, rock towers and waterfalls – as well as endemic flora (golden slipper orchid) and rare fauna (mountain eagles, peregrine falcons), is a wonderful place to explore for a few days. The **tourist office** (☎051 626 380, 838 90 04; www.logarska -dolina.si; Logarska Dolina 9; ☺9am-6pm Jul & Aug, 9am-3pm Apr-Jun & Sep) is in a small wooden kiosk opposite the Hotel Plesnik car park.

❂ Sights & Activities
The tourist office can organise any number of activities – from guided mountaineering and rock climbing (per hour €25) to paragliding (€60). It also rents mountain bikes (per hour/day €3/12). The valley has the very basic **ski grounds** (☎838 90 04; www.logarska -dolina.si; day pass adult/child €10/7), a 1km-long slope and 15km of cross-country ski trails served by two tows.

Logarska Dolina Country Park   PARK
The country park (Krajinski Park Logarska Dolina) (open year-round; from April to September at weekends in October) cars and motorcycles entering the park must pay €6 and €4 respectively; pedestrians and cyclists always get in free. A road goes past a chapel and through the woods to the 90m **Rinka Waterfall** (Slap Rinka) at 1100m, but there are plenty of trails to explore and up to 20 other waterfalls in the area.

The bottom of the Rinka Waterfall is a 10-minute walk from the end of the valley road. The climb to the top takes about 20 minutes. It's not very difficult, but it can get slippery. From the top to the west you can see three peaks reaching higher than 2250m: Kranjska Rinka, Koroška Rinka and Štajerska Rinka. Until 1918 they formed the triple border of Carniola (Kranjska), Carinthia (Koroška) and Styria (Štajerska). Ask the tourist office for the *Trail around Logarska* brochure, which will take you through the valley for 7km in around two hours.

Opposite Dom Planincev is a trail leading to **Sušica Waterfall** and **Klemenča Cave**, both at about 1200m.

Matkov Kot
VALLEY

Another magnificent and much less explored valley is 6km-long Matkov Kot, which runs parallel to Logarska Dolina and the border with Austria. Reach here by road by turning west as you leave Logarska Dolina.

🍴 Sleeping & Eating

Hotel Plesnik
HOTEL €€€

(☎839 23 00; www.plesnik.si; Logarska Dolina 10; s €89-96, d €144-154; P@☀) A 30-room hotel in the centre of the valley with a pool, sauna, a fine restaurant (open 8am to 10pm) and lovely public area, the Plesnik pretty much *is* Logarska Dolina. Its annex, the Vila Palenk (singles/doubles €79/126), with 11 rooms done up in generic 'Alpine style', takes the overflow.

Lenar Farmhouse
FARMSTAY €

(☎838 90 06; www.lenar.si; Logarska Dolina 11; r per person €27-29, apt for 3 €60; P) This farmhouse has four rooms and a couple of apartments in a lovely peasant's cottage, a couple of kilometres south from the valley entrance. Horse riding can be arranged here (€15 per hour).

Pension Na Razpotju
PENSION €€

(☎839 16 50; www.logarska-narazpotju.si; Logarska Dolina 14; s/d €50/80; P@) A very comfortable pension set back from the main road, 'At the Crossroads' has 21 beds.

Dom Planincev
MOUNTAIN HUT €

(☎070 847 639, 584 70 06; www.domplanincev.si; Logarska Dolina 15a; per person €18; ☉late Apr–Oct; P) This wooden mountain hut 2.5km from Rinka has a relaxed, rustic feel to it and sleeps up to 32 people.

Planšarija Logarski Kot
MOUNTAIN HUT €

(☎041 210 017, 838 90 30; info@logarska.si; per person €18; ☉late Apr–Oct; P) Close to the falls, this locally run hut has accommodation for two dozen hikers.

Orlovo Gnezdo
CAFE €

(Eyrie; ☎031 269 785; ☉10am-6pm) In the valley itself there's the Orlovo Gnezdo, a simple cafe-pub with snacks in a tall wooden tower overlooking the falls and reached by a steep set of steps.

ℹ Getting There & Around

Logarska Dolina isn't well served by public transport. You can reach Celje (€7.20, two hours) on a daily weekday bus in season.

You can rent bicycles (per hour/day €3/12) from both the park entrance and the tourist office. The latter also has electric bikes (per hour €14).

KOROŠKA

The truncated province of Koroška is essentially just three valleys bounded by the Pohorje Massif on the east; the last of the Karavanke peaks, Mt Peca, on the west; and the hills of Kobansko to the north. The Drava Valley runs east to west and includes the towns of Dravograd, Muta and Vuzenica. The Mežica and Mislinja valleys fan out from the Drava; the former is an industrial area with such towns as Ravne, Prevalje and Črna na Koroškem, while the latter's main centre is Slovenj Gradec.

There is a reason Koroška is so small. In the plebiscite ordered by the victorious allies after WWI, Slovenes living on the other side of the Karavanke, the 120-km-long rock wall that separates Slovenia from Austria, voted to put their economic future in the hands of Vienna while the mining region of the Mežica Valley went to Slovenia. As a result, the Slovenian nation lost 90,000 of its nationals (7% of the population at the time) as well as the cities of Klagenfurt (Celovec) and Villach (Beljak) to Austria.

Understandably, the results of that vote have never sat very well with the Slovenes on the southern side of the mountains. Still, Koroška holds a special place in the hearts and minds of most Slovenes. The Duchy of Carantania (Karantanija), the first Slavic state dating back to the 7th century, was centred here, and the word 'Carinthia' is derived from that name.

Slovenj Gradec
☎02 / POP 8340 / ELEV 410M

Slovenj Gradec isn't the 'capital' of Koroška – that distinction goes to the industrial centre of Ravne na Koroškem to the northwest – but it is certainly the province's cultural and recreational heart. A large number of museums, galleries and historical churches line its main square, while the sporting opportunities in the Pohorje Massif to the east are many.

Slovenj Gradec's main street is Glavni trg, a colourful long 'square' lined with old town houses and shops. The bus station is at Pohorska cesta 15, about 500m northeast of the TIC. Slovenj Gradec is not on a train line.

History

The history of Slovenj Gradec is closely tied to Stari Trg, a suburb southwest of the Old Town where there was a Roman set-

UNDER THE LINDEN TREES

Slovenia's national tree, the stately linden (or common lime) and its heart-shaped leaf have become something of a symbol of Slovenia and Slovenian hospitality.

The linden (*lipa*) grows slowly for about 60 years and then suddenly spurts upward and outwards, living to a ripe old age. It is said that a linden grows for 300 years, stands still for another 300 and takes 300 years to die.

Linden wood was used by the Romans to make shields and, as it is easy to work with, artisans in the Middle Ages carved religious figures from it, earning linden the title *sacrum lignum*, or 'sacred wood'. Tea made from the linden flower, which contains aromatic oils, has been used as an antidote for fever and the flu since at least the 16th century. More importantly, from earliest times the linden tree was the focal point of any settlement in Slovenia – the centre of meetings, arbitration, recreation and, of course, gossip. The tree, which could never be taller than the church spire, always stood in the middle of the village, and important decisions were made by town elders at a table beneath it.

In fact, so sacred is the linden tree to Slovenes that its destruction is considered a serious offence. In discussing the barbarous acts committed by the Italians during the occupation of Primorska between the wars, one magazine article passionately points out that 'Kobarid had to swallow much bitterness...The fascists even cut down the linden tree...'

Slovenia's oldest linden is the 800-year-old Najevska Lipa under Koroška's Mt Peca, where Slovenian politicians meet in July. We give it another century.

tlement called Colatio that existed from the 1st to the 3rd centuries (though there is no trace of it now). At that time an important Roman road from Celeia (Celje) to Virunum (near Klagenfurt in Austria) passed through Colatio. Slovenj Gradec was an important trade centre in the Middle Ages and minted its own coins. Later it became an important cultural and artistic centre with many artisans and craft guilds. Among the prominent Habsburg nobles based in Slovenj Gradec over the centuries were members of the Windisch-Grätz family, a variant of the German name for the town (Windisch Graz).

👁 Sights

Koroška Regional Museum   MUSEUM
(Koroški Pokrajinski Muzej; ☑884 20 55; http://gostje.kivi.si/muzej; Glavni trg 24; adult/child/family €2/1.50/5; ⊙9am-6pm Tue-Fri, 10am-1pm & 2-5pm Sat & Sun) This museum (on the 2nd floor of the former town hall) has exhibits devoted to the history of Slovenj Gradec and the Koroška region – from painted beehive panels to models of wartime hospital rooms and schools run by Partisans. There's also a very good archaeological collection focusing on the Roman settlement of Colatio. It includes jewellery and other effects taken from a Slavic burial ground at Puščava near Castle Hill (Grajski Grič) to the west.

Koroška Gallery of Fine Arts   GALLERY
(Koroška Galerija Likovnih Umetnosti; ☑882 21 31, 884 12 83; www.glu-sg.si; adult/student & child/family €2/1.50/5; ⊙9am-6pm Tue-Fri, 10am-1pm & 2-5pm Sat & Sun) The Koroška Gallery of Fine Arts, on the 1st floor of the former town hall, counts among its permanent collection African folk art, bronze sculptures by Franc Berneker (1874–1932) and naive paintings by Jože Tisnikar (1928–98). Tisnikar is among the most interesting and original artists in Slovenia, and his obsession with corpses, distorted figures and oversized insects is at once disturbing and funny. Outside the town hall is the **Venetian Horse**, a life-size work by contemporary sculptor/designer Oskar Kogoj, and something of a symbol for Slovenj Gradec.

Soklič Museum   MUSEUM
(Sokličev Muzej; ☑884 15 05; Trg Svobode 5; ⊙by appointment) The items on display at the Soklič Museum on the 2nd floor of the presbytery were amassed by Jakob Soklič (1893–1972), a priest who began squirreling away bits and bobs in the 1930s. Among the mediocre watercolours and oils of peasant idylls and the umpteen portraits of composer Hugo Wolf (born nearby in 1860), are green goblets and beakers from nearby Glažuta (an important glass-manufacturing town in the 19th century), local embroidery, religious artefacts and some 18th-century furniture.

ŠTAJERSKA & KOROŠKA SLOVENJ GRADEC

Slovenj Gradec

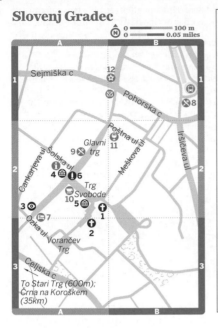

N 0 — 100 m
0 — 0.05 miles

Church of St Elizabeth CHURCH
(Cerkev Sv Elizabete; Trg Svobode) The sombre Church of St Elizabeth was built in 1251 and is the town's oldest structure. Aside from the Romanesque nave and a couple of windows, almost everything here is baroque, including the massive gold altar and pulpit, and the altar paintings done by local artist Franc Mihael Strauss (1647–1740) and his son Janez Andrej Strauss (1721–82).

Church of the Holy Spirit CHURCH
(Cerkev Sv Duha; Trg Svobode) The Church of the Holy Spirit (1494) has an interior covered with Gothic frescoes by Andrej of Otting. The 27 panels on the north wall represent the Passion of Christ; the scenes on the archway are of the Final Judgment. There's a peephole to view them (partially) when the church is locked.

🏃 Activities

Slovenian Alpine Trail HIKING
The Slovenian Alpine Trail passes through Stari Trg and the centre of Slovenj Gradec before continuing up to Mala Kopa (1524m), where it meets the E6. There is a Category II, 48-bed mountain hut at 1102m to the northwest called **Koča pod Kremžarjevim Vrhom** (☎041 832 035, 884 48 83; ⊗Wed-Mon

late Apr–Sep, Sat & Sun Oct–late Apr). The **E6** heads north through Vuhred and Radlje ob Dravi to Austria, and the Slovenian Alpine Trail carries on eastward to Rogla and Maribor. There is more accommodation on Velika Kopa at 1377m at the 68-bed **Grmovškov Dom pod Veliko Kopo** (☎041 601 832, 883 98 60; ⊗year-round). If you are going to do a fair amount of hiking in the western Pohorje, pick up a copy of the 1:50,000-scale *Pohorje* GZS map (€8.50).

Kope SKIING
(☎882 27 40; www.pohorje.org; day pass adult/child/student & senior €26/18/23) Three ski slopes are within striking distance of Slovenj Gradec, but the closest is Kope, with skiing above the Mislinja Valley on the western edge of the Pohorje Massif. The ski grounds have 8.5km of runs, 15km of cross-country trails and eight lifts on Mala Kopa and Velika Kopa peaks. To reach Kope, follow the Velenje road (No 4) for 3km south and then turn east. The ski area is another 13km at the end of the road.

🛏 Sleeping & Eating

Hotel Aerodrom HOTEL €€
(☎885 05 00; www.aerodrom-sg.si; Mislinjska Dobrava 110; s/d €52/75; P❄@🖥) It's a bit of a schlep 6km southeast of Slovenj Gradec, but

the four-star Aerodrom with a dozen rooms is head and shoulders above any other accommodation in the area.

Medeni Raj Camping Ground CAMPGROUND €
(☑885 05 00; www.aerodrom-sg.si; Mislinjska Dobrava 110; campsite per person €7, bungalows €40; ☺mid-Mar–mid-Oct) Sweet Paradise is a small, friendly place with sites for tents and caravans, and six bungalows set among the pine trees of Turiška Vas, just beyond the Aerodrom hotel in Mislinjska Dobrava.

Hotel Slovenj Gradec HOTEL €€
(☑883 98 50; www.vabo.si; Glavni trg 43; s/d/tr €36/70/93; [P][※][☎]) The only hotel option in town is this bland 68-room property with rather gloomy rooms and long, dark corridors that seem to go on forever. It deeply cries out for a makeover.

Pizzerija Apachi PIZZA €
(☑883 17 84; Pohorska cesta 17b; pizza €4.50-6; ☺7am-11pm Mon-Thu, 7am-1am Fri & Sat, noon-10pm Sun) This pizzeria with a 'cowboys and Indians' theme (go figure) is next to the bus station.

Gostilna Murko SLOVENIAN €€
(☑883 81 03; Francetova cesta 24; meals from €18; ☺8am-10pm) About 400m north of the centre on the Mislinja River, Gostilna Murko is a four-star roadside inn popular with Austrian tourists on the go.

Slaščičarna Šrimpf CAFE €
(☑884 14 82; Glavni trg 14; ☺8.30am-8pm Mon-Sat, noon-8pm Sun) This long-established cafe draws the crowds with its fabulous cakes. Try the *zagrebska* (€1.70), a rich concoction of custard, cream, chocolate and flaky pastry.

☕ Drinking & Entertainment

Mestna Kavarna CAFE
(☑884 51 09; Trg Svobode 7; ☺7am-10.30pm Mon-Thu, 6.30am-1am Fri, 8am-1am Sat, 8.30am-10pm Sun) This updated yet old-style cafe on the corner of Glavni trg is the most comfortable place in town to tip back a coffee or maybe something stronger.

Pod Velbom PUB, CAFE
(☑041 654 843; Glavni trg 1; ☺6.30am-midnight Mon-Thu, 6.30am-2am Fri, 9am-2am Sat, 4pm-midnight Sun) If you're looking for some company, the best place for meeting people in the centre of Slovenj Gradec is this pub-cafe; enter from Poštna ulica.

Slovenj Gradec Cultural Centre CULTURAL CENTRE
(Kulturni Dom Slovenj Gradec; ☑884 11 93; Francetova ulica 5) Classical music concerts are sometimes held at the Church of St Elizabeth and this centre, which also has a small cinema showing films between 7pm and 9pm Friday to Sunday.

ℹ Information

Mladinska Knjiga (☑881 22 83; Glavni trg 18; ☺8am-6.30pm Mon-Fri, 8am-noon Sat) Stocks regional maps and guides.

Nova Ljubljanska Banka (Glavni trg 30)

Post Office (Francetova cesta 1) At the northern end of Glavni trg.

Tourist Information Centre Slovenj Gradec (TIC; ☑881 21 16; www.slovenjgradec.si; Glavni trg 24; ☺8am-4pm Mon-Fri, 9am-noon Sat & Sun) On the ground floor of the former town hall.

ℹ Getting There & Around

Destinations served by bus from Slovenj Gradec include Celje (€6, 1½ hours), Gornji Grad (€6.30, 1½ hours, 57km, 1.31pm Monday to Saturday), Ljubljana (€9.90, two hours, up to three daily) and Maribor (€7.20, two hours, two or three daily).

You can call a taxi in Slovenj Gradec on ☑041 645 901.

Prekmurje

Best Places to Eat

» Gostilna Lovenjak (p199)

» Gostišče Oaza (p202)

Best Places to Stay

» Hotel Štrk (p199)

Why Go?

Prekmurje is Slovenia's forgotten corner – mostly a broad, farmed plain 'beyond the Mura River' (as its name suggests). Relatively isolated until the 1920s, Prekmurje has preserved its traditional music, folklore, architecture and a distinct local dialect.

Until the end of WWI, most of Prekmurje belonged to the Austro-Hungarian crown and it still has a small Magyar minority. In many ways Prekmurje looks and feels more like Hungary than Slovenia, with its white storks, large thatched farmhouses, substantial Roma population, and the occasional Hungarian-style *golaž* (goulash) cooked with paprika.

For visitors, the province is a springboard into Austria or Hungary, and a place to relax and enjoy taking the waters at the thermal spas, and indulge in the rich local pastry *gibanica*.

When to Go
Murska Sobota

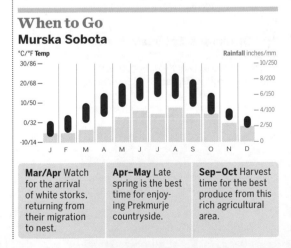

Mar/Apr Watch for the arrival of white storks, returning from their migration to nest.

Apr–May Late spring is the best time for enjoying Prekmurje countryside.

Sep–Oct Harvest time for the best produce from this rich agricultural area.

Murska Sobota & Around

♪02 / POP 11,614 / ELEV 189M

Slovenia's northernmost city, Murska Sobota sits on a plain flatter than a *palačinka,* the pancake filled with jam or nuts and topped with chocolate that is so popular here. The city itself has little to recommend it except for its odd architectural mix of neoclassical, Secessionist and 'socialist baroque' buildings. But the surrounding countryside, pottery villages and thermal spas make it a good springboard for the entire region.

History

The town of Murska Sobota was once little more than a Hungarian market town until the opening of the railway in 1907, which linked Murska Sobota with Šalovci in Hungary proper. With the formation of the Kingdom of Serbs, Croats and Slovenes in 1918 and the transfer of territory, Murska Sobota found itself more or less in the centre of Prekmurje and development really took off.

Prekmurje Highlights

1 Satisfy that sweet tooth with a helping of calorific *prekmurska gibanica,* pastry with poppy seeds, walnuts, fruit, cheese and cream

2 Take the waters at the **spa resort** (p200) at Radenci

3 Visit Prekmurje's last remaining **floating mill** (p200) on the Mura River at Ižakovci, near Veržej

4 Admire the wonderful 14th-century frescoes at the **Church of St Martin** (p199) in Martjanci

5 Marvel at the arrival of the **storks** (p199), those big white birds with long skinny legs responsible for the population explosion

Murska Sobota

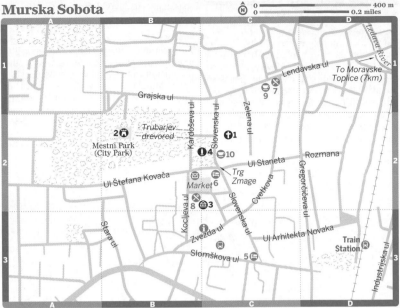

Murska Sobota

◎ Sights

1 Evangelical Church	C2
2 Murska Sobota Castle	B2
3 Murska Sobota Gallery	C2
Murska Sobota Regional Museum (see 2)	
4 Victory Monument	C2

▣ Sleeping

5 Hotel Diana	C3
6 Hotel Zvezda	C2

✖ Eating

7 Mini Restavracija Rajh	C1
8 Okrepčevalnica Grill	B2

◷ Drinking

9 Bar Sukič	C1
10 City	C2

◎ Sights

Murska Sobota Castle CASTLE
(Grad Murska Sobota) Renaissance-style Murska Sobota Castle, a sprawling manor house from the mid-16th century, houses the award-winning **Murska Sobota Regional Museum** (Pokrajinski Muzej Murska Sobota; ☏527 17 06; www.pok-muzej-ms.si; Trubarjev drevored 4; adult/child €3/2; ◷9am-5pm Tue-Fri, 9am-1pm Sat & Sun Sep-Jun, 10am-4pm Tue-Fri, 9am-noon Sat & Sun Jul & Aug), which tells the story of life along the Mura River, from prehistoric times to the present.

Victory Monument MONUMENT
In Mestni Park the Victory Monument is an impressive stone grouping Yugoslav Partisans and Soviet soldiers. Opposite the park is the neo-Gothic **Evangelical Church** (1910), the main Lutheran seat in Slovenia. The muted interior is a welcome change from the overwrought baroque decor found in most Catholic churches.

Murska Sobota Gallery GALLERY
(Galerija Murska Sobota; ☏522 38 34; www.galerija-ms.si; Kocljeva ulica 7; admission varies; ◷10am-6pm Tue-Fri, 9am-noon Sat Sep-Jun, 10am-4pm Tue-Fri, 9am-noon Sat Jul & Aug) The Murska Sobota

Gallery, the best gallery in Prekmurje, has a permanent collection of 550 works (mostly sculpture) as well as rotating exhibits.

Parish Church of St Martin CHURCH

The Parish Church of St Martin in Martjanci, 4km north of Murska Sobota on the road to Moravske Toplice, contains wonderful 14th-century frescoes painted on the sanctuary's vaulted ceiling and walls. Look for the centuries-old graffiti on the east wall.

🛏 Sleeping

The closest campground is Camp Terme 3000 (p202) at Moravske Toplice, 7km to the northeast.

Hotel Štrk HOTEL €€

(📋525 21 58; www.gostilna-lovenjak.com; Polana 40; s/d €46/76; [P][❄][@][🏊]) The accommodation part of the Lovenjakov Dvor (Lovenjak Court) tourist house, 4km northeast of Murska Sobota, boasts special features – from furnishings from a nearby castle (No 24), views of nesting storks (No 21), and thermal water in the pool from Moravske Toplice.

Hotel Diana HOTEL €€

(📋514 12 00; www.hotel-diana.si; Slovenska ulica 52; s/d €50/82; [P][❄][@][🏊]) Rooms at Murska Sobota's anchor hotel are bright and functional. It has a glassed-in swimming pool, sauna and fitness room as well as a decent pizzeria (pizzas €5 to €7).

Terme Banovci CAMPGROUND €

(📋513 14 00; www.terme-banovci.si; campsite per person €13; ☺late Mar-Oct; [P][🏊]) Some 59 of the 130 sites at this small spa near Veržej, 13km south of Murska Sobota, are reserved for

naturists. The price includes entry to the spa's thermal and swimming pools.

Hotel Zvezda HOTEL €€

(📋539 15 73; www.hotel-zvezda.si; Trg Zmage 8; s/d €31/52) This 36-room *caravanserai* is just a bunch of rooms above a pub-restaurant of the same name. Still, the price is right.

Eating

[TOP CHOICE] Gostilna Lovenjak SLOVENIAN €

(📋525 21 53; starters €6.50-12.70, mains €7.50-16.10; ☺11am-10pm Mon-Thu, 11am-midnight Fri & Sat, 11am-6pm Sun) This atmospheric *gostilna* serves such Prekmurje favourites as *bograč golaž* (Hungarian-style goulash soup), roast suckling pig served with noodles and indecently rich *prekmurska gibanica*. There's a Sunday buffet and live music at weekends.

Gostilna Rajh SLOVENIAN €€

(📋543 90 98; Soboška ulica 32; meals from €20; ☺10.30am-10pm Tue-Sat, 11am-4pm Sun) In Bakovci, a village 5km to the southwest, this *gostilna* specialises in local dishes and boasts a large cellar of regional wines.

Okrepčevalnica Grill BALKAN €

(📋524 18 50; Kocljeva ulica 5; dishes from €3.50; ☺6am-6pm Mon-Fri, 6.30am-1pm Sat) This inexpensive *bife* (snack bar) in the market south of Trg Zmage serves fish dishes as well as Balkan-style grills.

Mini Restavracija Rajh RESTAURANT €

(📋523 12 38; Cvetkova ulica 21; starters €4-7, pizza & pasta €4.80-7.30; ☺10am-10pm Tue-Fri, from 11.30am Sat, from 4pm Sun) A self-styled 'mini-restaurant' on the corner of Lendavska ulica, Rajh is an upmarket *špagetarija* and *picerija*.

WHITE STORKS

The white stork (*Ciconia cicconia*), or *beli štrk* in Slovene, is Prekmurje's most beloved symbol. Country people consider it a symbol of luck and honour for a pair to nest on their rooftop. The storks arrive in spring and spend the warm summer months here. Come mid-August, they migrate south on a 12,000km trek to sub-Saharan Africa for the winter, returning in the spring.

Storks build their nests on church steeples, rooftops or telephone poles. The nest is repaired every year, and can weigh as much as 500kg. Storks live on a diet of worms, grasshoppers, frogs and small rodents. If food is scarce, however, it is not unknown for parents to turf their fledglings out of the nest.

Slovenia's stork population (around 250 breeding pairs) has grown over the past two decades. Nevertheless, the white stork remains a vulnerable species primarily because its hunting and breeding grounds – the meadows – are being destroyed, dried out and regulated.

POTTERY TOWNS OF PREKMURJE

Explore some of Prekmurje's less-frequented towns and discover thermal spas, pottery workshops and a floating mill.

From Murska Sobota, head north along Route 232, then from Martjanci head east along Route 442 to the thermal spa of **Moravske Toplice**. Tešanovci, a couple of kilometres east, is noted for its *lončarstvo* (pottery).

About 2.5km further east is the village of **Bogojina** and its **Parish Church of the Ascension**, which was redesigned by Jože Plečnik around 1926. The interior is an odd mixture of black marble, brass, wood and terracotta; the oak-beamed ceiling is fitted with Prekmurje ceramic plates and jugs, as is the altar.

Filovci, 2km past Bogojina, is famed for its *črna keramika* (black pottery). **Keramika Bojnec** (☑041 330 987; www.bojnec.com; Filovci 20; admission €2.50), 200m southwest of the main road, invites visitors to watch them work at the ancient kiln in the *skanzen* (open-air museum displaying village architecture) over the road.

Carry on to Dobrovnik, which has a couple of decent roadside *gostilna* and then southwest through Beltinci to **Ižakovci**, which has one of the last floating mills on the Mura, the **Island of Love Mill** (Otok Ljubezni Mlin; ☑02-541 35 80; www.beltinci.si; Mladinska ulica 2; admission €2.50; ⊗9am-6pm Apr-Jun, Sep & Oct, 9am-8pm Jul & Aug), including a small museum and a raft ride across the Mura. Murska Sobota is just 8km northwest.

☐ Drinking

City   CAFE

(Slovenska ulica 27; ⊗7am-9pm Mon-Fri, to 1pm Sat & Sun) Essentially a stylish cafe with drinks, City also serves snacks and is a convenient distance to the Murska Sobota Regional Museum.

Bar Sukič   CAFE, BAR

(☑523 12 58; Lendavska ulica 14; ⊗5.30am-10pm Mon-Fri, 6am-3pm Sat) This convivial cafe-bar has a large open terrace fronting the main thoroughfare into town.

❶ Information

Nova Ljubljanska Banka (Trg Zmage 7)
Post Office (Trg Zmage 6)
SKB Banka (Kocljeva ulica 9)
Tourist Information Centre Murska Sobota (☑534 11 30; tic.sobota@siol.net; Zvezda ulica 10; ⊗9am-7pm Mon-Fri, 8am-1pm Sat) Just north of the bus station.

❶ Getting There & Around

BUS Buses leave regularly for Radenci (€2.75, 20 minutes, 19km), Maribor (€6.30, 1¼ hours) and Moravske Toplice (€1.80, 15 minutes). Other destinations include Dobrovnik (€2.70, 30 minutes, 18km) and Ljubljana (€16.80, 4¼ hours) via Maribor and Celje.

TRAIN Murska Sobota has rail connections to Ljubljana (€12 to €14, four hours) and Maribor (€6.80 to €8.50, 1¾ hours, 98km) and Vienna,

Austria. From Murska Sobota the train carries on to Budapest, Hungary.

BICYCLE Rent bikes from **Freerider** (☑524 15 68; www.freerider-on.net; Cvetkova ulica 2; regular/mountain bikes per hr €3/5, per day €10/18; ⊗10am-6pm Mon-Fri, 10am-1pm Sat).

TAXI You can order a taxi on ☑051 300 601.

Radenci

☑02 / POP 2200 / ELEV 208M

Radenci is best known for its health spa resort, Terme Radenci, parts of which still feel like a full-of-itself 19th-century spa town. The spa dominates activities for visitors, but when most Slovenes hear the name they think of Radenska Tri Srca – the 'Radenci Three Hearts' mineral water that's bottled here and consumed in every restaurant and cafe in the land.

🏃 Activities

Spas

Terme Radenci   SPA

(☑520 27 20; www.zdravilisce-radenci.si; Zdraviliško naselje 12; sauna 3hr/day €13/17.50; ⊗pools 9am-9pm Sun-Thu, 9am-10pm Fri & Sat, sauna 4-9pm Mon-Thu, 2-10pm Fri & Sat, 2-9pm Sun) The Radenci Thermal Spa opened in 1882 and has three claims to fame: water rich in carbon dioxide for drinking; mineral-laden thermal water (41°C) for bathing; and sulphurous mud from Lake Negova for therapeutic and beauty treatments.

Today, thoroughly modern blocks overlook the few remaining older Victorian-style buildings and a large wooded park. There are 10 pools of varying sizes, including large indoor and outdoor thermal pools with temperatures of 30°C to 33°C. Guests of Terme Radenci get free use; outsiders pay €9.50 per day. There are also various saunas and the **Corrium Wellness Centre**.

Other Activities

The tennis courts just southeast of the Terme Radenci hotel complex can be rented for €6/10 per hour during the day/night from May to September (€16 per hour the rest of the year). Rackets (€2) and balls are available from the **tennis school** (lessons per hr €25; ⊙9am-9pm).

The spa rents **bicycles** for €2.50/5.50/8.50 per hour/three hours/day. Cycling excursions can be made into the surrounding wine country; head southwest along the *vinska cesta* (wine road) for about 4km to Janžev Vrh and an old vineyard cottage called Janžev Hram. The region's most celebrated wine is the sparkling Zlata Radgonska Penina.

🛏 Sleeping

Private rooms are available on Panonska cesta to the west and south of the spa's main entrance. There are two four-star hotels, both owned by the thermal spa, and next door to each other.

Hotel Izvir HOTEL €€€
(☑520 27 20; Zdraviliško naselje 12; s €66-71, d €112-122) The smaller and quieter of Radenci's hotels, with a slick modern exterior and well-presented rooms.

Hotel Radin HOTEL €€€
(☑520 27 22; Zdraviliško naselje 12; s €70-75, d €120-130) Radenci's largest hotel – Hotel Radin is comfortable and well-organised, although it does have the occasional hint of conference centre about it.

🍴 Eating & Drinking

Restavracija Park SLOVENIAN €€
(☑520 10 00; set lunch/dinner €8.50/19; ⊙10am-9pm Tue-Sun) In the heart of the Terme Radenci resort's large wooded park and serving local specialities, the aptly named Restavracija Park is a pleasant place for a meal in summer.

Pub Kavarna Vikend PUB
(☑566 93 95; Panonska cesta 2; ⊙7am-11pm Mon-Thu, 7am-midnight Fri, 8am-midnight Sat, 9am-11pm Sun) This convivial pub-cafe with a large open-air terrace is just opposite the bank and post office, and around the corner from the main entrance to the Terme Radenci spa.

❶ Information

Nova Ljubljanska Banka (Panonska cesta 7) Near the main entrance to the Terme Radenci spa.

Post Office (Panonska cesta 5)

❶ Getting There & Away

BUS The bus station is opposite the main entrance to the Terme Radenci spa. There are daily buses to Gornja Radgona (€1.80, eight minutes, hourly), Ljubljana (€16, four hours, twice daily) via Maribor (€5.60, one hour) and Celje (€10.30, 2¼ hours), and half a dozen buses to Murska Sobota (€2.30, 15 minutes).

TAXI Call ☑031 457 777 or ☑031 671 076 for a taxi.

Moravske Toplice

☑02 / POP 760 / ELEV 201M

The thermal spa of Moravske Toplice, 7km northeast of Murska Sobota, boasts the hottest water in Slovenia: 72°C at its source but cooled to a body temperature of 38°C for use in its many pools and basins. Though it's one of the newest spas in the country – the spring was discovered in 1960 during exploratory oil drilling – many young Slovenes consider the clientele too old for their liking, preferring the small, partly *au naturel* spa at Banovci to the southwest. But Moravske Toplice is every bit a health resort geared for recreation, with enough upgraded sports facilities to cater to every taste.

🏊 Activities

Terme 3000 SPA
(☑512 22 00; www.terme3000.si; Kranjčeva ulica 12; ⊙8am-9pm May-Sep, 9am-9pm Oct-Apr) The Terme 3000 spa complex has 26 indoor and outdoor pools filled with thermal water, slides, a water tower and even a sound-and-light show. The thermal water is recommended for relief of rheumatism and certain minor skin problems. Guests at the resort have free use of the pools and saunas; otherwise they cost €12/8.50 (reduced after 3pm) per adult/child. The resort also has

a golf course, tennis courts, a fitness room and saunas.

Terme Vivat

SPA

(✆538 21 29; www.vivat.si; Ulica ob Igrišču 3; full day/after 3pm adult €10/3.50, child €6/5; ⊙8am-8pm Mon-Thu, 8am-11pm Fri & Sat, 8am-9pm Sun) Terme Vivat has thermal indoor and outdoor pools (connected by a swimming channel), saunas and an ambitious wellness centre.

🛏 Sleeping

The TIC can organise private rooms for around €17 per person; apartments for two cost from €30 to €50, depending on the length of stay.

Terme 3000

RESORT €€€

(✆512 22 00; www.terme3000.si) All the accommodation at Terme 3000 share the same contact numbers; prices vary according to the season and all prices quoted here except the camping ground are half board. The spa's 7-hectare camping ground, **Camp Terme 3000** (✆512 22 00; per person €16-17), can accommodate 800 guests and is open year-round. Use of the swimming pool nearby is included in the price. The attractive **bungalows** (✆512 22 00; half-board s €52-66, d €102-110; P@⛲) at the resort's Prekmurje Village (Prekmurska Vas) are done up to look like traditional peasant cottages, with thatched roofs, cool white-washed walls and a total of 78 double rooms. At the **Hotel Termal** (✆512 22 00; half-board s €78-84, d €132-144; P✳@⛲⛲) about half of the 116 rooms have balconies, and all offer good-standard tourist-class offerings. The vast **Hotel Livada Prestige** (✆512 22 00; half-board s €100-105, d €170-182, ste €115-290; P✳@⛲⛲) has 122 five-star rooms; many have thermal water piped straight into the bathrooms for your own private spa experience. Both hotels have several indoor and outdoor pools.

🍴 Eating

Gostilna Kuhar

SLOVENIAN €€

(✆548 12 15; Kranjčeva 13; meals from €15; ⊙9am-11pm Tue-Sun) Opposite the Terme 3000's main entrance, Gostilna Kuhar is a decent, convenient place in which to sample Prekmurje's cuisine. It also has accommodation.

Gostišče Oaza

SLOVENIAN €€

(✆051 383 141; mains from €11; ⊙8.30am-10pm Tue-Thu, 8.30am-midnight Fri & Sat, 10am-10pm Sun) Enjoy excellent local dishes while overlooking a tiny lake in Mljatinci, just south of the pottery village Tešanovci about 3km southeast of Moravske Toplice.

ℹ Information

Nova Ljubljanska Banka (Kranjčeva ulica; ⊙8am-noon & 3-5pm Mon-Fri) At the entrance to the Terme 3000 spa.

Post Office (Kranjčeva ulica 5; ⊙8-9.30am & 10am-6pm Mon-Fri, 8am-noon Sat) On the main road.

Tourist Information Centre Moravske Toplice (TIC; ✆538 15 20; www.moravske-toplice. com; Kranjčeva ulica 3; ⊙8am-8pm Mon-Fri, 7am-3pm Sat, 8am-2pm Sun Jul & Aug, shorter hrs Sep-Jun) On the main road northwest of the entrance to the Terme 3000 complex.

ℹ Getting There & Around

Buses leave from Kranjčeva ulica up to six times a day for Murska Sobota (€1.80, 10 minutes, 7km) and Dobrovnik (€2.70, 10 minutes, 19km).

The TIC rents bicycles for €2/9 per hour/day.

Understand Slovenia

population per sq km

SLOVENIA	ITALY	ZAGREB

≈ 100 people

Slovenia Today

Baby, It's Cold Outside

» Population: 2.05 million

» Area: 20,273 sq km (0.2% of Europe's total land mass)

» GDP: US$49.6 billion

» GDP per capita: €18,675 (84% of EU average)

» GDP growth: -1.1%

» Inflation: 2.5%

» Unemployment: 9.1%

Now is the winter of Slovenia's discontent, a country not used to hearing the 'dis' word much since independence. But perhaps reaching full maturity at 21 has forced it to put away childish things and confront some less-than-attractive realities. Take the economy... Slovenia was the wealthiest republic of the former Yugoslavia; with only 8% of the national population, the industrious Slovenes produced up to 20% of Yugoslavia's GDP and exported more than a quarter of its goods. And in 2007 Slovenia was the first of the former communist countries of Eastern Europe to adopt the euro. Now it faces the possibility of a 'Greek scenario' and may become yet another EU country to need a bailout. The problems lie with the nation's banks (the government has already provided 1% of GDP to the biggest one, Nova Ljubljanska Banka), a lack of foreign investment and a contracting economy that has seen growth fall from a dizzying 7% in 2007 to below nothing now.

Change of Guard

The year 2012 saw two important changes on the political stage. In parliament, a new government was installed, a five-party coalition led by conservative Prime Minister Janez Janša of the Slovenian Democratic Party (SDS), who had been a gadfly to the communist leaders in the 1980s as a journalist, and was prime minister for four years until 2008. Austerity reforms introduced by Janša, including spending cuts of up to 10% and a constitutional amendment requiring all governments to run a balanced state budget, prompted some 10,000 demonstrators to take to the streets of Ljubljana and Maribor, accusing the government of corruption and demanding Janša's resignation. Less than a week later, the man

Common Courtesy

» Do not refer to Slovenia as being part of Eastern Europe or – God forbid – the Balkans, which Slovenes think start at the Croatian border.

» Diners at the same table always wish one another 'Dober tek!' (Bon appetit!) before starting a meal.

» Some Slovenes enjoy a špička – slang for a little glass of schnapps – during the day as a pick-me-up, and you'll probably receive the invitation 'Pridite na kupico' ('Come and have a drop'). It's your call.

Top Icons

» **Kozolec** Distinctive rack used for drying hay that is the ultimate Slovenian symbol.

» **Potica** A nut roll eaten at all festive occasions.

» **Triglav** The nation's tallest peak (2864m) which every Slovene is expected to climb.

ethnic groups
(% of population)

if Slovenia were 100 people

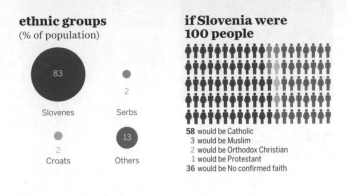

- 83 Slovenes
- 2 Serbs
- 2 Croats
- 13 Others

58 would be Catholic
3 would be Muslim
2 would be Orthodox Christian
1 would be Protestant
36 would be No confirmed faith

who assumed premiership after Janša's first term, left-leaning Borut Pahor, unseated President Danilo Türk in a landslide victory. Fasten those seatbelts, it's going to be a bumpy ride.

Me & My Sausage

Slovenia has always been very protective of what it has and why not? Although good things do come in small packages, Slovenia is an itty-bitty place. Take Lipizzaner horses, for one example. Although the gorgeous white creatures are bred in locations around the world, including Austria and Hungary, the breed takes it name from the Slovenian village of Lipica (Lipizza in Italian) and is considered a national animal here. And just to send the message home, Slovenia has put a pair of Lipizzaners on the verso of its €0.20 coin. Then there's the dispute with Croatia over where to draw the border in Piran Bay, which has in the past affected Croatia's bid to join the EU. It's now in international arbitration. And that's not the only battle Slovenia is fighting with its neighbour to the south. The second one involves something as sacred to many Slovenes as borders and horseflesh. We're talking sausages, in this case the much loved *kranjska klobasa* (Carniolan sausage) for which Slovenia is seeking EU Protected Designation of Origin status. Under PDO rules that would mean only the Slovenian variety could bear the name. Thing is, Croatia makes its own version and is crying foul, a word that some might use to describe what the EU says is 'pasteurised sausage made with coarsely minced pork and pork fat eaten after briefly warming in hot water.' Hot dog!

Slovenia ranks 154 in size – just between El Salvador and French-ruled New Caledonia – out of a total 234 nations and dependencies on earth.

Top Books

» **Black Lamb and Grey Falcon** (Rebecca West) Limited but insightful references to Slovenia in a lengthy look at Yugoslavia between the wars.

» **Forbidden Bread** (Erica Johnson Debeljak) Slovenia through the eyes of a young American woman who follows her poet-lover to his homeland.

» **Slovenia and the Slovenes: A Small State and the New Europe** (James Gow & Cathie Carmichael) Excellent analyses of Slovenian history, politics, culture and the arts.

Top Films

» **Kruh in Mleko** (*Bread and Milk*, 2001) Small-town family.

» **Rezerni Deli** (*Spare Parts*, 2003) Trafficking of illegal immigrants through Slovenia.

» **Petelinji Zajtrk** (*Rooster's Breakfast*, 2007) Bittersweet romance with lots of laughs.

History

Slovenia is as old as the hills and as new as tomorrow. Slovenia the *narod* (nation of people) can trace its origins back at least a millennium and a half. But Slovenia the *nacija*, or nation-state, is a much more recent entity.

As elsewhere in Europe, Slovenia's beginnings involved the mass migration of a nomadic people, the wandering Celts, the subjugation by and – it must be said – the civilising influence of the Romans, followed by the arrival of the Slavic tribes, who would unite and look after themselves for a brief time. But by the late 13th century the rich and powerful Habsburgs would move in and not vacate the premises for more than six centuries. Slovenia would enjoy a certain amount of autonomy as part of the kingdom and later the Socialist Republic of Yugoslavia. But it would not be not until June 1991 that the nation's 'new day' as an independent republic would arrive.

The Romans

When the Romans arrived in what is now Slovenia in the 2nd century BC they were not the region's first 'visitors'. During the Bronze Age (around 2000 to 900 BC), marsh dwellers farmed and raised cattle in the area south of present-day Ljubljana and at Lake Cerknica. But around 700 BC, these marsh people were overwhelmed by Illyrian tribes from the south who brought iron tools and weapons. They themselves were subdued a century and a half later by Celtic tribes pushing down from the north towards the Balkans. They established the Noric kingdom, the first 'state' on Slovenian soil.

In 181 BC the Romans set up the colony of Aquileia (Oglej in Slovene) on the Gulf of Trieste in order to protect the empire from such tribal incursions. In the next century, the Romans annexed the Noric kingdom and moved into the rest of Slovenia and Istria. From their military set-

A primitive bone flute discovered in 1995 in a cave at Divje Babe, near the town of Cerknica in Primorska, dates back some 35,000 years and is thought to be the world's oldest known musical instrument.

TIMELINE

2000–900 BC	400 BC	1st century AD
Bronze Age settlers build wooden huts on stilts, farm, raise cattle, and produce coarse pottery in the Ljubljana Barje, a marshy area south of present-day Ljubljana.	Continental Celtic tribes led by the Norics establish a kingdom called Noricum on Slovenian soil near the present-day city of Celje in central Štajerska.	The Romans move into Slovenia from Italy and annex Noricum, marking the beginning of Roman occupation that would last for almost half a millennium.

tlements the important towns of Emona (Ljubljana), Celeia (Celje) and Poetovio (Ptuj) developed.

The Early Slavs

In the middle of the 5th century AD, the Huns, led by Attila, invaded Italy via Slovenia, attacking Poetovio, Celeia and Emona along the way. On their heels came the Germanic Ostrogoths and then the Langobards, who occupied much of Slovenian territory. The last major wave was made up of the early Slavs.

The ancestors of today's Slovenes arrived from the Carpathian Basin in the 6th century and settled in the Sava, Drava and Mura River valleys and the eastern Alps. In their original homelands the early Slavs were a peaceful people, living in forests or along rivers and lakes, breeding cattle and farming by slash-and-burn methods. They were a superstitious people who saw *vile* (both good and bad fairies or sprites) everywhere and paid homage to a pantheon of gods and goddesses. As a social group they made no class distinctions, but chose a leader – a *župan* (now the word for 'mayor') or *vojvoda* (duke) – in times of great danger. During the migratory periods, however, they became more warlike and aggressive.

From Duchy to Kingdom

In the early 7th century the Alpine Slavs were united under their leader, Duke Valuk, and joined forces with the Frankish kingdom. This Slavic tribal union became the Duchy of Carantania (Karantanija), the first Slavic state.

Within a century, a new class of ennobled commoners called *kosezi* had emerged, and it was they who publicly elected and crowned the new *knez* (grand duke). Such a process was unique in the feudal Europe of the early Middle Ages.

Reminders of the Roman Presence

» Citizen of Emona statue in Ljubljana

» Roman necropolis at Šempeter near Celje

» Mithraic shrines outside Ptuj

HISTORY THE EARLY SLAVS

THE TALE IN THE PAIL

Hallstatt is the name of a village in the Salzkammergut region of Austria where objects characteristic of the early Iron Age (from about 800 BC to 500 BC) were found in the 19th century. Today the term is used generically for the late Bronze and early Iron Age cultures that developed in Central and Western Europe from about 1200 to 450 BC.

Many regions of Slovenia were settled during this period, particularly Dolenjska and Bela Krajina. Burial mounds – more than two dozen in Novo Mesto alone – have yielded swords, helmets, jewellery and especially *situlae* – pails (or buckets) that are often richly decorated with lifelike battle and hunting scenes. Hallstatt art is very geometric, and typical motifs include birds and figures arranged in pairs. The *Vače situla* in the National Museum of Slovenia in Ljubljana is a particularly fine example.

5th century
Around AD 450, the Huns, led by Attila, invade Italy via Slovenia, attacking the Roman settlements of Poetovio (Ptuj), Celeia (Celje) and Emona (Ljubljana) en route.

6th century
Early Slavic tribes, divided into two distinct but related groups, the Slaveni and the Antes, settle in the valleys of the Sava, Drava and Mura Rivers and the eastern Alps.

MAJA HAUSMEISTER / GETTY IMAGES ©

» Celje Old Castle (p187)

In 748 the Frankish empire of the Carolingians incorporated Carantania as a vassal state called Carinthia and began converting the people to Christianity. By the early 9th century, religious authority on Slovenian territory was shared between Salzburg and the Patriarchate (or Bishopric) of Aquileia, now in Italy. The weakening Frankish authorities began replacing Slovenian nobles with German counts, reducing the local peasantry to serfdom. The German nobility was thus at the top of the feudal hierarchy for the first time in Slovenian lands. This would later become one of the key obstacles to Slovenian national and cultural development.

With the total collapse of the Frankish state in the second half of the 9th century, a Carinthian prince named Kocelj established a short-lived (869–74) independent Slovenian 'kingdom' in Lower Pannonia, the area stretching southeast from Styria (Štajerska) to the Mura, Drava and Danube Rivers. But German King Otto I would soon bring this to an end after defeating the Magyars in the mid-10th century.

Lake Balaton in Hungary, which the early Slavs reached in their roamings, takes its name from the Slovenian word *blato* (mud).

German Ascendancy

The Germans decided to re-establish Carinthia, dividing the area into a half-dozen border regions (*krajina*) or marches. These developed into the Slovenian provinces that would remain basically unchanged until 1918: Carniola (Kranjska), Carinthia (Koroška), Styria (Štajerska), Gorica (Goriška) and the so-called White March (Bela Krajina).

A drive for complete Germanisation of the Slovenian lands began in the 10th century. Land was divided between the nobility and various church dioceses, and German gentry were settled on it. The population remained essentially Slovenian, however, and it was largely due to intensive educational and pastoral work by the clergy that the Slovenian identity was preserved.

The proto-democratic process that elected the grand duke of Carantania was noted by the 16th-century French political theorist Jean Bodin, whose work is said to have been a key reference for Thomas Jefferson when he wrote the American *Declaration of Independence* in 1775–76.

Between the 10th and 13th centuries most of Slovenia's castles were built and many important Christian monasteries – such as Stična and Kostanjevica – were established. Towns also began to develop as administrative, trade and social centres from the 11th century.

Early Habsburg Rule

In the early Middle Ages, the Habsburgs were just one of many German aristocratic families struggling for hegemony on Slovenian soil. But as dynasties intermarried or died out, the Habsburgs consolidated their power. Between the late 13th century and the early 16th century, almost all the lands inhabited by Slovenes passed into Habsburg hands.

By this time Slovenian territory totalled about 24,000 sq km, about 15% larger than its present size. Not only did more towns and boroughs receive charters and rights, but the country began to develop economically with the opening of ironworks (eg at Kropa) and mines (eg at

7th century	748	869–74	late 13th century
A loose confederation of Slavic tribes establishes the Duchy of Carantania, the world's first Slavic political entity, and centres its capital somewhere near Celovec, now Klagenfurt in Austria.	The Carolingian empire of the Franks incorporates Carantania as a vassal state called Carinthia; with the establishment of a formal church, the Christianisation of the Slovenes begins.	Carinthian Prince Kocelj rules a short-lived Slovenian 'kingdom' in Lower Pannonia, the area that stretches southeast from Styria (Štajerska) to the Mura, Drava and Danube Rivers.	The first feudal holdings on Slovenian territory – the provinces of Carniola, Gorizia, Istria, Carinthia and Styria – fall under Habsburg control and remain in their hands until WWI.

Idrija). This economic progress reduced the differences among the repressed peasants, and they united against their feudal lords.

Raids, Revolts & Reformation

Attacks by the Ottoman Turks on southeastern Europe in the early 15th century helped to radicalise landless peasants and labourers, who were required to raise their own defences *and* continue to pay tribute and work for their feudal lords. As a result, dozens of peasant uprisings and revolts erupted on Slovenian territory, reaching their peak between the late 15th and 16th centuries. Together with the Protestant Reformation, they are considered a watershed of the Slovenian national awakening.

In most of the uprisings, peasant 'unions' demanded a reduction in feudal payments and the democratic election of parish priests. Castles were occupied and pulled down and lords executed but none of the revolts succeeded as such.

The Protestant Reformation in Slovenia was closely associated with the nobility from 1540 onward and was generally ignored by the rural population except for those who lived or worked on lands owned by the church. But the effects of this great reform movement cannot be underestimated. It gave Slovenia its first books in the vernacular, thereby lifting the status of the language and thus affirming Slovenian culture.

Habsburg Reforms & Napoléon

Reforms introduced by Habsburg Empress Maria Theresa (1740–80) included the establishment of a new state administration with a type of provincial government; the building of new roads; and the introduction of obligatory elementary school in German, and state-controlled secondary schools. Her son, Joseph II (1780–90), went several steps further. He abolished serfdom in 1782, paving the way for the formation of a Slovenian bourgeoisie, and allowed complete religious freedom for Calvinists, Lutherans and Jews. He also made primary education in Slovene compulsory. As a result of these reforms, agricultural output improved, manufacturing intensified and there was a flowering of the arts and letters in Slovenia.

But the French Revolution of 1789 convinced the Austrians that reforms should be nipped in the bud, and a period of reaction began that continued until the Revolution of 1848. In the meantime, however, there was a brief interlude that would have a profound effect on Slovenia and its future. After defeating the Austrians at Wagram in 1809, Napoléon decided to cut the entire Habsburg Empire off from the Adriatic. To do this he created six 'Illyrian Provinces' from Slovenian and Croatian regions, and made Ljubljana their capital.

The early Magyars were such fierce fighters that a common Christian prayer during the Dark Ages was 'Save us, O Lord, from the arrows of the Hungarians.'

HISTORY RAIDS, REVOLTS & REFORMATION

Ivan Cankar's *Hlapec Jernej in Njegova Pravica* (*The Bailiff Yerney and His Rights*), a tale of the unequal relationship between servant and master, is read as a metaphor for Slovenia under Habsburg rule.

1408	1478–1573	1540–85	16th century
Ottoman Turks start their attacks on southeastern Europe, which continue for over two centuries and take them to the gates of Vienna several times.	Peasant-led agrarian riots are at their peak; together with the Protestant Reformation in the middle of the 16th century, they are considered a watershed of the Slovenian national awakening .	The first printed books appear in Slovene, including a catechism published by Primož Trubar, a complete translation of the Bible by Jurij Dalmatin, and a grammar of Slovene in Latin.	The Catholic-led Counter-Reformation is in full swing throughout Slovenia; the systematic Germanisation of Slovenia's culture, education and administration begins under the Habsburgs.

Although the Illyrian Provinces lasted only from 1809 to 1813, France instituted a number of reforms, including equality before the law and the use of Slovene in primary and lower secondary schools and in public offices. Most importantly, the progressive influence of the French Revolution brought the issue of national awakening to the Slovenian political arena for the first time.

Romantic Nationalism & the 1848 Constitution

The period of so-called Romantic Nationalism (1814–48), also known as the Vormärz (pre-March) period in reference to the revolution that broke out across much of Central Europe in March 1848, was one of intensive literary and cultural activity and led to the promulgation of the first Slovenian political program. Although many influential writers published at this time, no one so dominated the period as the poet France Prešeren (1800–49). His bittersweet verse, progressive ideas, demands for political freedom and longings for the unity of all Slovenes caught the imagination of the nation then and ever since.

In April 1848 Slovenian intellectuals drew up their first national political program under the banner Zedinjena Slovenija (United Slovenia). It called for the unification of all historic Slovenian regions within an autonomous unit under the Austrian monarchy, the use of Slovene in all schools and public offices, and the establishment of a local university. The demands were rejected, as they would have required the reorganisation of the empire along ethnic lines. Slovenes of the time were not contemplating total independence. Indeed, most looked upon the Habsburg Empire as a protective mantle for small nations against larger ones they considered predators such as Italy, Germany and Serbia.

The only tangible results for Slovenes in the 1848 Austrian Constitution were that laws would henceforth be published in Slovene and

SLOVENIA'S NATIONAL ANTHEM

The seventh stanza of France Prešeren's popular poem *Zdravljica* (*A Toast*) forms the lyrics of Slovenia's national anthem:

> God's blessing on all nations,
> Who long and work for that bright day,
> When o'er earth's habitations
> No war, no strife shall hold its sway;
> Who long to see
> That all men free
> No more shall foes, but neighbours be.

1782	1809	1848
Habsburg Emperor Joseph II abolishes serfdom, paving the way for the growth of a Slovenian bourgeoisie, and grants complete religious freedom to Calvinists, Lutherans and Jews.	Ljubljana is named the capital of the French-ruled Illyrian Provinces (1809–13), created by Napoléon from Slovenian and Croatian regions in a bid to cut the Habsburgs off from the Adriatic.	Slovenian intellectuals issue a national political program, United Slovenia, calling for the unification of all historic Slovenian regions within an autonomous unit under the Austrian monarchy.

STEVE OUTRAM / GETTY IMAGES ©

» Cooperative Bank, Ljubljana

that the Carniolan (and thus Slovenian) flag should be three horizontal stripes of white, blue and red. But the United Slovenia program would remain the basis of all Slovenian political demands up to 1918, and political-cultural clubs and circles began to appear all over the territory. Parties first appeared toward the end of the 19th century, and a new idea – a union with other Slavs to the south – was propounded from the 1860s onward.

The Kingdom of Serbs, Croats & Slovenes

With the defeat of Austria-Hungary in WWI and the subsequent dissolution of the Habsburg dynasty in 1918, Slovenes, Croats and Serbs banded together and declared the independent Kingdom of Serbs, Croats and Slovenes, under Serbian King Peter I. Post-war peace treaties had given large amounts of Slovenian and Croatian territory to Italy (Primorska and Istria), Austria (Koroška) and Hungary (part of Prekmurje), and almost half a million Slovenes now lived outside the borders.

The kingdom was dominated by Serbian control, imperialistic pressure from Italy and the notion of Yugoslav unity. Slovenia was reduced to little more than a province in this centralist kingdom, although it did enjoy cultural and linguistic autonomy, and economic progress was rapid.

In 1929 Peter I's son King Alexander seized power, abolished the constitution and proclaimed the Kingdom of Yugoslavia. But he was assassinated five years later during an official visit to France, and his cousin, Prince Paul, was named regent. The political climate changed in Slovenia when the conservative Clerical Party joined the new centralist government in 1935, proving hollow that party's calls for Slovenian autonomy. Splinter groups began to seek closer contacts with the workers' movements; in 1937 the Communist Party of Slovenia (KPS) was formed under the tutelage of Josip Broz Tito (1892–1980) and the Communist Party of Yugoslavia (KPJ).

WWII & the Partisan Struggle

Yugoslavia stayed out of WWII until April 1941 when the German army invaded and occupied the country. Slovenia was split up among Germany (Štajerska, Gorenjska and Koroška), Italy (Ljubljana, Primorska, Notranjska, Dolenjska and Bela Krajina) and Hungary (Prekmurje). To counter this, the Slovenian Communists and other left-wing groups formed a Liberation Front (Osvobodilne Fronte, or OF), and the people took up arms for the first time since the peasant uprisings. The OF, dedicated to the principles of a united Slovenia in a Yugoslav republic, joined the all-Yugoslav Partisan army of the KPJ, which received assistance from the Allies and was the most organised – and successful – of any resistance movement during WWII.

Josip Broz Tito was born in 1892 in Kumrovec, just over the Štajerska border in Croatia, to a Slovenian mother and a Croatian father.

Neil Barnett's relatively slim biography *Tito*, an entertaining and timely read, offers a new assessment of the limits of holding a state like Yugoslavia together by sheer force of personality.

HISTORY THE KINGDOM OF SERBS, CROATS & SLOVENES

1867	1918	1929	1937
A number of Slovenes are incorporated into Hungary with the Compromise of 1867, an agreement creating the Dual Monarchy of Austria (the empire) and Hungary (the kingdom).	Austria-Hungary loses WWI and the political system collapses with the armistice of 11 November; the Serbia-dominated Kingdom of Serbs, Croats and Slovenes is established.	King Alexander seizes power, abolishes the constitution and proclaims the Kingdom of Yugoslavia – only to be assassinated five years later by a Macedonian terrorist in France.	The Communist Party of Slovenia (KPS) forms under the tutelage of Josip Broz Tito and the Communist Party of Yugoslavia (KPJ).

After Italy capitulated in 1943, the anti-OF Slovenian Domobranci (Home Guards) were active in Primorska and, in a bid to prevent the communists from gaining political control in liberated areas, began supporting the Germans. Despite this assistance and the support of the fascist groups in Croatia and Serbia, the Germans were forced to evacuate Belgrade in 1944. Slovenia was not totally liberated until May 1945.

The following month, as many as 12,000 Domobranci and anti-communist civilians were sent back to Slovenia from refugee camps in Austria by the British. Most of them were executed by the communists over the next two months.

Postwar Division & Socialist Yugoslavia

The status of the liberated areas along the Adriatic, especially Trieste, was Slovenia's greatest postwar concern. A peace treaty signed in Paris in 1947 put Trieste and its surrounds under Anglo-American administration (the so-called Zone A) and the Koper and Buje (Istria) areas under Yugoslav control in Zone B. In 1954 Zone A (with both its Italian and ethnic Slovenian populations) became the Italian province of Trieste. Koper and a 47km-long stretch of coast later went to Slovenia while the bulk of Istria went to Croatia. The Belvedere Treaty (1955) guaranteed Austria its 1938 borders, including most of Koroška.

Tito had been elected head of the assembly, providing for a federal republic in November 1943. He moved quickly after the war to consolidate his power under the communist banner. Serbian domination from Belgrade would continue, though, and in some respects be even more centralist than under the Kingdom of Yugoslavia.

Tito distanced himself from the Soviet Union as early as 1948, but isolation from the markets of the Soviet bloc forced him to court the West. Yugoslavia introduced features of a market economy, including workers' self-management. Economic reforms in the mid-1960s as well as relaxed police control and border controls brought greater prosperity and freedom of movement, but the Communist Party saw such democratisation as a threat to its power. What were to become known as the 'leaden years' in Yugoslavia lasted throughout the 1970s until Tito's death in 1980.

Crisis, Renewal & Change

In 1987 the Ljubljana-based magazine *Nova Revija* published an article outlining a new Slovenian national program, which included political pluralism, democracy, a market economy and independence, possibly within a Yugoslav confederation. The new liberal leader of the Slovenian communists, Milan Kučan, did not oppose the demands, and opposition parties began to emerge. But the de facto head of the central government

Slovenia 1945: Memories of Death and Survival after World War II, by John Corsellis & Marcus Ferrar, is the harrowing story of the forced return to Slovenia and execution of thousands of members of the anti-Communist Domobranci after WWII.

France Štiglic's 1955 film *Dolina Miru (Valley of Peace)* is the bittersweet story of two children, an ethnic German boy and a Slovenian girl, trying to find a haven during the tumult of WWII.

1945	1948	1956	1980
Occupied Slovenia is liberated by the Partisans in May and 12,000 Domobranci and anti-communist civilians are executed the following month; Slovenia is included in the Federal People's Republic of Yugoslavia.	Yugoslavia distances itself from and then breaks with the Soviet Union; exclusion from the markets of the Soviet bloc forces Tito to look to the West.	Tito, in association with India's first prime minister Jawaharlal Nehru and the president of Egypt Gamal Abdul Nasser, founds the Non-Aligned Movement.	Tito, his direct involvement in domestic policy and governing somewhat diminished, dies at age 87, opening the floodgates that lead to the dissolution of the federal republic in the next decade.

in Belgrade, Serbian communist leader Slobodan Milošević, resolved to put pressure on Slovenia.

In June 1988 three Slovenian journalists working for the weekly *Mladina* (*Youth*) – including the current prime minister, Janez Janša – and a junior army officer who had given away 'military secrets' were tried by a military court and sentenced to prison. Mass demonstrations were held throughout the country.

In the autumn, Serbia unilaterally scrapped the autonomy of Kosovo (where 80% of the population is ethnically Albanian) granted by the 1974 constitution. Slovenes were shocked by the move, fearing the same could happen to them. A rally organised jointly by the Slovenian government and the opposition in Ljubljana early in the new year condemned the move.

In the spring of 1989 the new opposition parties published the May Declaration, demanding a sovereign state for Slovenes based on democracy and respect for human rights. In September the Slovenian parliament amended the constitution to legalise management of its own resources and peacetime command of the armed forces. Serbia announced plans to hold a 'meeting of truth' in Ljubljana on its intentions. When Slovenia banned it, Serbia and all the other republics except Croatia announced an economic boycott of Slovenia, cutting off 25% of its exports. In January 1990, Slovenian delegates walked out on a congress of the Communist Party, thereby sounding the death knell of the party.

Independence

In April 1990 Slovenia became the first Yugoslav republic to hold free elections. Demos, a coalition of seven opposition parties, won 55% of the vote, and Kučan, head of what was now called the Party of Democratic Renewal, was elected president. The Slovenian parliament adopted a 'declaration on the sovereignty of the state of Slovenia'. Henceforth Slovenia's own constitution would direct its political, economic and judicial systems; federal laws would apply only if they were not in contradiction to it.

On 23 December 1990, 88.5% of the Slovenian electorate voted for an independent republic, effective within six months. The presidency of the Yugoslav Federation in Belgrade labelled the move secessionist and anti-constitutional. Serbia took control of the Yugoslav monetary system and misappropriated almost the entire monetary issue planned for Yugoslavia in 1991 – US$2 billion. Seeing the writing on the wall, the Slovenian government began stockpiling weapons, and on 25 June 1991 Slovenia pulled out of the Yugoslav Federation for good. 'This evening dreams are allowed', President Kučan told a jubilant crowd in Ljubljana's Kongresni trg the following evening. 'Tomorrow is a new day.'

Best Preserved Castles in Slovenia

» Ljubljana Castle
» Bled Castle
» Ptuj Castle
» Celje Castle
» Predjama Castle

1988	1989	1990	June/July 1991
The sentencing of three Slovenian journalists and a junior army officer for passing on 'military secrets' brings mass demonstrations; independent political parties are established.	The May Declaration calls for a sovereign state for Slovenes based on democracy and respect for human rights.	Slovenian electorate overwhelmingly votes for an independent republic to go into effect within six months; Belgrade brands the action secessionist and anti-constitutional and raids the state coffers of US$2 billion.	Slovenia quits the Yugoslav Federation; fighting erupts when the Yugoslav army marches on Slovenia and meets resistance from the Territorial Defence Forces; the war lasts 10 days and leaves 66 people dead.

WAVING THE FLAG

Slovenia had to come up with a national flag and seal at rather short notice after independence and not everyone was happy with the results. Some citizens said that the flag resembled a football banner while others complained the seal was too close to that of neighbouring countries such as Croatia.

Though the flag's colours – red, white and blue – were decided in 1848, the national seal was a new design. In order to clear up any confusion, the government information office offered Slovenes and the world an explanation of 'what it all means' on two levels.

'On a national level, the outline of Triglav above a wavy line represents a recognisable sign of the Slovenian regional space, which has been created between the mountain world to the north and west, the Adriatic Sea to the south and the plains of the former Pannonian Sea to the east. The three six-pointed stars of the Counts of Celje symbolise the cultural-statesmanship tradition of the Slovenian lands in relation to their inclusion in the currents of European history.'

And then there's the 'universal' explanation… 'The symbol of a mountain with a water surface along the foothills is a universal archetype symbolising the basic equilibrium of the world. On a human level it also demonstrates the balance between man and woman and, on a planetary level, the balance between civilisation and nature. Such a symbol is understandable to people irrespective of their cultural background since it touches a primal exemplar rooted deep in the subconscious. In addition it is a sign of the future as a postmodern time which once again respects equilibrium on every level. The three gold stars above symbolise spiritual-ethical principles in relation to which the equilibrium is restored. The triangular disposition is a symbol of pluralistic dynamics.'

So now we know.

Indeed it was. On 27 June the Yugoslav army began marching on Slovenia but met resistance from the Territorial Defence Forces, the police and the general population. Within several days, units of the federal army began disintegrating; Belgrade threatened aerial bombardment and Slovenia faced the prospect of total war.

The military action had not come totally unprovoked. To dramatise their bid for independence and to generate support from the West, which preferred to see Yugoslavia continue to exist in some form or another, Slovenian leaders attempted to take control of the border crossings first. Belgrade apparently never expected Slovenia to resist, believing that a show of force would be sufficient for it to back down.

As no territorial claims or minority issues were involved, the Yugoslav government agreed on 7 July to a truce brokered by leaders of what was then the European Community (EC). Under the so-called Brioni Declaration, Slovenia would put further moves to assert its independence on

1992	2004	2007	2008
The EC formally recognises independent Slovenia; Slovenia is admitted to the United Nations as the 176th member-state; Serbia and Montenegro's bid for admission as the Federal Republic of Yugoslavia is rejected.	Slovenia enters the EU as a full member along with nine other countries and becomes the first transition country to graduate from borrower status to donor partner at the World Bank.	Slovenia becomes the first of the 10 new EU states to adopt the euro, its fourth currency (after Yugoslav dinar, tolar scrip and tolar) since independence.	In its most prestigious and high-profile role thus far, Slovenia assumes the presidency of the EU Council in the first half of 2008.

hold for three months provided it was granted recognition by the EC after that time. The war had lasted just 10 days and taken the lives of 66 people.

The Road to Europe

Belgrade withdrew the federal army from Slovenian soil on 25 October 1991, less than a month after Slovenia introduced its own new currency – the tolar. In late December, Slovenia got a new constitution that provided for a bicameral parliamentary system of government. The head of state, the president, is elected directly for a maximum of two five-year terms. Milan Kučan held that role from independence until 2002, when the late Janez Drnovšek (1950–2008), a former prime minister, was elected. Diplomat Danilo Türk served as president from 2007 to 2012, when he was unseated by former prime minister Borut Pahor, who garnered more than 67% of the vote. Executive power is vested in the prime minister and his cabinet. The current prime minister is Janez Janša, who was returned to power in 2012.

In May 2004, Slovenia entered the EU as a full member

The EC formally recognised Slovenia in January 1992, and it was admitted to the UN four months later as the 176th member-state. In May 2004, Slovenia entered the EU as a full member and less than three years later adopted the euro, replacing the tolar as the national currency.

2010
The Slovenian parliament ratifies a border arbitration deal with Croatia vital for Zagreb's EU membership bid, but a popular referendum calling for international arbitration passes by just over 51%.

2012
Janez Janša resumes the premiership after 3½ years in opposition, and his political opponent and predecessor, former prime minister Borut Pahor, unseats President Danilo Türk in a landslide victory.

» Slovenian parliament building, Ljubljana

Slovenian Way of Life

Slovenes are a sophisticated and well-educated people. They have a reputation for being sober-minded, hard-working, dependable and honest – perhaps a result of all those years under the yoke of the Germanic Habsburgs. But they retain something of their Slavic character, even if their spontaneity is a little more premeditated and their expressions of passion a little more muted than that of their Balkan neighbours. Think quietly conservative, deeply self-confident, broad-minded and tolerant. And mostly happy – though the current economic climate is trying even the most stalwart of optimists.

Slovenes are gifted polyglots, and almost everyone speaks some English, German and/or Italian. The fact that you will rarely have difficulty in making yourself understood and will probably never 'need' Slovene shouldn't stop you from learning a few phrases of this rich and wonderful language, which counts as many as three dozen dialects and boasts not just singular and plural but the 'dual' number in which things are counted in twos (or pairs) in all cases. Any effort on your part to speak the local tongue will be rewarded 100-fold. *Srečno* (Good luck)!

Cleveland, Ohio, in the USA is the largest 'Slovenian' city outside Slovenia; other American cities with large concentrations of ethnic Slovenes are Pittsburgh, Pennsylvania, and Chicago, Illinois.

Lifestyle

The population of Slovenia is divided almost exactly in half between those who live in towns and cities and those who live in the country. But in Slovenia, where most urban dwellers still have some connection with the countryside – be it a village house or a *zidanica*, a cottage in one of the wine-growing regions – the division is not all that great. And

---

TWO LITTLE MAGIC WORDS

If you really want to understand Slovenes and *Sloventsvo* ('Slovene-ness', for lack of a better term), there are two Slovenian words that will help. The first is *priden*, an adjective translated as 'diligent', 'industrious', 'hard-working' and – tellingly – 'well-behaved'. Erica Johnson Debeljak, long-term Slovenia resident and author of the seminal memoir *Forbidden Bread*, writes that *priden* 'comes close to defining the essence of the Slovenian soul'. Doing a spot of DIY, neighbour? How *priden* of you! Expecting that second child, you two? Aren't we *pridni*!

The second word is *hrepenenje*, a noun expressing a more complicated concept. The dictionary says it means 'longing' or 'yearning' but that's only half the story. In truth, it's the desire for something seemingly unattainable and the sorrow that accompanies it. '*Hrepenenje* is the exclusive property of the dispossessed,' writes Johnson Debeljak, citing 'the country's agonising history of border changes, emigration, alienation and powerlessness within a larger unit.' The medieval tale *Lepa Vida* can be seen as the very embodiment of this 'melancholic yearning'.

with the arrival of large malls on the outskirts of the biggest cities and a Mercator supermarket in virtually every village, the city has come to the countryside.

Most Slovenes believe that the essence of their national character lies in nature's bounty. For them a life that is not in some way connected to the countryside is inconceivable. At weekends many seek the great outdoors for some walking in the hills or cross-country skiing. Or at least a spot of gardening, which is a favourite pastime.

It's not hard to reach deep countryside here. Forest, some of it virgin, and woodland covers 58% of the country, the third-most forested country in the EU after Finland and Sweden. And the figure jumps to 66% if you include land reverting to natural vegetation and agricultural plots that have not been used for more than two decades. Land under agricultural use is rapidly diminishing and now accounts for just over a quarter of the total.

With farmhouse stays a popular form of accommodation in Slovenia, it's relatively easy to take a peek inside a local home. What you'll see generally won't differ too much from what you'd see elsewhere in Central and Western Europe, though you may be surprised at the dearth of children. Slovenes don't have many kids – the nation has one of Europe's lowest rates of natural population increase and women usually give birth on the late side (the average age is over 28). Most families tend to have just one child and if they have a second one it's usually almost a decade later. And the names of those kids? Overwhelmingly Franc and Janez for boys and Marija and Ana for girls.

Population & Multiculturalism

According to the most recent national field census figures, just over 83% of Slovenia's two million people claim to be ethnic Slovene, descendants of the South Slavs who settled in what is now Slovenia from the 6th century AD.

'Others' and 'unknown ethnic origin', accounting for almost 17% of the population, include (in descending order) ethnic Serbs, Croats, Bosnians, Albanians, those who identify themselves simply as 'Muslims' and many citizens of former Yugoslav republics who 'lost' their nationality after independence for fear that Slovenia would not grant them citizenship. The status of many as noncitizens in Slovenia – the so-called *izbrisani,* or 'erased' – remains extremely controversial.

The Italians (0.1% of the population) and Hungarians (0.3%) are considered indigenous minorities with rights protected under the constitution, and each group has a special deputy looking after their interests in parliament. Census figures put the number of Roma, mostly living in Prekmurje, at about 3500, although unofficial estimates are double or even triple that number.

Ethnic Slovenes living outside the national borders number as many as 400,000, with the vast majority in the USA and Canada. In addition, 50,000 or more Slovenes live in the Italian regions of Gorizia (Gorica), Udine (Videm) and Trieste (Trst), another 15,000 in Austrian Carinthia (Kärnten in German, Koroška in Slovene) and 5000 reside in southwest Hungary.

Sport

In the land of its birth, *smučanje* (skiing) remains the king of sports. The national heroes have been Primož Peterka, ski-jumping World Cup winner in the late 1990s, and extreme skier Davo Karničar, who made the first uninterrupted descent of Mt Everest on skis in 2000. More recent people to follow have been Robert Kranjec, who won the ski-flying World Championship in 2012, and Filip Flisar, who took out the ski-cross World

The French novelist Charles Nodier (1780–1844), who lived and worked in Ljubljana from 1811 to 1813 during the period of the so-called Illyrian Provinces, described Slovenia as 'an Academy of Arts and Sciences' because of the people's flair for speaking foreign languages.

Every third Slovene regularly takes part in some sort of active leisure pursuit; 3500 sport societies and clubs count a total membership of 400,000 – 20% of the population – across the nation.

SLOVENIA AT THE OLYMPICS

Slovenia punches well above its weight when it comes to winning Olympic medals. At the 2008 Olympic Games in Beijing, Team Slovenia took gold in the men's hammer throw, two silver medals (women's 200m freestyle swimming and laser sailing) and a bronze each in women's half-heavyweight judo and men's 50m rifle shooting. At the 30th Olympiad in London in 2012, Slovenia won gold in women's half-middleweight judo, silver in men's hammer throw and a bronze each in men's 50m rifle shooting and men's double scull rowing.

Cup the same year. Two women have also helped put Slovenian skiing on the world map. The first is Petra Majdič who, in 2006, was the first Slovenian skier to win a medal in a World Cup cross-country race and has gone on to collect two dozen more. She took bronze in the classic sprint at the 2010 Winter Olympics in Vancouver after falling and breaking several ribs, winning the admiration of her countrymen. The second is Tina Maze, who won two silvers at Vancouver and is the current world champion in giant slalom.

Until not so long ago Slovenia was one of the few countries in Europe where *nogomet* (football) was not a national passion. But interest in the sport increased after the national team's plucky performance in the 2000 European Championship. In the qualifying match for the 2010 World Cup, Slovenia beat Russia at home 1-0 and the national team started packing its bag for South Africa, its second appearance at a World Cup since independence. There Slovenia won their opening game against Algeria 1-0, tied with the US 2-2 but lost to England 1-0 before being eliminated.

There are 10 teams in the First Division (Prva Liga), with NK Maribor, Olimpija Ljubljana and NK Domžale consistently at the top of the league.

In general *kosarka* (basketball) is the most popular team sport here, and the Union Olimpija team reigns supreme; Slovenia hosts the prestigious EuroBasket world championship in September 2013. Other popular spectator sports are *odbojka* (volleyball) and *hokej na ledu* (ice hockey), especially since Anže Kopitar, perhaps the best-known Slovenian athlete in the world, helped the Los Angeles Kings of the US National Hockey League win their first Stanley Cup ever.

For the latest on Union Olimpija and Slovenian basketball see the Eurobasket (www.eurobasket.com/Slovenia/basketball.asp) website.

Religion

Although Protestantism gained a very strong foothold in Slovenia in the 16th century, the majority of Slovenes – just under 58% – identified themselves as Roman Catholic in the most recent census. The archbishop of Ljubljana and primate of Slovenia is Anton Stres.

Other religious communities in Slovenia include Muslims (2.5%), Eastern Orthodox Christians (2.3%) and Protestants (1%). Most Protestants belong to the Evangelical (Lutheran) church based in Murska Sobota in Prekmurje. Slovenia's first mosque has been given the green light after decades of wrangling and will be built in the Bežigrad district of northern Ljubljana.

Jews have played a very minor role in Slovenia since they were first banished from the territory in the 15th century. In 2003 the tiny Jewish community of Slovenia received a Torah at a newly equipped synagogue in Ljubljana, the first since before WWII. The chief rabbi of Slovenia is currently based in Trieste.

Arts

Literature
Medieval to Modern

Like that of cultures everywhere, Slovenian literature, among the oldest in the Slavic world, is heavily influenced by the nation's history.

The oldest example of written Slovene can be found in the so-called Freising Manuscripts (Brižinski Spomeniki) from around AD 970. They contain a sermon on sin and penance and instructions for general confession. Oral poetry, such as the seminal *Lepa Vida (Fair Vida)*, a tale of longing and nostalgia, flourished throughout the Middle Ages, but it was the Reformation that saw the first book in Slovene, a catechism published by Primož Trubar in 1550. Almost everything else published until the late 18th century was in Latin or German, including an ambitious account of Slovenia, *The Glory of the Duchy of Carniola* (1689), by Janez Vajkard Valvasor (1641–93), from which comes most of our knowledge of Slovenian history, geography, culture and folklore before the 17th century.

The Enlightenment gave Slovenia its first dramatist (Anton Tomaž Linhart), poet (Valentin Vodnik) and modern grammarian (Jernej Kopitar). But it was during the so-called National Romantic Period that Slovenian literature gained its greatest poet of all time: France Prešeren. In the latter half of the 19th century, Fran Levstik (1831–87) brought the

FRANCE PREŠEREN: A POET FOR THE NATION

Slovenia's most beloved poet was born in Vrba near Bled in 1800. Most of his working life was spent as an articled clerk in the office of a Ljubljana lawyer. By the time he had opened his own practice in Kranj in 1846 he was already a sick and dispirited man. He died three years later.

Although Prešeren published only one volume of poetry in his lifetime (*Poezije*, 1848), he left behind a legacy of work printed in literary magazines. His verse set new standards for Slovenian poetry at a time when German was the literary *lingua franca*, and his lyric poems, such as the masterpiece *Sonetni Venec* (*A Garland of Sonnets*, 1834), are among the most sensitive and original works in Slovene. In later poems, such as his epic *Krst pri Savici* (*Baptism by the Savica Waterfall*, 1836), he expressed a national consciousness that he tried to instil in his compatriots.

Prešeren's life was one of sorrow and disappointment. The sudden death of his close friend and mentor, the literary historian Matija Čop, in 1835 and an unrequited love affair with an heiress called Julija Primic brought him close to suicide. But this was when he produced his best poems.

Prešeren was the first to demonstrate the full literary potential of the Slovenian language, and his body of verse – lyric poems, epics, satire, narrative verse – has inspired Slovenes at home and abroad for generations.

writing and interpretation of oral folk tales to new heights with his legends about the larger-than-life hero Martin Krpan, but it was Josip Jurčič (1844–81) who published the first novel in Slovene, *Deseti Brat (The 10th Brother)* in 1866.

Contemporary Literature

The early 20th century was dominated by two men who single-handedly introduced modernism into Slovenian literature: the poet Oton Župančič (1878–1949) and the novelist and playwright Ivan Cankar (1876–1918). The latter has been called 'the outstanding master of Slovenian prose' and works like his *Hlapec Jernej in Njegova Pravica (The Bailiff Yerney and His Rights*, 1907), influenced a generation of young writers.

Slovenian literature immediately before and after WWII was influenced by socialist realism and the Partisan struggle as exemplified by the novels of Lovro Kuhar-Prežihov Voranc (1893–1950). Since then, however, Slovenia has tended to follow Western European trends: late expressionism, symbolism (poetry by Edvard Kocbek, 1904–81) and existentialism (novels by Vitomil Zupan, 1914–87, and the drama of Gregor Strniša, 1930–87).

The major figures of Slovenian post-modernism since 1980 are the novelist Drago Jančar (1948–) and the poet Tomaž Šalamun (1941–). Young talent to watch out for today includes authors dealing with very sensitive issues such as racism and relations with the former Yugloslav republics. The first novel by Andrej E Skubic (1967–), *Fužinski Bluz (Fužine Blues*, 2004), takes place on the day of the first football match between independent Slovenia and Yugoslavia. Goran Vojnovič (1980–) wrote a satire called *Čefurji Raus!* (2009), which is translated as *Southern Scum Out!* and refers to those from the other former Yugoslav republics living in Slovenia.

Music

As elsewhere in Central and Eastern Europe, music – especially the classical variety – is very important in Slovenia. There is a network of music schools at the secondary level across the nation, and attendance at concerts and recitals is high in cities and towns.

Contemporary classical composers whose reputations go well beyond the borders of Slovenia include Primož Ramovš, Marjan Kozina, Lojze Lebič and the ultramodernist Vinko Globokar, who was born in France. Aldo Kumar has received awards for his theatre and film compositions; Milko Lazar is one of the more interesting composer-musicians to emerge in recent years. Opera buffs won't want to miss out on the

> Slovenia is the third-smallest literature market in Europe (a fiction 'bestseller' means 500 to 800 copies sold) and in the EU only the Danes borrow more library books than the Slovenes, where the annual average is 10 books per person.

> The leader of celebrated punk band Laibach, Tomaž Hostnik, died tragically in 1982 when he hanged himself from a *kozolec*, the traditional Slovenian hayrack.

FOLK MUSIC

Ljudska glasba (folk music) has developed independently from other forms of music over the centuries. Traditional folk instruments include the *frajtonarica* (button accordion), *cimbalom* (a stringed instrument played with sticks), *bisernica* (lute), *zvegla* (wooden cross flute), *okarina* (clay flute), *šurle* (Istrian double flute), *trstenke* (reed pipes), Jew's harp, *lončeni bajs* (earthenware bass), *berdo* (contrabass) and *brač* (eight-string guitar).

Folk-music performances are usually local affairs and are very popular in Dolenjska and especially Bela Krajina. There's also been a modern folk-music revival in recent years. Listen for the groups Katice and Katalena, who play traditional Slovenian music with a modern twist, and Terra Folk, a quintessential world-music band.

chance to hear Marjana Lipovšek and Argentina-born Bernarda Fink, the country's foremost mezzo-sopranos.

Popular music runs the gamut from Slovenian *chanson* (eg Vita Mavrič) and folk to jazz and mainstream polka best, exemplified by the Avsenik Brothers Ensemble. However, it was punk music in the late 1970s and early 1980s that put Slovenia on the world stage. The most celebrated groups were Pankrti, Borghesia and especially Laibach, and they were imitated throughout Eastern Europe. The most popular rock band in Slovenia today remains Siddharta, formed in 1995 and still going strong.

Architecture

Examples of Romanesque architecture can be found in many parts of Slovenia and include the churches at Stična Abbey in Dolenjska, at Muta and Dravograd in Koroška, and at Podsreda Castle in Štajerska.

Much of the Gothic architecture in Slovenia is of the late period; the earthquake of 1511 took care of many buildings erected before then (although both the Venetian Gothic Loggia and Praetorian Palace in Koper date back a century before). Renaissance architecture is mostly limited to civil buildings (eg townhouses in Škofja Loka and Kranj, Brdo Castle in Gorenjska).

Italian-influenced baroque of the 17th and 18th centuries abounds in Slovenia, particularly in Ljubljana (eg the Ursuline Church of the Holy Trinity and the cathedral). Classicism prevailed in architecture here in the first half of the 19th century; the Kazina building in Ljubljana's Kongresni trg is a good example.

The turn of the 20th century was when the Secessionist (or art nouveau) architects Maks Fabiani and Ivan Vurnik began changing the face of Ljubljana (Miklošičev Park, the Prešeren monument, the Cooperative Bank on Miklošičeva cesta) after the devastating earthquake of 1895. But no architect has had a greater impact on his city or nation than Jože Plečnik (p42), a man whose work defies easy definition.

Postwar architecture is generally forgettable – Edvard Ravnikar's Trg Republike in Ljubljana is a blight on the national capital – but among the most interesting contemporary architects working today are the award-winning team of Rok Oman and Špela Videčnik, whose OFIS Architects designed the extraordinary Ljubljana City Museum (2004), the Maribor football stadium (2009), and participated in building the landmark Cultural Centre of European Space Technologies (KSEVT) in Vitanje in 2012.

Painting & Sculpture

The visual arts play an important role in the lives of many Slovenes; the nation counts some three dozen permanent art museums and galleries, and hundreds more temporary exhibition spaces.

Excellent examples of Gothic painting and sculpture include the carved altar in the Church of the Virgin Mary at Ptujska Gora, the frescoes in the Church of St John the Baptist in Bohinj, and the Dance of Death wall painting at the Church of the Holy Trinity in Hrastovlje. Important painters of this time were Johannes de Laibaco (John of Ljubljana), who decorated the Church of the Assumption in Muljava; Jernej of Loka, who worked mostly around Škofja Loka; and Johannes Aquila of Radgona, who did the frescoes in the magnificent church at Martjanci.

For baroque sculpture, look at Jožef Straub's plague pillar in Maribor, the golden altar in the Church of the Annunciation at Crngrob, or the work of Francesco Robba in Ljubljana (Carniolan Rivers fountain at the National Gallery). Fortunat Bergant, who painted the Stations of the Cross in the church at Stična Abbey, was a master of baroque painting.

The bilingual *Slovenian Folk Songs/Slovenske Ljudske Pesmi* (ed Marko Terseglav) is a good introduction to what was (and sometimes still is) sung up in them thar hills.

ARTS

Valvasor's explanation of how the water system in Lake Cerknica worked earned him membership in 1688 in the Royal Society in London, the world's foremost scientific institution at the time.

Architectural Guide to Ljubljana, by Janez Koželj and Andrej Hrausky, is a richly illustrated guide to more than 100 buildings and other features in the capital, with much emphasis on architect extraordinaire Jože Plečnik.

ARTS

SLAVOJ ŽIŽEK: PHILOSOPHER

Slovenia's best-known son has authored some 60 philosophical works and starred in several films, including the recently released *The Pervert's Guide to Ideology*.

How does it feel to be the most famous Slovene outside the borders? Fame... The irony of it all! That's not true in the USA. That would be the ice hockey star Anže Kopitar or maybe Donald Trump's wife who Germanised her name from Melanija Knavs to Melania Knauss. Maybe she thought it sounded better to be Austrian. You know, *Sound of Music*, Vienna waltzes, the Blue Danube...

And your place in Slovenia? OK, I am Slovene – whatever that means. The official line here is that we are a nation of poets, modest and good. But bad Slovenia is miserly, very Catholic, authoritarian and mean-spirited. An illustration: a fairy appears to a Slovenian farmer and tells him he can have anything he wants but his neighbour will get double. 'OK, take one of my eyes,' he says.

OK, the meaning of life. Discuss. A philosopher knows that asking the right question is more important than providing an answer. My first duty is to disturb the commonplace. And to make you understand what deep shit you are in.

You have quite a following among younger people. How so? Maybe they are tired of postmodern liberal culture and know change is on the way. Look at Occupy Wall St. Or maybe they think I'm a good stand-up philosopher and like my references to popular culture. Not everyone thinks being called 'the Borat of philosophy' is criticism.

So nothing to do with the Lady Gaga 'affair' then? A hoax circulated by my enemies and reported in the media. Imagine me debating the problems of feminist writing with Lady Gaga! But I'm still getting emails from young men asking for an introduction. I imagine writing back that my friend Lady G has said for them to send a sample of their writing and a photograph of themselves naked. I love the idea of being the mediator of a mess, to introduce disorder and then just disappear.

When not in Ljubljana, you might find me in... Škocjan Caves. I once read that Dante used the place as a model for his description of hell.

Steve Fallon

The most important painters of the 19th century include the impressionists Rihard Jakopič, Matija Jama, Ivan Grohar and Matej Sternen, who exhibited together in Ljubljana in 1900. In the 20th century, the expressionist school of Božidar Jakac and the brothers France and Tone Kralj gave way to the sculptors Alojzij Gangl, Franc Berneker, Jakob Savinšek and Lojze Dolinar. Favourite artists to emerge after WWII include Janez Bernik, Rudi Španzel and Jože Tisnikar.

From the 1980s and onward postmodernist painting and sculpture has been dominated by the artists' cooperative Irwin, part of the wider multimedia group Neue Slowenische Kunst (NSK). Among notable names today are the artist Tadej Pogačar, sculptor Marjetica Potrč and video artists Marko Peljhan and Marina Gržinič.

Cinema

Slovenia was never on the cutting edge of film-making as were some of the former Yugoslav republics (such as Croatia). However, it still managed to produce award-winning films such as Jože Gale's *Kekec* (1951) and France Štiglic's *Dolina Miru* (*Valley of Peace*, 1955).

What is now touted as the 'Spring of Slovenian Film' in the late 1990s was heralded by two films: *Ekspres, Ekspres* (*Express, Express*, 1997) by Igor Šterk, an award-winning 'railroad' film and farce, and *Autsajder* (*Outsider*, 1997), by Andrej Košak, about the love between a Slovenian girl and Bosnian 'outsider'.

Subsequent successes include: *Kruh in Mleko* (*Bread and Milk*, 2001), the tragic story of a dysfunctional small-town family by Jan Cvitkovič; Sašo Podgoršek's *Sladke Sanje* (*Sweet Dreams*, 2001), a coming-of-age piece set in 1970s Yugoslavia; and Damjan Kozole's *Rezerni Deli* (*Spare Parts*, 2003) about the trafficking of illegal immigrants through Slovenia from Croatia to Italy by a couple of embittered misfits. More recent (and lighter) fare is Cvitkovič's *Odgrobadogroba* (*Grave Hopping*, 2006), an Oscar-nominated tragicomedy about a professional funeral speaker; *Petelinji Zajtrk* (*Rooster's Breakfast*, 2007), a romance by Marko Naberšnik set in Gornja Radgona on the Austrian border in northeast Slovenia; and *Stanje Šoka* (*State of Shock*, 2012) by Andrej Košak, which is about a time-travelling Yugoslav 'model worker' who wakes up in independent Slovenia.

The website of the Slovenian Film Fund (www.film-sklad.si) will tell you everything you need to know about films and filming in Slovenia.

ARTS

The Slovenian Table

Little Slovenia can boast an incredibly diverse cuisine, with as many as two dozen different regional styles of cooking – from Prekmurje in the northeast to Slovenian Istria in the southwest. Until recently, except for a few national favourites such as *žlikrofi* (stuffed pasta) from Idrija and *jota* (hearty bean soup) from Istria or the Karst, and incredibly rich desserts like *gibanica* from Prekmurje and *kremna rezina* from Bled, you were not likely to encounter many of these regional specialities on restaurant menus. But all that is changing as Slovenia reclaims (and often redefines) its culinary heritage. Whatever you do, don't miss an opportunity to try some of these delights in a Slovenian home, where food is paramount.

There are several truisms concerning Slovenian cuisine. In general, it is plain and simple, pretty heavy and fairly meaty. And it is heavily influenced by its neighbours' cooking styles. From Austria, there's sausage *(klobasa),* strudel *(zavitek)* filled with fruit, nuts and/or curd cheese *(skuta),* and Wiener schnitzel *(dunajski zrezek).* The ravioli-like *žlikrofi, njoki* (potato dumplings) and *rižota* (risotto) obviously have Italian origins, and Hungary has contributed *golaž* (goulash), *paprikaš* (piquant chicken or beef 'stew') and *palačinke* (thin pancakes filled with jam or nuts and topped with chocolate). From Croatia and the rest of the Balkans have come such popular grills as *čevapčiči* (spicy meatballs of beef or pork) and *pljeskavica* (meat patties). But that's only part of the story.

> *Slovenian Cookery: Over 100 Classic Dishes* by Slavko Adamlje is a practical illustrated guide to Slovenian cuisine.

When to Eat

On the whole Slovenes are not big eaters of breakfast *(zajtrk),* preferring a cup of coffee at home or on the way to work. Instead, many people eat a light meal *(malica)* at around 10.30am. Lunch *(kosilo)* is traditionally the main meal in the countryside, and it's eaten at noon if *malica* has been skipped. Sometimes it is eaten much later – sometimes in the middle of the afternoon. Dinner *(večerja)* – a supper, really – is less substantial when eaten at home, often just sliced meats, cheese and salad.

Where to Eat

Restaurants go by many names in Slovenia, and the distinctions are not always very clear. At the top of the heap, a *restavracija* is a restaurant where you sit down and are served by a waiter. A *gostilna* or *gostišče* has waiters too, but it's more like an inn, with rustic decor and usually traditional Slovenian dishes. A *samopostrežna restavracija* is a self-service establishment where you order from a counter and carry your food on a tray. An *okrepčevalnica* and a *bife* serve simple fast food such as grilled meats and sausages. A *krčma* may have snacks, but the emphasis here is on drinking (usually alcohol). A *slaščičarna* sells sweets and ice cream whereas a *kavarna* provides coffee and pastries. A *mlečna restavracija*

> *The Food and Cooking of Slovenia* by Janez Bogataj is a richly illustrated and instructive tome that divides Slovenia into two dozen culinary regions – from Haloze and Koroška to Soča and the Karst – and takes the reader along for the ride.

SLOVENIA'S TOP SIX RESTAURANTS

The following half-dozen eateries not only serve local and regional specialities but make a positive obsession – very much to their credit – out of using only locally sourced ingredients. It's all part of the slow-food, local-only trend taking Slovenia by storm. And at times the food can be truly awesome.

Gostilna Lectar (p74) Arguably Gorenjska's best restaurant, the 'Gingerbread' in Radovljie serves enlightened Slovenian dishes amid authentic farmhouse decor.

Gostilna na Gradu (p55) Slovenian-sourced breads, cheeses and meats prepared to time-tested recipes in Ljubljana Castle.

Gostilna Repnik (p72) The specialities at this eatery just outside Kamnik are homemade soups, pâtés and harder-to-find dishes such as rabbit.

Hiša Franko (p104) Impeccable tasting menus in Kobarid, strong on locally sourced ingredients that change seasonally.

Strud'l (p89) Modern take on traditional farmhouse cooking in Bohinska Bistrica near Lake Bohinj.

Topli Val (p104) One of our favourite 'destination' eateries, the 'Warm Wave' in Kobarid serves superb Adriatic fish and seafood dishes and boasts an enviable wine list.

(milk bar) sells yoghurt and other dairy products as well as *krofi* (jam-filled doughnuts).

Almost every sit-down restaurant in Slovenia has a menu with dishes translated into English, Italian, German and sometimes French and Russian. It's important to note the difference between *pripravljene jedi* or *gotova jedilna* (ready-made dishes) such as goulash or stew that are just heated up and *jedi po naročilu* (dishes made to order). Lists of *danes priporočamo* or *nudimo* (daily recommendations or suggestions) are frequently in Slovene only. Many restaurants and inns have an inexpensive *dnevno kosilo* (set-lunch menu).

It's important to know that not many Slovenes eat in city-centre restaurants unless they have to because of work or because they happen to be entertaining after office hours. At the weekend, most will head 5km or 10km out of town to a *gostilna* or *gostišče* that they know will serve them good, home-cooked food and local wine at affordable prices.

What to Eat
Bread

Nothing is more Slovenian than bread *(kruh)*, and it is generally excellent, especially wholewheat bread *(kmečki temni kruh)*. Real treats are the braided loaves made around Christmas, not dissimilar to Jewish challah, and 'mottled bread' *(pisan kruh)* in which three types of dough (usually buckwheat, wheat and corn) are rolled up together and baked.

Soup

Most Slovenian meals start with *juha* (soup) – of which there are said to be a hundred different varieties – year-round but especially in winter. As a starter, this is usually chicken or beef broth with little egg noodles *(kokošja* or *goveja juha z rezanci)*. More substantial varieties include *jesprenj* (barley soup); *jota,* a very thick potage of beans, sauerkraut or sour turnip, sometimes potatoes and smoked pork or sausage; and *obara,* a stew, often made with chicken or veal.

Štajerska's distinctive *bučno olje* (pumpkin-seed oil) is not just an excellent condiment on salads but can also be poured over ice creams and sprinkled with green pumpkin seeds or cracked walnuts.

TASTY TRAVEL

Slovenes eat something nobody else does: *polh* (dormouse or loir), a tree-dwelling nocturnal rodent not unlike a squirrel that grows to about 30cm long and sleeps through several months of the year. But unless you are in Notranjska, where it was once a staple, during the loir-hunting season in late September and have friends there, it's unlikely you'll get to taste this incredible edible varmint.

Like the French, Slovenes have a taste for horse flesh – literally – and are especially fond of *žrebe* (colt). They like the taste (it's sweeter than beef or mutton), the low fat and the deep, almost ruby-red colour. You can try it most easily as a burger at a fast-food outlet called Hot Horse (p58) in Ljubljana's Park Tivoli.

Meat & Fish

It's the fiercely cold northeast wind in the Karst region called the *burja* that gives air-dried *pršut* its distinctive taste.

For most Slovenes, a meal is incomplete without *meso* (meat). The pig is king in Slovenia and *svinjina* (pork) rules, though *teletina* (veal), *govedina* (beef) and, in season, *divjačina* (game), such as *srna* (deer) and *fazan* (pheasant), are also eaten. Indeed, even *konj* (horse) finds its way to the Slovenian table. *Piščanec* (chicken) is not as common as *puran* (turkey) on a Slovenian menu, while *gos* (goose), *jagnjetina* (lamb) and *koza* (goat) are rarely seen.

Some excellent prepared meats are *pršut,* air-dried, thinly sliced ham from the Karst region that is related to Italian *prosciutto,* and *divjačinska salama* (salami made from game), popular in Gorenjska. Slovenes are big eaters of *riba* (fish) and *morski sadež* (shellfish), even far from the coast. *Postrv* (trout), particularly the variety from the Soča River, is superb.

Groats

Distinctively Slovenian dishes are often served with *žganci,* groats made from barley or corn but usually *ajda* (buckwheat). A real rib-sticker is *ajdovi žganci z ocvirki,* a kind of dense buckwheat porridge with the savoury addition of *ocvirki* (pork crackling or scratchings).

Dessert

Why goose on 15 November? According to legend, Martin, the man who would be saint, hid himself in a flock of geese when the faithful were looking for him to tell him he'd just been made a bishop.

Slovenian cuisine boasts several calorific desserts. *Potica,* a national institution, is a kind of nut roll (although it's often made with savoury fillings as well) eaten after a meal or at teatime. *Prekmurska gibanica,* from Slovenia's easternmost province, is a rich concoction of pastry filled with poppy seeds, walnuts, apples and/or sultanas and cheese and crowned with cream. *Blejska kremna rezina* is a layer of vanilla custard topped with whipped cream and sandwiched between two layers of flaky pastry.

Snacks

The most popular street food in Slovenia is a Balkan import called *burek* – flaky pastry sometimes stuffed with meat but more often cheese or even apple – that is a cousin of Turkish *börek*. It's sold at outdoor stalls or kiosks and is very cheap and filling. Other cheap *malice* (snacks) available on the hoof are *čevapčiči, pljeskavica* (spicy meat patties), *ražnjiči* (shish kebab) and pizza (which sometimes appears spelled in Slovene as *pica*).

Vegetarian & Vegan

Slovenia is hardly a paradise for vegetarians, but there are a couple of meat-free eateries in Ljubljana, and you're sure to find a few meatless dishes on any menu. *Štruklji,* dumplings made with cheese and often flavoured with chives or tarragon, are widely available, as are dishes like *gobova rižota* (mushroom risotto) and *ocvrti sir* (deep-fried cheese). Slovenes love fresh *solata* (salad) – a most un-Slavic partiality – and you can get one anywhere, even in a countryside *gostilna*. In season (usually late summer and autumn) the whole country indulges in *jurčki* (wild cep or Portobello mushrooms) in soups or salads or grilled.

Mushroom picking is almost a national pastime in the hills and forests of Slovenia in summer and autumn.

Wine

Vino (wine) has been made in what is now Slovenia since the arrival of the Celts in the 5th century BC, and many of the country's wines are of a very high quality indeed. Be warned, though, that cheaper 'open wine' *(odprto vino)* sold by the decilitre (0.1L) in bars and restaurants are usually rot-gut. For more detailed information, contact the **Wine Association of Slovenia** (Vinska Družba Slovenije; ✆01-244 18 00; www.vinskadruzba.si; Kongresni trg 14).

Slovenes usually drink wine with meals or socially at home; it's not very common to see people sit down to a bottle at a cafe or pub. As elsewhere in Central Europe, a bottle or glass of mineral water is ordered along with the wine when eating. It's a different story in summer, when *brizganec* or *špricar* (spritzers or wine coolers) of red or white wine mixed with mineral water are consumed in large quantities. Wine comes in 0.75L bottles or is ordered by the deci (decilitre, 0.1L). A normal glass of wine is about *dva* deci (0.2L).

You'll find some excellent recipes from around Slovenia in English at www.slovenia.si/en/visit/cuisine/recipes.

Wine Regions

Slovenia has three major wine-growing regions. Podravje (literally 'on the Drava'), encompassing the Prekmurje and Štajerska Slovenija (Slovenian Styria) districts, extends from northeast Štajerska into Prekmurje and produces whites almost exclusively, including Laški Rizling (welschriesling) and Renski Rizling (a true German riesling), Beli Pinot (pinot blanc), Traminec (gewürztraminer) and Šipon (furmint).

Posavje is the region running from eastern Štajerska across the Sava River into Dolenjska and Bela Krajina and includes the Bizeljsko-Sremič, Dolenjska and Bela Krajina districts. This region produces both whites and reds, but its most famous wine is Cviček, a distinctly Slovenian dry light red – almost rosé – wine with a low (8.5% to 10%) alcohol content. Reds include ruby-red Metliška Črnina (Metlika black) and whites such as the sweet Rumeni Muškat (yellow muscatel).

The Primorska wine region, which encompasses the districts of Slovenska Istra (Slovenia Istria), Kras (Karst), Vipavska Dolina (Vipava Valley) and the celebrated Goriška Brda (Gorica Hills), excels at reds, the most famous being Teran, a ruby-red, peppery wine with high acidity made from Slovenian Refošk (Refosco) grapes in the Karst region. Other wines from this region are Malvazija (malvasia), a yellowish white from Slovenian Istria that is light and dry, and red merlots, especially the ones from the Vipava Valley and Goriška Brda.

The oldest vine in the world, planted more than four centuries ago and still producing grapes and wine, is in Maribor.

A MATCH MADE IN HEAVEN

The pairing of food with wine is as great an obsession in Slovenia as it is in other wine-producing countries. Most people know that *pršut* with black olives and a glass of Teran is a near-perfect match, but what is less appreciated is the wonderful synergy other wines from the Karst – red Rebula, even white Malvazija – enjoy with these two foodstuffs. With heavier and/or spicier meat dishes such as goulash and salami, try Cviček. Malvazija, a yellowish white from the coast, is good with fish, as is Laški Rizling. And with sweet food such as strudel and *potica*, it's got to be a glass of late-harvest Rumeni Muškat.

THE SLOVENIAN TABLE

Most of the wine-producing districts have a *vinska cesta* (wine route) or two that you can follow in a car or on a bicycle. Many are outlined on the website of the Slovenian Tourist Board (www.slovenia.info). Along the way, you can stop at the occasional *klet* (cellar) that offers wine tastings or at a *vinoteka* in wine towns.

Choosing Wine

On a Slovenian wine label, the first word usually identifies where the wine is from and the second identifies the grape varietal: Vipavski merlot, Mariborski traminec etc. But this is not always the case, and some wines bear names according to their place of origin, such as Jeruzalemčan, Bizeljčan or Haložan.

Slovenia's version of *appellation d'origine contrôlée* (AOC) is *zaščiteno geografsko poreklo* (ZGP), a trademark protection that guarantees provenance and sets the limits to three quality levels. Some 9% is designated *vrhunsko vino* (premium wine), 54% is *kakovostno vino* (quality wine) and 27% is *deželno vino* (regional wine), not dissimilar to French *vin du pays*. The last 10% are wines classified as *priznano tradicionalno poimenovanje* (recognised traditional designation) such as Cviček, Teran, Metliška Črnina, Belokranjec and Bizeljčan. Wines can be red, white or rosé, and dry, semidry, semisweet or sweet. Very roughly, anything costing more than about €6 in the shops is a serious bottle of Slovenian wine; pay more than €10 and you'll be getting something very fine indeed and for €15 to €20, wines are super-premium.

One excellent Slovenian sparkling wine that employs the demanding *méthode classique* is Zlata Radgonska Penina from Gornja Radgona in Slovenian Styria, which is based on Chardonnay and Beli pinot. Kraška Penina, a sparkling Teran, is unique. Late-harvest dessert wines include Rumeni Muškat from Bela Krajina and Slovenian Istria.

Beer

Pivo beer is very popular in Slovenia, especially with younger people. Štajerska *hmelj* (hops) grown in the Savinja Valley are used locally, and are also widely sought by brewers from around the world. They have been described as having the flavour of lemongrass.

Slovenia has two major brewers, both of which are owned by the Laško brewery in the town of the same name south of Celje. Laško produces the country's two most popular brands: Laško Zlatorog and Union (which is brewed in Ljubljana). Both brands are standard pilsners, with a light golden colour and a hoppy, almost bitter taste. Of the two, Zlatorog is by far the most popular, with a reputation as the beer of choice for young professionals, hipsters and beer connoisseurs of all stripes. Union is generally seen as the working man's beer – the right choice for a bender, when just about anything will do. That said, we like them both and have a hard time telling them apart.

Laško also makes a popular, sweetish dark beer *(temno pivo)* called, appropriately enough, Laško Dark. It's frequently available on tap in bars and pubs. Union makes a very popular, low-alcohol (2.5%) shandy called Radler, flavoured with orange, lemon or grapefruit and available in cans and bottles. Another popular beer blend, Bandidos, throws in other alcohols, including tequila.

In a *pivnica* (pub), *točeno pivo* (draught beer) is ordered as a *veliko pivo* ('large beer'; 0.5L) or *malo pivo* ('small beer'; 0.3L). Both locally brewed and imported beers are also available at pubs, shops and supermarkets in 0.5L bottles or 0.3L cans.

TOP
PRODUCERS

The Wines of Slovenia by Julij Nemanič, which focuses on the top 60 producers in the country, is an excellent single source of viticulture and wine in Slovenia.

You'll learn lots more about Slovenian viticulture, regions and wine labelling by visiting www. matkurja.com/ projects/wine.

FOOD FESTIVALS FOR ALL SEASONS

As is the case the world over, Slovenia marks holidays and important dates with special dishes. At pre-Lenten carnivals *krofi* (jam-filled doughnuts) are enjoyed while Easter is marked by decorated Easter eggs and a ham cooked with herbs or *pršut* from Istria with black olives. And a Slovenian Christmas wouldn't be complete without a *potica* (nut roll).

Although it's not a public holiday, St Martin's Day (11 November) is important as on this day the winemakers' *mošt* (must; fermenting grape juice) officially becomes wine. In the evening families traditionally dine on goose with *mlinci* (thin dried flat bread) and red cabbage and drink new wine.

The selection of fresh vegetables and fruit is not great in the dead of winter but come spring and a cycle of bounty begins: from wild asparagus (Istria) and *ledenka* (ice lettuce) grown in the Trnovo district of Ljubljana to strawberries (Janče) and cherries (Goriška Brda), through all the stone fruits to apples (Kozjansko), chestnuts and nuts. And then there's the second national sport: mushroom-gathering.

Food festivals, usually timed to welcome the seasonal arrival of a certain fruit, vegetable, nut, wine or even fish, are among the red-letter days of the annual calendar in Slovenia and should not be missed should you be in the area. The following is just a sampling of what to expect.

March

Sevnica Salami Festival (Sevniška Salamijada; www.obcina-sevnica.si; Sevnica)

April

Nature & Wine Festival (www.klet-brda.com/en/goriska-brda-region/events; Medana)

May

Rebula Wine & Olive Oil Festival (Praznik Rebule in Oljčnega Olja; www.klet-brda.com/en/goriska-brda-region/events; Višnjevik)

Wine Spring (Vinska Vigred; www.metlika-turizem.si; Metlika)

June

Cherry Festival (Praznik Češenj; www.klet-brda.com/en/goriska-brda-region/events; Dobrovo)

Cviček Wine Festival (Cviičkarija; ☎+386 41 615 295; Čatež)

July

Polenta Festival (Praznik Polente; www.praznik-polente.si; Šempas)

August

Fishermen's Festival (Ribiški Praznik; www.izola.info; Izola)

Peach Festival (Praznik Breskev; www.novagorica-turizem.com; Prvačina)

Teran Wine & Pršut Festival (Praznik Terana in Pršuta; www.praznikteranainprsuta.si; Dutovlje)

September

Pumpkin Festival (Bučarija ; www.td-smartno.si; Šmartno ob Paki)

Plum Days (Češpovi Dnevi; www.slivje.si; Slivje)

October

Kozjansko Apple Festival (Prazni Kozjanskega Jabolka; www.kozjanski-park.si; Podsreada)

November

Must Festival (Moštna Gavna; www.ravne.si; Prevalje)

THE SLOVENIAN TABLE

Brandy

An alcoholic drink as Slovenian as wine is *žganje,* a strong brandy or *eau de vie* distilled from a variety of fruits. Common types are *slivovka* (made with plums), *češnjevec* (with cherries), *sadjevec* (with mixed fruit) and *brinjevec* (with juniper). A favourite type is *medeno žganje* (or *medica*), which is fruit brandy flavoured with honey – a kind of mead. One of the most unusual (if not the best) is Pleterska Hruška, a pear brandy (also called *viljamovka*) made by the Carthusian monks at the Pleterje monastery near Kostanjevica na Krki in Dolenjska.

Survival Guide

Directory A–Z

Accommodation

Accommodation in Slovenia runs the gamut from riverside camping grounds, hostels, mountain huts, cosy *gostišča* (inns) and farmhouses, to elegant castle hotels in Dolenjska and Štajerska, and five-star hotels in Ljubljana, so you'll usually have little trouble finding accommodation to fit your budget, except perhaps at the height of the season (July and August) on the coast, at Bled or Bohinj, or in Ljubljana.

Virtually every municipality levies a tourist tax of between €0.50 and €1 per person per night. For stays of less than three nights, many pensions and almost all private rooms charge 30% to 50% more, although the percentage usually drops on the second night.

Camping

There's a *kamp* (camping ground) in virtually every corner of the country; seek out the Slovenian Tourist Board's *Camping in Slovenia* brochure. Some rent inexpensive bungalows.

Camping grounds generally charge per person. Prices vary according to the site and the season, but expect to pay anywhere from €5 to €17.50 per person (children are usually charged 20% to 50% of the adult fee). Most official camping grounds offer discounts of 5% to 10% to holders of the Camping Card International (CCI).

Almost all sites close between mid-October and mid-April. Camping 'rough' is illegal in Slovenia.

Farmhouses

Hundreds of working farms in Slovenia offer accommodation to paying guests,

either in private rooms in the farmhouse itself or in Alpine-style guesthouses. Many farms offer outdoor sport activities and allow you to help out with the farm chores if you feel so inclined.

Expect to pay about €15 per person in a room with shared bathroom and breakfast (from €20 for half-board) in the low season (September to mid-December and mid-January to June), rising in the high season (July and August) to a minimum of €17 per person (from €25 for half-board). Apartments for groups of up to eight people are also available. There's no minimum stay, but you usually must pay 30% more if you stay fewer than three nights.

For more information, contact the **Association of Tourist Farms of Slovenia** (Združenje Turističnih Kmetij Slovenije; ☑041 435 528, 03-425 55 11; www.farmtourism.si; Trnoveljska cesta 1) or check out the Slovenian Tourist Board's *Friendly Countryside* brochure, which lists upwards of 300 farms with accommodation.

Hostels & Student Dormitories

Slovenia has a growing stable of excellent hostels including Ljubljana's trendy **Celica** (Map p38; ☑230 97 00; www.hostelcelica.com; Metelkova ulica 8; dm €17-21, dm €19-25, s/d/tr cell €53/60/70; P @ 🛜), the **MCC** (Map p186; ☑490 87 42; www.hostel-celje.com; Mariborska cesta 2; s/d €29/36, dm €18; 🛜) in Celje, the **Situla** (Map p148; ☑394 20 00; www.situla.si; Dilančeva ulica 1; dm €13.50-19, d €35-60, s/tr/q €25/57/76; P @ 🛜) in Novo Mesto and the **Pekarna** (☑059 180 880; www.mkc-hostelpekarna.si; Ob železnici 16; dm/s/d €17/21/42; 🛜) in Maribor. Throughout the country there are *dijaški dom* (college dormitories) or *študentski dom* (student residences) moonlighting as hostels for visitors in July and August. Unless stated otherwise hostel rooms share bathrooms. Hostels usually cost from €15 to €26; prices are at their highest in July and August and during the Christmas break.

Some three dozen hostels nationwide are registered or affiliated with the Maribor-based **Hostelling International Slovenia** (Popotniško Združenje Slovenije; ☎ 02-234 21 37; www.youth-hostel.si; Gosposvetska cesta 84). In Ljubljana contact Erazem. You are not required to have a Hostelling International (HI) card to stay at hostels in Slovenia, but it sometimes earns a discount or cancellation of the tourist tax.

Hotels

Rates at Slovenia's hotels vary seasonally, with July and August the peak season and September/October and May/June the shoulder ones. Ski resorts such as Kranjska Gora and Maribor Pohorje also have a peak season from December to March. In Ljubljana prices are generally constant throughout the year, though weekends are often cheaper at top-end hotels. Many resort hotels, particularly on the coast, are closed in winter.

Mountain Huts

Mountain huts are ranked according to category in Slovenia. A hut is Category I if it is at a height of over 1000m and is more than one hour from motorised transport. A Category II hut is within one hour's walking distance from motorised transport. A Category III hut can be reached by car or cable car directly.

A bed for the night runs from €18 to €27 in a Category I hut, depending on the number of beds in the room, and from €12 to €20 in a Category II. Category III huts are allowed to set their own prices but usually cost less than Category I huts.

Pensions & Guesthouses

Pensions and guesthouses go by several names in Slove-

nia. A *penzion* is, of course, a pension, but more commonly it's called a *gostišče* – a rustic restaurant with *prenočišče* (accommodation) attached. They're more expensive than hostels but cheaper than hotels, and might be your only option in small towns and villages. Generally speaking, a *gostilna* serves food and drink only, but some might have rooms as well. The distinction between a *gostilna* and a *gostišče* isn't very clear – even to most Slovenes.

Private Rooms & Apartments

You'll find private rooms and apartments through tourist offices and travel agencies in most towns. The Slovenian Tourist Board's brochure *Rates for Accommodation in Private Rooms and Apartments* provides photos and the location of the house along with rates.

You don't have to go through agencies or tourist offices; any house with a sign reading 'Sobe' or 'Zimmer frei' means that rooms are available. Depending on the season, you might save yourself a little money by going directly.

In Slovenia, *registered* private rooms and apartments are rated from one to four stars. Prices vary greatly according to the town and season, but typical rates range from around €15 to

€30 for a single and €25 to €40 for a double.

The price quoted is usually for a minimum stay of three nights. If you're staying a shorter time, you'll have to pay 30% and sometimes as much as 50% more the first night and 20% to 30% extra the second. The price never includes breakfast (from €4 to €6 when available) or tourist tax.

Some agencies and tourist offices also have holiday apartments available that can accommodate up to six people. One for two/four people could go for as low as €35/50.

Business Hours

» The *delovni čas* (opening times) are usually posted on the door. *Odprto* is 'open', *zaprto* is 'closed'.

» Grocery stores and supermarkets usually open from 8am to 7pm weekdays and 8am until 1pm on Saturday. In winter they may close an hour earlier. Some branches of Mercator supermarket open Sunday mornings.

» Restaurant hours vary tremendously but essentially are from 10am or 11am to 10pm or 11pm daily. Bars are equally variable but are usually open 11am to midnight Sunday to Thursday and to 1am or 2am on Friday and Saturday.

» Bank hours are generally from 8am or 8.30am to 5pm weekdays (often with a lunchtime break from 12.30pm to 2pm) and (rarely) from 8am until noon or 1pm on Saturday.

» The main post office in any city or town opens from 8am to 6pm or 7pm weekdays and 8am until noon or 1pm on Saturday.

» Museums are usually open from 10am to 6pm Tuesday to Sunday. Winter hours may be shorter (sometimes weekends only) outside the big cities and towns.

PRACTICALITIES

» The metric system is used for weights and measures.

» Plug your hair dryer or laptop into a standard European adapter with two round pins before connecting to the electricity supply (220V, 50Hz AC).

» Stay up to date with the following: **Slovenia Times** (www.sloveniatimes.com), a fortnightly English-language magazine usually distributed for free; **Sinfo** (www.ukom.gov.si), a free government-produced monthly magazine about Slovenian politics, environment, culture, business and sport; and **Slovenian Business Report** (www.sbr.si), a quarterly publication with a cover price of €12 but usually available for free at top-end hotels.

» Listen to the news bulletin broadcast in English year-round at 10.30pm on Radio Slovenija 1 (88.5, 90.0, 90.9, 91.8, 92.0, 92.9, 94.1, 96.4 MHz FM and 918 kHz AM). In July and August Radio Slovenija 1 and Radio Slovenija 2 (87.8, 92.4, 93.5, 94.1, 95.3, 96.9, 97.6, 98.9 and 99.9 MHz FM) broadcast a weather report in English at 7.10am and Radio 2 broadcasts traffic conditions after each news bulletin from Friday afternoon to Sunday evening. In summer Radio Slovenia International (RSI) has hourly news bulletins in English and German on 91.1, 93.4, 98.9 and 102.8 MHz FM. Visit the **RTV Slovenija** (www.rtvslo.si) website.

Children

Travelling with children in Slovenia poses very few problems: they receive discounts on public transport and entry to museums and attractions; shops like DM, the nationwide German-owned health and cosmetic store with five dozen branches across the country, stock basic supplies for children; and the general public attitude to kids is enthusiastic. Outside upmarket hotels, babysitters are almost impossible to organise.

All car-rental firms in Slovenia have children's safety seats for hire for around €35 per rental; by law children must use such seats until age 12. Make sure you book them in advance. Likewise, book high chairs and cots (cribs); they're standard in some restaurants and hotels, but numbers are often limited.

When touring around don't try to overdo things; packing too much into the time available can cause problems. Although the **Slovenian Ethnographic Museum** (Slovenski Etnografski Muzej; Map p38; ☑300 87 45; www.etno-muzej.si; Metelkova ulica 2; adult/student & senior €4.50/2.50, last Sun of month admission free; ⏰10am-6pm Tue-Sun) in Ljubljana has

wonderful and very colourful hands-on exhibits for kids, balance a morning there with an afternoon at the **Ljubljana Zoo** (Živalski Vrt Ljubljana; www.zoo-ljubljana.si; Večna pot 70; adult/child €7/5; ⏰9am-7pm May-Aug, 9am-6pm Apr & Sep, 9am-5pm Mar & Oct, 9am-4pm Nov-Feb) on Rožnik Hill or at the huge **Atlantis water park** (☑585 21 00; www.atlantis-vodnomesto.si; BTC City, Šmartinska cesta 152; day pass adult/child Mon-Fri €14.60/12.30, Sat & Sun €16.70/14.50; ⏰9am-9pm Mon-Thu, 9am-10pm Fri-Sun) in the BTC City shopping mall. Include children in the trip planning; if they've helped to work out where you will be going, they'll be much more interested when they get there.

Lonely Planet's *Travel with Children* is a good source of information.

Customs Regulations

Duty-free shopping within the European Union was abolished in 1999, and Slovenia, as an EU member, adheres to those rules. You cannot buy tax-free goods in, say, Austria, Italy or Hungary and take them to Slovenia. However, you can still enter Slovenia

with duty-free items from countries outside the EU. The usual allowances apply: 200 cigarettes, 50 cigars, 100 cigarillos or 250g of loose tobacco; 2L of wine and 1L of spirits; 50g of perfume and 250cc of eau de toilette. The total value of the listed items must not exceed €175/90 for those over/under 15 years of age.

Discount Cards
Camping Card International

The **Camping Card International** (CCI; www.campingcardinternational.com) is available free from local automobile clubs, local camping federations such as the UK's **Caravan Club** (www.caravanclub.co.uk) and sometimes on the spot at selected campgrounds. They incorporate third-party insurance for damage you may cause, and many campgrounds in Slovenia offer discounts of 5% or 10% if you sign in with one. For a list, contact the **Caravaning Club Slovenije** (CCS; www.ccs-si.com)

Hostel Card

No hostel in Slovenia requires you to be a Hostelling International (HI) cardholder or a member of a related association, but they sometimes offer a discount if you are. **Hostelling International Slovenia** (Popotniško Združenje Slovenije; 🖉02-234 21 37; www.youth-hostel.si; Gosposvetska cesta 84) in Maribor sells hostel cards for those aged up to 15 (€5.50), 16 to 29 (€7.50) and over 30 (€9.20).

Student, Youth & Teacher Cards

The **International Student Identity Card** (ISIC; www.isic.org; €10) provides bona fide students many discounts on certain forms of transport and cheap admission to museums and other sights. If you're aged under 26 but not a student, you can apply for ISIC's International Youth Travel Card (IYTC; €10) or the Euro<26 card (€17) issued by the European Youth Card Association (EYCA), both of which offer the same discounts as the student card. Teachers can apply for the International Teacher Identity Card (ITIC; €12).

Electricity

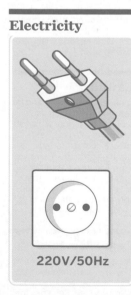

220V/50Hz

Embassies & Consulates

Australian Consulate (🖉01-425 42 52; Dunajska cesta 50, Ljubljana; ◷9am-1pm Mon-Fri)

Austrian Embassy (🖉01-479 07 00; Prešernova cesta 23, Ljubljana; ◷8am-noon Mon-Thu, 8-10am Fri) Enter from Veselova ulica.

Canadian Consulate (🖉01-252 44 44; 12th fl, Trg Republike 3, Ljubljana; ◷9am-noon Mon-Fri)

Croatia Embassy (🖉01-425 62 20; Gruberjevo nabrežje 6, Ljubljana; ◷9am-1pm Mon-Fri)

Croatian Consulate (🖉02-234 66 86; Trg Svobode 3, Maribor; ◷10am-1pm Mon-Fri)

French Embassy (🖉01-479 04 00; Barjanska cesta 1, Ljubljana; ◷8.30am-12.30pm Mon-Fri)

German Embassy (🖉01-479 03 00; Prešernova cesta 27, Ljubljana; ◷9am-noon Mon-Thu, 9-11am Fri)

Hungarian Embassy (🖉01-512 18 82; Ulica Konrada Babnika 5, Ljubljana; ◷8am-5pm Mon-Fri)

Irish Embassy (🖉01-300 89 70; 1st fl, Palača Kapitelj, Poljanski nasip 6, Ljubljana; ◷9.30am-12.30pm & 2.30-4pm Mon-Fri)

Italian Embassy (🖉01-426 21 94; Snežniška ulica 8, Ljubljana; ◷9-11am Mon-Fri)

Italian Consulate (🖉05-627 37 49; Belvedere 2, Koper; ◷9-11am Mon-Fri)

Dutch Embassy (🖉01-420 14 61; 1st fl, Palača Kapitelj, Poljanski nasip 6, Ljubljana; ◷9am-noon Mon-Fri)

New Zealand Consulate (🖉580 30 55; Verovškova ulica 57, Ljubljana; ◷8am-3pm Mon-Fri)

South African Consulate (🖉200 63 00; Pražakova ulica 4, Ljubljana; ◷3-4pm Tue) In Kompas building.

UK Embassy (🖉01-200 39 10; 4th fl, Trg Republike 3, Ljubljana; ◷9am-noon Mon-Fri)

American Embassy (🖉01-200 55 00; Prešernova cesta 31; ◷9-11.30am & 1-3pm Mon-Fri)

Food & Drink

Slovenia has a highly developed cuisine. For more on food and wine in Slovenia, see The Slovenian Table (p224).

Gay & Lesbian Travellers

Slovenia has no sodomy laws. There's a national gay rights law in place that bans discrimination in employment and other areas on the basis of sexual preference, and homosexuals are allowed in the military. In recent years a highly visible campaign against homophobia has been put in place across the country. Outside Ljubljana, however, there is little evidence of a gay presence, much less a lifestyle.

Roza Klub (Klub K4; Map p38; 🖉438 02 61; www.klubk4.org; Kersnikova ulica 4; ◷10pm-6am Sun Sep-Jun) in Ljubljana is made up of the gay and lesbian branches of **KUC** (www.skuc.org), which stands for Študentski Kulturni Center (Student Cultural Centre) but is no

---

EATING PRICE RANGES

The following price ranges refer to a two-course, sit-down meal, including a drink, for one person.

€ < €15

€€ €16–30

€€€ > €31

Many restaurants offer an excellent-value set menu of two or even three courses at lunch.

longer student-orientated as such. It organises the gay and lesbian **Ljubljana Pride parade** (www.ljubljanapride. org) in late June and the **Gay & Lesbian Film Festival** (www.ljudmila.org/siqrd/fglf) in late November/early December. The gay male branch, **Magnus** (skucmag nus@hotmail.com), deals with AIDS prevention, networking and is behind the Kulturni Center Q (Q Cultural Centre) in Ljubljana's **Metelkova Mesto** (Metelkova Town; Map p38; www.metelkova.org; Masarykova cesta 24), which includes Klub Tiffany for gay men and Klub Monokel for gay women. Lesbians can contact the Ljubljana-based (and ŠKUC-affiliated) **LL** (www.ljudmila.org/lesbo) through the latter.

The website of the **Slovenian Queer Resources Directory** (www.ljudmila.org/siqrd) contains a lot of stuff, both serious and recreational, but is in Slovene only. Much more up to date and reliable for entertainment venues and parties is the **Slovenia for Gay Travelers** (www.sloveniaforgaytravel ers.com) website. **Out in Slovenia** (www.outinslovenija .com), the first sports and recreational group for gays and lesbians in Slovenia, is where to go for the latest on outdoor activities and events. **Narobe** (Upside Down; www.narobe.si), a monthly publication, is in Slovene only, though you might be able to at least glean from the listings.

It's not a helpline as such but for advice ring **Mavrična Svetovalnica** (Rainbow Counselling; ☑031 258 685; ☺6-8pm Mon, Wed & Fri).

Insurance

A travel insurance policy to cover theft, loss and medical problems is a good idea. There is a wide variety of policies available, so check the small print. EU citizens on public health insurance

schemes should note that they're generally covered by reciprocal arrangements in Slovenia.

Some insurance policies specifically exclude 'dangerous activities', which can include motorcycling and even trekking, so check the small print.

You may prefer a policy that pays doctors or hospitals directly rather than you having to pay on the spot and claim later. If you have to claim later, make sure you keep all documentation. Some policies ask you to call back (reverse charges) to a centre in your home country, where an immediate assessment of your problem can be made. Check that the policy covers ambulances or an emergency flight home.

Paying for your airline ticket with a credit card often provides limited travel accident insurance, and you may be able to reclaim the payment if the operator doesn't deliver. Ask your credit-card company what it will cover.

Internet Access

Virtually every hotel and hostel in the land now has internet access – a computer for guests' use (free or for a small fee), wi-fi or both. Most of the country's tourist information centres offer free (or very cheap) access, many libraries in Slovenia have free terminals, and most cities and towns have at least one internet cafe (though they usually only have a handful of terminals), or even free wi-fi in town squares.

If you want to get online anywhere, you can get a Paket Mobi USB modem for your laptop for €15, with monthly connection fees from €29.

Language Courses

The most famous and prestigious place to learn Slovene is the **Centre for Slovene**

as a Second/Foreign Language (Center za Slovenščino kot Drugi/Tuji Jezik; Map p44; ☑01-241 86 47; www.centerslo. net; Kongresni trg 12) at the University of Ljubljana. There are a number of courses available, including two- and four-week summer ones in July of 30 and 80 hours respectively for €270 and €580, and an intensive 12-week course (220 hours; €1300). Prices exclude room and board. The centre also sponsors free 1½-hour introductory lessons in Slovene for tourists at 5pm on Wednesday from May to September at the **Slovenian Tourist Information Centre** (STIC; ☑306 45 76; www. slovenia.info; Krekov trg 10; ☺8am-9pm Jun-Sep, 8am-7pm Oct-May) in Ljubljana.

Private schools offering courses in Slovene in Ljubljana include the academic **Miklošič Educational Centre** (Map p38; ☑01-230 76 02; www.ism.si; Miklošičeva cesta 26), with courses of 30/85 hours starting at €240/590, and **Mint International House Ljubljana** (Map p38; ☑01-300 43 00; www.mint. si; 1st fl, Kersnikova ulica 1), with courses of 51/63 hours costing from €277/333. Individual lessons cost from €33 an hour.

Laundry

Launderettes are few and far between. The best place to seek out do-it-yourself washers and dryers is at hostels, college dormitories and camping grounds. There are a few expensive commercial laundries in Ljubljana that will do your laundry reasonably quickly; hotel laundry services are more costly.

Legal Matters

Persons violating the laws of Slovenia, even unknowingly, may be expelled, arrested or imprisoned. Penalties for possession, use or trafficking

ADDRESSES & PLACE NAMES

Streets in Slovenian towns and cities are well signposted, although the numbering system can be a bit confusing with odd and even numbers sometimes running on the same sides of streets and squares.

In small towns and villages, streets are usually not named and houses are just given numbers. Thus Ribčev Laz 13 is house No 13 in the village of Ribčev Laz on Lake Bohinj. As Slovenian villages are frequently made up of one road with houses clustered on or just off it, this is seldom confusing.

Places with double-barrelled names such as Novo Mesto (New Town) and Črna Gora (Black Hill) start the second word in lower case (Novo mesto, Črna gora) in Slovene, almost as if the names were Newtown and Blackhill. This is the correct Slovene orthography, but we've opted to go with the English-language way of doing it to avoid confusion.

Slovene frequently uses the possessive (genitive) case in street names. Thus a road named after the poet Ivan Cankar is Cankarjeva ulica and a square honouring France Prešeren is Prešernov trg. Also, when nouns are turned into adjectives they often become unrecognisable. The town is 'Bled', for example, but 'Bled Lake' is Blejsko Jezero. A street leading to a castle (grad) is usually called Grajska ulica. A road going in the direction of Trieste (Trst) is Tržaška cesta, Klagenfurt (Celovec) is Celovska cesta and Vienna (Dunaj) is Dunajska cesta. The words 'pri', 'pod' and 'na' in place names mean 'at the', 'below the' and 'on the' respectively.

---

of illegal drugs in Slovenia are strict, and convicted offenders can expect heavy fines and even jail terms. The permitted blood-alcohol level for motorists is 0.05%, and it is strictly enforced, especially on motorways. The age of consent for all sexual activity (ie heterosexual and homosexual) is 15 years.

Money

» Slovenia uses the euro as its legal tender.

» One euro is divided into 100 cents. There are seven euro notes, in denominations of €5, €10, €20, €50, €100, €200 and €500. The designs on the recto (generic windows or portals) and verso (imaginary bridges, a map of the EU) are exactly the same in all 15 countries and symbolise openness and cooperation.

» The eight coins in circulation are in denominations of €1 and €2, then one, two, five, 10, 20 and 50 cents. The 'heads' side of the coin, on which the denomination is shown, is identical throughout the euro zone; the 'tails' side is particular to each

member-state, though euro coins can be used anywhere where euros are legal tender, of course.

» In Slovenia, the €1 coin (silver centre with brassy outer ring) portrays the Protestant reformer and translator Primož Trubar (1508–86) and the Latin inscription *Stati Inu Obstati* (To Exist and Persevere). The verso of the €2 coin (brassy centre ringed with silver) shows the poet France Prešeren (1800–49) and a line from his poem 'Zdravljica' ('A Toast'), which forms part of the Slovenian national anthem.

» On the three lowest-denomination coins – €0.01, €0.02 and €0.05 (all copper) – are a stork, the stone where the 8th-century Carantanian dukes were installed, and *The Sower* by painter Ivan Grohar (1867–1911). The other three coins are brass. On the €0.10 coin is a design for a parliament by architect Jože Plečnik (1872–1957) that was never built and the words 'Katedrala Svobode' (Cathedral of Freedom). The €0.20 coin features a pair of Lipizzaner horses prancing. The stunning and very symbolic

€0.50 coin shows Mt Triglav, the Cancer constellation (under which independent Slovenia was born) and the words 'Oj Triglav moj dom' ('O Triglav, my home').

ATMs

Automated teller machines (ATMs) – called *bančni avtomat* – are ubiquitous throughout Slovenia. If you have a card linked to either the Visa/Electron/Plus or the MasterCard/Maestro/Cirrus network then you can withdraw euros anywhere. Both Abanka and SKB Banka ATMs are linked to both networks but some smaller banks only link to one or other of the networks.

Credit Cards

Visa, MasterCard/Eurocard and American Express credit cards are widely accepted at hotels, restaurants, shops, car-rental firms, petrol stations and travel agencies. Diner's Club is also accepted but less frequently.

Visa cardholders can get cash advances from any Abanka branch, Eurocard/MasterCard holders from a Nova Ljubljanska Banka or SKB Banka. American

Express clients can get an advance from the main office of **Atlas Express** (☎01-430 77 20; Slovenska cesta 56; ⏰8am-5pm Mon-Fri) in Ljubljana, but the amount is usually limited to €600 in travellers cheques for Green Card holders, €1200 for Gold Card holders and €3600 for Platinum Card holders. American Express customers who want to report a lost or stolen card or travellers cheques should also call here or on ☎01-568 0300. They can both replace cards (although you must know the account number) and make refunds for lost or stolen American Express travellers cheques.

If you have problems with your Visa card, call the **A Banka Visa Centre** (☎01-471 81 00) in Ljubljana. Eurocard and MasterCard holders should call **Nova Ljubljanska Banka** (☎476 39 00; www.nlb.si; Trg Republike 2; ⏰8am-6pm Mon-Fri) or **SKB Banka** (☎01-433 21 32). **Diners Club** (☎01-589 61 33) is based in Bežigrad, a northern suburb of Ljubljana.

Moneychangers

It is easy to change cash and travellers cheques at banks, post offices, tourist offices, travel agencies and private exchange offices. Look for the words *menjalnica* or *devizna blagajna* to guide you to the correct place or window. Most banks take a *provizija* (commission) of 1% on travellers cheques but usually nothing at all on cash. Tourist offices, travel agencies and exchange bureaus usually charge around 3%. Hotels can take as much as 5%.

Taxes & Refunds

Value-added tax (known as *davek na dodano vrednost* or DDV in Slovenia) is applied to the purchase of most goods and services at a standard rate of 20% (eg on alcoholic drinks, petrol and so on) and a reduced rate of 8.5% (eg on accommodation, food, books, museum entrance

fees etc). It is usually included in the quoted price of goods but not always.

Visitors who are not residents of the European Union can claim refunds on total purchases of around €65 (not including tobacco products or spirits) issued on one or more receipts by the same retailer/shop on the same day as long as they take the goods out of the country (and the EU) within 90 days. In order to make the claim, you must have a DDV-VP form or Global Tax-Free Shopping refund cheque correctly filled out by the salesperson at the time of purchase and have it stamped by a Slovenian customs officer at the border. You can then collect your refund – minus handling fee – from selected offices or have it deposited into your credit-card account. For information and the location of refund offices contact **Global Refund** (☎01-513 22 60; www.globalrefund.com; Goriška ulica 17) in Ljubljana.

TIPPING

When a gratuity is not included in your bill, which may or may not be the case, paying an extra 10% is customary. If service is outstanding, you could go as high as 15%. With taxi drivers, you usually just round up the sum.

Post

The Slovenian postal system (Pošta Slovenije), recognised by its bright yellow logo, offers a wide variety of services – from selling stamps and telephone cards to making photocopies and changing money. Newsstands also sell *znamke* (stamps). Post offices can sell you boxes.

Postal Rates

Domestic mail costs €0.20 to €0.30 for up to 20g depending on the size, €0.41 for up to 50g and €0.48 for up to 100g. Postcards are €0.26. For international mail, the

rate is €0.45 for 20g or less, €0.92 for up to 100g and €0.35 for a postcard.

Sending & Receiving Mail

» Look for the sign 'Pisma – Paketi' if you've got a *pismo* (letter) or *paket* (parcel) to post.

» *Poštno ležeče* (poste restante) is kept at the main post office of a city or town. In the capital, address it to Glavni Pošta, Slovenska cesta 32, 1101 Ljubljana, where it will be held for 30 days.

Public Holidays

Slovenia celebrates 14 *prazniki* (holidays) each year. If any of them fall on a Sunday, then the Monday becomes the holiday.

» **New Year's holidays** 1 & 2 January

» **Prešeren Day** (Slovenian Culture Day) 8 February

» **Easter & Easter Monday** March/April

» **Insurrection Day** 27 April

» **Labour Day holidays** 1 & 2 May

» **National Day** 25 June

» **Assumption Day** 15 August

» **Reformation Day** 31 October

» **All Saints Day** 1 November

» **Christmas Day** 25 December

» **Independence Day** 26 December

Although it's not a public holiday, St Martin's Day (11 November), the day that fermenting grape juice officially becomes new wine, is almost marked as such; just about everyone has a sip or three.

On the eve of St Gregory's Day (11 March), children in certain Gorenjska villages – Železniki is the most famous – set afloat hundreds of tiny boats bearing candles.

On Palm Sunday (the Sunday before Easter), people carry a complex arrangement of greenery, wood shavings and ribbons called a *butara* to church to be blessed. They end up as home decorations or are placed on the graves of relatives.

Many towns celebrate Midsummer's Night (Kresna Noč; 23 June) with a large bonfire, and St John's Eve (30 April) is the night for setting up maypoles and more bonfires. A *žegnanje* is a fair or celebration held on the feast day of a church's patron saint. Naturally a lot of them take place throughout Slovenia on 15 August, the feast of the Assumption of the Virgin Mary.

Safe Travel

Slovenia is not a violent or dangerous society. Police say that 90% of all crimes reported in Slovenia involve theft, so take the usual precautions. Be careful of your purse or wallet in busy areas like bus and train stations, and don't leave it unattended on the beach, or in a hut while hiking. Lock your car, park in well-lit areas and do not leave valuables visible. Bike theft is also on the increase. Secure it at all times.

Alcohol may not be purchased from a shop, off-license or bar for consumption off the premises between the hours of 9pm and 7am. You can drink to your heart's content in restaurants and bars.

Telephone

Public telephones require a *telefonska kartica* or *telekartica* (telephone card) available at post offices and some newsstands. Phonecards cost €2.70/4/7.50/14.60 for 25/50/100/300 *impulzov* (impulses, or units). A three-minute local call costs €0.09 during peak times (7am to 7pm weekdays) and €0.07 at off-peak times.

A three-minute call from Slovenia to Austria, Croatia, Italy or Hungary will cost €0.37; to much of Western

Europe, including the UK, as well as Canada and the USA, it's €0.42; to Australia €1.15; and to New Zealand, South Africa and most of Asia €1.71. Rates are 20% cheaper on most calls between 7pm and 7am every day. Slovenian call boxes do not display their telephone numbers, so it's impossible for the other party to phone you back.

To call Slovenia from abroad, dial the international access code, ☑386 (the country code for Slovenia), the area code (minus the initial zero) and the number. There are six area codes in Slovenia (☑01 to ☑05 and ☑07). To call abroad from Slovenia, dial ☑00 followed by the country and area codes and then the number. Numbers beginning with ☑80 are toll-free.

Mobile Phones

Network coverage amounts to more than 95% of the country. Mobile numbers carry the the prefix ☑030 and ☑040 (SiMobil), ☑031, ☑041, ☑051 and ☑071 (Mobitel), and ☑070 (Tušmobil).

Slovenia uses GSM 900, which is compatible with the rest of Europe and Australia but not with the North American GSM 1900 or the Japanese system. SIM cards with €5 credit are available for around €15 from **SiMobil** (www.simobil.si), **Mobitel** (www.mobitel.si) and **Tušmobil** (www.tusmobil.sil). Top-up scratch cards are available at post offices, newsstands and petrol stations.

All three networks have outlets throughout Slovenia, including in Ljubljana:

Mobitel Centre (Mobitelov Center; ☑01-472 24 76; www.

mobitel.si; Trg Ajdovščina 1; ⊘8am-8pm Mon-Fri, 8am-1pm Sat) Trubarjeva cesta (☑031 357 555; Trubarjeva cesta 40; ⊘9am-7pm Mon-Fri)

Simobil (Halo Centre; ☑01-430 01 77; www.simobil.si; Slovenska cesta 47; ⊘8am-7pm Mon-Fri) Čopova cesta (☑01-426 71 02; Čopova cesta 4; ⊘8am-7pm Mon-Fri, 9am-1pm Sat)

Tušmobil (☑01-600 6000; www.tusmobil.sil; Bratislavska cesta 9; ⊘9am-9pm Mon-Fri, 8am-9pm Sat, 9am-3pm Sun) In the BTC City shopping mall.

Time

Slovenia lies in the Central European time zone. Winter time is GMT plus one hour while in summer it's GMT plus two hours. Clocks are advanced at 2am on the last Sunday in March and set back at the same time on the last Sunday in October.

Like some other European languages, Slovene tells the time by making reference to the next hour – not the previous one as in English. Thus 1.15 is 'one-quarter of two', 1.30 is 'half of two' and 1.45 is 'three-quarters of two'.

Tourist Information

The **Slovenian Tourist Board** (Slovenska Turistična Organizacija | STO; ☑01-589 18 40; www.slovenia.info; Dunajska cesta 156) based in Ljubljana is the umbrella organisation for tourist promotion, and produces a number of excellent brochures, pamphlets and booklets in English.

USEFUL TELEPHONE NUMBERS

Domestic Directory Assistance (☑1188)

International Directory Assistance (☑1180)

International Operator/Collect Calls (☑115)

Time/Speaking Clock (in Slovene) (☑195)

Walk-in visitors in Ljubljana can head to the **Slovenian Tourist Information Centre** (STIC; ☑306 45 76; www.slovenia.info; Krekov trg 10; ☺8am-9pm Jun-Sep, 8am-7pm Oct-May). In addition, the STO oversees another five dozen or so local tourist offices and bureaus called 'tourist information centres' (TICs) across the country; there are smaller, independent or community-run offices in other cities and towns. In the unlikely even that the place you're visiting doesn't have either, seek assistance at a branch of one of the nationwide travel agencies (eg Kompas) or from hotel or museum staff.

The best office in Slovenia for face-to-face information is the **Ljubljana Tourist Information Centre** (TIC; ☑306 12 15; www.visitljubljana.si; Adamič-Lundrovo nabrežje 2; ☺8am-9pm Jun-Sep, 8am-7pm Oct-May) run by the Ljubljana Tourist Board (Zavod za Turizem Ljubljana). The staff know everything about the capital and almost as much about the rest of Slovenia. There's a branch at the train station.

Travellers with Disabilities

Facilities found throughout Slovenia include public telephones with amplifiers, pedestrian crossings with beepers, Braille on maps at city bus stops, occasional lifts in pedestrian underpasses, sloped pavements and ramps in government buildings, and reserved spaces in many car parks. An increasing number of hotels have at least one room designed especially for disabled guests

(bathrooms big enough for a wheelchair user to turn around in, access door on bath tubs, grip bars alongside toilets etc).

The **Paraplegics Association of Slovenia** (Zveza Paraplegikov Republike Slovenije; ☑01-432 71 38; www.zveza-paraplegikov.si; Štihova ulica 14) in Ljubljana looks after the interests and special needs of paraplegics and tetraplegics, and produces a guide for its members in Slovene only (although their English-language website is fairly complete). Another active group is the Ljubljana-based **Slovenian Association of Disabled Students** (Društvo Študentov Invalidov Slovenije; ☑01-565 33 51; www.dsis-drustvo.si; Kardeljeva ploščad 5). Some towns and cities produce useful brochures describing which local sights and attractions are accessible by wheelchair. Ask the TIC.

Visas

Virtually everyone entering Slovenia must have a valid passport, although citizens of the EU as well as Switzerland need only produce their national identity card on arrival for stays of up to 30 days. It's a good idea to carry your passport or other identification at all times.

Citizens of virtually all European countries as well as Australia, Canada, Israel, Japan, New Zealand and the USA do not require visas to visit Slovenia for stays of up to 90 days. Those who do require visas (including South Africans) can get them at any Slovenian embassy or consulate for up to 90 days. They cost €35 regardless of

the type or length of validity. You'll need confirmation of a hotel booking plus one photo and may have to show a return or onward ticket.

Your hotel, hostel, camping ground or private room arranged through an agency will register your name and address with the municipal *občina* (government) office as required by law. That's why they have to take your passport away – at least for the first night. If you are staying elsewhere (eg with relatives or friends), your host is supposed to take care of this for you within three days.

If you want to stay in Slovenia longer than three months, the easiest thing to do is simply cross the border into Croatia and return (it won't work with Austria, Italy or Hungary as they are all EU countries too). Otherwise you will have to apply for a temporary residence permit at the Ministry of the Interior's **Department for Foreigners** (Oddelek za Tujce; ☑01-306 32 61; Tobačna ulica 5; ☺8am-noon & 1-3pm Mon & Tue, 8am-noon & 1-6pm Thu, 8am-1pm Fri, 8am-noon Sat) just south of Park Tivoli in Ljubljana.

Women Travellers

Travelling as a single woman in Slovenia is no different from travelling in most Western European countries. If you can handle yourself in the very occasional less-than-comfortable situation, you'll be fine.

In the event of an emergency call the **police** (☑113) any time or the **SOS Helpline** (☑080 11 55; www.drustvo-sos.si; ☺noon-10pm Mon-Fri, 6-10pm Sat & Sun).

Transport

GETTING THERE & AWAY

Entering the Country

Border formalities with Slovenia's fellow European Union neighbours – Italy, Austria and Hungary – are now virtually nonexistent. Croatia is entering the EU in July 2013 and plans to implement the Schengen border rules soon after. Until then expect a somewhat closer inspection of your documents – national ID (for EU citizens) or passport and, in some cases, a visa when travelling to/from Croatia.

Passport

Virtually everyone entering Slovenia must have a valid passport, although citizens of the EU as well as Switzerland need only produce their national identity card on arrival for stays of up to 30 days. It's a good idea to carry your passport or other identification at all times.

Air

Airports & Airlines

Slovenia's only international airport receiving regular scheduled flights is Ljubljana's **Jože Pučnik Airport** (LJU/Aerodrom Ljubljana; ☑04-206 19 81; www.lju-airport.si/eng; Zgornji Brnik 130a, Brnik)

at Brnik, 27km north of Ljubljana. In the arrivals hall there's a **Slovenia Tourist Information Centre desk** (STIC; ☉11am-11pm Mon, Wed & Fri, 10am-10pm Tue & Thu, 10.30am-10.30pm Sat, 12.30pm-12.30am Sun), a hotel-booking telephone and an ATM. Some nine car-rental agencies, including Atet, Avis, Budget, Europcar and Hertz, have outlets opposite the terminal.

From its base at Brnik, the Slovenian flag-carrier, **Adria Airways** (JP; ☑01-369 10 10, 080 13 00; www.adria -airways.com), serves some 20 European destinations on regularly scheduled flights. Adria connections include three or four daily from Munich, Frankfurt and Zürich; daily from Amsterdam and London (Luton); and useful connections to other former Yugoslav capitals.

Other airlines with regularly scheduled flights to and from Ljubljana include:
Air France (AF; ☑01-244 34 47; www.airfrance.com/si) Daily flights to Paris (CDG).
ČSA Czech Airlines (OK; ☑04-206 17 50; www.czechair lines.com) Flights to Prague.
EasyJet (EZY; ☑04-206 16 77; www.easyjet.com) Low-cost daily flights to London Stansted.
Finnair (AY; ☑in Helsinki 358-9-818 888; www.finnair.com) Flights to Helsinki.
Lufthansa (LH; ☑01-434 72 46; www.lufthansa.com; Gosposvetska cesta 6) Code-shared flights with Adria.

CLIMATE CHANGE & TRAVEL

Every form of transport that relies on carbon-based fuel generates CO_2, the main cause of human-induced climate change. Modern travel is dependent on aeroplanes, which might use less fuel per kilometre per person than most cars but travel much greater distances. The altitude at which aircraft emit gases (including CO_2) and particles also contributes to their climate change impact. Many websites offer 'carbon calculators' that allow people to estimate the carbon emissions generated by their journey and, for those who wish to do so, to offset the impact of the greenhouse gases emitted with contributions to portfolios of climate-friendly initiatives throughout the world. Lonely Planet offsets the carbon footprint of all staff and author travel.

JAT Airways (JU; ☎01-231 43 40; www.jat.com) Daily flights to Belgrade.

Montenegro Airlines (YM; ☎04-259 42 52; www.mon tenegroairlines.com) Twice weekly flight to Podgorica.

Turkish Airlines (TK; ☎04-206 16 80; www.turkishairlines. com) Flights to Istanbul.

Land

Slovenia is well connected by road and rail with its four neighbours – Italy, Austria, Hungary and the Balkans. Bus and train timetables sometimes use Slovenian names for foreign cities.

Bus

Most international buses arrive and depart from **Ljubljana bus station** (Avtobusna Postaja Ljubljana; ☎234 46 00; www.ap-ljubljana. si; Trg Osvobodilne Fronte 4; ⏱5.30am-10.30pm Sun-Fri, 5am-10pm Sat).

CROATIA, BOSNIA & HERCEGOVINA, & SERBIA

Koper, Piran and Portorož are the ports of entry from Croatian Istria and points further south by bus. A bus leaves Koper daily on Monday and Friday at 10.10am for Rijeka (€12.50, two hours) and there are buses at 7.30am weekdays and again at 2pm daily to Pula (€16.50, 2½ hours) via Poreč, Umag and Rovinj.

From Ljubljana count on at least two daily departures to Belgrade, Serbia (€38.70 to €40.70, eight hours). Buses depart from Ljubljana daily for Rijeka (€16.70 to €25.70, 2½ hours) and Split (€43.20, 10 hours) in Croatia, where you can change for Dubrovnik (€20.40, 4½ hours). There are also daily buses to Sarajevo in Bosnia & Hercegovina (€44.70 to €48.70, 9½ to 12 hours) and Banja Luka (€27.20, 5½ hours).

ITALY

Buses from Koper to Trieste (€3, one hour) run along the coast via Ankaran and Muggia Monday to Saturday. There's a direct year-round service from Ljubljana to Trieste (€11.60, 2½ hours). Two daily buses at 5.10am and 8.15am link Ljubljana with Mestre (€25, four hours) near Venice.

Hourly buses link the train stations in the Italian city of Gorizia with Nova Gorica (€1, 25 minutes) just across the border.

GERMANY & AUSTRIA

From Germany, **Deutsche Touring** (☎in Frankfurt 069-790 35 01; www.deutsche -touring.com) operates a daily overnight bus between Frankfurt and Ljubljana (adult one way/ return €90/139, under 26 & student one way/return €81/125, 11½ hours), via Stuttgart, Ulm and Munich. The northbound bus leaves Ljubljana on Thursday, Friday and Saturday.

There's a daily overnight bus from Maribor across Austria to Munich, Stuttgart and Frankfurt (€95, 14 hours).

HUNGARY

The Hungarian town of Rédics is only 7km to the north of Lendava, in northeastern Slovenia, which can be reached from Murska Sobota (€3.60, 30 minutes, 29km). Two buses a day link Murska Sobota and Ljubljana (€16, four hours). From Rédics, trains go to Zalaegerszeg (795Ft, 1¼ hours) for connections to Budapest.

Car & Motorcycle

Slovenia maintains some 150 border crossings with its neighbours, but not all are open to citizens of 'third countries' (ie those not from either side). On country maps and atlases, those marked with a circle and a line are international ones; those with just a circle are local ones.

Train

Slovenian Railways (Slovenske Železnice, SŽ; ☎01-291 33 32; www.slo-zeleznice.si) links up with the European railway network via Austria (Villach, Salzburg, Graz, Vienna), Germany (Munich, Frankfurt), Czech Republic (Prague), Croatia (Zagreb, Rijeka), Hungary (Budapest), Italy (Venice), Switzerland (Zürich) and Serbia (Belgrade).

International direct trains include EuroCity (EC) ones linking Ljubljana with Vienna as well as Salzburg and Munich. InterCity (IC) trains connect Maribor with Vienna and Graz, and Ljubljana with Villach, Zagreb and Belgrade. Express trains run via Ljubljana between Zürich and Belgrade, Vienna and Zagreb, Munich and Zagreb, and Munich and Rijeka. EuroNight (EN) between Budapest and Venice go via Ljubljana and Zagreb.

Seat reservations (€3.50), compulsory only on trains to and from Italy, are included in the ticket price. On night trains, sleepers and couchettes are available.

DISCOUNTS & PASSES

Undiscounted international tickets on Slovenian Railways trains are valid for two months. Certain fares bought at special offer are valid for one month, while others are valid only for the day and train indicated on the ticket. Half-price tickets are available to children between the ages of six and 12 years.

A Global Pass from **InterRail** (www.interrailnet.com) covers some 30 European countries and can be purchased by nationals of European countries (or residents of at least six months). A pass offers 1st-/2nd-class travel for five days within a 10-day period (€289/219), 10 days within a 22-day period (€429/315), 22 continuous days (€549/409), or one month (€709/525). Discounts are available for those under 26.

InterRail now offers a 'One Country Pass' valid for rail travel in Slovenia only.

ROAD DISTANCES (KM)

	Bled	Bovec	Celje	Črnomelj	Koper	Kranj	Kranjska Gora	Ljubljana	Maribor	Murska Sobota	Nova Gorica	Novo Mesto	Postojna	Ptuj
Bovec	83													
Celje	131	207												
Črnomelj	147	223	130											
Koper	156	161	185	193										
Kranj	27	102	105	123	131									
Kranjska Gora	39	45	161	178	186	58								
Ljubljana	59	134	76	93	107	33	89							
Maribor	181	257	54	198	234	156	212	126						
Murska Sobota	245	320	118	266	298	219	275	189	64					
Nova Gorica	156	72	185	193	90	131	168	107	236	299				
Novo Mesto	127	202	95	32	171	101	157	69	151	246	173			
Postojna	102	131	131	139	59	77	133	53	182	245	60	118		
Ptuj	184	260	58	179	237	159	215	129	29	64	238	148	183	
Slovenj Gradec	164	188	50	191	217	138	185	108	71	135	218	146	163	75

It would be impossible for a standard **Eurail pass** (www.eurailnet.com) to pay for itself in Slovenia. But if you are a non-European resident, you may consider one of its combination tickets allowing you to travel over a fixed period for a set price. These include the Hungary N' Slovenia/ Croatia and Austria N' Slovenia/Croatia passes, offering five/10 days of travel within two months on those countries' rail networks for adults US$258/421 and youths US$214/349; children aged four to 11 travel half-price. Buy the pass before you leave home.

CROATIA, BOSNIA & HERCEGOVINA, & SERBIA

From Croatia, there are seven trains a day to Ljubljana from Zagreb via Zidani Most (€12.20, two hours, 141km), two a day from Rijeka (€12.60, two hours, 135km) via Postojna, and five a day from Split (€47.80, eight to 12 hours, 456km), with a change at Zagreb. There are five trains a day from Belgrade, Serbia (€44.20, nine to 10 hours, 569km) via

Zagreb. There are also two trains a day from Sarajevo in Bosnia & Hercegovina (€43.20, 12 hours, 670km) with a change at Zagreb.

ITALY

The EN *Venezia* runs between Ljubljana and Venice (four hours) and though the normal one-way fare is €25, there's also a few Smart Price tickets available for €15 on some trains. Another possibility is to go first to Nova Gorica (€8, three hours), walk to Gorizia then take an Italian train to Venice (about €8).

GERMANY & AUSTRIA

There are three direct trains a day between Ljubljana and Munich (€72.40, six hours) via Villach and Salzburg; one carries on to Frankfurt (€144.40, 10 hours). There is also a train from Salzburg (€19, four hours) to Ljubljana and another from Villach (€18.20, two hours).

To get to Vienna (€61.80, six hours) from Ljubljana there is the direct EC *Emona*, or five other trains which require a change at Maribor. Graz (€31.40, three hours)

trains include a change at Maribor.

While fares to Vienna and Graz from Ljubljana and Maribor are high, so-called SparSchiene fares as low as €19 (valid for travel in one direction in 2nd class) apply on certain trains at certain times. Also, a *Praga Spezial* fare is available for only €29 to those travelling to Prague via Salzburg, but the number of these discounted tickets per train is limited.

HUNGARY

The EN *Venezia* links Ljubljana with Budapest (€49.80, nine hours) via Zagreb. The IC *Citadella* goes via Ptuj and Hodoš. There are Budapest Spezial fares available for as low as €29/39 one way/ return on certain trains and at certain times.

SWITZERLAND

The overnight MV414/415 links Ljubljana directly with Zürich (€89.60, 14½ hours) via Schwarzach-St Veit; the *SparSchiene* (€29) and *SparNight* (with couchette €39) offer enormous savings on the standard fare.

Sea

The **Prince of Venice** (☏05-617 80 00; www.kompas-online.net) is a 39.6m-long, high-speed catamaran that runs day trips between Izola and Piran and Venice from April to October. It departs Izola at 8am (Piran at 7.30am) and arrives in Venice at 11am; the return journey departs at 5pm and arrives back at Izola/Piran at 8pm. The schedule changes according to the season, but essentially there are sailings on Saturday from mid-April to October, with between seven and 15 sailings a week from May to September. Less-frequent sailings to/from Piran are between late June and mid-September. An adult return ticket costs €50 to €65 (children aged three to 14 pay half-price) depending on the season and day, including a tour of Venice. There are various family packages available. An adult one way costs €35 to €45. Tickets can be purchased at **Kompas** (www.kompas.si) and various other travel agencies along the coast.

From late May to late September, **Venezia Lines** (☏in Italy 039 41 272 2646; www.venezialines.com) runs a similar service from Piran, departing at 8.30am and returning at 7.30pm on selected Wednesdays, Thursdays and Saturdays. Tickets, which cost from €46/89 one way/return for adults (children aged three to 13 pay half-price), are available through several travel agencies in Piran and Portorož, including **Maona Tourist Agency** (www.maona.si).

A third vessel, the 42m-long catamaran **Dora** (☏05-674 71 60; www.topline.si), sails from Piran to Venice at 8am on Saturday from early May to late September, returning at 5pm. The adult fare is €65, with children aged three to 13 paying half-price.

A service run by **Trieste Lines** (www.triestelines.it; one way/return €8.50/15.70) links Portorož and Trieste between one and four times a day from May to September. Buy tickets (one way/return €7.10/13.10) from the **Atlas Express** (☏674 67 72; atlas.portoroz@siol.net; Obala 55; ☻9am-4pm Mon-Fri, 10am-1pm Sat) in Portorož or the **TIC** (☏673 44 40, 673 02 20; www.portoroz.si; Tartinijev trg 2; ☻9am-8pm summer, 9am-5pm winter) in Piran.

GETTING AROUND

Air

Slovenia has no scheduled domestic flights, but a division of Adria Airways called **Aviotaxi** (☏041 636 420, 04-236 34 60; www.adria-airways.com) flies chartered four-seater Piper Turbo Arrows on demand to airports and aerodromes around the country. Sample return fares for three passengers from Brnik airport are €95 to Bled, €134 to Bled and Bohinj, €172 to Slovenj Gradec and €369 to Portorož or Maribor.

Bicycle

Cycling is a popular way of getting around. Bikes can be transported for €2.80 in the baggage compartments of IC and regional trains. Larger buses can also carry bikes as luggage. Cycling is permitted on all roads except motorways. Larger towns and cities have dedicated bicycle lanes and traffic lights.

Bicycle rental places are generally concentrated in the more popular tourist areas such as Ljubljana, Bled, Bovec and Piran, though a fair few cycle shops and repair places hire them out as well. Expect to pay from €1/5 per hour/day; some places may ask for a cash deposit or a piece of ID as security.

Bus

You can buy your ticket at the *avtobusna postaja* (bus station) or simply pay the driver as you board. In Ljubljana you should book your seat (€1.20/3.70 domestic/international) one day in advance if you're travelling on Friday, or to destinations in the mountains or on the coast on a public holiday. Bus services are severely restricted on Sunday and holidays (less so on Saturday).

A range of bus companies serve the country, but prices are uniform: €3.10/5.60/9.20/16.80 for 25/50/100/200km of travel.

Some bus stations have a *garderoba* (left-luggage office) and charge €2 per hour. They often keep bank hours; if it's an option, a better bet is to leave your things at the train station, which is usually nearby and keeps longer hours. If your bag has to go in the luggage compartment below the bus, it will cost €1.25 extra.

Timetables in the bus station, or posted on a wall or column outside, list all desti-

BUS TIMETABLE ABBREVIATIONS

D Monday to Friday

D+ Monday to Saturday

N Sunday

NP Sunday and holidays

So Saturday

SoNe Saturday and Sunday

SoNP Saturday, Sunday and holidays

Š Monday to Friday when schools are in session

ŠP Monday to Friday during school holidays

V Daily

nations and departure times. If you cannot find your bus listed or don't understand the schedule, get help from the *blagajna vozovnice* (information or ticket window), which are usually one and the same. *Odhodi* means 'departures' while *prihodi* is 'arrivals'.

Car & Motorcycle

Automobile Association

Slovenia's national automobile club is the **AMZS** (Avto-Moto Zveza Slovenije; ☑530 53 00; www.amzs.si; Dunajska cesta 128), based in Ljubljana. For emergency roadside assistance, call ☑19 87 anywhere in Slovenia. All accidents should be reported to the police on ☑113 immediately.

Driving Licence

Foreign driving licences are valid for one year after entering Slovenia. If you don't hold a European driving licence, obtain an International Driving Permit (IDP) from your local automobile association before you leave.

Fuel

Petrol stations are usually open from about 7am to 8pm Monday to Saturday, though larger towns have 24-hour services on the outskirts.

The price of *bencin* (petrol) is on par with the rest of Continental Europe: EuroSuper 95 costs around €1.50 per litre, with diesel at €1.40.

Hire

Renting a car in Slovenia allows access to cheaper out-of-centre hotels and farm or village homestays. Rentals from international firms such as Avis, Budget, Europcar and Hertz vary in price; expect to pay from €40/210 a day/week, including unlimited mileage, collision damage waiver (CDW), theft protection (TP), Personal Accident Insurance (PAI) and taxes. Some smaller agencies have

somewhat more competitive rates; booking on the internet is always cheaper.

Insurance

Third-party liability insurance is compulsory in Slovenia. If you enter the country in your own car and it is registered in the EU, you're covered. Other motorists must buy a **Green Card** (www.cobx.org) valid for Slovenia at the border.

Parking

You must pay to park in the centre of most Slovenian towns. 'Pay and display' parking coupons (from €0.30 per hour) are sold at vending machines (no change). In Ljubljana there are underground car parks where fees are charged (€1.50 to €1.70 for the first hour and €0.50 to €1.50 per hour after that depending on the time of day).

Road Conditions & Tolls

Roads in Slovenia are generally excellent. Driving in the Julian Alps can be hair-raising, with a gradient of up to 18% at the Korensko Sedlo Pass into Austria, and a series of 49 hairpin bends on the road over the Vršič Pass from Gorenjska into Primorska. Many mountain roads are closed in winter and some well into early spring. Motorways and highways are well signposted, but secondary and tertiary roads not always so; take a good map or GPS navigation device (available from car-rental agencies).

There are two main motorway corridors – between Maribor and the coast (via the impressive flyover at Črni Kal) and from the Karavanke Tunnel into Austria to Zagreb in Croatia – intersecting at the Ljubljana ring road, with a branch from Postojna to Nova Gorica. Motorways are numbered from A1 to A10.

Major international roads are preceded by an 'E'. The most important of these are

the E70 to Zagreb via Novo Mesto, the E61 to Villach via Jesenice and the Karavanke Tunnel, the E57 from Celje to Graz via Maribor, and the E59 from Graz to Zagreb via Maribor. National highways contain a single digit and link cities. Secondary and tertiary roads have three digits.

Private-car ownership is high so expect a lot of traffic congestion, especially in summer and on Friday afternoons when entire cities and towns head for the countryside.

Tolls are no longer paid separately on the motorways. Instead all cars must display a *vinjeta* (road-toll sticker) on the windscreen. They cost €15/30/95 for a week/month/full year for cars and €7.50/25/47.50 for motorbikes and are available at petrol stations, post offices and certain newsstands and tourist information centres. These stickers will already be in place on a rental car; failure to display such a sticker risks a fine of up to €300.

Road Rules

Drive on the right. Speed limits for cars and motorcycles (less for buses) are 50km/h in towns and villages, 90km/h on secondary and tertiary roads, 100km/h on highways and 130km/h on motorways.

Seat belts are compulsory, and motorcyclists must wear helmets. All motorists must illuminate their headlights throughout the day – not just at night. The permitted blood-alcohol level for drivers is 0.05%.

Hitching

Hitchhiking remains a popular way to get around for young Slovenes, and it's generally easy – except on Friday afternoon, before school holidays and on Sunday, when cars are often full of families. Hitching from bus stops is fairly common, otherwise use

National Rail Network

motorway access roads or other areas where the traffic will not be disturbed.

Hitching is never entirely safe in any country in the world, and we don't recommend it. Travellers who decide to hitch should understand that they are taking a small but potentially serious risk. People who do choose to hitch will be safer if they travel in pairs and should let someone know where they are planning to go. In particular, it is unwise for females to hitch alone; women are better off hitching with a male companion.

Train

Slovenian Railways (Slovenske Železnice, SŽ; ☏01-291 33 32; www.slo-zeleznice.si) runs trains on 1228km of track, about 40% of which is electrified. Very roughly, figure on covering about 60km/h to 65km/h except on the ICS express trains, which hurtle between Ljubljana and Maribor (€13.60, 1¾ hours) at an average speed of 90km/h. In the summer months an ICS train links Koper with Maribor (€23.80, four hours) via Ljubljana (€13.60, two hours).

» The provinces are served by *regionalni vlaki* (regional trains) and *primestni vlaki* (city trains), but the fastest are InterCity trains (IC).

» An 'R' next to the train number on the timetable means seat reservations are available. If the 'R' is boxed, seat reservations are obligatory.

» Purchase your ticket before travelling at the *železniška postaja* (train station) itself; buying it from the conductor on the train costs an additional €2.50. Invalid ticket or fare dodging earn a €40 fine.

» A *povratna vozovnica* (return ticket) costs double the price of a *enosmerna vozovnica* (a single ticket). A 1st-class ticket costs

TRAIN TIMETABLE SYMBOLS

⊗ Mon-Fri (except public holidays)

✗ Mon-Sat (except public holidays)

⊗ Mon-Sat and public holidays

Ⓥ Sat & Sun

Ⓥ Sat, Sun & public holidays

Ⓟ Sun and public holidays

7 No Sun service

† Public holidays

50% more than a 2nd-class one.

» Travelling by train in Slovenia is about 35% cheaper than going by bus. A 100km journey costs around €6 in 2nd class.

» You'll find luggage lockers at train stations in Celje, Divača, Koper, Ljubljana, Maribor, Nova Gorica, Postojna and Sežana. The daily charge is €2 to €8 according to locker size.

Train Timetables

Departures and arrivals are announced by loudspeaker or on an electronic board and are always on a printed timetable somewhere in the station. Those headed *Odhod* or *Odhodi Vlakov* are departures; *Prihod* or *Prihodi Vlakov* indicate arrival. Other useful words are *čas* (time), *peron* (platform), *sedež* (seat), *smer* (direction) and *tir* (rail).

Slovenian Railways (Slovenske Železnice, SŽ; ☑01-291 33 32; www.slo-zeleznice.si) have a useful online timetable, which includes fares. It's also possible to buy a hard copy, *Vozni Red Slovenske Železnice* (€4.20), or an abridged version listing main routes (€1).

Discounts & Passes

There's a 30% discount on return weekend fares and ICS fares.

Slovenian Railways sells the InterRail Country Pass Slovenia from **InterRail** (www.interrailnet.com), which is valid for rail travel in Slovenia only and available to residents of any European country (excluding Slovenia). The pass, which includes travel on ICS trains, is available for three/four/six/eight days of travel within one month for €63/78/104/122; those under 26 years of age pay €42/51/68/80.

Language

WANT MORE?

For in-depth language information and handy phrases, check out Lonely Planet's *Central Europe phrasebook*. You'll find it at **shop.lonelyplanet.com**, or you can buy Lonely Planet's iPhone phrasebooks at the Apple App Store.

Slovene belongs to the South Slavic language family, along with Croatian and Serbian (although it is much closer to Croatia's north-western and coastal dialects). It also shares some features with the more distant West Slavic languages through contact with a dialect of Slovak. Most adults speak at least one foreign language, often English, German or Italian.

If you read our coloured pronunciation guides as if they were English, you'll be understood. Note that oh is pronounced as the 'o' in 'note', ow as in 'how', uh as the 'a' in 'ago', zh as the 's' in 'pleasure', r is rolled, and the apostrophe (') indicates a slight y sound. The stressed syllables are indicated with italics.

The markers (m/f) and (pol/inf) indicate masculine and feminine forms, and polite and informal sentence options respectively.

BASICS

Hello.	*Zdravo.*	zdra·vo
Goodbye.	*Na svidenje.*	na svee·den·ye
Excuse me.	*Dovolite.*	do·vo·lee·te
Sorry.	*Oprostite.*	op·ros·tee·te
Please.	*Prosim.*	pro·seem
Thank you.	*Hvala.*	hva·la
You're welcome.	*Ni za kaj.*	nee za kai
Yes.	*Da.*	da
No.	*Ne.*	ne

What's your name?
Kako vam/ti
je ime? (pol/inf)
ka·ko vam/tee
ye ee·me

My name is ...
Ime mi je ...
ee·me mee ye ...

Do you speak English?
Ali govorite
angleško?
a·lee go·vo·ree·te
ang·lesh·ko

I don't understand.
Ne razumem.
ne ra·zoo·mem

ACCOMMODATION

campsite	*kamp*	kamp
guesthouse	*gostišče*	gos·teesh·che
hotel	*hotel*	ho·tel
youth hostel	*mladinski hotel*	mla·deen·skee ho·tel

Do you have a ... room?	*Ali imate ... sobo?*	a·lee ee·ma·te ... so·bo
cheap	*poceni*	po·tse·nee
double	*dvoposteljno*	dvo·pos·tel'·no
single	*enoposteljno*	e·no·pos·tel'·no

How much is it per ...?	*Koliko stane na ...?*	ko·lee·ko sta·ne na ...
night	*noč*	noch
person	*osebo*	o·se·bo

I'd like to share a dorm.
Rad/Rada bi delil/
delila spalnico. (m/f)
rad/ra·da bee de·leew/
de·lee·la spal·nee·tso

Is breakfast included?
Ali je zajtrk
vključen?
a·lee ye zai·tuhrk
vklyoo·chen

Can I see the room?
Lahko vidim sobo?
lah·ko vee·deem so·bo

| I'll have ... | Jaz bom ... | yaz bom ... |
| Cheers! | Na zdravje! | na zdrav·ye |

I'd like the ..., please.	Želim ..., prosim.	zhe·leem ... pro·seem
bill	račun	ra·choon
menu	jedilni list	ye·deel·nee leest

breakfast	zajtrk	zai·tuhrk
lunch	kosilo	ko·see·lo
dinner	večerja	ve·cher·ya

LANGUAGE DIRECTIONS

Question Words

How?	Kako?	ka·ko
How much/ many?	Koliko?	ko·lee·ko
What?	Kaj?	kai
When?	Kdaj?	gdai
Where?	Kje?	kye
Which?	Kateri/ Katera? (m/f)	ka·te·ree/ ka·te·ra
Who?	Kdo?	gdo
Why?	Zakaj?	za·kai

DIRECTIONS

Where's the ...?
Kje je ...? kye ye ...

What's the address?
Na katerem naslovu je? na ka·te·rem nas·lo·voo ye

Can you show me (on the map)?
Mi lahko pokažete (na zemljevidu)? mee lah·ko po·ka·zhe·te (na zem·lye·vee·doo)

How do I get to ...?
Kako pridem do ...? ka·ko pree·dem do ...

Is it near/far?
Ali je blizu/daleč? a·lee ye blee·zoo/da·lech

(Go) Straight ahead.
(Pojdite) Naravnost naprej. (poy·dee·te) na·rav·nost na·prey

Turn	Obrnite	o·buhr·nee·te
left/right	levo/desno	le·vo/des·no
at the ...	pri ...	pree ...
corner	vogalu	vo·ga·loo
traffic lights	semaforju	se·ma·for·yoo

behind	za/zadaj	za/za·dai
far (from)	daleč (od)	da·lech (od)
here	tu	too
in front of	spredaj	spre·dai
near (to)	blizu (do)	blee·zoo (do)
opposite	nasproti	nas·pro·tee
there	tam	tam

EATING & DRINKING

What is the house speciality?
Kaj je domača specialiteta? kai ye do·ma·cha spe·tsee·a·lee·te·ta

What would you recommend?
Kaj priporočate? kai pree·po·ro·cha·te

Do you have vegetarian food?
Ali imate vegetarijansko hrano? a·lee ee·ma·te ve·ge·ta·ree·yan·sko hra·no

Key Words

bottle	steklenica	stek·le·nee·tsa
breakfast	zajtrk	zai·tuhrk
cold	hladen	hla·den
delicatessen	delikatesa	de·lee·ka·te·sa
dinner	večerja	ve·cher·ya
food	hrana	hra·na
fork	vilica	vee·lee·tsa
glass	kozarec	ko·za·rets
hot	topel	to·pel
knife	nož	nozh
lunch	kosilo	ko·see·lo
market	tržnica	tuhrzh·nee·tsa
menu	jedilni list	ye·deel·nee list
plate	krožnik	krozh·neek
restaurant	restavracija	res·tav·ra·tsee·ya
spoon	žlica	zhlee·tsa
wine list	vinska karta	veen·ska kar·ta
with	z	zuh
without	brez	brez

Meat & Fish

beef	govedina	go·ve·dee·na
chicken	piščanec	peesh·cha·nets
clams	školjke	shkol'·ke
cod	oslič	os·leech
fish	riba	ree·ba
ham	šunka/ pršut	shoon·ka/ puhr·shoot
lamb	jagnjetina	yag·nye·tee·na
pork	svinjina	svee·nyee·na
poultry	perutnina	pe·root·nee·na
prawns	škampi	shkam·pee
squid	lignji	leeg·nyee

trout	*postrv*	pos·*tuhrv*
veal	*teletina*	te·*le*·tee·na

Fruit & Vegetables

apple	*jabolko*	ya·bol·ko
apricot	*marelica*	ma·re·lee·tsa
beans	*fižol*	fee·zhoh
carrots	*korenje*	ko·re·nye
cauliflower	*cvetača/ karfijola*	tsve·*ta*·cha/ kar·fee·*yo*·la
cherries	*češnje/ višnje*	chesh·nye/ veesh·nye
grapes	*grozdje*	groz·dye
hazelnuts	*lešniki*	lesh·nee·kee
orange	*pomaranča*	po·ma·*ran*·cha
peach	*breskev*	bres·kev
pear	*hruška*	hroosh·ka
peas	*grah*	grah
pineapple	*ananas*	a·na·nas
plum	*češplja*	chesh·plya
potatoes	*krompir*	krom·*peer*
pumpkin	*bučke*	booch·ke
raspberries	*maline*	ma·lee·ne
spinach	*špinača*	shpee·na·cha
strawberries	*jagode*	ya·go·de
walnuts	*orehi*	o·re·hee

Other

bread	*kruh*	krooh
butter	*maslo*	mas·lo
cheese	*sir*	seer
eggs	*jajca*	yai·tsa
pasta	*testenine*	tes·te·*nee*·ne
pepper	*poper*	po·per
rice	*riž*	reezh
salad	*solata*	so·*la*·ta
salt	*sol*	soh
soup	*juha*	yoo·ha
sugar	*sladkor*	slad·kor

Drinks

beer (lager)	*svetlo pivo*	svet·lo pee·vo
beer (stout)	*temno pivo*	tem·no pee·vo
coffee	*kava*	ka·va
juice	*sok*	sok
lemonade	*limonada*	lee·mo·*na*·da

milk	*mleko*	mle·ko
plum brandy	*slivovka*	slee·vov·ka
red wine	*črno vino*	chuhr·no vee·no
sparkling wine	*peneče vino*	pe·ne·che vee·no
tea	*čaj*	chai
water	*voda*	vo·da
white wine	*belo vino*	be·lo vee·no

EMERGENCIES

Help!	*Na pomoč!*	na po·*moch*
Go away!	*Pojdite stran!*	poy·*dee*·te stran
Call ...!	*Pokličite ...!*	pok·lee·chee·te ...
a doctor	*zdravnika*	zdrav·nee·ka
the police	*policijo*	po·lee·*tsee*·yo

I'm lost.
Izgubil/ Izgubila sem se. (m/f) eez·goo·*beew*/ eez·goo·*bee*·la sem se

I'm ill.
Bolan/Bolna sem. (m/f) bo·*lan/boh*·na sem

It hurts here.
Tukaj boli. too·kai bo·*lee*

I'm allergic to ...
Alergičen/ Alergična sem na ... (m/f) a·*ler*·gee·chen/ a·*ler*·geech·na sem na ...

Where are the toilets?
Kje je stranišče? kye ye stra·*neesh*·che

SHOPPING & SERVICES

Where is a/the ...?	*Kje je ...?*	kye ye ...
bank	*banka*	ban·ka
market	*tržnica*	tuhrzh·nee·tsa
post office	*pošta*	posh·ta
tourist office	*turistični urad*	too·rees·teech· nee oo·rad

Signs

Informacije	Information
Izhod	Exit
Moški	Men
Odprto	Open
Prepovedano	Prohibited
Stranišče	Toilets
Vhod	Entrance
Zaprto	Closed
Ženske	Women

yesterday	včeraj	vche·rai
today	danes	da·nes
tomorrow	jutri	yoo·tree

Monday	ponedeljek	po·ne·de·lyek
Tuesday	torek	to·rek
Wednesday	sreda	sre·da
Thursday	četrtek	che·tuhrt·tek
Friday	petek	pe·tek
Saturday	sobota	so·bo·ta
Sunday	nedelja	ne·de·lya

January	januar	ya·noo·ar
February	februar	fe·broo·ar
March	marec	ma·rets
April	april	a·preel
May	maj	mai
June	junij	yoo·neey
July	julij	yoo·leey
August	avgust	av·goost
September	september	sep·tem·ber
October	oktober	ok·to·ber
November	november	no·vem·ber
December	december	de·tsem·ber

Numbers

1	en	en
2	dva	dva
3	trije	tree·ye
4	štirje	shtee·rye
5	pet	pet
6	šest	shest
7	sedem	se·dem
8	osem	o·sem
9	devet	de·vet
10	deset	de·set
20	dvajset	dvai·set
30	trideset	tree·de·set
40	štirideset	shtee·ree·de·set
50	petdeset	pet·de·set
60	šestdeset	shest·de·set
70	sedemdeset	se·dem·de·set
80	osemdeset	o·sem·de·set
90	devetdeset	de·vet·de·set
100	sto	sto

I want to make a telephone call.
Rad/Rada bi telefoniral/ telefonirala. (m/f) — rad/ra·da bee te·le·fon·nee·row/ te·le·fon·nee·ra·la

Where can I get internet access?
Kje lahko dobim internet povezavo? — kye lah·ko do·beem een·ter·net po·ve·za·vo

I'd like to buy ...
Rad/Rada bi kupil/ kupila ... (m/f) — rad/ra·da bee koo·peew/ koo·pee·la ...

I'm just looking.
Samo gledam. — sa·mo gle·dam

Can I look at it?
Ali lahko pogledam? — a·lee lah·ko po·gle·dam

How much is this?
Koliko stane? — ko·lee·ko sta·ne

It's too expensive.
Predrago je. — pre·dra·go ye

TIME & DATES

What time is it?
Koliko je ura? — ko·lee·ko ye oo·ra

It's (one) o'clock.
Ura je (ena). — oo·ra ye (e·na)

half past seven
pol osem (literally 'half eight') — pol o·sem

| in the morning | zjutraj | zyoot·rai |
| in the evening | zvečer | zve·cher |

TRANSPORT

When does the ... leave?	Kdaj odpelje ...?	gdai od·pe·lye ...
boat	ladja	la·dya
bus	avtobus	av·to·boos
ferry	trajekt	tra·yekt
plane	avion	a·vee·on
train	vlak	vlak

One ... ticket to (Koper), please.	... vozovnico do (Kopra), prosim.	... vo·zov·nee·tso do (ko·pra) pro·seem
one-way	Enosmerno	e·no·smer·no
return	Povratno	pov·rat·no

1st/2nd class	prvi/drugi razred	puhr·vee/droo·gee raz·red
bus station	avtobusno postajališče	av·to·boos·no po·sta·ya·leesh·che
first/last	prvi/zadnji	puhr·vee/zad·nyee
ticket office	prodaja vozovnic	pro·da·ya vo·zov·neets
train station	železniška postaja	zhe·lez·neesh·ka pos·ta·ya

I want to go to ...
Želim iti ...   zhe·*leem* ee·tee ...

How long does the trip take?
Koliko traja   ko·*lee*·ko tra·ya
potovanje?   po·to·*va*·nye

Do I need to change?
Ali moram presesti?   a·lee mo·ram pre·ses·tee

Can you tell me when we get to ...?
Mi lahko poveste   mee lah·ko po·ves·te
kdaj pridemo ...?   gdai pree·de·mo ...

Stop here, please.
Ustavite tukaj,   oos·ta·vee·te too·kai
prosim.   pro·seem

I'd like to   Rad/Rada bi   rad/ra·da bee
hire a ...   najel/   na·yel/
                    najela ... (m/f) na·ye·la ...

bicycle   kolo   ko·lo

car   avto   av·to

motorcyle   motorno kolo   mo·tor·no ko·lo

Where's a service station?
Kje je bencinska   kye ye ben·*tseen*·ska
črpalka?   *chuhr*·pal·ka

I need a mechanic.
Potrebujem   po·tre·*boo*·yem
mehanika.   me·ha·nee·ka

PLACE NAMES & THEIR ALTERNATIVES

(C) Croatian, (Cz) Czech, (E) English, (G) German, (H) Hungarian, (I) Italian, (P) Polish

Beljak – Villach (G)
Benetke – Venice (E), Venezia (I)
Bizeljsko – Wisell (G)
Bohinj – Wochain (G)
Brežice – Rhain (G)
Budimpešta – Budapest (H)
Čedad – Cividale (I)
Celovec – Klagenfurt (G)
Celje – Cilli (G)
Cerknica – Cirkniz (G)
Črnomelj – Tschernembl (G)
Dolenjska – Lower Carniola (E)
Dunaj – Vienna (E), Wien (G)
Gorenjska – Upper Carniola (E)
Gorica – Gorizia (I)
Gradec – Graz (G)
Gradež – Grado (I)
Idrija – Ydria (G)
Istra – Istria (E)
Izola – Isola (I)
Jadran, Jadransko Morje – Adriatic Sea (E)
Kamnik – Stein (G)
Kobarid – Caporetto (I)
Koper – Capodistria (I)
Koroška – Carinthia (E), Kärnten (G)
Kostanjevica – Landstrass (G)
Kranj – Krainburg (G)
Kranjska – Carniola (E), Krain (G)
Kras – Karst (E)
Kropa – Cropp (G)
Krnski Grad – Karnburg (G)
Lendava – Lendva (H)
Lipnica – Leibnitz (G)
Ljubljana – Laibach (G), Liubliana (I)
Metlika – Möttling (G)
Milje – Muggia (I)

Murska Sobota – Muraszombat (H)
Notranjska – Inner Carniola (E)
Nova Gorica – Gorizia (I), Görz (G)
Otočec – Wördl (G)
Oglej – Aquileia (I)
Piran – Pirano (I)
Pleterje – Pletariach (G)
Pliberk – Bleiburg (G)
Portorož – Portorose (I)
Postojna – Adelsberg (G)
Praga – Prague (E), Praha (Cz)
Ptuj – Pettau (G)
Radgona – Bad Radkersburg (G)
Radovljica – Ratmansdorf (G)
Reka – Rijeka (C), Fiume (I)
Ribnica – Reiffniz (G)
Rim – Rome (E), Roma (I)
Rogaška Slatina – Rohitsch-Sauerbrunn (G)
Rosalnice – Rosendorf (G)
Seča – Sezza (I) Peninsula
Sečovlje – Sicciole (I)
Škocjan – San Canziano (I)
Sredozemsko Morje – Mediterranean Sea (E)
Štajerska – Styria (E), Steiermark (G)
Soča – Isonzo (I)
Stična – Sittich (G)
Strunjan – Strugnano (I)
Trbiž – Tarvisio (I)
Trst – Trieste (I)
Tržaški Zaliv – Gulf of Trieste (E), Golfo di Trieste (I)
Tržič – Monfalcone (I)
Varšava – Warsaw (E), Warszawa (P)
Videm – Udine (I)
Vinica – Weinitz (G)
Železna Kapla – Eisenkappel (G)

GLOSSARY

(m) indicates masculine gender, (f) feminine gender and (n) neutral

AMZS – Avto-Moto Zveza Slovenije (Automobile Association of Slovenia)

bife – snack and/or drinks bar
breg – river bank
burja – bora (cold northeast wind from the Adriatic)

c – abbreviation for cesta
čaj – tea
cerkev – church
cesta – road

DDV – davek na dodano vrednost (value-added tax, or VAT)
delovni čas – opening/ business hours
dijaški dom – student dormitory, hostel
dolina – valley
dom – house; mountain lodge
Domobranci – anti-Partisan Home Guards during WWII
drevored – avenue
dvorana – hall

fijaker – horse-drawn carriage

gaj – grove, park
gledališče – theatre
gora – mountain
gostilna – innlike restaurant
gostišče – inn with restaurant
gozd – forest, grove
grad – castle
greben – ridge, crest
GZS – Geodetski Zavod Slovenije (Geodesic Institute of Slovenia)

Hallstatt – early Iron Age Celtic culture (800–500 BC)
hiša – house
hrib – hill

izvir – source (of a river, stream etc)

jama – cave
jezero – lake

Karst – limestone region of underground rivers and caves in Primorska
kavarna – coffee shop, cafe
klet – cellar
knjigarna – bookshop
knjižnica – library
koča – mountain cottage or hut
kosilo – lunch
kot – glacial valley, corner
kotlina – basin
kozolec – hayrack distinct to Slovenia
kras – karst
krčma – drinks bar (sometimes with food)
lekarna – pharmacy

LPP – Ljubljanski Potniški Promet (Ljubljana city bus network)

mali (m) **mala** (f) **malo** (n) – little
malica – midmorning snack
menjalnica – private currency exchange office
mesto – town
morje – sea
moški – men (toilet)
most – bridge
muzej – museum

na – on
nabrežje – embankment
narod – nation
naselje – colony, development, estate
nasip – dike, embankment
novi (m) **nova** (f) **novo** (n) – new

občina – administrative division; county or commune; city or town hall
odprto – open

okrepčevalnica – snack bar
Osvobodilne Fronte (OF) – Anti-Fascist Liberation Front during WWII
otok – island

pivnica – pub, beer hall
pivo – beer
planina – Alpine pasture
planota – plateau
pletna – gondola
pod – under, below
polje – collapsed limestone area under cultivation
pot – trail
potok – stream
potrditev – enter/confirm (on ATM)
prazniki – holidays
prehod – passage, crossing
prekop – canal
prenočišče – accommodation
pri – at, near, by
PZS – Planinska Zveza Slovenije (Alpine Association of Slovenia)

reka – river
restavracija – restaurant
rob – escarpment, edge

samopostrežna restavracija – self-service restaurant
samostan – monastery
Secessionism – art and architectural style similar to art nouveau
skanzen – open-air museum displaying village architecture
slaščičarna – shop selling ice cream, sweets
smučanje – skiing
STO – Slovenska Turistična Organizacija (Slovenian Tourist Board)
sobe – rooms (available)
soteska – ravine, gorge
sprehajališče – walkway, promenade
stari (m) **stara** (f) **staro** (n) – old

stena – wall, cliff
steza – path
stolp – tower
štruklji – dumplings
Sv – St (abbreviation for saint)
SŽ – Slovenske Železnice (Slovenian Railways)

terme – Italian word for 'spa' used frequently in Slovenia
TIC – Tourist Information Centre
TNP – Triglavski Narodni Park (Triglav National Park)

toplarji – double-linked hayracks, unique to Slovenia
toplice – spa
trg – square

ul – abbreviation for ulica
ulica – street

vas – village
večerja – dinner, supper
veliki (m) **velika** (f) **veliko** (n) – great, big
vila – villa
vinoteka – wine bar
vinska cesta – wine road
vinska klet – wine cellar

vrata – door, gate
vrh – summit, peak
vrt – garden, park

zaprto – closed
zdravilišče – health resort, spa
zdravstveni dom – medical centre, clinic
žegnanje – a patron's festival at a church or chapel
ženske – women (toilet)
žičnica – cable car
zidanica – a cottage in one of the wine-growing regions

Behind the Scenes

SEND US YOUR FEEDBACK

We love to hear from travellers – your comments keep us on our toes and help make our books better. Our well-travelled team reads every word on what you loved or loathed about this book. Although we cannot reply individually to postal submissions, we always guarantee that your feedback goes straight to the appropriate authors, in time for the next edition. Each person who sends us information is thanked in the next edition – the most useful submissions are rewarded with a selection of digital PDF chapters.

Visit **lonelyplanet.com/contact** to submit your updates and suggestions or to ask for help. Our award-winning website also features inspirational travel stories, news and discussions.

Note: We may edit, reproduce and incorporate your comments in Lonely Planet products such as guidebooks, websites and digital products, so let us know if you don't want your comments reproduced or your name acknowledged. For a copy of our privacy policy visit lonelyplanet.com/privacy.

OUR READERS

Many thanks to the travellers who used the last edition and wrote to us with helpful hints, useful advice and interesting anecdotes:

Helen Berrieman, David Bosomworth, David Budgen, Matthew Bunney, Andy Davies, Leandro Fantuzzi, Val Fletcher, Jennifer Franciska Gráf, Ruth Hazi, Frances Jaffe, Rok Jarc, Michelle Langelier, Rien Linthout, Robert Maisano, Mark Mclain, Sandra Melvold, Peter Millard, Milena Praprotnik, Ana Ribeiro, Tine Rus, Ciska Tillema, Lyn Wills

AUTHOR THANKS

Mark Baker

I would like to thank the helpful staff at the Slovenian Tourist Board, including Ljubljana-based Ana Vugrin and Alenka Hribar in Kamnik, as well as Simona Berden at the Ljubljana municipal office and Domen Kalajzic and his staff in Bled. Thanks, too, to my co-authors, Steve Fallon and Paul Clammer, for making this edition such a smooth ride.

Paul Clammer

In Slovenia, thanks to Simon Zagoricnik in Lucija, Matic Leskosek in Bovec and especially Klemen Sagadin in Celje. Anton Plankar was generous with his help at Ljubljana bus station, and Katja Batagelj likewise at Postojna. Thanks also to Verica Leskovar at Ljubljana Tourism. Desk-bound thanks to my co-authors Mark Baker and Steve Fallon for their helpful suggestions and easy working style. Finally, thanks and love to Helena, Megan and Tabitha for giving me a roof over my head to write the project up.

Steve Fallon

A warm *najlepša hvala* to Petra Čuk, late of the Vila Bled, Domen Kalajžič in Bled, and both Petra Stušek and Verica Leskovar at the Ljubljana Tourist Board. Dušan Brejc of the Wine Association of Slovenia helped with the right vintage(s) and I am grateful. As always, my efforts here are dedicated to my partner, Michael Rothschild.

ACKNOWLEDGMENTS

Climate Map Data Climate map data adapted from Peel MC, Finlayson BL & McMahon TA (2007) 'Updated World Map of the Köppen-Geiger Climate Classification', Hydrology and Earth System Sciences, 11, 1633¬44.

Cover photograph: Lake Bled, Gorenjska, Guy Edwardes/Getty Images.

THIS BOOK

This 7th edition of Lonely Planet's *Slovenia* guidebook was researched and written by Mark Baker, Paul Clammer and Steve Fallon. The previous two editions were written by Steve Fallon. This guidebook was commissioned in Lonely Planet's London office, and produced by the following:

Commissioning Editors
Joe Bindloss, Helena Smith

Coordinating Editors
Lauren Hunt, Gina Tsarouhas

Coordinating Cartographer
Csanad Csutoros

Coordinating Layout Designer Nicholas Colicchia

Managing Editors Brigitte Ellemor, Annelies Mertens

Managing Cartographers Anthony Phelan, Diana Von Holdt

Managing Layout Designer Chris Girdler

Senior Editor Andi Jones

Assisting Editors Carolyn Bain, Rebecca Chau, Erin Richards

Assisting Cartographer Samantha Tyson

Cover Research Naomi Parker

Internal Image Research Aude Vauconsant

Language Content Branislava Vladisavljevic

Thanks to Dan Austin, Penny Cordner, Ryan Evans, Larissa Frost, Laura Jane, Jouve India, Asha Ioculari, Kate McDonell, Trent Paton, Raphael Richards, Averil Robertson, Amanda Sierp, Fiona Siseman, Andrew Stapleton, Lieu Thi Pham, Martine Power, Gerard Walker, Danny Williams, Wendy Wright

Index

262